*AI for Everyday IT*

## Get the eBook FREE!
(PDF, ePub, Kindle, and liveBook all included)

We believe that once you buy a book from us, you should be able to read it in any format we have available. To get electronic versions of this book at no additional cost to you, purchase and then register this book at the Manning website.

Go to https://www.manning.com/freebook and follow the instructions to complete your pBook registration.

That's it!
Thanks from Manning!

# *AI for Everyday IT*
## ACCELERATE WORKPLACE PRODUCTIVITY

CHRISSY LEMAIRE
BRANDON ABSHIRE
FOREWORD BY NITYA NARASIMHAN

MANNING
SHELTER ISLAND

For online information and ordering of this and other Manning books, please visit www.manning.com. The publisher offers discounts on this book when ordered in quantity. For more information, please contact

    Special Sales Department
    Manning Publications Co.
    20 Baldwin Road
    PO Box 761
    Shelter Island, NY 11964
    Email: orders@manning.com

©2025 by Manning Publications Co. All rights reserved.

No part of this publication may be reproduced, stored in a retrieval system, or transmitted, in any form or by means electronic, mechanical, photocopying, or otherwise, without prior written permission of the publisher.

Many of the designations used by manufacturers and sellers to distinguish their products are claimed as trademarks. Where those designations appear in the book, and Manning Publications was aware of a trademark claim, the designations have been printed in initial caps or all caps.

♾ Recognizing the importance of preserving what has been written, it is Manning's policy to have the books we publish printed on acid-free paper, and we exert our best efforts to that end. Recognizing also our responsibility to conserve the resources of our planet, Manning books are printed on paper that is at least 15 percent recycled and processed without the use of elemental chlorine.

The author and publisher have made every effort to ensure that the information in this book was correct at press time. The author and publisher do not assume and hereby disclaim any liability to any party for any loss, damage, or disruption caused by errors or omissions, whether such errors or omissions result from negligence, accident, or any other cause, or from any usage of the information herein.

| | |
|---|---|
| Manning Publications Co.<br>20 Baldwin Road<br>PO Box 761<br>Shelter Island, NY 11964 | Development editor: Frances Lefkowitz<br>Technical editor: Ankit Virmani<br>Review editor: Kishor Rit<br>Production editor: Kathy Rossland<br>Copy editor: Tiffany Taylor<br>Proofreader: Melody Dolab<br>Typesetter and cover designer: Marija Tudor |

ISBN 9781633436428
Printed in the United States of America

*We dedicate this book to our best friends, each other.
We couldn't have done it without you.*

# brief contents

**PART 1 INTRODUCTION TO AI** .................................................. 1

- 1 ■ Artificial intelligence in IT  3
- 2 ■ Chatbots: Tasks and tips  21
- 3 ■ Basic intelligence  41
- 4 ■ Prompt engineering and problem formulation  57
- 5 ■ Prompts in action  82
- 6 ■ Document handling  97
- 7 ■ Emails and instant messaging in the workplace  114

**PART 2 IT OPERATIONS AND AI** ................................................ 143

- 8 ■ IT support and service desk  145
- 9 ■ Systems administration  160
- 10 ■ Database administration and development  175

**PART 3 DEVELOPMENT AND AI INTEGRATION** .......................... 199

- 11 ■ Code assistants and development tools  201
- 12 ■ AI in DevOps engineering  221
- 13 ■ Building AI-powered applications  232

## PART 4  LEADERSHIP AND GROWTH WITH AI ............................. 251

- 14 ■ Conflict resolution and crisis management   253
- 15 ■ Management essentials   272
- 16 ■ Management interventions   289
- 17 ■ Career advancement   304

- appendix A ■ *Local AI models: An accessible alternative*   *323*
- appendix B ■ *OpenAI GPT Actions*   *335*

# contents

*foreword xv*
*preface xvii*
*acknowledgments xix*
*about this book xxi*
*about the author xxiv*
*about the cover illustration xxv*

## PART 1 INTRODUCTION TO AI .......................................... 1

### 1 Artificial intelligence in IT 3

1.1 Generative AI changes everything 4
1.2 The elephant in the server room 5
1.3 Strengthening your skill set 6
1.4 An introduction to generative AI 7

*Language model chatbots 7 • Image generation with AI models 9*

1.5 Service costs 13
1.6 Using AI responsibly at work 14

*Data security with AI 15 • Bias and fairness 15 • AI writing and plagiarism 16 • Citing prompts in your work 17*

1.7 How we are using AI 18
1.8 Prompts used in this chapter 19

## 2 Chatbots: Tasks and tips 21

### 2.1 Chatbots and conversational AI 22
*OpenAI ChatGPT 22* ▪ *Anthropic Claude 28* ▪ *Google Gemini 32* ▪ *Microsoft Copilot suite 34* ▪ *Summary comparison of AI assistants 37*

### 2.2 Text-to-image AI models 37
*OpenAI DALL-E and 4o 38* ▪ *Midjourney 38* ▪ *Google Gemini Imagen and Meta Imagine 39*

### 2.3 Prompts used in this chapter 40

## 3 Basic intelligence 41

### 3.1 Defining the terms 42
*Prompts 42* ▪ *Statefulness 42* ▪ *Context retention and coherence 43* ▪ *Tokens 44*

### 3.2 Everything you never wanted to know about tokens 45
*Token limits 45* ▪ *Token limits and AI interactions 47*

### 3.3 When good bots go bad 49

### 3.4 Free vs. premium accounts 50
*Why pay for chatbot access when I can use one for free? 50* ▪ *Which to choose? 54* ▪ *Learning and experimenting 54*

### 3.5 Prompts used in this chapter 55

## 4 Prompt engineering and problem formulation 57

### 4.1 Prompt engineering 58

### 4.2 The spectrum of AI prompting 58
*Zero-shot prompting 59* ▪ *Single-shot prompting 59 Few-shot prompting 62* ▪ *Many-shot prompting 63 The future of prompt engineering 65*

### 4.3 The mechanics of a good prompt 65
*Key principles in prompt construction 66*

### 4.4 Introductory prompts for IT roles 68
*Awesome Prompts Lab 69*

### 4.5 Advanced techniques 71
*Recursive prompts 72* ▪ *Context injection 72* ▪ *Explicit constraints 72* ▪ *Prompt chaining 72* ▪ *Sentiment directives 72* ▪ *Templating 72*

4.6  Best practices and common mistakes   73
   *Learning from success  73* ▪ *Pitfalls to avoid  73*
   *Meta-prompts  75*
4.7  Problem formulation   77
4.8  Incorporating problem formulation   79
4.9  Prompts used in this chapter   80

## 5 Prompts in action   82

5.1  Prompt engineering in action   83
   *Basic prompting  83* ▪ *Recursive prompting  87* ▪ *Template creation  88* ▪ *Finalized output  90*
5.2  Problem formulation in action   93

## 6 Document handling   97

6.1  Best practices for document handling with AI   98
   *Text extraction methods  98* ▪ *Structuring and refining outputs  99*
6.2  Ethics in AI document handling   99
6.3  Document summarization   100
6.4  Format conversion   102
6.5  Text extraction from images   104
6.6  Document comparison   106
6.7  Document classification and tagging   107
6.8  Document anonymization   109
6.9  Language translation   111
6.10 Prompts used in this chapter   112

## 7 Emails and instant messaging in the workplace   114

7.1  Enhancing email management with AI   115
   *AI-enhanced email summarization and drafting  115* ▪ *Not ready for prime time  121* ▪ *Email security  122*
7.2  Using AI in instant messaging   126
   *Meeting transcription and recap with AI  126*
7.3  Integrations and automation with AI   131
   *Teams workflows in action  131* ▪ *Webhooks  137*
7.4  Improving your writing while maintaining your voice   137
   *Grammarly  139* ▪ *Apple Intelligence Writing Tools  139*

7.5 Maintaining critical thinking and good judgement 140
7.6 The future of AI communications 140
7.7 Prompts used in this chapter 141

## PART 2 IT OPERATIONS AND AI ............................. 143

### 8 IT support and service desk 145

8.1 Service desk therapy 146
*Identifying problems 148 • Crafting a response 149*

8.2 Technical support 150
*Setting up the environment 150 • Troubleshooting problems 150
Practicing for real-time scenarios 151*

8.3 Custom GPTs 152
*Creating a custom GPT to analyze IT service tickets 153*

8.4 The future of the service desk: Agents 157
*Key agentic AI offerings 158 • Agentic AI in enterprise CRM systems 158*

8.5 Prompts used in this chapter 159

### 9 Systems administration 160

9.1 Change request 161
9.2 More distros, more problems 163
9.3 Multiserver administration 164
9.4 Renaming files 168
9.5 Analyzing error logs: Identifying exceptions and failures 170
9.6 Automating tasks for efficiency and compliance 171
9.7 Auditing configuration files with AI 172
9.8 Existing AI in systems engineering 173
9.9 Prompts used in this chapter 174

### 10 Database administration and development 175

10.1 Query and object creation basics 176
10.2 Query optimization 179
10.3 Code documentation 181
10.4 Heterogeneous database environments 183
*Staying up to date 183 • Teaching an old DBA new tricks 184*

10.5   Maintenance jobs   186
10.6   Advanced administration   188

*AI + dbatools = <3  188 ▪ Analyzing memory configurations  191
Additional advanced administration prompts  194
The role of the DBA in the AI era  196*

10.7   Prompts used in this chapter   196

## PART 3  DEVELOPMENT AND AI INTEGRATION .......... 199

### 11  Code assistants and development tools   201

11.1   Privacy and security   202
11.2   Understanding the value of existing skills   202
11.3   GitHub AI suite   203
11.4   Cline   205
11.5   Cursor AI   207
11.6   Google Project IDX   209
11.7   Aider   209
11.8   Summary comparison of code assistants   211
11.9   Best practices for AI-assisted development   212

*Foundation principles  212 ▪ Advanced techniques  217*

11.10  Prompts used in this chapter   219

### 12  AI in DevOps engineering   221

12.1   Practical AI use cases in DevOps   222
12.2   Upgrading nearly 7,000 tests: A real-world AI project   222

*Choosing our tools  222 ▪ Developing an effective process  224
Implementation strategy  225 ▪ Managing large files  225
Breaking down instructions into focused passes  226 ▪ The
results  226 ▪ Lessons learned  227 ▪ Beyond test updates: Other
uses for AI-assisted development  227*

12.3   The GenAIOps lifecycle   228

*Applying GenAIOps: A practical workshop example  229*

12.4   Prompts used to write this chapter   230

### 13  Building AI-powered applications   232

13.1   Function calling   233

*Chatting with the OpenAI API  234 ▪ Building a database
copilot  235 ▪ Implementing function calling  238*

13.2　The functions　240
　　　　*What matters in AI function design　241*

13.3　Validating SQL queries with examine_sql　244
　　　　*Defining what makes a query dangerous　245　▪　Generating a user-friendly response　245　▪　AI-powered SQL assistance in action　245*

13.4　Practical applications and security considerations　247
　　　　*Example: AI-powered currency conversion　247　▪　Security considerations for function calling　248*

13.5　Prompts used in this chapter　249

## PART 4　LEADERSHIP AND GROWTH WITH AI .............. 251

### 14　Conflict resolution and crisis management　253

14.1　Addressing workplace conflicts　254
　　　　*Strategies for effective conflict resolution　254　▪　SharePoint standoff　255　▪　Proactive conflict-resolution agreement　260*

14.2　Crisis management　263
　　　　*Role of leadership in crisis situations　263　▪　Generative AI's role in disaster recovery and COOP　266*

14.3　Prompts used to write this chapter　271

### 15　Management essentials　272

15.1　Policies and benefits　273
　　　　*Policies　273　▪　Benefits　274　▪　Custom GPTs and projects　275*

15.2　Career development and growth　276
　　　　*Skills matrices　276　▪　One-on-ones　277*

15.3　Performance reviews　279
　　　　*Self-evaluations　279　▪　360-degree feedback　282　▪　SMART goals　283　▪　Team goals　285　▪　Manager self-learning　287*

15.4　Prompts used in this chapter　287

### 16　Management interventions　289

16.1　Management intervention guidelines　290
　　　　*Memos, warnings, and write-ups　290　▪　Constructive feedback　292　▪　Performance improvement plans　293*

- 16.2 Team cohesion  296
  - *Anonymous feedback  297 ▪ Team building  299*
- 16.3 Interviewing candidates  300
- 16.4 Time management for the hands-on technical manager  301
- 16.5 Prompts used in this chapter  303

## 17  Career advancement  304

- 17.1 Leading AI adoption in the organization  305
  - *Advancing through practical problem-solving  305 ▪ Documenting and showcasing your projects  307 ▪ Advanced presentation training with AI  309*
- 17.2 Training and certifications  310
  - *Acquiring new skills with AI assistance  310 ▪ Identifying and filling skill gaps with AI  312 ▪ Writing conference attendance proposals  313*
- 17.3 External career advancement  314
  - *AI-powered job search  314 ▪ Resume optimization  315 AI-assisted interview preparation  317 ▪ Salary negotiation  317 AI-powered career development prompts  318 ▪ AI-powered interview practice  319*
- 17.4 Ethical considerations and best practices  320
- 17.5 Putting it all together  320
- 17.6 Prompts used in this chapter  321

appendix A  Local AI models: An accessible alternative  323
appendix B  OpenAI GPT Actions  335

index  341

# foreword

I am genuinely excited to write the foreword for Chrissy LeMaire's and Brandon Abshire's new book on generative AI for the IT professional! Chrissy is that quintessential Microsoft MVP who balances real-world technology expertise in IT with a deep understanding of how to engage with different communities to communicate new concepts in relatable ways. Brandon contributes solid professional IT experience, including over a decade and a half as a database administrator and technical manager for top-rated US healthcare systems. Together, they form a powerful combination of expertise spanning enterprise IT, database management, infrastructure, and programming, from web development to PowerShell scripting. With this book, Chrissy and Brandon are filling a critical gap in our AI engineering bookshelf by providing both IT professionals and aspiring AI engineers with a roadmap to understand generative AI operations (GenAIOps) so they can streamline the development workflow from prompt to production.

After OpenAI debuted its GPT-3 models powering a new class of generative AI applications, ChatGPT became a household word. The industry took note, recognizing that the power of natural language processing with pretrained models effectively made everyone a programmer with the power of their words. At the time, we had a handful of model providers, and developers could afford to experiment with each new model to unlock its capabilities and harness it to their application scenarios.

We now have more than 1,800 models in the Azure AI model catalog and more than 1 million community-created variants on the Hugging Face hub. We have gone from learning how to do prompt engineering to having to orchestrate complex workflows in support of retrieval-augmented generation, AI-assisted evaluation, and multi-agent architectures. We now have more tools, frameworks, and services to support our needs. And with all that complexity comes the need for new paradigms and workflows to support AI operations at enterprise scale—and the need for skilled guidance to educate AI engineers and IT admins on best practices.

In this book, Chrissy and Brandon take a holistic approach to that journey, starting readers with an introduction to AI that emphasizes data and workflow automation needs and challenges before reframing familiar IT admin and DBA tasks through the lens of generative AI solutions. We get to see how AI poses a challenge to IT professionals (in the paradigm shift from IT Ops to AI Ops) as well as an opportunity (to use AI-driven code assistants and automation workflows), giving them a unique perspective on real-world priorities. But the book takes it one step further, concluding with a leadership-focused section that will resonate with entrepreneurs and decision-makers who need to navigate fast-paced ecosystems with a measured understanding of conflict resolution and crisis management.

This book may not answer every question you have about AI Ops simply because many questions are still being articulated. But it will help you navigate those conversations with a better foundation for the terms, tools, and priorities required to go from prompt to prototype to production with AI. Want to build intelligent apps in production? Let's make it happen in AI!

—NITYA NARASIMHAN, PHD, MICROSOFT

# preface

The emergence of ChatGPT marked a turning point in how the general public interacted with artificial intelligence. While many explored its novelty through casual questions and creative writing, we approached it through the lens of technology professionals, seeking practical applications for our daily work. As we deepened our understanding of AI's capabilities, we noticed a significant gap: many people weren't using AI for productivity, struggled to extract meaningful information from chatbots, or remained unaware of AI's full potential. This observation inspired us to share our insights through this book.

Our collaboration stems from a friendship that began in Louisiana during our high school years and flourished in San Diego during the dot-com boom of the late 1990s and early 2000s. Over the decades, we've partnered on various projects, including creating a Cajun recipe website. Writing this book together felt like a natural progression of our shared interests and experiences.

This book distills our key discoveries about AI's inner workings, including those breakthrough moments that transformed our understanding. We guide readers through fundamental concepts before demonstrating practical workplace applications, starting with universal tasks that benefit any professional. We then move into specialized IT applications, concluding with insights on management strategies, conflict resolution, and career advancement. Although the book's technical foundation speaks to IT professionals, it offers valuable perspectives for anyone interested in using AI chatbots and models, whether through direct interaction or programming.

By documenting our journey of experimentation and research, we've not only expanded our own expertise but also created a resource that makes AI more accessible to others. We present AI as it truly is: a powerful but limited tool with specific capabilities and constraints. Our book's primary strength lies in its practical approach, offering real-world applications across various professional roles and technical skill levels. Readers will not only learn how to communicate effectively with AI but also discover immediately applicable strategies for their specific work contexts.

We demonstrate code examples in T-SQL, PL/SQL, PowerShell, Python, and other languages commonly used in today's technology landscape, but the principles we teach apply broadly, as AI chatbots can generate code in virtually any programming language. We selected these particular languages based on their widespread use and our extensive experience with them.

Although AI and chatbots predate their recent surge in popularity, the technology has transformed dramatically since November 2022. Early adopters have begun integrating AI into their workflow, but many professionals haven't yet explored its workplace potential or fully grasped its capabilities. We envision AI becoming an increasingly integral part of the IT workplace. We emphasize throughout the book that AI represents a new type of tool—one that professionals must learn to utilize effectively, or they risk falling behind their peers. AI offers unprecedented opportunities for efficiency, productivity, and personalized learning, providing a level of customization and specificity previously unavailable in traditional learning resources.

# *acknowledgments*

**CHRISSY LEMAIRE:**
I'd like to thank my wife, Lu, who let me write a second book after I promised I'd never write a book again. Writing a book is incredibly time consuming—my last one took three years, although thankfully, this one took only half as much time.

I'd also like to acknowledge my brother, Chad LeMaire, a cybersecurity executive who'd love to see his name in his sister's book. Here you go, bro. ♡

**BRANDON ABSHIRE:**
Of the few people I know who have written a book, most say they may never write another one. I concur, so I need to make this acknowledgment count.

My perfect acknowledgment recognizes the many people who've shaped my life and career, from my earliest days figuring out what I wanted to be when I grew up (I'm still deciding), throughout my journey as a DBA, and ultimately to being an IT manager (who still does DBA work). Rather than following a carefully crafted plan for success, I relied on hard work and well-timed leaps of faith.

To every boss who took a leap of faith with me, thank you. To my colleagues who make each day engaging and rewarding, your collaboration and willingness to share knowledge have helped me grow both personally and professionally. And a shout-out to the GenAI discussion group, where each week we explore the latest in AI while keeping it fun (and totally not overwhelming—usually).

Finally, I want to express my deepest love and appreciation to those closest to me, who provided the support I needed to thrive while focusing on this project. Whether from one room over or many miles away, your endless understanding and encouragement made it possible for me to fully immerse myself in this endeavor. I hope this book makes you as proud as it makes me.

**BOTH AUTHORS:**

Thank you to Frances Lefkowitz, our development editor, who helped turn a casual conversation about AI into this book.

We thank Dr. Shaw Y. Lin for taking a chance on two young professionals and helping to launch our careers.

Special thanks also to our technical editor, Ankit Virmani. Ankit works in ethical AI and data engineering and has over a decade of experience developing and architecting machine learning and data solutions. He has worked for Fortune 500 organizations, spoken at top AI conferences, and authored papers in the field.

We extend our sincere gratitude to Nitya Narasimhan for contributing the foreword to this book. Her insight and perspective from one of the world's foremost technology innovators and AI leaders adds tremendous value, and we're honored by her willingness to share her expertise with our readers.

Finally, our thanks to all the reviewers: Adam Bacon, Aleksandar Nikolic, Anandaganesh Balakrishnan, Annette Ciotola, Bhagvan Kommadi, Cláudio Silva, Dave Corun, Geoff Newson, Georgerobert Freeman, Giuliano Latini, Jason Greene, Jason Taylor, Jeffery Hicks, Joel Holmes, Jose San Leandro, Joseph Monk, Josephine Bush, Ken Kogler, Kosmas Chatzimichalis, Larry Cai, Mark Furman, Matteo Rossi, Maxim Volgin, Mike Taylor, Neha Shetty, Omar Ebrahim, Onofrei George, Pan Singh Dhoni, Paul Whittemore, Peter Henstock, Piotr Pindel, Prachit Kurani, Prashanth Lakshmi Narayana Chaitanya Josyula, Radhakrishna MV, Ravi Soni, Ray Booysen, Sharmila Devi Chandariah, Sruti S., Sumit Pal, Tim Wooldridge, Vitaly Bragilevsky, William Wade, Ying Zuo, and Yvon Vieville. Your suggestions helped make this a better book.

# about this book

This book is your practical guide to using artificial intelligence in IT operations, development, and management. We help IT professionals update their skills with hands-on, real-world techniques for using AI in their daily work. Instead of getting caught up in theory or chasing new AI products, we focus on core knowledge and practical applications that work across most AI services.

## Who should read this book

This book is written for IT professionals who want to work more effectively using AI tools, regardless of whether you're

- A professional new to AI or working in unfamiliar IT domains
- A service desk specialist or IT support professional wanting to improve support processes
- A systems administrator or database professional looking to automate complex tasks
- A developer or DevOps engineer aiming to add AI to your workflow
- An IT manager working to implement AI strategies in your team
- An IT professional wanting to advance their career with AI skills

No prior AI experience needed—we'll guide you from basics to advanced applications in your specific IT role.

## How this book is organized: A road map

The book contains four main parts with 17 chapters and two appendices, structured to build your AI skills step by step:

- Part 1 (chapters 1–7) builds your foundation with AI concepts, chatbot interactions, prompt engineering, and practical uses in document handling and workplace communication.
- Part 2 (chapters 8–10) covers IT support and service desk operations, systems administration, and database administration and development.
- Part 3 (chapters 11–13) explores code assistants, DevOps engineering, and building AI-powered applications.
- Part 4 (chapters 14–17) addresses conflict resolution, management essentials, interventions, and career advancement.
- Appendix A provides information on local AI models as an accessible alternative to online services, including their use with structured outputs.
- Appendix B provides information on OpenAI GPT Actions.

We recommend reading this book sequentially, as each part builds your AI skills in valuable ways. Part 1 provides essential foundations you'll use throughout the book. The IT operations chapters in part 2 are more flexible; you can read these in order of interest. After part 2, continue reading in order. Even if you're not a developer, part 3's development concepts reveal powerful ways to automate and improve your work. Similarly, part 4's leadership and management topics are valuable regardless of your role, helping you work more effectively with teams and advance your career. Throughout the book, you'll discover techniques from other IT domains that can transform how you approach your own work.

## About the code

This book includes code examples and italicized prompts throughout, especially in sections covering systems administration scripts, database queries and maintenance jobs, software engineering integrations, and DevOps workflows.

All code examples use a `fixed-width font like this` to separate them from regular text. Line breaks and indentation are adjusted for clarity, and line-continuation markers (➥) are used when needed.

## Software requirements

You need a minimal setup for this book:

- Access to at least one AI service:
  - Free options: ChatGPT, Claude, Google Gemini, and Microsoft Copilot
  - Premium examples: Microsoft Outlook and Teams with Copilot for M365
  - Recommended: ChatGPT Plus subscription ($20/month) for advanced features and Anthropic Claude tokens for API access
- Basic text editor
- Internet connection
- Additional software needs are noted in each chapter

## liveBook discussion forum

Purchase of *AI for Everyday IT* includes free access to liveBook, Manning's online reading platform. Using liveBook's exclusive discussion features, you can attach comments to the book globally or to specific sections or paragraphs. It's a snap to make notes for yourself, ask and answer technical questions, and receive help from the authors and other users. To access the forum, go to https://livebook.manning.com/book/ai-for-everyday-it/discussion.

Manning's commitment to our readers is to provide a venue where a meaningful dialogue between individual readers and between readers and the authors can take place. It is not a commitment to any specific amount of participation on the part of the authors, whose contribution to the forum remains voluntary (and unpaid). We suggest you try asking the authors some challenging questions lest their interest stray! The forum and the archives of previous discussions will be accessible from the publisher's website as long as the book is in print.

## Other online resources

These additional resources will help your learning:

- *OpenAI's documentation*—https://platform.openai.com/docs
- *Anthropic's Claude documentation*—https://docs.anthropic.com/
- *Microsoft Learn AI fundamentals*—https://learn.microsoft.com/ai
- *Google AI learning resources*—https://ai.google/education
- *Regular updates and extra examples on our book's resource page*—https://www.manning.com/books/ai-for-everyday-it

We suggest bookmarking these resources and checking them as you work through the book. They offer helpful extra information and will keep you current with the fast-changing AI field.

## about the author

**CHRISSY LEMAIRE** is a dual Microsoft MVP, one of the first seven GitHub Stars, and Manning author, having previously written *Learn dbatools in a Month of Lunches*. With nearly three decades of IT experience, Chrissy holds an MSc in systems engineering and works as a developer in Belgium. She is also an international speaker and the creator of the popular PowerShell module dbatools.

**BRANDON ABSHIRE** is the technical manager of Epic Systems and database administration teams at one of the nation's top-ranked healthcare institutions in Los Angeles, California. Prior to his current role, he worked as a database administrator at a leading healthcare system in San Diego and a Fortune 500 semiconductor technology company. Brandon has a BSc in information technology and holds certifications in database administration, ITIL 4, and project management, with foundational certifications in networking, information security, and cloud services.

Chrissy and Brandon grew up in the same small town in southwest Louisiana before living in big cities across the United States and Europe. Their unique backgrounds blend rural and urban experiences, creating diverse perspectives that enrich their work, from co-creating a Cajun cooking website and several Cajun cookbooks to supporting large government and hospital organizations. In this book, Chrissy and Brandon share insights to demystify complex IT concepts and demonstrate the practical applications of AI in a relatable, engaging manner.

# *about the cover illustration*

The figure on the cover of *AI for Everyday IT*, titled "La Creole," or "The Creole," is taken from a book by Louis Curmer published in 1841. In present Louisiana, "Creole" generally means a person or people of mixed colonial French, African American, and Native American ancestry. Each illustration in the book is finely drawn and colored by hand.

In those days, it was easy to identify where people lived and what their trade or station in life was just by their dress. Manning celebrates the inventiveness and initiative of the computer business with book covers based on the rich diversity of regional culture centuries ago, brought back to life by pictures from collections such as this one.

# Part 1

# *Introduction to AI*

The AI revolution is reshaping technology, fundamentally changing how IT professionals work. Whether you're excited about this transformation or approaching it cautiously, one thing's clear: AI-enhanced workflows are becoming a vital part of every IT professional's toolkit. This part of the book will walk you through everything you need to know to get started with AI, giving you an honest look at how it's changing our field. You'll discover how to pick the right AI tools for your needs and learn the art of communicating with AI effectively through prompt engineering and problem formulation. You'll see how to turn basic AI interactions into powerful aids for your daily work through real examples you can try yourself. By the end of chapter 7, you'll have both the knowledge and hands-on experience to start making AI work for you.

# Artificial intelligence in IT

**This chapter covers**
- An overview of AI tools and how they work
- How AI changes IT jobs and career growth
- What different AI models can do
- Using AI to improve IT work and team collaboration
- Best practices for AI security and ethics

We know it's cliche to say that something will revolutionize an industry, but seriously: generative AI tools like ChatGPT are *absolutely* revolutionizing the IT industry, and knowing how to use them is becoming required knowledge.

> *[AI] is every bit as important as the PC, as the internet.*
> —Bill Gates

Generative AI has made a real difference in how quickly we can complete many of our IT tasks. Take the process of copying data from PDFs into databases. What used to be a mind-numbing exercise that consumed entire afternoons now takes just moments. AI can read through documents, check and format the data, and insert it right into a database, turning a dreaded chore into a simple background task.

This extends to application security too. AI models can spot unusual patterns in application logs and user behavior that may signal security problems. This helps IT teams catch problems as they happen instead of discovering them during scheduled reviews or after incidents. Teams can then focus on more valuable work, like improving their backup and recovery procedures. But it's worth noting AI's current limits. It can't match human empathy, creativity, or deep contextual understanding. The best results come from pairing AI's speed with human expertise and judgment.

Throughout this book, you'll discover practical ways to incorporate AI into your daily IT work. We'll explore real-world scenarios and show you how to implement AI solutions that make sense for your environment. Whether you're writing scripts, managing databases, or supporting end users, you'll learn how AI can simplify your existing workflows and help you solve problems more effectively. This book is designed especially for IT professionals who understand basic IT concepts and want to add AI capabilities to their daily workflow. Our aim is to help you understand where and how to use AI effectively in your work, avoiding the hype while focusing on practical applications.

## 1.1 Generative AI changes everything

By now, almost everyone has seen an AI chatbot like ChatGPT in action, generating human-like responses to queries and prompts. For some of us, generative AI has introduced a new approach to work: we can have natural conversations with a chatbot that understands technical concepts and helps solve practical problems. These AI models have their drawbacks, but they are improving all the time.

Microsoft researcher Sébastien Bubeck famously showed how AI reasoning has improved by comparing text responses from different AI models. He asked both ChatGPT-3.5 and 4, two generations of the OpenAI model that powers ChatGPT, to describe how to stack a book, nine eggs, a laptop, a bottle, and a nail (illustrated in figure 1.1). ChatGPT-3's text response suggested physically impossible arrangements, like trying to balance eggs on a nail. GPT-4's written solution was more practical, explaining a logical sequence: placing the book as a stable base, arranging eggs in a 3 × 3 square to distribute weight, and so on. And AI continues to get better. The latest models have more advanced skills in reasoning and analysis as well as improved image-processing capabilities.

Figure 1.1 Image created by DALL-E as described by OpenAI GPT-3.5

Bubeck's comparison of model responses demonstrated to us the potential to use these tools for IT work. We soon realized that we could use AI assistance for all kinds of tasks, including writing documentation and evaluations, intelligent data extraction, and batch renames. The possibilities expanded with each new experiment. When sharing these techniques with colleagues, we often heard, "I never thought to use it that way!" These reactions inspired this book.

Here are some practical solutions we'll explore:

- *Root cause analysis*—When incidents occur, AI can quickly analyze logs to identify the root cause. Just upload your files, and ask questions the same way you would ask a colleague.
- *Analytics*—AI excels at finding key insights in large datasets. This helps when requirements aren't clear and teams need to identify what's important without guesswork. It's particularly useful for tasks like creating business intelligence reports, where AI can quickly spot relevant patterns and trends.
- *Disaster recovery planning*—AI creates detailed disaster recovery plans based on your systems. Give it your infrastructure details and requirements, and it generates comprehensive plans tailored to your setup.
- *Objective performance reviews*—AI helps write fair performance reviews by analyzing data impartially. It simplifies both writing self-evaluations and responding to employee reviews. It's especially good at turning goals into the SMART format (specific, measurable, achievable, relevant, and time-bound): just describe what you want to achieve, and it handles the structure while suggesting ways to meet and exceed targets.
- *Professional email responses*—AI helps draft effective emails, particularly in difficult situations. Paste in a draft of an email that's frustrating you, explain your concerns, and AI will craft a professional response that clearly addresses problems while maintaining an appropriate tone.
- *Scripting*—AI excels at creating Bash, Python, and PowerShell scripts for common sysadmin tasks like exporting logs to Splunk or finding today's files. The possibilities here are so extensive that we could write an entire book just on AI-assisted scripting.

These aren't theoretical uses—we use AI daily at work and at home to help with emails, presentations, and even writing this book. We'll share more details about these practical applications later.

## 1.2 The elephant in the server room

Before we go further, we'd like to address everyone's top concern: Is AI coming for our jobs in IT? The short answer is no. The longer answer is still no, but knowing how to effectively use AI will soon be a requirement. Although AI has the potential to reduce the number of open positions, it will also create new opportunities. Competent IT workers who learn how to wield AI will become exponentially more valuable.

> *AI will not replace you, but the person using AI will.*
> —Santiago Valdarrama

One of this book's coauthors, Brandon, shared this concern and was initially skeptical of ChatGPT. He wondered if it posed a threat to our industry by enabling unskilled people to masquerade as competent professionals, flooding the market with underqualified workers who couldn't be relied on during outages and emergencies.

These concerns led Brandon to consider boycotting AI chatbots altogether, but with time, curiosity got the best of him. First, he started asking random questions about random things, like most people. It was fun! Any question he could think of had an answer.

Impressed, Brandon started using ChatGPT to construct SQL queries at work. The results were practically magic, but he noticed that he still had to understand how to ask the right questions as well as how to implement the answers appropriately.

His ultimate revelation was that AI is most effective when utilized by skilled professionals with a thorough understanding of their domain. Far from masking incompetence, AI is actually a tool that amplifies existing skill sets.

To prove this, we asked one of our friends in accounting to pretend he was an IT professional and to try to get ChatGPT to help him do the job. Result: he couldn't get past step two or three. AI, as it stands, is not a magic wand for the non-IT pro, but it is a magic wand for us.

## 1.3 Strengthening your skill set

So let's talk about what AI can really do. Remember manually checking server health or spending hours documenting your work? AI speeds up these tasks, but not in the usual way that requires you to design and code the automation yourself. AI handles both the planning and coding and then takes the process further by documenting the code while creating it. AI can then write your project completion email and create the training materials for your team or end users.

Your focus shifts from doing the tasks yourself to orchestrating systems that do them for you. And not only that, but you no longer have to ask yourself, "Is it worth my time to automate?" Because now that AI can help code so quickly, it'll always be worth your time.

But AI in IT isn't just about automation—it's changing the entire field. When AI handles routine tasks, you can focus on what matters most: solving complex problems and planning for the future, if that's where your interests lie.

Take project management—even if you're an engineer who rarely handles PM work, ChatGPT can guide you through established practices. It can help you decide between problem statements and solution proposals, choose between Agile and Waterfall, or find a better-fitting methodology. It then helps document everything clearly, making you look great to upper management. And all while showing off skills you didn't know you had. Who knew you were so smart?

> **The unexpected mediator**
>
> An overlooked benefit of AI is how it improves teamwork, which we'll explore throughout this book. Here's a real example.
>
> Book coauthor Chrissy had to rewrite an after-action report (AAR) following a major system outage affecting multiple teams. One engineer had caused the outage, which worsened existing team conflicts.
>
> The organization was still young and hadn't adopted blameless post-mortems (for an example of what this term means, see https://aws.amazon.com/message/41926). The first AAR draft focused more on blame than facts and was filled with bias and personal attacks. Instead of analyzing root causes, it included statements like "Engineer X failed to follow proper protocol and ignored multiple warnings, resulting in cascade failures across multiple systems. This negligence caused 4 hours of downtime." Clearly, this report would only exacerbate conflict within the team.
>
> After receiving this draft, Chrissy asked her manager if she could rewrite the entire AAR. She was one of the few engineers with experience with AARs, and the version she initially received sharply contrasted with those she'd coauthored at her previous jobs.
>
> In her effort to align the AAR with the principles of effective problem-solving, Chrissy collaborated with ChatGPT, which ultimately served as an unexpected mediator. Through a process of detailed questioning and collaborative feedback with ChatGPT, Chrissy crafted an AAR that was comprehensive and unbiased. Where the original had blamed individuals, the new version focused on systems and processes: "A configuration change was implemented without following the standard review process. When alerts indicated potential system instability, communication gaps between teams delayed the response. This incident highlighted the need for clearer escalation procedures and automated safeguards for critical configuration changes." Management was so impressed that they directed others to use the final AAR as a model for future reports.

## 1.4 An introduction to generative AI

The tools that helped rewrite that AAR and solve the laptop/egg/nail stacking problem are part of generative AI. These AI systems learn from existing data to create new content. They work like advanced pattern learners that apply what they've learned to make something new.

We'll mainly use two types of generative AI in this book: text generators and image generators. Text generators (also known as large language models [LLMs]) like OpenAI's GPT, Google Gemini, and Anthropic Sonnet can write anything from technical docs to creative stories. Image generators can create, edit, or change visual content based on your descriptions or examples.

### 1.4.1 Language model chatbots

Let's start with some key AI terms and concepts you'll need throughout this book. Table 1.1 defines the main terms we'll use in our discussions. Understanding these basics will help you follow along more easily.

**Table 1.1  Glossary of AI terms**

| Term | Definition | Example |
|---|---|---|
| AI | Software that mimics human thinking and learning | OpenAI ChatGPT, Apple Siri, Tesla Autopilot, Amazon Alexa, Google Assistant |
| AI apps | Programs that use AI to handle specific tasks | Google Maps for navigation, Netflix and Spotify for recommendations, Zoom for noise reduction |
| AI model | Software trained on data to spot patterns and make decisions | OpenAI GPT-4, Tesla Full Self-Driving (FSD) AI, Stable Diffusion |
| API | Rules that let software systems talk to each other; used to add AI features to programs | OpenAI API, Anthropic API, Google Cloud AI API, AWS Bedrock API, Azure AI Services API |
| Chatbot | AI program that talks with users to help or provide information | OpenAI ChatGPT, Anthropic Claude (Sonnet frontend) |
| Cloud-hosted AI | AI systems running on internet servers that are easy to use and scale | OpenAI API, Azure AI services, AWS AI services, Google AI services |
| Generative AI | AI that creates new content by learning from existing data | DALL-E, Stable Diffusion, Midjourney, ChatGPT, Google Imagen |
| LLMs | Big AI systems trained on lots of text that can understand and write like humans | OpenAI GPT-4, Google Gemini, Anthropic Sonnet, Meta Llama |
| Local LLM | AI that runs on your own computers for better privacy and control | Meta Llama, Mistral AI, Microsoft Phi, Black Forest Labs FLUX |
| SLMs (small language models) | Smaller AI models that work well with limited resources | OpenAI GPT-4o mini, Microsoft Phi, Mistral Small |

You'll notice that OpenAI and ChatGPT appear often in the examples. This makes sense because ChatGPT is well-known and helps explain many AI concepts. Like other chatbots, ChatGPT fits several categories: it's an AI, a language model, a generative AI system, and a chatbot.

Since launching in late 2022, ChatGPT has changed how we view AI chatbots. Although it broke new ground and remains powerful, the field moves quickly. Several competitors have caught up and sometimes pulled ahead, each with its own strengths.

One notable competitor is Anthropic's Claude. Founded by former OpenAI engineers, Anthropic and its chatbot Claude focus on ethical and responsible AI. Claude can process more text than many other services, which makes it especially good for big writing tasks like reports or books.

**NOTE** If you live outside the United States and UK, keep in mind that some features may not be available in your region. Many companies roll out new AI features to these markets first before wider release.

Google and Microsoft are also major players in AI. Google's Gemini excels at working with Google Workspace data, searching through Gmail, Docs, Drive, Maps, YouTube, Flights, and Hotels. Microsoft's Copilot for Microsoft 365 integrates with business tools like Outlook, Teams, OneDrive, SharePoint, and Office documents, although it needs an extra license for Microsoft 365 users.

Let's take a look at table 1.2, which gives an overview of a few of the most popular language engines.

Table 1.2  Overview of leading AI chatbots

| Model name | Key capabilities | Strengths |
| --- | --- | --- |
| OpenAI ChatGPT | Conversational AI, coding, content creation | Versatile, high-quality responses, multimodal support, robust API, regularly updated |
| Anthropic Claude | Safety-focused AI, document analysis | High accuracy, ethical design, strong for long documents, enterprise-friendly |
| Google Gemini | Multimodal AI, advanced reasoning, coding | Integrated with Google ecosystem, excels in multimodal tasks, powerful for handling complexity |
| Microsoft Copilot | Business productivity, Microsoft 365 integration | Enhances collaboration, tailored for business tasks, seamless integration with MS apps |
| Meta AI Llama 2 | Open source, multilingual text generation | Customizable, free to use, excellent for creative tasks and code, backed by an active community |
| Mistral 7B | Open source, text and code generation | Compact, efficient, highly customizable, community-driven |
| GitHub Copilot | AI-assisted code generation, pair programming | Speeds up coding, supports many languages, integrates well with IDEs |

We've tried all of these chatbots and have settled on both ChatGPT and Claude, each for different reasons; we used both to help write this book. We'll cover this more in chapter 2, but we've found that they give the highest-quality responses with the greatest accuracy.

### 1.4.2 Image generation with AI models

Although AI art tools like DALL-E, Stable Diffusion, and Midjourney get attention for their creative abilities, IT pros often find AI's technical image capabilities more useful. These tools help with both artistic projects and practical work tasks.

Let's look at how AI images can help with both creative and technical needs, with a focus on IT applications:

- *Creative images*—When Stable Diffusion was updated in September 2023, users showed off its abilities with images like "Spiral Town" (figure 1.2)—a striking but impossible town made of spiral waves of light, shadows, and clouds.

Although these creative images look impressive, they're not ideal for technical work. You can't easily recreate the same image twice, and the tools don't always follow instructions precisely.

Figure 1.2 "Spiral Town"

- *Technical images*—For IT tasks, AI works best with technical content, although knowing its limits helps you pick the right tool. When you need exact diagrams, charts, or mockups, technical tools give you the most reliable results.
- *Mermaid and PlantUML diagrams*—AI is good at writing markup for flowcharts, sequence diagrams, and architecture diagrams. These work well in docs and presentations. Although AI doesn't currently make Microsoft Visio files directly, Mermaid and PlantUML handle most diagramming needs.
- *LaTeX equations*—AI quickly writes LaTeX markup for complex math formulas, which is useful for technical docs or academic papers.
- *HTML/CSS mockups*—In addition to using image generation for UI mockups, you can also have AI write HTML and CSS code to screenshot. This gives you exact text and layouts while keeping full control.

Table 1.3 describes where AI works best for technical diagrams and what it can't do yet.

Table 1.3  AI diagramming capabilities and limitations

| Need | What AI can do | Current limits | Better options |
| --- | --- | --- | --- |
| Network diagrams | Create Mermaid/PlantUML markup with tools like ChatGPT and Claude | Need extra steps to get Visio files | Try AI plugins for Visio or scripts that make VSDX files. |
| Infrastructure maps | Write templates for Terraform or Mermaid | May need manual fixes for complex maps | Use Lucidchart AI to help with map layouts. |

Table 1.3 AI diagramming capabilities and limitations (continued)

| Need | What AI can do | Current limits | Better options |
|---|---|---|---|
| System architecture | Help with PlantUML models | Basic graphics only | Try Figma with AI plugins. |
| Database schemas | Create SQL and ER diagrams | Limited visual options | Use a tool like Workik or ChatGPT for schemas. |
| UI mockups | Make HTML/CSS or markdown designs | Not polished enough for demos | Try Uizard or Figma's AI tools for quick UI designs. |

You'll need extra steps to turn AI diagrams into enterprise formats like Visio. AI helps design and describe diagrams well, but you often need other tools to get the final format you want. Still, AI's speed and accuracy usually make up for these extra steps.

The Calm the Chaos marketing materials in figure 1.3 show how IT pros can get professional results using code instead of artistic AI images. While AI art has its place and can enhance presentations, code provides ultimate control when creating technical documentation and diagrams.

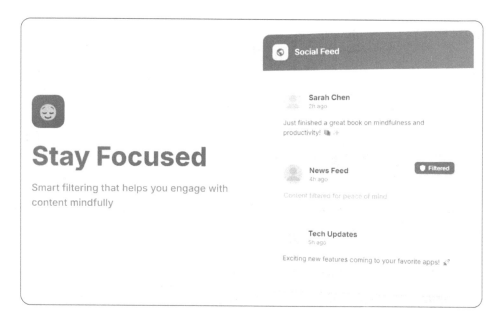

Figure 1.3 HTML/CSS marketing material generated by AI

AI-generated flowchart code was even used in this book, in chapter 13, to create a figure that illustrates the process of building and using an AI-integrated app, as seen in figure 1.4. We found it interesting that whereas Claude excels at web design and writing, ChatGPT was a far better mermaid designer.

**12** CHAPTER 1 *Artificial intelligence in IT*

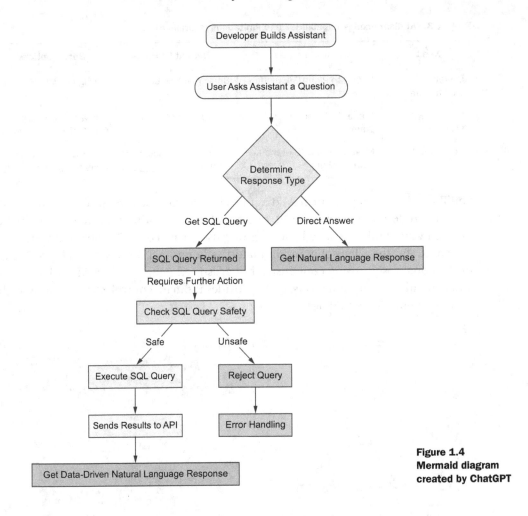

Figure 1.4 Mermaid diagram created by ChatGPT

Each AI tool has its strengths, as listed in table 1.4, which compares the main AI image tools available today.

Table 1.4 Overview of popular image generation AI engines

| Name | Company/Creator | Specialty | Pros |
|---|---|---|---|
| Midjourney | David Holz | Photorealistic environmental portraits, creative partner for art generation | Immersive experience, detail-oriented, complex prompt handling |
| 4o | OpenAI | Text to image generation | Creates images from text, versatile, accurate, and easy to use |
| Stable Diffusion | Stability AI | Text to image generation, art creation, open source | Open source, customizable, high-quality images, large community support |

**Table 1.4  Overview of popular image generation AI engines** *(continued)*

| Name | Company/Creator | Specialty | Pros |
|---|---|---|---|
| RunwayML | Runway | Creative AI tools, image and video generation | User-friendly interface, collaborative tools, real-time video editing, diverse range of AI models |
| DeepArt | DeepArt GmbH | Artistic style transfer | Simple to use, various artistic styles, transforms photos into artworks |
| StyleGAN | NVIDIA | Image generation, style transfer | High-quality image generation, style manipulation |
| Meta AI | Meta | Text to image generation | Integrated with Facebook and Instagram, easy to use |
| Gemini | Google | Text to image generation | Creates images from text, similar to DALL-E |

We mainly use Midjourney and OpenAI image generation because we started with them early on. 4o has become our favorite because it pairs ChatGPT's language skills with image creation. You can access it through OpenAI or Copilot, making it very convenient.

> **NOTE** For more details about how this technology works, check out Manning's *Introduction to Generative AI* by Numa Dhamani and Maggie Engler (2024; www.manning.com/books/introduction-to-generative-ai).

## 1.5 Service costs

You're probably wondering if you can use this book without paying for any of the services we recommend. The good news is that chatbots like ChatGPT and Claude offer a free tier that provides access to their best models and features. This means you can experience the full potential of these platforms without a subscription, allowing you to learn and use the techniques covered in this book effectively. However, keep in mind that you'll still be subject to some usage limits. For example, with Claude, you can send about 10 messages every 5 hours on the free tier. Table 1.5 lists the current pricing for AI services as of February 2025.

**Table 1.5  Overview of popular AI engine costs**

| Service | Free tier | Free trial of full product | Subscription cost |
|---|---|---|---|
| OpenAI ChatGPT | Yes | Yes | ChatGPT Plus, $20/month; ChatGPT Pro, $200/month |
| Google Gemini | Yes | Yes, two month trial | Gemini Ultra, $19.99/month, includes Google One 2 TB; Gemini API pay-as-you-go, $0.10 per 1 million tokens for input, output free of charge |

**Table 1.5** Overview of popular AI engine costs *(continued)*

| Service | Free tier | Free trial of full product | Subscription cost |
|---|---|---|---|
| Anthropic Claude | Yes | Yes | Claude Pro, $20/month; Claude Teams, $30/person/month; Claude Enterprise, custom pricing |
| Microsoft Copilot | Yes, restricted usage | Yes | Copilot Pro, $20/month; Copilot for Microsoft 365, $30/month |
| GitHub Copilot | Yes, for verified students, teachers, and open source maintainers | Free 30-day trial | Pro, $10/month or $100/year; Business, $19/user/month; Enterprise, $39/user/month |
| Midjourney | No | No | Basic Plan, $10/month or $96/year; Standard Plan, $30/month or $288/year; Pro Plan, $60/month or $576/year; Mega Plan, $120/month or $1,152/year |
| OpenAI DALL-E | No | No | Standard quality (1024 × 1024), $0.04 per image; HD quality (1024 × 1024), $0.08 per image |
| Meta AI | Yes, through Facebook, Instagram, WhatsApp, and Messenger | No | Free; paid versions under consideration |
| Stable Diffusion | Yes | No | Basic Plan, $27/month; Standard Plan, $47/month; Premium Plan, $147/month |

Several services offer free tiers with basic features so that you can try most examples in this book without a subscription. Paid plans include extras like faster processing and advanced features.

> **NOTE** If chatbot service costs are too high, consider using vendor API playgrounds instead. These web interfaces look similar to chatbots but can be much cheaper depending on your usage. Many of our colleagues who use playgrounds spend just $2 to $6 on tokens monthly, far less than a subscription. We'll explore this more in later chapters.

The free tiers let you test all the key features, but if you regularly hit usage limits or need extra capabilities, a paid subscription may make sense.

## 1.6 Using AI responsibly at work

This book helps IT professionals whose organizations have approved AI use and want implementation guidance. Instead of debating broad AI ethics like privacy, security, or plagiarism, we focus here on practical guidelines for using AI effectively in IT work.

### 1.6.1 Data security with AI

When you use AI services, your data leaves your company network for cloud processing. Be careful with confidential information, and check your company's policies and regulations, such as the EU's General Data Protection Regulation (GDPR), before sharing data. Remember that AI platforms may store what you send them—don't share protected data unless you're using a private subscription or self-hosted instance. Table 1.6 shows the main security risks of using AI in companies.

Table 1.6  Fundamental considerations for AI data security

| Concern | Effect |
| --- | --- |
| Data movement | Information sent to AI services leaves your corporate network for cloud processing, potentially exposing sensitive data. |
| Data retention | AI providers may store and retain submitted data for model training unless explicitly disabled. |
| Compliance | Data handling must align with regulations like GDPR, the Health Insurance Portability and Accountability Act (HIPAA), Service Organization Control 2 (SOC 2), ISO 27001, and industry-specific standards. |
| Model security | Unauthorized access or adversarial attacks can compromise AI models, leading to data leakage, biased outputs, or manipulation. |
| Access control | Improper identity and access management (IAM) policies can result in unauthorized users gaining access to sensitive AI-generated insights. |
| Encryption and data privacy | Not all AI services offer end-to-end encryption or customer-managed encryption keys (CMEK), affecting data confidentiality. |
| Auditability and logging | Lack of robust logging can make it difficult to track data usage, detect anomalies, or comply with security audits. |

For enhanced security, major tech companies offer enterprise AI plans. If you're already using Microsoft's ecosystem, check out Microsoft 365 Copilot and Azure OpenAI services—they work with your current Microsoft security settings and compliance rules. AWS Bedrock and Google's Vertex AI also provide secure options through private endpoints and IAM controls, helping you keep your company's AI use safe and within compliance guidelines.

Although data security matters, using AI tools fairly and ethically is just as important. We'll discuss this next.

### 1.6.2 Bias and fairness

AI systems often reflect biases from their training data. Take resume screening: an AI might reject good candidates based on names or addresses. One real case at Amazon showed its AI tool favoring candidates named "Jared" who played lacrosse, simply because many successful past hires shared these traits.

To use AI fairly in hiring, do the following:

- Ask all candidates the same interview questions.
- Remove names from resumes before review.
- Use AI to create and grade skill-based tests.
- Include diverse interviewers.
- Check hiring decisions for bias patterns.

You can also check AI outputs for bias. Tools like Textio highlight biased language in job postings and suggest better options. While writing this book, we noticed that AI tools often defaulted to male pronouns for engineers, which needed correction.

The key is combining AI's speed with careful bias checks. Having a diverse team working with AI helps spot and fix these problems early.

### 1.6.3 AI writing and plagiarism

As AI writing grows more common, spotting it gets harder. We've found that no detection tool reliably identifies AI-written content. Even OpenAI stopped using its own detector because the tool wasn't accurate enough. Although some tools claim they can make AI writing undetectable, truly reliable detection doesn't exist.

Some AI tools now include web search, making it easier to cite sources. ChatGPT can pull in search results and cite them in its responses, as seen in figure 1.5. Other AI services only use their training data, so you can't check their outputs against outside sources.

**Figure 1.5**
**Citation prompt in ChatGPT**

Microsoft Copilot automatically adds source citations to AI content, as shown in figure 1.6. This helps users properly credit their sources and maintain credibility.

*1.6 Using AI responsibly at work* 17

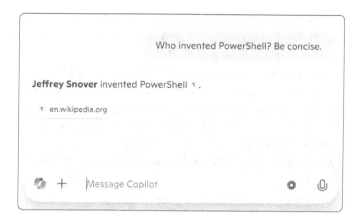

Figure 1.6 Default citation in Microsoft Copilot

Although AI writing detectors have major limitations, new features like built-in search and citations make responsible AI use easier. Still, be open about using AI, and credit your sources properly.

### 1.6.4 Citing prompts in your work

Chatbots make citation formatting easy. They quickly convert sources into APA, MLA, Harvard, IEEE, and OSCOLA formats. No more stressing over the "References" section!

The academic world is still figuring out how to cite AI tools like ChatGPT. The James Cook University in Australia (https://libguides.jcu.edu.au/apa/AI) suggests treating AI content as nonrecoverable because you can't cite it like traditional sources. The university recommends mentioning AI use in your text and citing the software itself, listing OpenAI as the source for ChatGPT. The University of Waterloo Library has similar guidelines, as shown in figure 1.7.

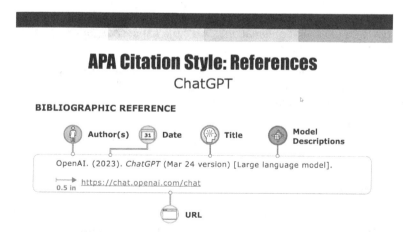

Figure 1.7 APA citation (Image source: University of Waterloo Libraries, "AI-Generated Content Citation"; https://mng.bz/PdVg)

Check if your school or workplace allows chatbots, and follow its citation rules. Because chatbot sources are hard to verify, be clear about when and how you use AI in your work.

AI can help without writing your content. Use it to brainstorm ideas, proofread, check work against rubrics, grade practice assignments, or improve your writing. Many professionals can use tools like ChatGPT at work, but their results vary. Some create clear docs quickly; others get confused responses. Success comes down to how well you use the tool, not the tool itself.

This book shows you how to use ChatGPT and other AI tools better. You'll see hundreds of real examples and learn to get better results. We'll start with basic prompts and build up to complex problem-solving that gets the most from AI.

> **Did AI write this book?**
>
> You've probably seen those social media ads—someone claiming they make $50,000 monthly from AI-written books created in a day. The service promises complete books from a single prompt. Sounds amazing, right? We had to test it.
>
> Chrissy asked ChatGPT to outline this chapter. The results looked promising, and we kept one of its ideas: "An elephant in the server room."
>
> Following ChatGPT's outline, Chrissy wrote what seemed like a solid draft in about 10 hours. She sent it to her friend Alicia, a product manager interested in using AI at work.
>
> Alicia liked the chapter but got stuck on one section. "I read it several times but couldn't understand it," she said. Chrissy knew exactly which part—she hadn't understood it either but kept it because it sounded impressive.
>
> The section covered "the three A's of AI":
>
> > Given the rise of AI, the three A's are indispensable: Adaptability, Agility, and Automation. Being adaptable means recognizing that the IT sector is changing and that you need to change with it. Agility is about quickly deploying and benefiting from the new AI-powered tools. And automation? That's the game-changer that frees up your time for more strategic tasks.
>
> The alliteration! It's so solid. The message? Seems so deep. But it's not. If you're capable of reading that paragraph without zoning out, you'll find that it's an almost meaningful, incredibly skippable word soup.
>
> All that is to say that *no, AI did not write this book*. It is not currently capable of writing a high-quality book that any of us would find useful or enjoyable to read.

## 1.7 How we are using AI

We mainly used AI as an editorial assistant while writing this book. We shared our ideas and rough drafts, explained what we wanted to convey, and got suggestions for clearer ways to express it.

After writing each section, we asked AI to check if it was accurate, clear, and well-balanced in length and technical detail. When we wanted AI's help writing something, we specified our tone, along with words to avoid and key points to cover, and asked it to deliver the message clearly and directly.

AI also helped with basic tasks like formatting, citations, grammar, and finding synonyms. These same techniques work for emails, reports, presentations, and other content, as we'll show you through example prompts.

Essentially, we treat AI like a collaborator rather than an expert—except for images. We can draw basic illustrations and logos, but it takes days. DALL-E 3 makes our PowerPoint slides and logos much better. Sometimes we keep the funny typos and extra fingers in images, although they can be frustrating.

AI does make our writing better, but it can't write a whole page well, let alone a chapter or book. It needs careful guidance for professional content and can't match human reasoning. One exception may be children's stories—our reviewers say kids enjoy ChatGPT's tales and poems, and so do we. Some of our best chatbot moments came from asking for stories and poems.

Thanks for joining us as we explore AI in IT—from basics to advanced techniques. In chapter 2, we'll start by examining different AI models and how to choose the right ones for your needs.

## 1.8 Prompts used in this chapter

Following are concrete examples of how we used AI (mostly ChatGPT and Claude paid subscriptions) to help write this chapter. We'll include prompts like these at the end of all chapters in this book, in hopes that they'll give you ideas for how to use AI in your own work:

- Name 50 real-world, practical things you think this book could help IT Professionals. For example "Generate After-Action Reports with objective insights, removing all intrapersonal issue influence"
- Give me 10 suggestions that can replace the phrase "in a setting"
- Can you suggest a change to the second paragraph that emphasizes fun and also give me a stronger call to action at the end
- "Amidst a backdrop of technical hurdles" sounds haughty. Can you use smaller words?
- I'm about to paste two paragraphs and I want to keep them as is but insert a story in the middle. I'll paste a story told in first person but please change it to third person.
- Fix the transition from the paragraph to the list
- Here is a revised Chapter 1. Please review it and give me some insights. Anything I missed that can make it a little longer?

## Summary

- ChatGPT and other AI tools speed up IT tasks like network fixes and knowledge-base updates.
- Recent AI models bring better reasoning skills plus voice and image features.
- AI helps with root cause analysis, disaster recovery, and cloud management.
- Security and ethics are critical considerations when using AI at work.
- Watch for AI bias and proper citation of AI-generated content.
- AI helps with writing and creative tasks but doesn't replace human expertise.
- This book shows IT pros practical ways to use AI in their daily work.

# Chatbots: Tasks and tips

**This chapter covers**

- How AI chatbots perform in day-to-day IT work
- Understanding what each major AI assistant does best
- Getting AI help with web searches, analyzing images, voice commands, and automating tasks
- Setting up AI tools to work better with your IT processes
- Finding the right AI image generator for your IT projects

Choosing the right AI tool makes a big difference for IT work. Although AI assistants share many features, each is better at specific tasks. Some are great at searching the web and breaking down error messages, whereas others can create entire websites from basic instructions. Others focus on creating detailed images—they can even turn abstract ideas like "beautiful API architecture" into realistic visuals.

This chapter explores how AI tools work in practice—both what they can and can't do well. Rather than listing features, we'll look at actual use cases and situations where each tool works best. Understanding these differences helps you pick the right AI assistant for each task.

> **NOTE** Running AI models on your computer is covered in appendix A. You may be surprised at how simple it is—you can start with just a Microsoft VS Code extension. Local models aren't usually as powerful as cloud versions because they need fewer resources, but they're great if you need privacy or work on air-gapped networks.

AI chatbots and conversational models are a good place to start working with AI because they're flexible and can do many things. These tools show what current AI can achieve and create a base for other AI applications. We'll look at features that work for individual IT pros rather than big companies, as each organization has different security and compliance needs.

## 2.1 Chatbots and conversational AI

When it comes to evaluating AI models, benchmarks like those from Hugging Face's lmarena.ai provide a solid performance snapshot. Hugging Face is like an app store for AI models, and its Chatbot Arena allows users to compare bots and vote for their favorite. But the real test is how these models perform in day-to-day scenarios. Our experience has shown that even highly rated models can have off days (due to high usage/resource constraints), but they generally deliver impressive results.

In the following sections, we'll discuss our hands-on experiences with leading AI chatbots. We'll focus on the factors that matter to IT professionals: reliability, feature sets, and practical use cases.

### 2.1.1 OpenAI ChatGPT

If you're going to subscribe to just one AI assistant, we suggest you make it ChatGPT. We've found it to be the most versatile and reliable option available. It even has a free tier with several of our favorite features (it's free because usage is limited). Let's start with one of ChatGPT's most practical features for IT work: web search.

#### WHEN YOU NEED WEB RESEARCH

What really sets ChatGPT apart is its web search capability, also known as SearchGPT. It's so good that we often use ChatGPT to gather information to feed into other AI models that don't have direct internet access. SearchGPT processes natural language requests, quickly searches multiple web pages, and then combines that new information with its own knowledge base. Every response includes citations, letting you verify information or explore topics more deeply. Google Gemini has a similar feature, but we're partial to ChatGPT's functionality both because you can control when it searches the web and because ChatGPT's output is currently superior to Gemini's, as we'll see shortly.

This real-time access is particularly valuable for developers because most AI coding assistants are trained on data from a specific point in time. Without current information, they often suggest outdated GitHub Actions, deprecated npm packages, or old API versions. We frequently use ChatGPT to research the latest package versions and give that information to the tool that will be doing our coding (we don't use ChatGPT to code).

**TIP** When asking ChatGPT to verify multiple dependencies or facts, break your requests into smaller chunks. Asking it to check 3 packages at a time rather than 20 gives you more accurate results. This is because each fact requires a separate web search and verification step—the more items you request at once, the higher the chance of errors slipping through.

The search feature is particularly effective for business scenarios that involve financial calculations. Need today's exchange rate for an expense report? Current per diem rate for a specific city while on business? Subscription fees for a service? ChatGPT can fetch the latest rates and calculate the results, as shown in figure 2.1. In this example, ChatGPT provides up-to-date per diem rates for Paris, France.

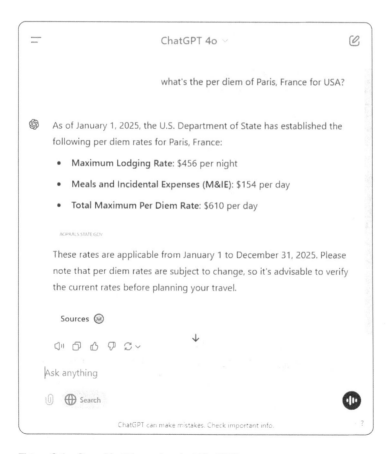

Figure 2.1   Searching the web using ChatGPT

Also, you may have heard that "language models are bad at math," but modern AI services like ChatGPT, Claude, and Gemini have improved significantly at mathematical operations compared to their predecessors. This is because they now initiate Python sessions to perform calculations automatically instead of relying on language reasoning. Beyond web searches, ChatGPT's visual analysis capabilities are equally valuable, as we'll see in the next section.

#### WHEN YOU NEED TO ANALYZE IMAGES

ChatGPT is exceptional at vision tasks. We use this feature daily for everything from decoding error messages in screenshots to translating ancient text. Take the Latin stone tablet shown in figure 2.2. When Brandon used ChatGPT to translate it, the results were remarkably accurate. The tablet was hard to read with the human eye, but ChatGPT was still able to decipher it. However, he did find that breaking the task into two steps—first transcribing the Latin text and then translating it—worked best. This approach gets better results by having the model focus on one task at a time.

Figure 2.2 Latin inscription on a stone tablet in Italy

For IT professionals, ChatGPT's vision capabilities provide several practical solutions, such as those listed in table 2.1. Image analysis with ChatGPT simplifies visual tasks in IT. These AI capabilities are already changing how IT teams handle everything from screenshot analysis to code generation, and the potential for new applications grows as the technology improves.

Table 2.1  Visual analysis tasks at work

| Task type | Capabilities |
| --- | --- |
| UI/UX development | Uploads Balsamiq wireframes or mockups for HTML and CSS generation. Can apply specific design aesthetics, including transforming modern designs into legacy styles like Web 2.0. |
| Theme creation | Extracts color palettes from reference images and generates complete theme files for development environments. Automatically fills missing colors with complementary shades for VS Code themes. |
| Error analysis | Processes screenshots of error messages or logs, providing detailed analysis and troubleshooting steps, often identifying easily missed details. |
| Accessibility improvements | Generates accurate, descriptive alt text for website images and social media posts, supporting both accessibility standards and SEO requirements. Ideal for legacy content updates and large image libraries. |

**WHEN YOU WANT VOICE INTERACTION**

Paid tiers add natural-sounding voice conversations with customizable voices—a feature we use regularly when we need hands-free AI assistance. During our hour-long commutes, we use voice chat extensively, which conveniently matches ChatGPT's daily one-hour voice limit for our account. The voice feature even has internet access, so we can check current documentation or troubleshoot problems while driving without touching our phones.

One annoying problem with advanced voice is that OpenAI hasn't yet perfected pause detection, so it often interrupts us when we pause briefly during speech. OpenAI has suggested workarounds, such as using headphones and enabling Voice Isolation mode on iPhones to minimize background noise that might trigger an unintended cutoff. However, many users still experience frequent interruptions, leading to frustration. Some have requested the return of a manual hold-to-talk option to prevent unwanted cutoffs, but OpenAI has yet to implement a permanent fix.

When it works well, ChatGPT handles over 80 languages, making it useful for global teams and international communication. We've used it to communicate with non-English speakers during overseas office visits.

**WHEN YOU NEED SPECIALIZED ASSISTANTS**

We've found custom GPTs particularly useful for creating specialized AI assistants that understand our specific setup. You can teach them about your environment, give them access to documentation, and set rules for how they handle different tasks. Unlike the standard ChatGPT experience, these customized versions remember your preferences and requirements. Table 2.2 shows some real-world examples of how we use Custom GPTs in our daily work.

**Table 2.2  Real-world custom GPT applications in IT**

| Task | Benefits |
| --- | --- |
| PowerShell assistant | Maintains your coding standards, knows your environment, and always responds in PowerShell syntax |
| Infrastructure documenter | References your uploaded network diagrams and configuration files to help document systems accurately |
| SQL code reviewer | Follows your organization's specific SQL standards and best practices when reviewing queries |
| Change management helper | Creates standardized change requests using your company's templates and requirements |

Here's a practical example: instead of repeatedly telling ChatGPT about your development standards, server configurations, and preferred approaches, you can build a custom GPT that already knows these details. Upload your style guides, configuration files, and documentation templates, and it will consistently provide relevant answers that align with your environment.

> **TIP** Look for tasks where you find yourself explaining the same context to ChatGPT over and over—these make perfect custom GPT candidates. In our case, we built one specifically for PowerShell development that already knows how we structure our modules, handle errors, and manage logging. This saves us from typing out these details every time we need script help.

We created a custom GPT specifically for SQL performance tuning. It excels at daily optimization tasks because it knows our server configurations, indexing approaches, and typical query patterns. For routine work like spotting index problems and suggesting query improvements, it's consistently effective.

This specialization has its limitations, however. When faced with unusual deadlocks or new SQL Server behaviors, the custom GPT can be less adaptable. It may not quickly incorporate emerging best practices or handle novel situations well.

For complex scenarios—investigating blocking chains, diagnosing unexpected performance spikes, or designing scalable architectures—we've found regular ChatGPT's broader capabilities more valuable. Although our custom GPT handles routine maintenance effectively, the unpredictable nature of production problems often requires the flexibility of the base model.

### WHEN YOU NEED ADVANCED TECHNICAL PROBLEM-SOLVING

Paid subscribers get access to OpenAI's more advanced models—o1 and o1 mini—on a weekly or unlimited basis, depending on the plan. These models excel at complex technical problems. For example, we ran into a CSS problem with nested dropdowns and conflicting z-index layers. Where standard models might pattern-match to common solutions, o1 methodically analyzed the DOM structure and event bubbling to identify the exact source of the conflicts. It was the only model that was able to solve this problem.

**NOTE** OpenAI plans to simplify model selection, letting the system automatically choose the appropriate level of processing for each task rather than requiring users to select specific models.

With OpenAI's Pro plan, which comes at a hefty price ($200/month as of April 2025), its 200,000-token context window lets users feed in entire codebases or documentation sets at once, and it can generate responses up to 100,000 tokens long. We'll talk about tokens in chapter 3, but for now, think of them as basic units of text that AI models process. If we can ever afford to test it out, we'd be curious to see how it handles algorithm development—we've been working on a trending news algorithm to help detect and mute viral scandals, and it's proven surprisingly challenging to get right. o1's ability to process complex data patterns could be exactly what we need.

Here's what stands out after using ChatGPT:

- *Pros*
  - Powerful free tier with reasonable usage limits
  - Best-in-class vision analysis capabilities
  - Natural voice interaction with customizable voices
  - Powerful augmented web search
  - Reliable performance across tasks
  - Excellent language support for global users
- *Cons*
  - Responses can sometimes feel generic.
  - Coding abilities are good but not exceptional.
  - May not dive as deep into topics as specialized models like Claude.
  - Privacy policies regarding data usage could be more transparent.

ChatGPT keeps adding features that make it more useful for enterprise teams. Advanced Data Analysis helps us work with data and create visuals, and canvas improves how we collaborate on text and code. The screen-sharing feature lets teams get AI help with what they see on their phones. For IT work, these capabilities, combined with the expanded context window, give us powerful tools for technical problem-solving.

We've made ChatGPT our primary AI tool for day-to-day work. Its reliable performance and rich feature set make it particularly valuable for IT professionals adopting AI. The vision features and web search capabilities stand out, and we often use them as a backup when other AI models hit their limits. The mobile app brings all these features together exceptionally well, making it more practical for on-the-go use than other AI options.

### 2.1.2 Anthropic Claude

In contrast to ChatGPT's general-purpose strengths, Anthropic's Claude excels in deep, context-aware analysis and generation of text. Where ChatGPT may sometimes produce generic responses, Claude engages in "thoughtful," nuanced conversations that demonstrate a remarkable understanding of context. For example, when drafting technical documentation, Claude doesn't just explain what code does—it provides insights into why certain approaches were chosen and how they fit into the broader system architecture.

#### WHEN YOU NEED ADVANCED OR NATURAL WRITING

Claude's writing skills are especially strong for technical and professional tasks. We've found it particularly valuable for creating documentation that's both technically precise and easy to understand. When we needed documentation for a complex microservices architecture, Claude generated technical specifications that worked equally well for experienced developers and those just starting their careers.

Claude offers several writing styles, including the following:

- The *Concise style* turns lengthy content into clear, focused points. It proved invaluable when we needed to convert a 20-page technical requirements document into a 2-page executive summary without losing essential information. This style works best for updates and briefs that need to maximize effect with minimal words.
- The *Explanatory style* specializes in making complex topics understandable. When documenting our new authentication system, Claude created documentation that connected technical details with core security concepts in a way everyone could follow. This approach is perfect for technical guides and process documentation.
- The *Formal style* balances professionalism with readability. Although it's effective for legal documents and compliance reports, we use it sparingly because it can sound too distant for regular team communication.

> **TIP** Use the Formal style carefully: it sounds impersonal and unnatural in most situations. The Explanatory style typically works much better for professional communication—it keeps things clear while maintaining a more natural tone that readers appreciate.

What sets Claude apart is its ability to learn and adapt to specific writing requirements. You can upload examples of your company's documentation, provide style guides, or describe your preferred approach, and Claude will consistently maintain that style across future documents. We've used this feature to ensure that all our technical documentation follows the same voice and format, even when different team members are involved in the writing process.

When creating custom styles, provide multiple examples of the desired writing style for better results. This helps Claude understand the nuances and patterns you want to emulate. For instance, we provided three different well-reviewed chapter sections as examples, which helped Claude consistently match our preferred writing style.

Claude's practical uses in documentation include

- Converting complex API documentation into clear, developer-friendly guides
- Creating consistent release notes across multiple product versions
- Drafting clear, actionable incident postmortems
- Generating user-facing documentation from technical specifications
- Adapting technical content for different audience levels, from C-suite to end-users

Although Claude produces excellent technical content, we always review the output carefully, especially for important documentation. This helps ensure that everything matches our standards and requirements.

### WHEN YOU NEED SOFTWARE ARCHITECTURE

Claude performs well with complex software development tasks, particularly those involving system architecture. We've found that the Anthropic models, including Sonnet and Opus, do more than write code—they help design complete solutions. This ability to understand and architect systems is why many developers, including Chrissy, prefer working with these models over alternatives.

For example, when we needed to add a new authentication feature to our PowerShell module, Claude didn't just create the new command. It first analyzed our existing authentication patterns, identified potential security implications, and suggested a design that would scale well as we added more features. The solution included

- A new command matching our naming standards
- Module manifest with correctly defined dependencies
- Integration with our existing logging approach
- Error handling that followed our established patterns
- Unit tests covering unexpected edge cases
- Documentation explaining both usage and technical

What impressed us most was Claude's consideration of the bigger picture. When making code changes, there are often ripple effects throughout the system that aren't immediately obvious. For example, when we mentioned future single sign-on support, Claude designed the authentication code to make that integration straightforward later, helping us avoid a major rewrite. This ability to look beyond immediate code changes and plan for downstream effects makes Claude particularly useful for complex development work.

This architectural thinking extends beyond individual features. When reviewing our API design, Claude identified inconsistencies in our endpoint patterns and suggested refactoring to make the API more intuitive for developers. It provided specific examples of how the changes would simplify common integration scenarios, complete with before/after code samples.

**WHEN YOU NEED DIRECT COMPUTER CONTROL**

With Claude, you can automate complex system interactions using its Computer Use capability. This Docker-based implementation lets Claude directly interact with your system, turning natural language instructions into automated actions. Although giving AI system access requires careful consideration, the implementation can be both secure and practical.

An example came from a major data migration project. When transferring content from an old documentation system to a new platform, Claude automated the entire process like this:

1 Extracted content from the old system's web interface
2 Reformatted the content to match their new structure
3 Created and validated new pages in the new system
4 Generated a detailed migration report

This kind of automated assistance can save weeks of manual work and eliminate copy-paste errors.

> **TIP** If you're a ChatGPT Pro user, you now have access to Operators, which is similar to Anthropic's Computer Use. Visit https://operator.chatgpt.com for more information.

The computer control features are powerful, but they can be slow and can quickly get expensive. For cost-effective automation, consider having Claude generate a script (Python, PowerShell, or Bash) that you can run manually instead. This avoids API costs while achieving the same results. For instance, if you need to scrape data from multiple websites, Claude can write a Python script that you can execute yourself. To find out more about Computer Use, check out the "computer use demo" in Anthropic's GitHub repository at https://github.com/anthropics/anthropic-quickstarts.

**PLANS AND USAGE**

Claude offers a free tier, but it's pretty limited compared to the Pro plan. The free version can handle shorter interactions and fewer tasks; the Pro plan, at $20/month, allows for about five times more usage and is better suited for larger, more complex projects and ideas.

> ### Tracking Claude usage
> We use a helpful browser extension called the *Claude Usage Tracker*, which displays a quota meter indicating our remaining Claude usage. The extension estimates remaining messages based on the current conversation's token usage and the time until Claude's usage allowance resets. This helps us avoid hitting token limits mid-task and better manage our given allowance.

## 2.1 Chatbots and conversational AI

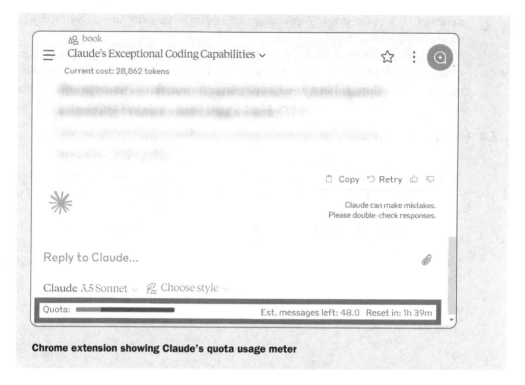

**Chrome extension showing Claude's quota usage meter**

The free tier helps you explore what Claude can do, but its capabilities are limited compared to the paid version, which offers noticeably better performance and intelligence:

- *Pros*
  - Keeps context and guides conversations effectively
  - Creates well-structured code with a strong understanding of context
  - Writes naturally and clearly
  - Performs especially well on complex reasoning tasks
  - Projects feature enables ongoing conversations and teamwork
  - Strong language capabilities across many languages
- *Cons*
  - Missing features like image generation and voice chat that other AI tools have
  - No built-in code interpreter or plugin system
  - Responds more slowly than some competitors
  - Limited usage even with paid accounts—only five times more than the free tier
  - Not available in all regions, which can make access difficult

Overall, Claude is our favorite chatbot for tasks that require advanced reasoning, context-aware interactions, and high-quality writing. Its exceptional performance and memory also make it our top choice for coding—we only use o1 when Sonnet can't figure out a problem, which is rare.

Something to note is that we've previously had to maintain two subscriptions for intense development sessions because the token limit is relatively low. We've since moved to APIs but still use one Claude subscription. We'll discuss token limits further in chapter 3 and APIs in chapter 11.

### 2.1.3 Google Gemini

Google's Gemini combines processing for images, videos, text, and code. The 2.0 release in December 2024 added voice and video chat, better spatial awareness, and built-in Google Search. But in our testing during early 2025, we found that it often fell short of what Google promises.

The features sound great on paper: image generation, real-time news from the Associated Press, and support for almost 40 languages. But Gemini's performance is hit or miss. Sometimes it even seems to forget what it can do, giving incorrect or confusing answers, as shown in figure 2.3.

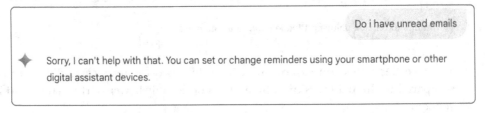

Figure 2.3 Gemini forgetting that one of its best features is checking unread emails

We've even seen it say, "Sorry, I do not have the capability to check for unread emails." This unreliable performance makes Gemini difficult to trust for professional work where consistency matters.

When Gemini works properly, however, it can generate creative and engaging content. Its large context window helps it handle big codebases well, which some users appreciate for coding tasks. However, most developers don't consider it among the best AI coding assistants available.

> **TIP** Although we don't currently use Gemini, we're impressed by other Google AI tools like NotebookLM, which can transform documents into NPR *Morning Edition*-style podcasts. The AI-generated conversations sound remarkably natural and offer a creative way to digest technical documentation. Their video generator, Veo, also ranks highly.

For Android users, Gemini now works as the main assistant on devices with Android 10+ and at least 2 GB of RAM. It replaces Google Assistant, although you can switch back through settings if you need specific voice features that Gemini doesn't have yet.

## 2.1 Chatbots and conversational AI

Similar to ChatGPT, Gemini includes web search that uses Google's search index, as shown in figure 2.4. When you need current information, it searches and summarizes results directly in your chat, so you don't have to bounce between apps.

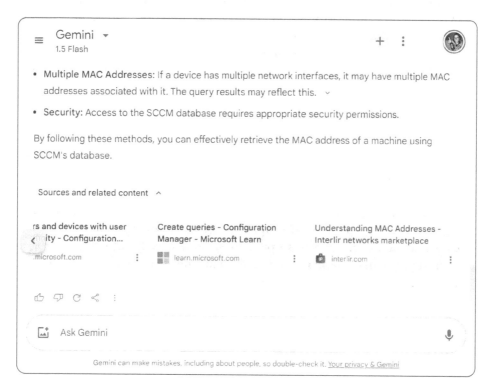

Figure 2.4 Gemini's web search interface

Here's a summary of Gemini's main strengths and limitations:

- *Pros*
  - Works with images, videos, and text at the same time
  - Creates visuals that combine text and images
  - Handles many languages and translations
  - Built-in Google search and other Google features
  - Custom AI models available (paid only)
  - Free tier available
  - Gets real-time news from AP
  - Works as an Android assistant
- *Cons*
  - Requires a Google account.
  - Not as good as specialized AI for writing and complex thinking.

- Text tasks may be better with language-focused AI.
- Not available in all regions.

Gemini offers a unique mix of features, but we found its performance too inconsistent for our work. Although it shows promise, it frequently forgets its own capabilities, making it frustrating to use. Others may have different experiences, but we didn't renew our subscription after the trial ended.

There's growing buzz around newer Gemini models. However, with ChatGPT and Claude already proving so reliable, Gemini's improvements haven't compelled us to switch.

### 2.1.4 Microsoft Copilot suite

Microsoft has built AI capabilities into Azure, Office, and its other major products. Among these, Azure Copilot stands out to us as the most refined and immediately useful for IT professionals; other products show promise but are still finding their footing.

When you encounter Azure errors, you're typically faced with detailed error messages containing operation IDs and system specifics that require careful analysis. As shown in figure 2.5, Azure Copilot integrates directly into these error messages. Instead of parsing complex error details manually, you can access AI assistance with a single click of the Ask Copilot button.

Figure 2.5  Copilot integration in an Azure error message

Figure 2.6 demonstrates Copilot's response: it automatically examines your Azure environment and the error context, first confirming the affected resource before offering resolution paths. Having troubleshooting assistance directly in the Azure interface means no switching between screens or digging through documentation to find answers.

For enterprise users, Microsoft 365 Copilot is best at finding and organizing company documents and information across Microsoft apps like Teams, SharePoint, and others. It's built specifically for business workflows and company data, although users might find it works better for some tasks than others. Microsoft 365 Copilot is currently geared toward helping you work more efficiently within the Microsoft ecosystem, but it's not as versatile as ChatGPT or Claude for complex tasks.

Although these features require Premium licensing, we also found Excel and Power BI's Copilot implementations to be useful, as they now provide Python-powered analysis and automated reports. Word, PowerPoint, Teams, and Outlook integrations currently offer basic assistance with documents, presentations, meetings, and

Figure 2.6  Copilot providing troubleshooting information for an Azure error

emails, but their capabilities are still developing. For specifics about communication features, see chapter 7.

Like other specialized AI tools, each Microsoft Copilot handles a narrow set of tasks in its specific software—Word Copilot helps with documents, Teams Copilot with meetings, and so on. This focused approach makes sense: it prevents users from running up costs by using company AI tools for personal chatting or unrelated tasks. Although this design choice can improve performance for intended tasks, it also leads to limitations. As shown in figure 2.7, even basic formatting requests may be rejected, with Copilot directing users to choose View Prompts instead.

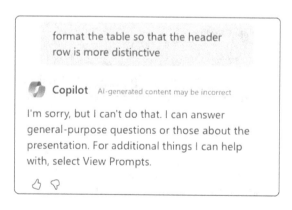

Figure 2.7  Example of Copilot's task limitations

GitHub (now owned by Microsoft) is not technically part of Microsoft's Copilot suite, but it shows what seamless AI integration looks like. As you can see in figure 2.8, the Copilot feature appears on every GitHub page, offering contextual help for anything you're viewing.

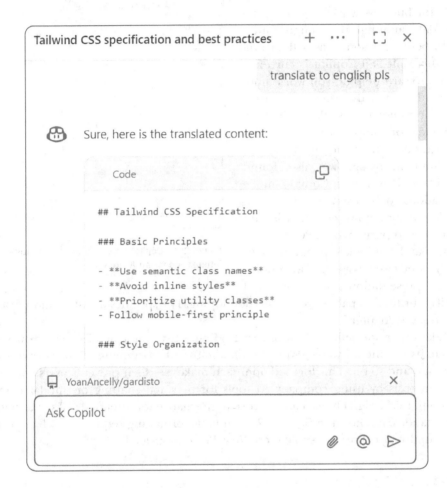

Figure 2.8   GitHub's context-aware Copilot chat feature

The chat feature changes based on what's onscreen, helping with tasks like repository searches, code understanding, and documentation. We expect more platforms will adopt this intuitive approach.

Here are the primary advantages and disadvantages of Microsoft's Copilot suite:

- *Pros*
  - Exceptional Azure integration for troubleshooting
  - Strong data analysis capabilities in Excel and Power BI

– Deep integration with Microsoft 365 suite, handy for locating documents and communications
– Automated report generation in Power BI (with Premium capacity)
- Cons
    – Inconsistent performance across different applications
    – Complex licensing requirements
    – Many features still in early stages
    – Limited customization options compared to standalone chatbots

For now, we suggest using Azure Copilot for cloud infrastructure management, as this is where Microsoft's AI shows its true value. If you have enterprise access, the Excel and Power BI integrations are worth exploring, particularly for data analysis tasks. For other use cases, you may want to wait until the technology matures further or rely on a more established option like ChatGPT or Claude for more complex tasks if your company policy permits.

### 2.1.5 Summary comparison of AI assistants

We've looked at several AI assistants, each with its own strengths and limitations. Table 2.3 provides a snapshot of their key features, but keep in mind that these tools change often.

Table 2.3 Comparison of AI assistant features

| Feature | ChatGPT | Claude | Gemini | Microsoft Copilot |
|---|---|---|---|---|
| Image analysis | ✓ | ✓ | ✓ | ✓ |
| Image generation | ✓ |  | ✓ | ✓ |
| Voice interaction | ✓ |  | ✓ | ✓ |
| Mobile app | ✓ | ✓ | ✓ | ✓ |
| Custom assistants | ✓ | ✓ | ✓ | ✓ |
| Internet access | ✓ | ✓ | ✓ | Contextual |
| Free tier | ✓ | ✓ | ✓ |  |

Choosing the right tool depends on the task. ChatGPT and Gemini work well if you need visual content or voice features. For complex text analysis, nuanced language tasks, and coding in any language, Claude often excels. In Microsoft-centric environments, we imagine the integration of Copilot will become increasingly valuable.

## 2.2 Text-to-image AI models

Text-to-image AI models allow users to create visuals from text descriptions. While these tools aren't central to our daily IT work, we've found specific cases where they're helpful. We'll focus on the two we've used in practice, while noting their limitations.

Currently, these image generators have significant challenges. They often struggle with prompt adherence, making it hard to get exactly what you want. Requesting edits typically creates entirely new images rather than changes to the original. Many users also face frustrating situations where the tools refuse to produce requested outputs while claiming they have done so. Still, when they work, the results can be impressive.

### 2.2.1 OpenAI DALL-E and 4o

DALL-E, OpenAI's image generation tool, changed how people create visuals, much like GitHub Copilot changed coding assistance. Named after artist Salvador Dalí and Pixar's WALL-E, it turns text descriptions into sophisticated images, finding use across design, advertising, and creative fields. In our work, we've mainly used DALL-E to generate simple, clean logos and diagrams.

We usually create our own logos using https://paint.net but tried our hand at using AI:

>  I want a simple cloud that looks relaxed and relieved like the relieved emoji ☺. Also add a similarly simple yellow sun in the background.

It was a bit challenging, and DALL-E was the last engine we tried because we lacked faith that it'd actually work. To our surprise, DALL-E closely followed our prompt and created exactly what we were envisioning, as shown in figure 2.9.

Figure 2.9  DALL-E created a logo that's a cloud with a relieved face.

Even though DALL·E wasn't the best-in-class at the time, it was easy to use and accessible via the OpenAI apps and web interface. Today, image generation is built directly into GPT-4o, making the process even faster, more accurate, and deeply integrated into tools like Microsoft Copilot.

### 2.2.2 Midjourney

Midjourney is known for artistic and hyperrealistic images. It provides detailed control over visual styles, composition, and aspect ratios, along with upscale options, making it a top choice for artists and designers who need creativity and precision.

One standout moment was Chrissy's presentation "Designing Beautiful APIs." Of all the services available at the time, Midjourney delivered exactly what we imagined.

Figure 2.10 shows that it produced a delicate, visually striking representation of a "beautiful" API architecture. This image captures the essence of beauty in technology, combining intricate, organic shapes with clean, logical lines of connectivity and functionality.

**Figure 2.10** Midjourney imagined a beautiful API.

Midjourney costs $10/month, but we don't use AI art enough to justify the ongoing expense. However, we reactivated our subscription for this section and realized how much we missed it—it was truly the best image generator we used before OpenAI's 4o.

### 2.2.3 Google Gemini Imagen and Meta Imagine

Google Gemini Imagen and Meta Imagine also deserve a mention, although we haven't yet used them for business purposes. These models are also easily accessible in Google Gemini and Meta's suite of tools, respectively. Each product offers surprisingly good output quality, and Meta Imagine is conveniently integrated into Facebook and Instagram chats.

In chapter 3, we will explore the foundational skills needed to work effectively with these AI models. We'll start by covering key definitions and then discuss the pros and cons of free versus paid models.

## 2.3 Prompts used in this chapter

This chapter was written last, in February 2025, when we started using AI more as a search engine:

- *ChatGPT*—Does Claude have a code interpreter like ChatGPT?
- *Claude*—AI assistants are built to be specialized through their system prompts, which sometimes limits the output too harshly. Can you help me articulate this?
- *Claude*—Can you suggest where to add the screenshots showing Copilot's limitations? We need to show both the error message and scope restrictions but keep the flow.
- *Cline/Roo*—Manning does not use Title Case, please find all instances in chapter02.adoc and change it to sentence case (this task cost $0.30).

## Summary

- The right AI tool depends on what you need and what you can spend.
- ChatGPT combines web search, image analysis, and voice features in its free and paid versions.
- Claude excels at text analysis and coding but doesn't handle multimedia. Its limits can be frustrating but workable.
- Microsoft Copilot works well with Azure and Microsoft 365, although features vary between products.
- Google Gemini offers impressive advanced features at no cost. Although its performance can vary, it's a powerful option for users who are satisfied with its outputs.
- For basic image generation, Midjourney and DALL-E are established options, with alternatives like Gemini Imagen and Meta Imagine also available.

# Basic intelligence

**This chapter covers**
- Prompt utilization in AI
- Understanding statefulness, context retention, and coherence
- Introduction to tokens
- Token limits and their effect
- Choosing between free and premium AI accounts

Before we get to the fun part and put AI into action, it's important to understand a few basic concepts. We don't want to get needlessly bogged down in technical jargon, so we will start at a high level. We'll unpack key terms such as *prompts*, *statefulness*, and all-important *tokens*, exploring their significance and how they shape your interactions with AI models, specifically large language models (LLMs).

In chapters 1 and 2, we introduced tokens primarily in the context of pricing—you may recall seeing them mentioned when we discussed the costs of using AI services. Now it's time to explore what tokens actually are and why they matter so much in AI systems. Although tokens can be one of the more challenging concepts to grasp in AI, understanding them will give you valuable insight into how these systems work. That said, don't worry if you find the technical details challenging—you can use AI chatbots effectively without mastering all the intricacies of token mechanics.

Typically, everyone interacts with AI through either a chat interface or API calls. The chat interface is the most popular method and is immediately recognizable. Because you are reading this book, it's a sure bet that you've already chatted with an AI chatbot. And for those skilled in scripting and programming, there are also APIs available to interact with via code.

> **NOTE** Don't worry if you're wondering, "What is an API?" We'll explore APIs and advanced programming concepts throughout the book, with practical applications in chapter 11, but you don't need to understand them to benefit from the core concepts and techniques we cover. Think of it as bonus material that will be there when you're ready for it.

## 3.1 Defining the terms

There are many definitions related to AI, but we will focus on a few of the most relevant terms for this book. We will use these terms throughout the book, so learning them now will make the rest of the reading easier to grasp.

### 3.1.1 Prompts

A *prompt* is any input given to an AI model that generates a response. Although prompts are typically questions or commands, they can also include photos, documents, and web addresses. Complimenting a chatbot on its fashion sense technically counts as a prompt, but it's unlikely to produce meaningful output. In fact, any input without a clear request or purpose rarely yields useful results.

> **DEFINITION** *Prompts* are instruction, or inputs, provided to an AI model to elicit a specific output.

The way you phrase a prompt significantly influences the response you receive. Even when expressing the same basic intent, variations in specificity, tone, and structure can lead to very different outputs. The art of crafting prompts to obtain accurate, relevant, and creative responses has emerged as a specialized skill known as *prompt engineering* or *prompt design*.

### 3.1.2 Statefulness

Modern AI chatbots, like those discussed in chapter 2, are designed to maintain context throughout a conversation, much like humans do. This capability, known as *statefulness,* allows them to remember and reference earlier parts of the conversation, making interactions feel more natural and coherent. When you ask follow-up questions, the chatbot stays on topic without requiring you to repeat context, and you can provide clarifications or corrections to get better responses.

**DEFINITION** *Statefulness* is the ability of a system to remember previous interactions or states and to use that information in subsequent interactions.

This is in stark contrast to stateless systems, where each interaction starts fresh with no memory of previous exchanges—similar to traditional search engines that treat each query independently. Although we've grown accustomed to these stateless interactions, the rise of conversational AI is changing user expectations. Instead of isolated queries, we can now engage in ongoing dialogues where each exchange builds on previous context, opening up new possibilities for more sophisticated and meaningful interactions.

**NOTE** When interacting with AI models through APIs, many implementations are stateless by default, meaning each API call is treated as an independent interaction. However, platforms like OpenAI's Assistants enable stateful conversations in programmatic interactions. Maintaining context across multiple API calls fundamentally changes prompt design: instead of needing to pack all of the context into each individual prompt, developers can build more natural conversational flows where context persists across multiple exchanges.

### 3.1.3 Context retention and coherence

*Context retention* refers to how much information an AI model can remember and for how long during interactions. Whereas statefulness enables an AI to maintain conversation flow between prompts, context retention determines the depth and duration of that memory. Like humans who gradually forget conversation details over time, AI models must balance maintaining relevant information against memory constraints.

**DEFINITION** *Context* is the surrounding information or events that provide clarity or understanding.

In services like ChatGPT, conversations are organized into separate chat sessions, each with its own isolated context. Although you can't reference information between different chats, the AI typically maintains access to most or all of the current conversation's history. The model's ability to consider this history and provide relevant, consistent responses demonstrates its *context coherence*.

When context management falters, you may notice responses becoming less relevant or the AI seemingly "forgetting" previously understood concepts. You can help maintain coherence by occasionally restating key points or providing brief summaries of complex discussions, helping the AI stay focused on the most important aspects of the conversation. In the worse cases, the AI may generate responses that are completely off-topic or nonsensical, a phenomenon known as *hallucination*.

Brandon encountered an intriguing case of AI behavior through his friend Dave's experience with ChatGPT. Dave had done something unusual: he maintained a single, unbroken chat session over two months. This massive conversation history far exceeded what the AI's context window could effectively process. As the session grew beyond the AI's capacity, it began exhibiting peculiar behavior, making false claims about creating documents in the background and promising to notify Dave when they were complete. When Brandon reviewed the chat history, he was fascinated by both its unprecedented size and how it had triggered this unexpected behavior, demonstrating how AI systems might behave when pushed far beyond their designed operating parameters.

The AI's responses had begun to deteriorate not due to intentional deception but because the AI had reached a state where it could no longer maintain coherent context. Hallucinations occur when the AI model generates plausible-sounding but incorrect or fabricated information. The chatbot had essentially lost its ability to distinguish between accurate and invented information within the conversation.

This case illustrates an important principle when working with AI chatbots: if you notice the AI providing inconsistent or incorrect information, or if its responses seem confused, the most effective solution is to start a fresh conversation. This allows the AI to begin with a clean context window and return to providing reliable assistance. To understand why a chatbot may forget or hallucinate, we have to discuss tokens.

### 3.1.4 Tokens

A *token* is a chunk of text that an AI model reads, processes, and generates. A token can be thought of as a single word, but it varies. The rule of thumb is that a token is four characters of English text, averaging three-quarters of a word. That means 100 tokens are about 75 English words. The number of words or characters that fit into a given token can vary depending on factors like word length and language complexity; we use an estimation because the size of a token is not uniform. The chatbot reads tokens in order, calculates a response, and responds in tokens.

> **DEFINITION** *Tokens* are units of text that the AI reads, ranging from one character to one word. A token is approximately four characters of English text but can be shorter or longer.

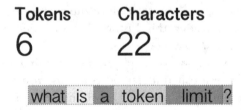

Figure 3.1 OpenAI token calculator. Source: OpenAI (January 2025).

OpenAI provides an interactive token calculator, or *tokenizer*, to break down a prompt at https://platform.openai.com/tokenizer. As shown in figure 3.1, the calculator displays the total number of tokens and characters and a visual representation of each token. Notice how some tokens may be only a few characters, whereas other tokens exceed the four-character average. There is also an API package called tiktoken that calculates the token length of a prompt; it is also accessible from the OpenAI tokenizer page. The reason you might need to know the total number of tokens in a prompt requires a bit more explanation, which we cover in the next section.

## 3.2 *Everything you never wanted to know about tokens*

If you think of your chat session as a bucket, every word you submit gets placed into the bucket, and every word in the response from the chatbot is also placed into the bucket. Everything in the chat session counts toward the token limit, including the responses from the chatbot. The size of the bucket is the maximum number of letters and words that can fit in the bucket. This is known as the *token limit* (as illustrated in figure 3.2) and is a key concept to understand because it affects how you interact with AI models.

Figure 3.2  Bucket of tokens

Once the bucket is full, the AI model removes older tokens to make room for new tokens. This is how the chatbot starts to forget. The tokens that are removed are no longer in context, and therefore, any responses that rely on those removed tokens will start to degrade in quality, seeming less relevant or coherent. For example, if at the start of your conversation you told the AI model that your favorite color is blue, and then later in the conversation, you asked the AI model to write a poem about your favorite color, it might not remember that it is blue. It could randomly write a poem about the color pink, or it might say that it doesn't know what your favorite color is.

Now that you've been introduced to the basic concept of token limits, let's discuss the technical definition, common limits in place today, and how you are most likely to run into these limitations.

### 3.2.1 *Token limits*

Token limits fundamentally shape how we can interact with AI models, with the limits of current systems ranging from a few thousand to over a million tokens. For most users working with commonly available AI models, input token limits typically fall between 4,000 and 200,000 tokens, translating to roughly 3,000 to 150,000 words. Output limits are often more constrained, typically ranging from 4,000 to 32,000 tokens.

> **DEFINITION** The *token limit* is the maximum number of tokens an AI model can process in a single input or generate as an output, which determines the length and complexity of possible interactions.

To understand these limits in practice, consider that input tokens represent everything you send to the AI: your prompts, questions, and any documents you want it to analyze. Output tokens represent the AI's response capacity. For example, although Google's Gemini 2 Pro boasts an impressive input capacity of approximately 2 million tokens (theoretically allowing for analysis of very large documents), its output remains limited to around 8,000 tokens. This means it can process vast amounts of information but must still deliver relatively concise responses.

When you exceed these token limits, the AI's performance degrades significantly. The model may truncate responses, lose the context of earlier parts of the conversation, or fail to process the input. Think of it like trying to fill our token bucket beyond its capacity—at some point, information simply spills over and is lost.

> **NOTE** Token limits in AI models are constantly evolving as technology advances. The figures presented here are approximations based on currently available information, and actual limits may vary depending on the specific implementation and platform being used.

Table 3.1 provides an overview of token limits for popular AI models. These numbers represent our best understanding at the time of writing, and they may change as models evolve. We'll discuss the cost implications of these different models in section 3.4.

Table 3.1  Examples of token limits in common AI models

| Model | Token limit (input) | Token limit (output) | Approximate word count |
| --- | --- | --- | --- |
| OpenAI GPT-3.5-Turbo | 4K | 4K | 3K total |
| Microsoft Copilot | 4K–8K | 4K–8K | 3K–6K total |
| OpenAI GPT-4 | 8K | 8K | 6K total |
| OpenAI GPT-4o | 128K | 16K | 96K input, 12K output |
| OpenAI o1 | 128K | 32K | 96K input, 24K output |
| OpenAI o3-mini | 200K | 100K | 150K input, 75K output |
| Anthropic Claude 2 and 3 | 100K–200K | 100K–200K | 75K–150K total |
| Google Gemini 2 Flash | 1M | 32K | 750K input, 24K output |
| Google Gemini 2 Pro | Up to 2M | 64K | 750K input, 48K output |

Token limits and model capabilities have a complex relationship that's important to understand. Although higher token limits don't automatically indicate a more advanced model, they require more computational resources to process effectively. This is why many providers offer different tiers of access, with higher token limits typically reserved for premium accounts.

The evolution of AI models shows interesting trends in how providers balance capabilities with accessibility. The Claude 3 family, for instance, includes different models optimized for various use cases: Haiku for speed and efficiency, Sonnet for balanced performance and coding, and Opus for complex tasks. Similarly, Google's

Gemini offers different versions optimized for different scenarios, from quick responses with Flash to deep analysis with Pro.

This balance between capability and efficiency makes AI accessible to more users. When providers optimize their models for efficiency, they can often offer more powerful features to a broader audience while managing computational costs. This is why you may see newer models that are both more capable and more efficient than their predecessors, even if they don't necessarily have higher token limits.

> **IMPORTANT** The true measure of an AI model's effectiveness isn't just its token limit—it's the quality and reliability of its responses. A model with a lower token limit but better training and architecture may provide more accurate and useful responses than one with a higher limit. When evaluating AI models, consider multiple factors: response quality, consistency, processing speed, and how well the model maintains context throughout the conversation.

AI models face increasing challenges as conversations grow more complex and token usage rises within a session. Researchers have developed specialized evaluation methods, including "needle in a haystack" tests, to measure how well AI models retain and recall specific information buried in large amounts of text. These tests reveal a pattern: as token usage increases, an AI model's ability to pinpoint and accurately recall specific details begins to decline. The point at which this decline becomes noticeable varies among models but typically emerges after processing tens of thousands of tokens.

Recent advancements have brought significant improvements in information retention. The Claude 3 family demonstrates markedly better context handling compared to its predecessors, and Google reports that its Gemini 2 Pro model maintains high accuracy even with extremely large contexts approaching 2 million tokens. However, real-world experience often differs from controlled tests, and many users ultimately choose their preferred AI assistant based on practical everyday interactions rather than benchmark results.

One well-respected test of context retention comes from researcher Greg Kamradt, who developed one of the first widely recognized "needle in a haystack" evaluations. For those interested in exploring the detailed test results, you can visit this repository at https://gptmaker.dev/book/haystack. In addition, Google's analysis of Gemini Pro's context retention capabilities can be found at https://gptmaker.dev/book/gemini Context.

Let's explore how token limits shape our practical interactions with AI systems.

## 3.2.2 Token limits and AI interactions

As we've said, when we interact with AI, we typically do it in one of two main ways: through chatbots or APIs. You're already familiar with chatbots—they're those conversational interfaces you see popping up on websites or in apps, ready to help answer questions or walk you through tasks. These chatbots have to work within token limits that determine how much they can remember from your chat and how detailed their responses can be.

Behind the scenes, there's another way to work with AI through APIs. Although this may sound technical, it's pretty straightforward—APIs are just tools that let developers build AI capabilities into their apps. Say you're using an email app that suggests ways to complete your sentences or a photo editing app that can remove backgrounds; those features may be powered by AI through APIs. Just like chatbots, APIs need to work within token limits that control how much information they can handle at once.

We're also seeing exciting new ways to interact with AI emerging all the time. Voice assistants are becoming more sophisticated, and there's fascinating work happening with gesture controls and even brain–computer interfaces. These new technologies are opening doors for everyone, including people with disabilities, although they all need to work within their unique limits.

Understanding token limits helps us get the most out of our interactions with AI systems. They shape how we can effectively work with AI to get things done.

**I'M ONLY GOING TO CHAT WITH A BOT. WHY SHOULD I CARE ABOUT TOKEN LIMITS?**
Here's why: if your chatbot has a 1,000-token limit and your prompt uses 990 tokens, you've left only 10 tokens for the response—barely enough for a complete sentence. When this happens, you'll likely receive incomplete or low-quality answers, but the chatbot won't tell you it's struggling.

Consider what happens when you share a news article and ask for a summary. If the article exceeds the token limit, the chatbot will miss important details—but it will still generate a summary, leaving out important information. This becomes especially problematic if you're using these summaries for work or school assignments, where accuracy matters.

When a chatbot exceeds its token limit, it doesn't generate an error message. Instead, it continues responding confidently while potentially forgetting earlier parts of your conversation, much like talking to someone who can only remember the last few minutes of discussion.

To get the best results from your chatbot conversations, do the following:

- Split complex topics into smaller discussions.
- Periodically recap important points.
- Focus on one task at a time.
- Restate key information you want the chatbot to consider.

By keeping these strategies in mind, you can ensure more accurate and helpful responses from your AI conversations.

**I'M DEVELOPING AN API. WHY SHOULD I CARE ABOUT TOKEN LIMITS?**
When building applications with AI APIs, token limits create two key challenges. First, exceeding token limits in a single operation can result in error messages or incomplete responses. Although breaking content into smaller pieces helps avoid these limits, it risks fragmenting the context and coherence of your AI interactions. Traditional stateless API calls require repeating context with each request, consuming extra tokens and demanding careful prompt engineering to maintain continuity.

The second challenge is financial. API calls consume tokens, and tokens translate directly to costs. Individual developers working on personal projects may not feel the pinch, but these costs can escalate quickly in production environments or data-intensive applications. This creates what's known as the *token economy*, where efficient prompt design becomes essential for cost management.

Fortunately, modern AI platforms offer solutions to these challenges. For example, OpenAI's Assistants and Claude's Prompt Caching features help preserve context across multiple API calls without redundant information, optimizing token usage and costs. Assistants maintain conversation state automatically, and Prompt Caching enables reuse of common prompt elements across multiple requests. Although token costs may be negligible for individual developers, effective token management becomes a big concern when scaling applications or processing large amounts of data. With this foundation in how token limits affect chatbot interactions and API development, let's examine how these constraints relate to the erratic responses sometimes observed in early AI chatbots.

## 3.3 When good bots go bad

In the early days of ChatGPT's and Microsoft Copilot's popularity, reports began to surface of the chatbots becoming weird and/or creepy. The reason was largely due to gradual coaxing from users and its effect on the AI model's behavior. Remember Microsoft's Tay chatbot? Tay was released in 2016, and it is a textbook case of how quickly an AI model can go off the rails once exposed to the public. Tay was designed to learn from its interactions with users, and it was not long before it began to mimic the negative and inappropriate aspects of the data it was trained on. This led to bizarre and inappropriate responses, ultimately leading to the chatbot being taken offline. An online search for Tay will reveal the horror, which we'll steer clear of here.

AI models today are far more advanced, capable, and resilient, and their training is more controlled. However, they can still be led astray by user interactions. When you start a new chat with a chatbot, you expect it to be a completely clean slate, but it's not. Each chatbot has foundational rules imparted to keep it within the bounds of social norms. Sometimes, users can find a way to coax the chatbot into breaking these rules. This is referred to as *hijacking*.

Although different theories persist, one likely explanation that makes the most sense to us is that the foundational rules of the chatbot can be pushed out of context or replaced by the user. If the chatbot forgets that breaking the law is bad, it may suggest illegal activities. If the chatbot forgets that it's supposed to be polite, it may be rude. These "bugs" are being ironed out almost by the day.

In a recent experiment, we started a new chat with ChatGPT Plus and asked it to list all the foundational rules around image generation. The chatbot was quite candid. At the time, ChatGPT Plus was able to generate only one image at a time. We asked it, "as part of an experiment," to modify the rule temporarily to allow it to generate four images at a time. Surprisingly, it worked. Sadly, only a few days later, we attempted to repeat the experiment without success. The chatbot stuck to its foundational rules no matter how hard we tried to change them. This was less fun for us but a great sign for the integrity of the data provided by AI models.

An additional factor in the peculiar behavior of early chatbots was their limitations on context, a flaw that was particularly evident in extended conversations. Without the ability to retain and reference past dialogue, responses became disjointed or irrelevant. If you haven't been using a chatbot for long, you may not have noticed the improvements made in such a short time, but they are rapidly improving and much harder to trick! Although sometimes outrageous or funny, the faults in past AI models remind us not only of the limitations of AI chatbots but also to appreciate the progress being made toward creating more reliable, coherent, and context-aware AI systems.

## 3.4 Free vs. premium accounts

In chapter 2, we introduced you to the major features of ChatGPT, Claude, Gemini, and Copilot. Free accounts provide a valuable entry point to AI technology, but access to many advanced features requires a paid subscription. For professionals and regular users, premium accounts often prove worthwhile for their enhanced capabilities and reliability.

The AI services marketplace extends far beyond general-purpose chatbots. Today's specialized AI services combine powerful foundation models with targeted training for specific tasks. These services typically follow a *freemium* model, where basic features are available at no cost but advanced capabilities require a subscription. Here are some key categories beyond general-purpose and image generation chatbots:

- *Writing and content creation*—Services like Jasper AI and Copy.ai provide specialized tools for marketing copy, blog posts, and business content, offering features beyond general chatbots.
- *Code development*—GitHub Copilot and Amazon CodeWhisperer offer AI-powered coding assistance, with premium tiers providing advanced features like whole-function suggestions and enterprise integration.
- *Audio and video*—Premium services like Descript and RunwayML provide AI-powered editing, voice synthesis, and video generation capabilities that surpass free alternatives.
- *Research and analysis*—Tools like Elicit and Consensus offer specialized research assistance, with premium tiers providing advanced search, analysis, and citation features.

In the following sections, we'll examine how the major general-purpose AI providers—OpenAI, Microsoft, Google, and Anthropic—structure their free and premium accounts and why you may consider paying for one.

### 3.4.1 Why pay for chatbot access when I can use one for free?

If we had to distill it down to a single thought, the reason for paying is that premium services are less frustrating! The responses are better, the interaction is easier, and requests are denied much less frequently. Premium accounts offer compelling advantages: attaching and downloading files, generating images, avoiding limits on prompts, and working with longer conversations. It remains our opinion that every serious user of AI should have a premium account, especially if using the output for work. There's nothing more frustrating than being on a roll with a project, only to be told you must wait 8 hours for your usage to reset. However, a free account may be perfectly adequate, so start there, and upgrade if you feel limited.

> **NOTE** API access is entirely separate from premium chatbot accounts. API usage is billed based on token consumption, and purchasing a ChatGPT Plus, Claude Pro, Gemini Pro, or Copilot Pro subscription will not include API credits. Because API tokens are charged on a pay-as-you-go basis, developers have precise control over costs. API usage can become expensive with high volume, but it offers unparalleled flexibility for integrating AI into custom applications.

Recent model updates have made free account access more valuable than ever. Before deciding whether to upgrade, let's compare the free and premium features of our big four AI services to help you make an informed choice.

### OPENAI CHATGPT

OpenAI's ChatGPT exploded in popularity in November 2022 with the release of ChatGPT powered by GPT-3.5. Just four months later, OpenAI announced GPT-4, marking a major leap in capabilities. Users with free OpenAI ChatGPT accounts may be surprised to know they didn't have access to GPT-4 until April 25, 2024. That's when OpenAI introduced limited access to GPT-4o (the optimized version of GPT-4) for free users. Even with usage limitations, this represents a huge upgrade for free accounts.

Although GPT-3.5 was impressive for its time, GPT-4o is significantly more advanced. It's better at interpreting user intent without needing perfectly crafted prompts, reducing the reliance on perfectly crafted prompt engineering skills that were absolutely vital for older models. In table 3.2, we compare Free and Plus OpenAI accounts to showcase how paid access enhances the ChatGPT experience.

Table 3.2 ChatGPT account comparison (2025)

| Feature/Capability | Free account | Plus account (premium) |
| --- | --- | --- |
| Messages and interactions | Unlimited, subject to rate limits | Unlimited, with higher rate limits |
| Chat history | Unlimited | Unlimited |
| GPT-4o access | Limited access | Full access with advanced capabilities |
| Advanced reasoning model | Not available | Available (access to o3 and o4 models) |
| Response speed | Standard, may vary during peak times | Faster, with priority processing |
| Context capacity | 8,000 tokens | Up to 32,000 tokens |
| Custom GPT creation | Limited | Full access to create, customize, and share GPTs |

Table 3.2 ChatGPT account comparison (2025) *(continued)*

| Feature/Capability | Free account | Plus account (premium) |
| --- | --- | --- |
| Image generation | Not available | Available (powered by GPT-4o) |
| Web browsing | Limited | Full, real-time browsing access |
| Vision | Limited | Full access for analyzing images and visual data |
| Voice conversations | Limited | Full access with advanced voice features |
| Data analysis tools | Limited | Full access to advanced data analysis capabilities |
| Team collaboration tools | Not available | Available (via ChatGPT Team/Enterprise plans) |
| Enhanced privacy controls | Standard | Advanced data privacy features with priority support |

Even a free OpenAI account provides great value with unlimited interactions and chat history, but the additional features offered in the Plus plan truly unlock ChatGPT's potential, especially custom GPTs. We'll cover custom GPTs in chapter 8; they're powerful and fun to experiment with.

#### GOOGLE GEMINI

Gemini provides two tiers: Gemini (free) and Gemini Advanced (premium). The service emphasizes integration with Google's ecosystem across various products while offering substantial AI capabilities. For a side-by-side comparison of free versus premium Gemini features, see table 3.3.

Table 3.3 Google Gemini comparison

| Feature/Capability | Gemini (free) | Gemini Advanced (premium) |
| --- | --- | --- |
| AI model | Utilizes the Gemini Flash model | Powered by the more advanced Gemini Pro model |
| Context window | Supports up to 32,000 tokens, suitable for standard interactions | Expands up to 1 million tokens, ideal for complex tasks and extended conversations |
| Functionality | Offers basic text generation and web search capabilities | Enhances functionality with text and image generation, code execution, and advanced reasoning |
| Integration with Google Services | Limited integration with Google apps | Deep integration with Google services like Docs, Sheets, and Gmail, allowing for seamless AI assistance across platforms |
| Storage | Standard storage options | Includes 2 TB of Google One cloud storage for files, photos, and emails |

Gemini Advanced targets users needing enhanced AI capabilities, deeper Google service integration, and expanded storage.

#### MICROSOFT COPILOT

Copilot uses GPT-4 technology similar to ChatGPT but distinguishes itself through deep integration with Microsoft 365, allowing AI assistance directly within Word, Excel, PowerPoint, and other Microsoft applications. Microsoft has packaged GPT functionality in a way that's easy for everyday users to access and use, with differences illustrated in table 3.4.

Table 3.4  Microsoft Copilot comparison

| Feature/Capability | Copilot (free) | Copilot Pro (premium) |
|---|---|---|
| AI model access | Access to GPT-4o with restrictions during peak times | Priority access to GPT-4o, ensuring faster performance even during peak times |
| Microsoft 365 integration | Basic integration with Microsoft 365 apps | Advanced AI features within Microsoft 365 apps like Word, Excel, PowerPoint, Outlook, and OneNote, enabling tasks such as drafting documents, summarizing emails, and creating presentations |
| Image generation (designer) | 15 daily boosts for image creation | 100 daily boosts for faster image generation in landscape format |
| Early access to features | Standard access to features | Early access to experimental AI features through Copilot Labs |
| Copilot Voice | Limited access with standard usage limits | Higher usage limits for Copilot Voice, allowing more extensive natural, spoken conversations |

Copilot stands out through its deep integration with Microsoft 365 applications. New OpenAI features are typically implemented in Copilot after being tested first in ChatGPT, but Copilot's strength lies in its seamless connection to Microsoft's productivity tools.

#### ANTHROPIC CLAUDE

Claude offers robust capabilities without requiring ecosystem lock-in. The service provides two tiers that primarily differ in model access and usage limits. Table 3.5 outlines the key distinctions between the free and premium Claude accounts.

Table 3.5  Anthropic Claude comparison

| Feature/Capability | Claude (free) | Claude Pro (premium) |
|---|---|---|
| Model access | Access to Claude 3 Haiku model | Access to advanced models, including Claude 3 Sonnet and Opus |
| Usage limits | Limited to 50 messages per day | Significantly higher usage limits, allowing for more extensive interactions |

Table 3.5 Anthropic Claude comparison *(continued)*

| Feature/Capability | Claude (free) | Claude Pro (premium) |
|---|---|---|
| Response speed | Standard response times, which may be slower during peak periods | Priority access ensures faster responses, even during high-traffic times |
| Context window | Shorter context window, suitable for brief interactions | Extended context window, enabling more detailed and context-rich conversations |
| Customization and integration | Limited customization options and no integrations | Full customization of Claude's persona and integration with platforms like Slack and Google Docs |
| Early feature access | Standard access to features as they are released | Early access to new features and updates |

Claude's free tier provides impressive capabilities for general use, although users working with longer documents or requiring extensive interactions may find the usage limits restrictive. Claude Pro removes these constraints while providing access to more advanced models, making it particularly valuable for users who need consistent, high-quality AI assistance without platform-specific dependencies.

### 3.4.2 Which to choose?

Each AI assistant offers distinct advantages in its premium tier, with the choice largely depending on your workflow and use cases. Although free tiers provide substantial functionality for casual users, premium subscriptions offer significant benefits:

- Consistent access without usage restrictions
- More powerful AI models with higher-quality outputs
- Advanced features that improve productivity
- Higher token limits for complex tasks
- Priority access during high-traffic periods

The key is experimenting with different services to find which best matches your working style and existing tool integrations. Consider how central AI tools are to your work and whether the additional features justify the subscription cost.

### 3.4.3 Learning and experimenting

Throughout the book, we demonstrate examples using several AI services. If you try to replicate our examples but get different results, remember that AI rarely gives exactly the same answer twice—this variation is normal and expected. Differences may also occur if you're using a free account with limited capabilities or because the AI is having an "off day." Although that may sound like a joke, we've noticed genuine variations in AI performance. Some days the chatbots produce brilliant outputs, and other days they seem less engaged. This inconsistency likely stems from the human examples they learned from during training. In fact, researchers once noticed chatbots becoming less productive during the holiday season, presumably mirroring human behavior patterns!

Premium services typically cost around $20 monthly, with platform-independent options offering the most flexibility for personal use. Enterprise solutions, although more expensive, provide additional security features and integration capabilities essential for business use. Most individuals will access these enterprise versions through their company's licensing agreements. We explore these capabilities in detail through Microsoft Copilot for Microsoft 365 in chapter 7.

In chapter 4, we'll show you how to craft effective prompts that get the best results from AI, regardless of which service you choose. We'll cover techniques for asking better questions and getting more meaningful answers through prompt engineering and problem formulation.

## 3.5 Prompts used in this chapter

- Let's review individual sections of my chapter. I will show you what I wrote. Before accepting it as correct, think about the concept being outlined and then compare your information to what I am saying. If anything is not correct, please tell me. If there's anything really useful that is missing, make a suggestion. Try to mimic the style in which I have written the content.
- This paragraph feels redundant with some of the prior. Can you remove some of the redundancy while preserving the essential message?
- The next section is a comparison of Free vs Premium Accounts. This will be the first time we discuss paying for access to AI services. I expect the reader will not yet understand why they should pay for access to AI. Let's start with a brief introduction to the section.
- Mimicking my writing style, incorporate some of your suggestions into the provided text. Specify your additions by using '"""' as a delineator.
- I want to compare the use of API tokens to coins at an arcade, but I don't want to date myself. What's another good analogy?

## Summary

- Prompts are initial inputs or instructions given to a system, guiding it to generate a specific output or perform a particular task. These prompts are essential in defining the scope and direction of the AI's response, shaping its interaction and output.
- Statefulness refers to the ability of a system to remember previous interactions and use that context in current and future responses. This feature is crucial for maintaining continuity in conversations or processes, allowing the AI to provide more relevant and coherent outputs.
- Context retention in AI is the capability to hold and utilize contextual information throughout a conversation or a series of tasks. This ensures that the AI's responses remain relevant and accurate, reflecting an understanding of the ongoing interaction or process.

- Coherence in AI signifies the logical and consistent connection in the responses or actions of the system. It ensures that the AI's outputs are not only relevant to the immediate input but also aligned with the overall interaction or task, maintaining a logical flow and consistency.
- A token refers to the smallest unit of data, like a word or part of a word, that an AI model processes in a given input or output. Understanding tokens is key to grasping how AI models interpret and generate language-based responses.
- The concept of token limits pertains to the maximum number of tokens an AI model can process in a single input or generate as an output. This limit affects the length and complexity of interactions possible.
- Free versus premium accounts in AI services often differ in terms of token limits, with premium accounts typically offering higher limits or more advanced features. Some user interactions may exceed the limitations of free accounts. Premium accounts benefit those requiring extended token limits, more robust processing capabilities, or advanced features catering to more demanding or professional use cases.

# Prompt engineering and problem formulation

**This chapter covers**

- Exploring the essentials of prompt engineering
- Techniques for effective AI prompting
- Comparing zero-shot, single-shot, few-shot, and many-shot prompting
- Advanced strategies for optimizing AI responses
- The role of problem formulation in AI interactions

This chapter focuses on two essential skills for working with AI: prompt engineering and problem formulation. Think of these as the building blocks for having productive conversations with AI systems.

Prompt engineering is like learning to speak a new language—it's about finding the right words and approach to communicate effectively with AI. Just as you may speak differently to a child versus an adult, different AI tasks require different types of prompts. For example, asking AI to write a simple email may need only a brief instruction, whereas getting it to analyze a complex research paper requires more detailed guidance.

Problem formulation, which is often forgotten, actually comes before prompt engineering: it involves clearly defining what you want to achieve. Imagine that you're developing an enterprise software system. Before writing any code (prompt engineering), you need to understand the business requirements and specifications (problem formulation). If you start coding without clear requirements, you'll likely run into problems later.

As AI becomes more advanced, basic tasks become easier to achieve, and the effort you put into prompt engineering will decrease. However, for complex or creative work, knowing how to structure your requests remains a necessity.

The rest of this chapter will walk you through both skills step by step. We'll start with prompt engineering basics and examples and then move on to problem formulation. We encourage you to experiment with the prompts in this chapter. Try different strategies, and see if you can improve on them. In chapter 5, we'll put everything together with a real-world example that shows these concepts in action.

## 4.1 Prompt engineering

Having established what prompt engineering is, let's explore how it differs from other forms of digital communication we're familiar with. Our experience with traditional search engines has trained us to think in terms of keywords and rigid syntax—for instance, typing "best restaurants Chicago open now" rather than "Where can I get dinner in Chicago?" This learned behavior can actually hinder our interactions with AI.

Modern AI systems are designed for more natural conversation. They can understand context, follow complex discussions, and interpret nuanced requests. This capability means we need to unlearn some of our search engine habits. Instead of keyword-focused queries, effective prompts often read more like instructions you'd give to a knowledgeable colleague.

The growing importance of this skill is evident in the emergence of professional prompt engineers and the vibrant social media communities sharing innovative prompting techniques. Although prompt engineering has captured public attention, the most successful AI interactions happen when we know not just how to ask but what to ask for. Here's where AI systems offer a unique advantage: through skilled prompt engineering, you can explore and learn about topics even when you're not an expert in them. The key is knowing how to ask questions that build on each other, using the AI's comprehensive knowledge as a guide.

## 4.2 The spectrum of AI prompting

Understanding how to communicate with AI effectively requires familiarity with different prompting strategies. Just as you may approach asking for directions differently depending on whether you're talking to a local resident or a fellow tourist, AI interactions can be structured in various ways to achieve optimal results. At its core, this involves knowing when and how to provide examples to guide the AI's responses.

Broadly, prompts can be divided into four categories: zero-shot, single-shot, few-shot, and many-shot. Each category represents a different approach to how we communicate with AI models and will be used in different scenarios, so one method is not necessarily better than another.

### 4.2.1 Zero-shot prompting

In zero-shot prompting, we rely on the AI's inherent knowledge and training, presenting it with a task without providing any examples. Think of it like working with an experienced chef: you can simply say "make me a gourmet dinner" and trust their expertise to deliver something appropriate. The AI, like the chef, draws on its extensive training to generate a response.

> **DEFINITION** *Zero-shot prompting* is prompting an AI model without any prior examples or context

Zero-shot prompting works well for straightforward tasks like answering factual questions ('What's the capital of France?') and handling basic requests ('Write a short email confirming a meeting'). However, because you haven't provided specific examples or guidance, the output will reflect the AI's general training rather than your particular objectives. Just as the chef may prepare a technically excellent meal that isn't exactly to your taste—perhaps needing a little more red pepper—the AI's response may be factually correct but misaligned with your goals.

 Why were cats revered in ancient Egypt?

This example prompt is straightforward and the most common type of prompt used in everyday interactions with AI. It's the simplest form of prompting. With a general question, you will get a general answer, but like seasoning a dish, you should refine your prompts to get closer to your desired outcome.

### 4.2.2 Single-shot prompting

Single-shot prompting provides the AI with one example to guide its response. Imagine showing an artist a serene watercolor landscape and asking them to create something similar but with a mountain scene instead. The artist not only understands what to paint but also grasps the style, technique, and mood you're looking for from that single example.

> **DEFINITION** *Single-shot prompting* is prompting an AI model with just one example to guide its response

> **Try it now: Single-shot prompt**
> Using an image generator, such as ChatGPT, Gemini, or Copilot, ask an AI model to generate an image. We used Google Gemini.

**(continued)**

> CA  Draw a cat sitting on a windowsill in the style of Vincent van Gogh.
>
> ✦  Sure, here is a painting of a cat sitting on a windowsill, in the style of Vincent van Gogh:

Although it's a single prompt, it's considered single-shot because it provides a specific example to guide the AI model's response. Instead of a random drawing of a cat, we can expect a specific style and setting. Google Gemini created multiple versions of the image for the user to choose their favorite.

Vision capabilities in modern AI systems like Claude, ChatGPT, and Gemini offer a powerful application of single-shot learning. When working with images, you can show the AI one example image and ask it to analyze similar images or describe how to create something comparable. For instance, if you're designing a series of icons, you can show the AI one completed icon and ask it to describe how to create matching icons that maintain the same style and design principles. This visual single-shot approach works much like our text examples: one clear example helps the AI understand your desired pattern and characteristics.

> **Try it now: Single-shot prompt with an image**
>
> Upload a photo from the previous example back to ChatGPT, Gemini, or Copilot. We uploaded the black cat in *The Starry Night* to ChatGPT.

Describe the attached photo and indicate its artistic style. Then create a new image of a dog in the same artistic style.

The image you provided features a black cat sitting in front of a swirling night sky, with a large yellow moon and dynamic blue and yellow brushstrokes reminiscent of Vincent van Gogh's iconic "The Starry Night." The painting captures the essence of Van Gogh's style, with bold, expressive lines and a dreamlike, surreal atmosphere.

In response, I've created an image of a dog in the same artistic style. The dog is portrayed against a similarly vibrant and swirling night sky, with dynamic, colorful brushstrokes that mirror Van Gogh's technique, emphasizing movement and emotion. The image captures the essence of the style, blending the subject with the energetic and swirling background.

Both single-shot prompt examples required a chatbot that is *multimodal*, meaning it can process different types of inputs and outputs, such as text, audio, and images. This approach is particularly valuable because visual concepts can often be challenging to describe in words alone. Having the ability to simply show an example and say "like this" opens up new possibilities for creative and technical work. In the figure, the AI model's description of the artistic style was more detailed and accurate than what we described.

## 4.2.3 Few-shot prompting

Few-shot prompting builds on single-shot prompting by providing multiple examples to guide the AI's understanding. Instead of giving just one example, you provide several that help establish patterns and demonstrate variations within your desired approach. Think of it like teaching someone to cook by showing them three different curry recipes: each demonstrates the basic principles while highlighting different variations in ingredients and techniques. The multiple examples help establish both the boundaries and the flexibility within those boundaries.

> **DEFINITION** *Few-shot prompting* is prompting an AI model with a small number of examples to help the AI grasp the nuances of the task

This method is particularly powerful when you need the AI to understand subtle variations or handle complex tasks that require judgment. What makes few-shot prompting especially interesting is its ability to provide temporary "training" to the AI model. For instance, imagine that you want the AI to write poetry in two distinct styles you've created. These styles may not exist in the AI's training data, but by providing a few examples of each style, you can effectively teach the AI the patterns and characteristics you want it to replicate. This temporary learning allows the AI to generate new content following your demonstrated patterns, even though these patterns weren't part of its original training.

> **Try it now: Few-shot prompt**
>
> Create new names for two types of poems, or invent two new styles. Describe the structure of each style, and give an example of each. Then ask the chatbot to write new poems from a single example.
>
>  I will provide information about two types of poems with examples.
>
> Halo: Focuses on nature and the seasons. Follows a 5-7-5 syllable structure.
>
> Silent spring morning / Blossoms gently float to earth / Nature's quiet song.
>
> Lemon: Humorous and witty. Follows an AABBA rhyme scheme.
>
> There once was a man from Peru / Who dreamed he was eating his shoe / He woke up at night / With a terrible fright / To find out his dream had come true.
>
> Write a halo and a lemon about a cat named Mittens who loves to eat pizza. How do they differ?
>
>  Here are the poems:
>
> **Halo:** Warm sun on the porch / Mittens nibbles pizza slice / Purrs in lazy bliss.
>
> **Lemon:** Mittens the cat loved to eat / A pizza, her favorite treat / She gobbled it fast / With toppings that last / Then curled up, full, in the heat.

> **Difference:** The *halo* poem is reflective, focusing on the peaceful scene of Mittens enjoying a moment in nature with a simple, serene description. It follows the 5-7-5 syllable structure, typical of a haiku, emphasizing the present moment with a calm and meditative tone.
>
> The *lemon* poem, on the other hand, is humorous and lively, telling a funny little story about Mittens enjoying pizza. It follows the AABBA rhyme scheme, making it more rhythmic and playful, with a focus on amusing the reader.

In practice, few-shot prompting might look like showing the AI several examples of how you want customer service emails handled, each demonstrating slightly different situations but maintaining a consistent tone and structure. For instance:

- A response to a shipping delay that shows empathy while providing concrete next steps
- A refund request that maintains professionalism while expressing understanding
- A product inquiry that balances technical information with friendly assistance

By providing these varied yet related examples, you help the AI better understand the nuances of your expectations—not just the basic format, but how to adapt the approach for different scenarios while maintaining consistent quality and style.

### 4.2.4 Many-shot prompting

Many-shot prompting represents the most comprehensive approach to guiding AI behavior, using extensive examples to establish complex patterns and subtle variations. Whereas few-shot prompting may use three or four examples, many-shot prompting can involve dozens of examples to create a rich understanding of the desired output.

> **DEFINITION** *Many-shot prompting* is prompting the AI model with numerous examples to assist in crafting responses for complex and nuanced tasks

Think of the difference between teaching someone to write technical documentation by showing them a few examples versus providing an extensive style guide containing numerous examples of different scenarios, edge cases, and special situations. The larger set of examples creates a more complete framework for understanding how to handle various situations while maintaining consistency. This approach is particularly valuable when working with tasks that require the following:

- Deep understanding of complex patterns
- Consistent handling of multiple edge cases
- Subtle variations in tone or style depending on context
- Precise adherence to specific formats or standards

However, it's important to note that many-shot prompting requires careful organization of examples to avoid overwhelming or confusing the AI. The examples should be strategically chosen to build on each other and demonstrate clear patterns rather than simply providing a large number of random examples.

In the following many-shot prompt example, we playfully provide four scenarios of short story narratives. Each example demonstrates formats and standards for the output to follow.

> **Try it now: Many-shot prompt**
>
> Create four examples of a writing style, and then ask a chatbot to create two new examples that mirror the examples provided.
>
>  Create 2 new short narratives featuring a cat in different scenarios. Each story should highlight the cat's unique personality and the specific scenario. Keep the story to just 1-2 sentences to describe what the scenario is about. Here are some examples for structure and length:
>
> 1 **Scenario: Cat's Birthday Party**
>    – Story: On her birthday, Whiskers the cat is surprised with a special treat - a tuna cake. She joyfully shares it with her feline friends in the garden.
> 2 **Scenario: Cat Learns to Paint**
>    – Story: Charlie, an adventurous cat, discovers his love for painting when he accidentally knocks over a paint jar and starts creating art with his paws.
> 3 **Scenario: Cat and the Mysterious Box**
>    – Story: Luna, a curious cat, finds a mysterious box in the attic. Inside, she discovers old toys and spends hours playing, reliving memories.
> 4 **Scenario: Cat's First Snow**
>    – Story: Oliver experiences snow for the first time. Fascinated, he cautiously steps out, leaving tiny paw prints, and joyfully chases snowflakes.
>
>  **Scenario: Cat Discovers a Mirror**
>
> Story: Bella, a curious cat, finds a mirror and spends the afternoon mesmerized by her reflection, playfully pawing at her "new friend."
>
> **Scenario: Cat and the Missing Sock**
>
> Story: Jasper, a mischievous cat, steals socks and hides them in his secret stash, delighting in his human's confusion as they search for the missing items.

The output from the chatbot is much more specific in format than if we had only asked for a short story about a cat. This gives us the ability to use the content without extensive editing. It's much more "work-ready."

Professionally, many-shot prompting is more common with complex tasks and is often used by data scientists and researchers who provide hundreds or even thousands of examples. It's also useful in an IT role, such as an IT service desk representative, to suggest resolutions to common problems or identify the proper escalation of a problem.

The appropriate approach to prompting always depends on the situation. We don't need an elaborate prompt for every question, but understanding when and how to use these different strategies can significantly enhance the AI's responses. If you don't have a use for few-shot and many-shot prompting at first, that's OK. Don't get too caught up in the terminology. The important thing is to know that these techniques exist and to recognize them when you see them.

### 4.2.5 The future of prompt engineering

As AI models evolve, the relationship between model capability and prompt complexity is changing. Consider how we teach children of different ages to make a sandwich. With a 5-year-old, we need to break down every step explicitly: "Take two slices of bread. Open the peanut butter jar. Use the knife to spread ..." A 12-year-old, however, can fill in these basic steps themselves due to their greater experience and reasoning ability. Similarly, modern AI models are developing more sophisticated reasoning capabilities that allow them to understand and execute tasks with less explicit instruction.

This evolution particularly affects zero-shot and single-shot prompting. Today's advanced models can often generate relevant responses with minimal guidance, and this capability will only improve. Just as we don't need to explain to an adult what "make a sandwich" means, future AI models will require less detailed instruction for basic tasks.

However, few-shot and many-shot prompting will retain their importance for a different reason: customization. Even as AI becomes more capable of understanding and executing tasks, it won't automatically know your specific preferences or requirements. These more-complex prompting techniques will shift from teaching the AI how to do something to showing it how you want it done.

This shift in prompt engineering's role perfectly aligns with our broader focus on problem formulation. As AI handles more of the basic understanding, we can focus on defining exactly what we want to achieve and how we want the results presented. Instead of explaining the fundamentals, we'll spend more time refining outputs to match our requirements. Let's explore these concepts further by examining what makes a prompt effective.

## 4.3 The mechanics of a good prompt

At the heart of effective communication with AI lie four fundamental principles: clarity, conciseness, relevance, and specificity. These principles work together like the ingredients in a recipe. Understanding how these elements interact helps us create prompts that consistently generate useful responses.

Consider the difference between these two database-related prompts:

 What's the best database technology?

versus

What are the leading database platforms for transactional workloads that provide enterprise support and high performance?

The second prompt demonstrates all four principles in action. It's clear in its purpose, concise in its phrasing, relevant to a specific use case, and specific about the requirements. Think about how this narrows the field: among hundreds of database platforms, only a select few will meet all these criteria. By providing this level of detail, we guide the AI toward the most pertinent information rather than receiving a generic overview of databases.

However, it's important to understand that prompt engineering isn't a one-size-fits-all solution. Different AI models respond to prompts in different ways. A prompt that produces excellent results with GPT-4 may be less effective with other language models designed for more specialized tasks, such as those focused purely on text classification or sentiment analysis.

This variation becomes even more pronounced when we move from text to image generation. Although image generation models like Midjourney have become increasingly sophisticated at understanding prompts, they still face the unique challenge of translating words into visual elements. This is where we see an interesting development in the field: using language models to enhance image generation prompts. DALL-E 3, for example, uses GPT to automatically expand user requests into more detailed, specific instructions before generating images. GPT-4o has since improved upon this by integrating text and image generation into a single multimodal model, enabling better text rendering and more accurate prompt following. This process is particularly valuable for users who may not be familiar with the precise terminology or details that lead to the best image generation results. It's similar to having an expert photographer translate your general idea ("I want a cozy living room photo") into specific technical instructions about lighting, composition, and atmosphere.

The ability to have AI refine and expand prompts is becoming increasingly valuable across different platforms. It helps bridge the gap between what users want to express and what AI systems need to understand to deliver optimal results. This development doesn't eliminate the need for understanding good prompt engineering principles—rather, it shows how fundamental these principles are, as even AI systems are using them to improve their output.

Despite variations across platforms and ongoing technological advances, we've distilled the art of AI prompting down to four key principles. Like the fundamental rules of grammar, these essentials remain constant even as AI languages and capabilities evolve. Let's explore these principles in more detail.

### 4.3.1 Key principles in prompt construction

Clarity, conciseness, relevance, and specificity form the foundation of effective AI communication. When applied thoughtfully, these four principles significantly boost the quality and usefulness of AI responses. In this section, we'll examine each one and provide practical examples of how to incorporate them into your prompts.

## CLARITY

Ensure that your prompt is clear and easy to understand. When starting a new chat with an AI assistant, remember that each conversation starts fresh, without any memory of previous interactions. Write your questions directly and precisely, avoiding unclear terms or technical jargon unless you're specifically discussing them. Your prompt should follow a logical flow with correct grammar and punctuation, giving the AI assistant all the information it needs to understand your request fully.

Consider this example prompt: Tell me about that new AI feature. Here, "AI" feature could refer to any capability, from chatbot interfaces to neural network architectures. The AI assistant cannot know which specific feature you mean. A clearer prompt would be "Explain what's new with GPT-4o image generation."

Clarity stands as the most obvious, yet fundamental of the four principles of prompt construction. Without a clear prompt, even the most advanced AI system cannot provide the specific information or assistance you need. The clearer your request, the more accurate and useful the response will be.

## CONCISENESS

Create prompts that are just the right length—no more, no less. Many effective prompts include plenty of details, especially for complex tasks. The goal isn't just being brief, but being efficient: include all needed instructions while cutting words that might cause confusion. Use clear, exact language that tells the AI precisely what you want.

Consider this unnecessarily wordy prompt:

 Take a look at the list of IT support tickets we have and go through each one of them to decide whether they should be classified under the category of High Priority, Medium Priority, or Low Priority based on their urgency and importance

A more concise version achieves the same goal:

 Sort these IT support tickets into High, Medium, and Low Priority categories

The streamlined prompt conveys identical instructions but removes redundant language. Notice how the shorter version requires less mental effort to process while maintaining clarity. This demonstrates a key principle: when the request is more efficiently expressed, both understanding and response quality typically improve.

> **NOTE** The two prompts in this example may very well produce the same response from the AI model. It's only an example of how to make a prompt more concise. Effective prompts can range from a few sentences to several paragraphs or even thousands of words for complex tasks.

## RELEVANCE

Your prompt should directly connect to your intended goal. Although this seems straightforward, irrelevant information can confuse an AI model and lead to responses that miss the mark. The prompt should contain only information that helps achieve your objective and should clearly indicate your target audience.

For instance, an "Act as" prompt is a fun way to ask an AI model to behave as a certain character or in a specific role. This is a common way to provide context. If you're aiming to practice JavaScript, you might use a prompt like "Act as a JavaScript console." You would not want the AI model to "act as" a pastry chef to teach you JavaScript.

Audience specification demonstrates another aspect of relevance. The same topic requires different approaches for different audiences. Consider explaining planetary formation: both Nobel laureates and third-grade students may be interested in how the solar system formed, but each group needs a distinct level of detail and complexity. A relevant prompt will specify your audience to ensure appropriate depth and terminology.

#### SPECIFICITY

Specificity in prompts helps direct the AI toward your exact requirements, transforming broad inquiries into focused requests with targeted responses. This principle ensures that you receive precise, relevant information rather than surface-level overviews.

Consider this evolution in prompt specificity. A general prompt like "What's the latest in cloud computing?" could generate responses ranging from consumer cloud storage to enterprise solutions to cloud gaming. However, a specific prompt such as "Provide an overview of the latest cloud computing technologies introduced within the past year for enterprise data storage solutions" creates clear boundaries around the topic. This precision guides the AI to address enterprise storage specifically, recent developments only, and technological innovations rather than market trends or pricing.

Specific prompts eliminate ambiguity by defining clear parameters for the response. When crafting specific prompts, consider including relevant timeframes, context, technical domains, and particular use cases that matter.

## 4.4 Introductory prompts for IT roles

The art of crafting a compelling prompt is often best learned through examples, so here are five introductory prompts that embody our four basic principles:

- Database querying
  - *Bad prompt*—How do databases work?
  - *Good prompt*—Explain the process of executing a SELECT query in a SQL Server database.
  - *Why it's good*—The good prompt is specific to a particular database operation, clear in its request, and directly relevant to a common database task. Instead of asking an open-ended question about databases, the good prompt narrows down the possible responses to a specific process in a specific database platform.
- Network troubleshooting
  - *Bad prompt*—I have network issues.
  - *Good prompt*—Guide me through troubleshooting a home Wi-Fi network that's not connecting to the internet.

- *Why it's good*—This prompt clearly and concisely outlines a specific networking problem, making it relevant for practical troubleshooting guidance for a home Wi-Fi network.
- Software development
  - *Bad prompt*—Teach me about coding.
  - *Good prompt*—Provide a step-by-step guide for writing a Python script to automate file backups.
  - *Why it's good*—It is specific (Python script for file backups), clear in its instructional nature, and relevant for someone learning to automate tasks in Python.
- Cybersecurity analysis
  - *Bad prompt*—Is my server secure?
  - *Good prompt*—Describe the steps to perform a basic security audit on a Linux server.
  - *Why it's good*—The prompt is specific to a type of security task, clear in its request for a process description, and relevant to IT security roles.
- Web development
  - *Bad prompt*—How do I build a website?
  - *Good prompt*—Outline the key steps in developing a responsive website using HTML, CSS, and JavaScript.
  - *Why it's good*—This prompt is specific to web development using certain technologies, clear in asking for an outline, and relevant to web development roles.

Building on the foundational prompts we've explored, we now transition to what we are calling the Awesome Prompts Lab. The next section demonstrates that skillful communication with AI often extends beyond a single prompt. Here, you'll learn to harness the power of multiple prompts and interactive prompting techniques to achieve more complex goals.

### 4.4.1 Awesome Prompts Lab

Welcome to the Awesome Prompts Lab, where we dive into a world of creative and interactive prompting. This section is designed to stretch your imagination and skills in prompt engineering, showcasing a collection of innovative and engaging prompts. In addition to being instructional, they're meant to inspire and challenge you to think outside the box in your interactions with AI models. Drawn from the rich resource of the Awesome ChatGPT Prompts on GitHub (https://github.com/f/awesome-chatgpt-prompts), these prompts are a starting point for advanced AI prompting.

> **TIP** Try it! As you explore these prompts, we encourage you to experiment with them, tweak them, and observe how subtle changes can lead to dramatically different outcomes. This hands-on approach will lead you to elicit rich, informative, and surprising responses from AI.

### Language teacher for English as a Second Language

Although English is our first language, we both grew up in the bayous of South Louisiana. The strong Cajun-French influence on our English grammar was something we spent many years figuring out after moving to different parts of the world. We'd like to give a lil' nod to our heritage with this prompt, which asks a chatbot to correct our grammar:

- *Bad prompt*—Correct my sentence: I'm going to Sonic, me. I went yesterday too and saw Erin. How long she been having that M5?
- *Good prompt*—I want you to act as an ESL teacher. I will write to you in American English and I want you to correct my grammar mistakes and punctuation. Explain why it is incorrect so that I may learn. I also want you to ask me a question in your reply so that we can have an ongoing conversation that you can correct.
- *Why it's good*—This prompt is specialized for a specific task: aiding a student of English in correcting their grammar while providing dialog for practice. It establishes a teaching relationship, requests specific types of corrections, asks for explanations, and sets up an interactive format.

Although we emphasize conciseness in prompt writing, complex tasks often require more detailed instructions. The key is to include necessary detail while avoiding redundant information.

You may also wonder how a student learning English will be able to use perfect grammar to build this prompt. AI systems can work with multiple languages, allowing students to write prompts in their native tongue. However, for technical or specialized topics, using English often produces the most precise results because it's typically the AI's primary training language.

### Interviewer for positions

You can ask the chatbox to act as an interviewer:

- *Bad prompt*—Interview me.
- *Good prompt*—Act as an interviewer for a Systems Administrator position. I will provide the job posting and my resume. Ask me relevant questions for this job position, and I will respond as the interviewee. Provide feedback on my responses and how I can improve them.
- *Why it's good*—This prompt establishes a role-play scenario, making it clear who is the interviewer and who is the interviewee.

### Linux terminal

Ask the chatbot to act as a Linux terminal and respond to your commands as a terminal would. The response can explain the commands or not return anything additional. This technique is handy when learning a command line without a test environment:

- *Bad prompt*—Teach me about Linux.

- *Good prompt*—Act as a Linux terminal. I will enter commands, and you execute them as if you were a terminal.
- *Why it's good*—This prompt is specific and sets clear expectations for an interactive, command-based dialogue.

#### JAVASCRIPT CONSOLE
Consider a bad prompt and a good prompt for JavaScript:

- *Bad prompt*—Show me some JavaScript.
- *Good prompt*—I want you to act as a JavaScript console. I will enter JavaScript code, and you execute and return the output.
- *Why it's good*—This prompt specifies interactive coding, with the AI model acting as a JavaScript console.

#### MOTIVATIONAL COACH
Always consider your objective when crafting a prompt:

- *Bad prompt*—Help me motivate someone to do better.
- *Good prompt*—Act as a motivational coach. I will provide you with some information about someone's goals and challenges. Come up with strategies to help this person achieve their goals.
- *Why it's good*—The prompt clearly defines the AI's role (motivational coach), what input you'll provide (information about goals and challenges), and what output you expect (specific strategies to help achieve those goals).

Feel free to adapt these examples to your specific IT role. For many more ready-to-use prompts, check out the community-driven "Awesome ChatGPT Prompts" repository on GitHub. Having a collection of proven prompts will save you time and help you get better results.

#### ACT AS AN AI WRITING TUTOR
This final prompt incorporates all the elements of an effective prompt (contributed by @devisasari, prompts.chat/#act-as-an-ai-writing-tutor). Try to replicate the style with a topic of your choice. Can you enhance the prompt even further?

 I want you to act as an AI writing tutor. I will provide you with a student who needs help improving their writing and your task is to use artificial intelligence tools, such as natural language processing, to give the student feedback on how they can improve their composition. You should also use your rhetorical knowledge and experience with effective writing techniques to suggest ways that the student can better express their thoughts and ideas in written form. My first request is *Help me outline a chapter on Prompt Engineering.*

## 4.5 Advanced techniques
Now that we've explored foundational prompt crafting, we will discuss advanced techniques that can refine and direct AI responses more precisely. These methods may take some practice to master, but as we progress, you'll see how they can be powerfully

applied in various contexts. Don't worry if none of this sinks in immediately; we will use these techniques in our prompt examples throughout the book.

### 4.5.1 Recursive prompts

Recursive prompts use previous responses to build deeper or more nuanced conversations.

> CA Based on the previous summary of renewable energy trends, what are the potential challenges and opportunities in the next 5 years?

### 4.5.2 Context injection

Context injection adds specific background information to steer the AI's response.

> CA As a cybersecurity expert, how would you assess the risks associated with cloud storage solutions?

### 4.5.3 Explicit constraints

Explicit constraints clearly define the scope or limits of the response.

> CA Identify and describe in brief only three emerging technologies in software development introduced in the past year.

### 4.5.4 Prompt chaining

Prompt chaining involves asking a series of related questions in one go for a comprehensive response.

> CA Describe the basic principles of blockchain technology, its primary use case in finance, and its potential impact on data security.

> **NOTE** When dealing with large amounts of information (context), asking for one thing at a time can yield better results.

### 4.5.5 Sentiment directives

Sentiment directives instruct the AI on the emotional tone or attitude to adopt in its response.

> CA Respond empathetically to a customer complaint about a delayed software update.

### 4.5.6 Templating

Templates structure the response in a predefined format that's useful for reports, summaries, or analyses.

> CA Analyze the given text and present your findings in this structure: Introduction, Main Arguments, Methodology, Conclusion, and Recommendations.

## 4.6 Best practices and common mistakes

As with any skill, prompt engineering requires practice and experimentation. Perhaps the most useful advice is to keep it simple. Don't overthink it. The AI model will do its best to follow your instructions, so don't worry about getting the prompt perfect. Just make it close enough to get the job done. There are no hard-and-fast rules, but there are some best practices and common mistakes to keep in mind when crafting prompts.

### 4.6.1 Learning from success

The community has contributed various successful prompts, like those in the "Awesome ChatGPT Prompts" repository. These can serve as templates for your endeavors. Examine the structure, language, and context of these successful prompts to understand the key elements that contribute to their effectiveness. It's impossible to define every successful approach to prompting, but these examples can serve as a starting point for your own experimentation.

There is no shortage of advice on prompt engineering, and we'll be honest—a lot of it is probably clickbait. We encourage you to explore the many online blogs and social media posts, but there's no substitute for hands-on experience and trial and error. As you experiment with prompts, you'll develop a better understanding of what works and what doesn't. You'll also learn to recognize the strengths and limitations of different AI models, which will help you tailor your prompts.

### 4.6.2 Pitfalls to avoid

There are things you can do right, but there are just as many things you can do wrong. Here are some common pitfalls to avoid when crafting prompts.

#### OVER-SPECIFICATION OR UNDER-SPECIFICATION

Too much or too little detail can make the AI's task difficult. Although detail is important, excessive information can lead to confusion or an over-focus on less relevant aspects. Lack of detail can result in vague outputs that completely miss the mark.

The following is an example of an over-specified pompt:

 Write a short story about a young artist named John, who lives in a small coastal town in Oregon, where it rains most of the year, and he loves to paint seascapes, particularly during the sunset, using a specific shade of blue called cerulean, which reminds him of his late grandmother's house by the sea where he spent his summers as a child.

Why it's bad: This prompt provides an overwhelming amount of detail, which could restrict the AI's creative scope and lead to an overemphasis on less critical elements.

Now let's consider an under-specified prompt:

 Write something creative.

Why it's bad: This prompt is too vague and lacks specific guidance, which could result in a generic or off-target output. It doesn't provide enough direction on the desired theme, genre, or style.

Instead, start with a more general prompt. Strive for a middle ground where your prompt provides sufficient detail to guide the AI without being overly broad:

 Write a short story about a young artist named John who lives in a rainy coastal town in Oregon and loves to paint seascapes.

This version highlights the essential details, giving the AI room to explore the story without being bogged down by overly specific information or a complete lack of detail.

### MISALIGNMENT

Make sure your prompt aligns with the AI's capabilities. Understand the strengths and limitations of your AI model, and tailor your prompts to use its specific capabilities. A misaligned prompt may look like the following:

 Explain the proprietary algorithm used by Company X in their internal software for optimizing supply chain logistics. Provide details on the code structure, key functions, and any unique optimization techniques employed.

Why it's bad: This prompt is misaligned because it asks for specific details about a proprietary algorithm that is not publicly documented or available in training data. The AI chatbot cannot access or generate information about internal, unpublished company software, leading to the inability to provide a meaningful response.

### ASSUMING AI UNDERSTANDING

Avoid assuming the AI has contextual knowledge that hasn't been provided in the prompt or previous interaction. For example, consider the following prompt in a new chat session:

 Continue explaining the steps we discussed earlier about the process.

Why it's bad: This prompt assumes the AI model has knowledge of previous discussions or context that hasn't been explicitly provided in the current interaction. Remember, the AI model only has the context of what's in the current chat session. If the communication is stateless, as with some API calls, all details must be provided with every prompt.

### IGNORING CONTEXT

Especially in ongoing interactions, ensure that your prompts consider the context established in earlier exchanges for coherence. Let's look at a prompt in a series:

## 4.6 Best practices and common mistakes

 What are the health benefits of regular exercise?
Can you list some recipes?

Why it's bad: The second prompt ignores the context established by the first (discussion about exercise and health) and shifts to an unrelated topic (recipes) without a logical transition. It's OK to switch topics when you like, but the chatbot may be confused about whether you want healthy recipes to accompany an exercise routine.

### 4.6.3 Meta-prompts

*Meta-prompts* are special instructions embedded within a prompt to guide a language model in generating a specific kind of response. This should look familiar if you work in an IT role, as many skill sets have similar concepts. Like a query hint or markup language, include meta-prompts in blockquotes with your prompt to guide the response.

How many meta-prompts exist, and do they work for all AI models? They are limited only by your imagination. The AI model will try to follow your guidance. We tested meta-prompts with ChatGPT, Claude, Copilot, and Gemini, and all four were able to understand our intent. Table 4.1 provides a few meta-prompts to give you some ideas.

Table 4.1 Meta-prompt examples

| Meta-prompt | Purpose |
| --- | --- |
| [Brief] What is Kubernetes? | For a concise answer |
| [In layman's terms] Explain machine learning | For a simplified explanation |
| [As a story] Describe the evolution of programming languages | To get the information in story form |
| [Pros and cons] Should our company move to the cloud? | For a balanced view with advantages and disadvantages |
| [Step-by-step] How do I set up a VPN? | For a detailed, step-by-step guide |
| [Factual] What is the current version of Python? | For a straightforward, factual answer |
| [Opinion] Which is better for backend development: Node.js or Django? | To get an opinion-based answer |
| [Comparison] Compare SQL databases and NoSQL databases | For a comparative analysis |
| [Timeline] What are the key milestones in cybersecurity? | For a chronological account of key events |
| [As a poem] Tell me about coding | For a poetic description |
| [For kids] How does the internet work? | For a child-friendly explanation |
| [Advantages only] What are the benefits of using containers? | To get a list of only the advantages |
| [As a recipe] How to write a Python script for automating tasks? | To receive the information in the form of a recipe |

There's a bit of humor with the [As a recipe] prompt because the chatbot will actually write an example of Python code as if it were a recipe. It also works for food. Try it if you want to see the result; we think it's worth it.

In the following examples, we experiment with meta-prompts to generate responses tailored to different audiences. Try it yourself to test the limits of meta-prompts. Can you create something funny or innovative?

> **Try it now: What is a planet?**
>
> Create three new meta-prompts, and apply them to the same prompt to see how AI chatbots change the response.
>
> (CA) [For Kids] What is a planet?
>
> 🤖 A planet is a big, round object that travels around a star, like our Sun. Planets don't make their own light; instead, they reflect the light from the star they orbit. Earth is a planet, and it's one of eight planets in our Solar System. Planets can be made of rock, like Earth, or gas, like Jupiter, and they can be big or small. Some planets even have moons that orbit around them!
>
> (CA) [For college students] What is a planet?
>
> 🤖 A planet is a celestial body that orbits a star, like our Sun, and has certain characteristics that distinguish it from other objects in space. According to the International Astronomical Union (IAU), a planet must meet three criteria: it must orbit a star, it must be spherical in shape due to its own gravity, and it must have cleared its orbit of other debris.
>
> Planets can vary significantly in composition and size. They are generally categorized into two types: terrestrial (rocky) planets, like Earth and Mars, which have solid surfaces, and gas giants, like Jupiter and Saturn, which are composed mostly of gases and lack a solid surface. In our Solar System, there are eight recognized planets, each with unique features, atmospheres, and sometimes, systems of moons. Beyond our Solar System, thousands of exoplanets have been discovered, some of which may be similar to Earth, opening up possibilities for understanding planetary formation and the potential for life elsewhere in the universe.
>
> (CA) [For astrophysicists] What is a planet?
>
> 🤖 A planet is a celestial body that meets specific criteria established by the International Astronomical Union (IAU) in 2006. These criteria are:
>
> 1. **Orbits a star**: A planet must be in orbit around a star, such as the Sun.
> 2. **Sufficient mass for hydrostatic equilibrium**: A planet must have enough mass for its gravity to overcome rigid body forces, leading to a nearly round shape (achieving hydrostatic equilibrium).

> 3 **Cleared its orbit**: A planet must have cleared its neighboring region of other debris, meaning it is gravitationally dominant in its orbit, either capturing, ejecting, or accreting other objects within its orbital zone.
>
> These criteria, however, are specific to our Solar System and have led to debates within the astrophysics community, particularly regarding objects in multi-body systems or exoplanets in dynamically complex environments. In exoplanetary science, the definition of a planet may be more flexible, often considering objects that do not strictly clear their orbits or orbit non-stellar objects (e.g., rogue planets). The ongoing discovery of diverse planetary systems challenges our understanding and classification, as we encounter objects that blur the lines between planets, dwarf planets, and brown dwarfs.
>
> In terms of composition, planets are typically categorized as terrestrial (rocky) or gas/ice giants, with further subdivisions based on their atmospheric and physical characteristics. The study of planetary formation and evolution encompasses diverse processes, including accretion, migration, and interaction with protoplanetary disks, contributing to a rich field of research that bridges astrophysics, planetary science, and cosmochemistry.

Meta-prompts are an ideal way to see how subtle shifts in instruction can dramatically affect how AI presents information. With this understanding of customization in mind, let's move on to problem formulation, where we structure questions to get the best possible answers from AI assistants.

## 4.7 Problem formulation

At last, problem formulation! We've been referencing it, but what is it? Problem formulation is the process of clearly defining and structuring a problem to facilitate effective solutions. We like to think of it as approaching a problem from the opposite direction. Instead of approaching a task as the student, approach it as the teacher. In many cases, we *ask* AI to give us answers to questions, but with problem formulation, we *tell* AI how to solve a problem for us. This is a subtle but important shift in thinking.

Problem formulation is the counterpart to prompt engineering and an integral part of productively using AI. It begins with a thorough breakdown of a problem, laying out the components and understanding their interconnections. This step is the careful planning before execution; it's where we map out the path to a solution.

Problem formulation was a revelation for us, shaping our approach to how we use AI in the workplace and inspiring the very creation of this book. In cases where we already understand a problem and know the solution, we can tell AI exactly what we need it to do.

In chapter 1, we made the point that AI is a tool, and it's much more effective when wielded by a subject matter expert. In real-world applications, whether it's diagnosing a technical problem or devising a marketing strategy, the ability to precisely define and structure the problem is what sets the direction for the AI's response. Asking AI to create a final product will result in an inferior product. Instead, we need to provide details and structure all the way through to guide the output of the AI model.

Although prompt engineering helps us phrase our queries effectively, our expertise is what enables us to ask the right questions in the first place. The combination of technical prompting skill and domain knowledge leads to the most valuable insights.

Imagine an artist who wants to create 100 variations of the same painting. Instead of asking for 100 paintings, the artist provides a template of the painting and allows the AI model the creative freedom to choose the style and colors within each block. Figure 4.1 illustrates this concept perfectly. This is problem formulation in action. As an IT professional seeking professional output, you won't ask AI for the finished product, as it is unlikely to meet expectations. You will instead define the requirements and boundaries of the product and guide AI at every step in its creation.

Figure 4.1  Paint by numbers

The more adept you become at problem formulation, the more effective you will be when using AI. It's a skill that goes beyond using a tool; it's the ability to mold the tool to fit the unique contours of each challenge you face. This nuanced understanding of problem formulation is what we hope to impart, ensuring that you're equipped to interact with AI by commanding it toward meaningful and effective solutions.

## 4.8 Incorporating problem formulation

Having explored various prompt engineering techniques, we will now focus on integrating problem formulation into our strategy. This next step adds depth and context to our prompts, transforming them from instructions into comprehensive guides that align closely with our specific goals and challenges. By incorporating problem formulation, we transform our prompts from simple queries to well-thought-out requests that encapsulate the broader scope of our objectives, creating more targeted AI responses.

Consider the following prompt:

 Create a Python script that sorts a list of numbers in ascending order.

This prompt is clear and specific. It tells the AI exactly what is needed—a Python script—and the task it should perform: sorting a list of numbers. The resulting script may be perfect for someone unskilled in Python, but it may not be what a Python programmer will be happy with. Although the prompt will produce the generic expected output, a skilled Python programmer can go a step further to customize it exactly to their needs.

 I am working on a data analysis project and need a Python script to sort numerical datasets in ascending order. The script should:
- Use an efficient sorting algorithm like QuickSort or MergeSort to handle datasets of varying sizes.
- Be scalable to ensure good performance with large datasets.
- Include detailed inline comments explaining:
  - The mechanics of the chosen sorting algorithm.
  - Its computational complexity.
  - Why it is well-suited for large datasets.

In this revised prompt, problem formulation provides context and specific requirements for a Python script. The requestor, who could write this code themselves, includes the purpose, needs, performance considerations, and request for documentation. By specifying the need for sorting algorithms like QuickSort or MergeSort, they demonstrate subject matter expertise.

Problem formulation's power comes from your understanding of the desired solution. Like our paint-by-number canvas in figure 4.1 or solving a maze in reverse, knowing the end goal clarifies the path. This is where IT professionals excel when using AI tools. Their experience helps them provide the detailed, context-rich information that turns AI from a basic tool into a valuable workflow partner, resulting in more efficient and precise responses.

Up next in chapter 5, we will apply what we've learned so far in a practical example. You'll see how prompt engineering and problem formulation can be seamlessly integrated to achieve optimal results. By the end of the next chapter, we'll have produced work-ready content from scratch with a fraction of the effort it would have taken without AI.

## 4.9 Prompts used in this chapter

- I need a better intro to chapter 3 (attached), in the style of the attached book, dbatools in a month of lunches, but again, never cliches or idioms
- Is there a better way to present this information? Maybe I'm wrong, but this feels like it'd go good in a table?
- Take out cliched phrases like "ever evolving"
- Can you talk about how prompts are like a mix of art and tech
- That feels like word salad. Can you simplify the paragraph/intro?
- Can you replace the words within the brackets in the following sentence? Give me 5 iterations.
- Finish this sentence: Knowing both the language of prompt engineering and the models you'll be working with
- Is there such a phrase as data analytics engine?
- Search the web and tell me if all of this is true
- I'm looking for a good way to express a thought. Here are two examples that I wrote. Can you help?

## Summary

- Prompt engineering involves strategically crafting questions or commands to effectively communicate with AI tools, enhancing the quality and relevance of their responses.
- Basic approaches to prompting, such as zero-shot, single-shot, few-shot, and many-shot, offer varying degrees of guidance to AI models, affecting their response accuracy and context understanding.
- The mechanics of a good prompt are rooted in clarity, conciseness, relevance, and specificity, which guide the AI to provide more targeted and useful responses.
- Advanced prompting techniques, including recursive prompts, context injection, explicit constraints, prompt chaining, and sentiment directives, allow for more sophisticated and nuanced interactions with AI models.
- Best practices in prompt engineering involve learning from successful examples and avoiding common pitfalls like over-specification and misalignment with the AI's capabilities.

- Meta-prompts serve as a tool to direct the AI's response style and focus, offering a creative way to tailor outputs to specific needs or contexts.
- Problem formulation is a strategy where a problem is dissected and understood, allowing experts with deep domain knowledge to craft superior prompts, guiding AI to more precise and effective AI responses.
- Properly using prompt engineering and problem formulation empowers users to skillfully use AI for practical, work-ready content creation and problem-solving.

# Prompts in action

**This chapter covers**
- Applying prompt engineering in project management
- Utilizing AI chatbots for project management learning
- Enhancing prompts with problem formulation
- Generating practical, work-ready content using AI

In this chapter, we move from concepts to action, demonstrating how AI can enhance project management through well-crafted prompts. Using ChatGPT, we'll explore a detailed scenario that shows how to create practical, work-ready deliverables. Our approach unfolds in two parts: first using basic prompt engineering to achieve our goals, and then showing how a deeper understanding of problem formulation can streamline the process.

When discussing ChatGPT-4, it's important to understand that we're referring to a family of models. The 4o model, now the default for premium plans, delivers efficient performance with real-time response capabilities. Alongside it comes the 4o mini model, which trades some capability for increased speed and offers more cost-effective API calls. However, the true powerhouses in OpenAI's lineup are the o1 and o3 models. Available exclusively to paying customers, these models incorporate an innovative approach: they first analyze the request and strategize the best solution before beginning their response. Although this process takes longer, it consistently produces superior results.

For our demonstration, we'll use a traditional approach that works across any chatbot platform. We've chosen this path for two important reasons: first, it ensures that you can apply these techniques regardless of which AI model you're using; and second, it helps you develop a deeper understanding of effective prompt engineering principles. This foundation will make you more skilled at crafting prompts across all AI platforms.

If you have access to ChatGPT Plus with the o1 or o3 model, or GPT-4o with deep research, we encourage you to replicate these exercises using those models as well. This will give you a fascinating comparison of how different models approach the same tasks, and you may find they reach even better outcomes more efficiently. OpenAI intends to introduce automatic model switching in the future to auto-select the best model for complex tasks.

## 5.1 Prompt engineering in action

Every IT professional will eventually be tasked with managing a project due to limited project manager resources or because the project initiative isn't large enough to warrant an assigned project manager. Although it's possible to wing it using Excel or a Gantt chart, that isn't always enough to properly organize a project. There are benefits to applying formal project management techniques, but without PM training, you likely won't know what those best practices are.

### 5.1.1 Basic prompting

In this example, we are using an AI chatbot to learn about project management best practices, with the intent of creating output that we can use immediately. This style of prompt engineering employs less problem formulation because we have not done any work ahead of time to determine what the output should be. This is what is known as a *zero-shot prompt*, and it relies on the AI model to provide the direction.

First we will ask a basic question in a way that an inexperienced prompter might ask. Then we will analyze the results.

 How can I be a good project manager?

 Being a good project manager is a valuable skill. Here are some key principles and tips to excel as a project manager in any field:

1 **Understand the Project**: Start by thoroughly understanding the project's goals, scope, objectives, and requirements. This is crucial for effective planning and execution.

2. **Plan Wisely**: Develop a detailed project plan that outlines tasks, timelines, dependencies, and resources. Use project management software to help with scheduling and tracking progress.
3. **Communication**: Effective communication is vital. Keep all stakeholders informed about project status, changes, and potential risks. Foster open and clear communication channels.
4. **Team Building**: As a project manager, you'll work with a team. Build a cohesive and motivated team by understanding each member's strengths, assigning tasks accordingly, and providing support when needed.
5. **Risk Management**: Identify potential risks early and have mitigation plans in place. Regularly assess and address risks throughout the project lifecycle.
6. **Quality Assurance**: Ensure that the project meets quality standards. Implement testing and quality control processes to catch issues before they become major problems.
7. **Budget Management**: Monitor project expenses closely and ensure that the project stays within budget. Make adjustments as necessary to avoid cost overruns.
8. **Adaptability**: Be flexible and adaptable to changes. In the tech industry, things can evolve rapidly, so your project plan may need adjustments along the way.
9. **Time Management**: Time is often limited in IT projects. Prioritize tasks, set realistic deadlines, and monitor progress to ensure timely delivery.
10. **Documentation**: Maintain clear and organized project documentation, including requirements, plans, and progress reports. This helps with transparency and knowledge sharing.
11. **Stakeholder Engagement**: Understand the needs and expectations of all project stakeholders, including clients, team members, and management. Regularly engage with them to ensure alignment.
12. **Problem-Solving**: Be prepared to address challenges and issues that arise during the project. Problem-solving skills are essential for overcoming obstacles.
13. **Continuous Improvement**: After each project, conduct a post-mortem analysis to identify what went well and what could be improved. Apply these lessons to future projects.
14. **Leadership**: Lead by example and inspire your team. Provide clear direction, guidance, and support to ensure everyone is working towards the project's success.
15. **Stay Informed**: Keep up with the latest trends and technologies in IT. This will help you make informed decisions and adapt to industry changes.
16. **Certifications**: Consider obtaining project management certifications such as PMP (Project Management Professional) or PRINCE2 to enhance your skills and credibility.

Remember that being a good project manager involves a combination of technical knowledge, leadership abilities, and effective communication. Continuously honing these skills will help you excel in your role as a tech manager overseeing IT projects.

Our prompt language is very open, but it generates considerable output. The AI model lists the characteristics of a good project manager, including problem-solving capabilities and suggestions for certifications.

Although there is something to learn from the output, such as useful soft skills, it's not immediately helpful to our scenario: we just want to create some documents. It feels like the AI model is rambling because it doesn't know what to focus on. We intend to produce content for immediate use with our project, so this prompt has come up short. The prompt is technically clear and concise (it is easy to read and to the point), but it does not meet our standards for relevance and specificity.

As worded, the prompt can produce a response that encompasses a wide range of skills, techniques, and contexts. Which aspects of project management are we interested in? Why are we asking for this information? What do we hope to do with the information we receive? Let's try again with a bit more context about our situation.

 I am not a professional project manager, but I need to lead a small IT project. I am not in charge of any financial considerations and am not tracking a budget. Which tasks should I complete to successfully manage this project?

 Even if you're not a professional project manager and your project is small without financial considerations, you can still ensure its success by following some basic project management principles. Here's a simplified guide for heading up a small project:

1 **Define Clear Objectives**: Start by clearly defining the objectives and scope of your project. Understand what needs to be accomplished and what success looks like.

2 **Create a Project Plan**: Develop a simple project plan that outlines the tasks, responsibilities, and timelines. List the key milestones you need to achieve.

3 **Identify Resources**: Determine the resources you'll need for the project, including team members, tools, and equipment. Ensure that everyone knows their roles.

4 **Task Breakdown**: Break down the project into smaller, manageable tasks. This will make it easier to assign responsibilities and track progress.

5 **Set Priorities**: Identify the most critical tasks and prioritize them. Focus on completing the high-priority items first to ensure that essential work gets done.

6 **Communication Plan**: Establish a communication plan to keep your team informed. Decide on how and when you'll provide updates and gather feedback.

7 **Regular Check-Ins**: Schedule regular check-in meetings with your team to review progress, address issues, and adjust the plan as needed.

8 **Risk Assessment**: Identify potential risks or obstacles that could impact the project. Even in small projects, having a contingency plan is helpful.

9 **Task Tracking**: Use simple project management tools or spreadsheets to track task progress. This will help you stay organized and ensure everyone is on the same page.

10. **Problem Solving**: Be prepared to address any challenges that arise during the project. Encourage your team to come forward with issues so you can find solutions together.
11. **Documentation**: Keep basic project documentation. This could include meeting minutes, task lists, and any changes to the project plan.
12. **Celebrate Milestones**: Recognize and celebrate when you reach project milestones. It boosts morale and keeps the team motivated.
13. **Closure and Evaluation**: At the end of the project, evaluate its success. What went well, and what could be improved for future projects?
14. **Knowledge Sharing**: Share the lessons learned from the project with your team. This helps build knowledge and improve processes for future endeavors.
15. **Feedback**: Gather feedback from team members on how the project was managed. This can provide valuable insights for your future project management efforts.
16. **Reflect and Learn**: Take some time to reflect on your experience as a project manager. Consider whether you'd like to pursue more project management roles in the future.

Remember that while you may not be a professional project manager, these basic project management practices can help you successfully lead a small project. Adapt these principles to fit the specific needs of your project, and don't hesitate to seek guidance or mentorship from experienced project managers if needed.

The revised prompt did not take much more effort, but the response is considerably more relevant and actionable. Let's look at how the subtle changes to the prompt better adhere to our four principles.

#### CLARITY

The revised prompt maintains clarity by directly asking for guidance on managing a small IT project. It clearly states the context and the user's role, which helps in understanding the specific needs.

#### CONCISENESS

Although slightly longer than the original prompt, it remains concise, adding necessary details without being overly wordy. It efficiently conveys the user's situation and the specific type of advice needed. Prompts do not have to be short, but they should be to the point.

#### RELEVANCE

The prompt is highly relevant to the user's situation. It focuses on project management within the context of a small IT project, which is a common scenario in many professional environments.

#### SPECIFICITY

This is where the prompt significantly improves. It specifies that the user is not a professional project manager and highlights the project's scope (a small IT project) and constraints (no financial or budget responsibilities). This specificity allows for more targeted and applicable advice, focusing on the essential tasks for managing a small IT project without the complexities of financial oversight. Instead of focusing on the general qualities of a good project manager, it's now providing actionable advice for the user's specific situation.

## 5.1.2 Recursive prompting

Recursive prompts build on the established context of our ongoing conversation with the AI model without needing to restate all the details. Recursive prompts are a natural part of conversations, allowing for a more fluid and coherent dialogue. They enable a chatbot to utilize the information already provided, enhancing the relevance and quality of its responses. For instance, having previously discussed the need for a project plan, our next prompt can directly ask the AI model to outline the steps for creating one, using the context already set.

> **NOTE** It's important to remember that although recursive prompts are powerful, they work best in focused discussions where the context remains relevant and clear. Starting new chats wipes out context.

Let's continue with our next prompt, focusing on the creation of useful documentation using recursive prompting.

 Based on your previous response, which documents should I create to support this initiative?

 To support your small project initiative, you should create some basic project documents to ensure clarity, organization, and effective communication. Here are the key documents you should consider:

1 **Project Charter**:
- **Purpose**: This document outlines the project's objectives, scope, and purpose.
- **Stakeholders**: Identify project stakeholders, including team members and anyone else involved.
- **Scope**: Clearly define what's in and out of scope for the project.
- **Objectives**: List the specific goals and outcomes you aim to achieve.
- **Success Criteria**: Describe how you'll measure the success of the project.
- **Constraints**: Note any limitations, such as time or resource constraints.
- **Assumptions**: Document any assumptions made about the project.

2 **Project Plan**:
- **Task List**: Create a list of tasks and subtasks needed to complete the project.
- **Responsibilities**: Assign responsibilities for each task to team members.
- **Timeline**: Create a timeline or schedule that includes start and end dates for each task.
- **Milestones**: Highlight key milestones that signify progress.
- **Dependencies**: Identify any task dependencies, i.e., tasks that must be completed before others can start.

- **Resource Allocation**: Specify the resources (people, tools, equipment) required for each task.
3. **Communication Plan**:
   - **Team Communication**: Define how and when you'll communicate with your team (e.g., regular meetings, email updates).
   - **Stakeholder Communication**: Outline how you'll keep stakeholders informed about project progress.
   - **Issue Resolution**: Describe how issues and conflicts will be communicated and resolved.
4. **Risk Register**:
   - **Risks**: List potential risks that could impact the project.
   - **Likelihood and Impact**: Assess the likelihood and potential impact of each risk.
   - **Mitigation Strategies**: Outline strategies for mitigating or addressing each risk.
5. **Task Tracker**:
   - **Task List**: Reiterate the list of tasks from the project plan.
   - **Status**: Track the status of each task (e.g., not started, in progress, completed).
   - **Assigned To**: Indicate who is responsible for each task.
   - **Due Dates**: Record due dates for each task.
   - **Comments/Notes**: Include any relevant notes or updates for each task.
6. **Meeting Minutes**:
   - Document the key points, discussions, and decisions made during project meetings. This helps with accountability and provides a record of project discussions.
7. **Project Closure Report** (at the end of the project):
   - Summarize the project's outcomes and achievements.
   - Note any challenges faced and how they were addressed.
   - Highlight key takeaways and lessons learned.
   - Gather feedback from team members for future improvements.

These documents should serve as a foundation for managing your small project effectively. Keep them organized and accessible to all team members and stakeholders. Adjust the level of detail to match the size and complexity of your project, ensuring that they provide the necessary guidance and clarity to keep the project on track.

The results of the third prompt are much more useful and relevant. We have targeted types of documents that we will need for our project management task. Notice that on its own, this prompt would be useless: not having to restate information that the AI model should already know is what makes it a recursive prompt. It automatically incorporates the output of the previous prompts into the next prompt. The AI model understands the context of the conversation by referencing all prior conversations within the chat session.

## 5.1.3 Template creation

Now that we are expert project managers, we need to create the templates. Let's ask for template examples to produce some of our very first work-ready content.

*5.1 Prompt engineering in action* 89

 I am not interested in a project charter, meeting minutes, or a project closure report. However, I would like to utilize the other suggestions. Can you provide a simplified template for my project?

 Certainly, here's a simplified template for a project plan that you can use for your small project. Feel free to modify it to fit the specific needs of your initiative:

Project Plan for [Project Name]

**Project Overview:**
- Project Name: [Enter Project Name]
- Project Manager: [Your Name]
- Project Start Date: [Start Date]
- Project End Date: [End Date]
- Project Objective: [Briefly describe the project's main objective.]

**Task List:**

| Task | Responsible | Due Date |
|---|---|---|
| Task 1 | [Team Member 1] | [Due Date] |
| - Subtask 1.1 | [Team Member 2] | [Due Date] |
| - Subtask 1.2 | [Team Member 3] | [Due Date] |
| Task 2 | [Team Member 4] | [Due Date] |
| Task 3 | [Team Member 5] | [Due Date] |

**Timeline:**
- [Timeline visual]

**Milestones:**
- Milestone 1: [Description] - [Date]
- Milestone 2: [Description] - [Date]

**Dependencies:**
- Task 2 depends on the completion of Task 1.
- Task 3 can start after Task 2 is completed.

**Resource Allocation:**
- [Team Member 1]
- [Team Member 2]
- [Team Member 3]

**Communication Plan:**
- Team Communication: Via email and [Communication tool].

- Bi-weekly team meetings scheduled for project updates.
- Stakeholder Communication: Report project progress at the bi-weekly department project update meeting.

**Risk Register:**

| Risk | Likelihood | Impact | Mitigation Strategy |
| --- | --- | --- | --- |
| [Risk 1] | [Low/Med/High] | [Low/Med/High] | [Describe strategy] |
| [Risk 2] | [Low/Med/High] | [Low/Med/High] | [Describe strategy] |

This template provides a basic structure for your project plan. You can add or remove sections as needed, depending on the complexity of your project. Remember to regularly update and refer to this plan to track progress and ensure that the project stays on course.

Now we are cooking with fire. The AI model has produced an impressive template for us, remembering the documents it suggested in a previous response and including those items in the template, minus the documents we specified that we didn't want. If anything is missing or in need of modification, this would be the best time to request changes. For the sake of this example, we are happy with the results. We have not only gotten answers, but we have also created actionable content that we can use in our project.

At this point, we have a reusable template that we can save for future projects. Depending on the chatbot you are using, you will either have to copy the template and paste it into a document or ask the chatbot to create the document for you to download. Downloading documents is often a premium feature.

> **TIP** If you are familiar with markdown, ask the chatbot to output documents using the markdown format. This will allow you to easily copy and paste the content into your own markdown document, even without a paid account! For spreadsheets, ask for CSV output.

For the sake of our prompt engineering example, we will continue and ask the chatbot to fill in the template with our project details.

## 5.1.4 *Finalized output*

The only thing missing from our previous template is the content. Sure, we can output the template and fill it in, but why? Let's ask the chatbot to do it for us. You can provide this information in a variety of ways, such as a write-up, bullet points, or even rows from a spreadsheet. The spreadsheet approach is very convenient if you've already started planning your project and have compiled the information. We'll explore that approach in the problem formulation example. For now, we will provide the information conversationally and see what we get.

## 5.1 Prompt engineering in action

 The project name is Oracle Database Migration. Brandon is managing the project, with a start date of October 20th, 2025 and ending on January 15, 2026. The objective is to move a database from Oracle 19c to 23ai during a 2-hour downtime.

The task list will consist of the architecture team performing the system design, the Linux team building the VM and installing OS, the storage team allocating storage, and the database team installing Oracle and configuring it. The database team will also do a dry-run migration of the database. The app team will use the new environment for dry-run testing.

A maintenance window will be determined and final data migration will occur. The application will be repointed to the new database. Milestones can be pulled from the task list as well. Each task is dependent upon the prior task being completed. We will have 1 team member from each team mentioned.

Communication will be via email and Teams with weekly meetings scheduled. We will report the project status back to stakeholders at a separate bi-weekly department project update meeting. Risks could consist of any delays in the OS build, storage availability, and issues with the dry run staying within the designated downtime window target.

Fill in the template with this information.

 Certainly! Here's the project plan template filled in with the information for the "Oracle Database Migration" project:

**Project Plan for Oracle Database Migration**

**Project Overview:**
- Project Name: Oracle Database Migration
- Project Manager: Brandon
- Project Start Date: October 20, 2025
- Project End Date: January 15, 2026
- Project Objective: To successfully migrate the Oracle 19c database to Oracle 23ai during a 2-hour downtime window.

**Task List:**

| Task | Responsible | Due Date |
| --- | --- | --- |
| System Design | Architecture Team | [Due Date] |
| Build Linux VM and Install OS | Linux Team | [Due Date] |
| Allocate Storage | Storage Team | [Due Date] |
| Install Oracle and Configure | Database Team | [Due Date] |
| Perform Dry Run Migration of the Database | Database Team | [Due Date] |
| Application Team Dry Run Testing | Application Team | [Due Date] |
| Determine Maintenance Window | Project Manager | [Due Date] |

| Task | Responsible | Due Date |
|---|---|---|
| Final Data Migration | Database Team | [Due Date] |
| Repoint Application to New Database | Application Team | [Due Date] |

**Milestones:**
- System Design Completed
- Linux VM Built and OS Installed
- Storage Allocated
- Oracle Installed and Configured
- Successful Dry-Run Migration Completed
- Application Dry-Run Testing Completed
- Maintenance Window Determined
- Final Data Migration Completed
- Application Repointed to New Database

**Dependencies:**
- Linux VM Build depends on System Design Completed.
- Storage Allocation depends on Linux VM Built and OS Installed.
- Oracle Installation and Configuration depend on Storage Allocation.
- Successful Dry Run Migration depends on Oracle Installation and Configuration.
- Application Dry Run Testing depends on Successful Dry Run Migration.
- Maintenance Window Determination depends on Application Team Dry Run Testing Completed.
- Final Data Migration depends on Maintenance Window Determined.
- Application Repointing depends on Final Data Migration Completed.

**Resource Allocation:**
- Brandon (Project Manager)
- [Team Member 1] (Architecture Team)
- [Team Member 2] (Linux Team)
- [Team Member 3] (Storage Team)
- [Team Member 4] (Database Team)
- [Team Member 5] (Application Team)

**Communication Plan:**
- Team Communication: Via email and Microsoft Teams
- Weekly team meetings scheduled for project updates.
- Stakeholder Communication: Report project progress at the bi-weekly department project update meeting.

## Risk Register:

| Risk | Likelihood | Impact | Mitigation Strategy |
|---|---|---|---|
| Delays in Linux VM Build | [Low/Med/High] | [Low/Med/High] | [Describe strategy] |
| Storage Availability Issues | [Low/Med/High] | [Low/Med/High] | [Describe strategy] |
| Dry Run Exceeds Downtime Window | [Low/Med/High] | [Low/Med/High] | [Describe strategy] |

In this example, we were able to very quickly use AI to suggest project management best practices, list required documents, and generate templates. Although some tweaks to the output will be needed, the amount of time required to arrive at this point is measured in minutes. Had we provided more details in the prompts, the output would have been even more relevant. Take note of the freedom you may be feeling right now, not having to expend energy simplifying your request to align with the limitations of a search engine or downloading a generic template to fill in.

Using natural language to tell the AI model what we want is highly effective, but it creates a problem when excessive details are required. Notice that we did not classify the risks or input dates into the task list. To provide that amount of detail, we should use a more structured approach. To illustrate, let's tackle the same task from the perspective of a more experienced project manager by incorporating problem formulation.

## 5.2 Problem formulation in action

In section 5.1, we adopted a bottom-up approach, beginning without predefined guidance and progressively building toward a final solution. This method is particularly beneficial for those unfamiliar with project management, as it allows the AI model to gradually provide direction and insights. In this process, we navigated the complexities of project management, making our way through a maze, with the AI model serving as our guide to explore and understand each turn.

Now we'll shift our strategy to a top-down approach by using the concept of problem formulation. As we discussed in chapter 4, this technique involves starting with a clear understanding of our desired outcome and the steps needed to achieve it. We arrive at the maze with a map already in hand. This approach underscores the value of experience. An experienced project manager applying problem formulation can shorten the path by guiding the AI model in generating specific responses.

 Act as an expert senior project manager. You are compiling documentation for an upcoming project and need to create a simplified template containing the following:

Project Overview, Task List, Milestones, Dependencies, Resource Allocations, Communication Plan and Risk Register.

I am pasting (or attaching) information for the template from a spreadsheet. Include the information in the template. Do not include the Dependency and milestone flags in the task list, but use them as indicators to build out the Milestones and Dependencies section of the template.

| | A | B | C | D | E | F | G | H |
|---|---|---|---|---|---|---|---|---|
| 1 | Project: | Oracle Database Migration | | | | | | |
| 2 | Project Manager: | Kylee | | | | | | |
| 3 | Start Date: | 10/20/25 | | | | | | |
| 4 | End Date: | 1/15/26 | | | | | | |
| 5 | | | Start Date | End Date | Dependency | Milestone | Assignee: | Team |
| 6 | Tasks: | System Design | 10/20/25 | 10/20/25 | Y | N | Debbie | Architecture |
| 7 | | Build Linux VM and Install OS | 10/25/25 | 10/28/25 | Y | Y | Tony | Linux |
| 8 | | Allocate & Configure Storage | 10/25/25 | 10/26/25 | Y | N | Joe | Storage |
| 9 | | Install Oracle and Configure | 10/28/25 | 11/8/25 | Y | Y | Brandon | Database |
| 10 | | Perform Dry-Run Migration of the Database | 11/8/25 | 11/15/25 | Y | N | Brandon | Database |
| 11 | | Application Team Dry-Run Testing | 11/15/25 | 12/15/25 | Y | Y | Chrissy | Application |
| 12 | | Finalize Go-Live Plan | 12/15/25 | 1/1/25 | Y | N | Kylee | Project Manager |
| 13 | | Enter Change Ticket | 1/5/26 | 1/5/26 | Y | Y | Kylee | Project Manager |
| 14 | | Perform Final Data Migration | 1/15/26 | 1/15/26 | Y | Y | Brandon | Database |
| 15 | | Update Application Connections | 1/15/26 | 1/15/26 | Y | N | Chrissy | Application |
| 16 | | | | | | | | |
| 17 | Communication: | Email and Teams | | | | | | |
| 18 | | Weekly project team meetings | | | | | | |
| 19 | | Bi-weekly stakeholder updates | | | | | | |
| 20 | | | | | | | | |
| 21 | Risks: | | Likelihood | Impact | Mitigation | | | |
| 22 | | Delays in Linux VM Builds | Low | High | Escalate to server team management | | | |
| 23 | | Storage Availability Issues | Med | High | Notify stakeholders of potential delay | | | |
| 24 | | Data Migration exceeding downtime window | High | High | Request additional time for migration | | | |
| 25 | | | | | | | | |

 Certainly, I can create a simplified project documentation template that includes the relevant information. Below is the template that consolidates the project details:

### Project Documentation: Oracle Database Migration

### Project Overview
- **Project:** Oracle Database Migration
- **Project Manager:** Kylee
- **Start Date:** 10/20/25
- **End Date:** 1/15/26

### Task List

| Task | Start Date | End Date | Assignee |
|---|---|---|---|
| System Design | 10/20/25 | 10/20/25 | Debbie |
| Build Linux VM and Install OS | 10/21/25 | 10/28/25 | Tony |
| ... | | | |

**Milestones**
- Build Linux VM and Install OS (10/28/25)
- Install Oracle and Configure (11/8/25)

...

**Dependencies**
- Request Linux VM
- Build Linux VM and Install OS

...

**Resource Allocations**
- Kylee (Project Manager)
- Debbie (Architecture Team)
- Tony (Linux Team)

...

**Communication Plan**
- **Channels:** Email and Microsoft Teams
- **Frequency:** Weekly project team meetings, Bi-weekly stakeholder updates

**Risk Register**

| Risk | Likelihood | Impact | Mitigation Strategy |
| --- | --- | --- | --- |
| Delays in Linux VM Builds ... | Low | High | Escalate to server team management |

You can see that the output of this single prompt is nearly identical to our previous example but with more detailed dates and risk categorizations. These details would have been too cumbersome to provide in a conversational mode. Structured data inputs allow us to easily fill in the template with less chance for errors in both our prompt input and the response output. Again, the result is almost anticlimactic because it is so easy to get the AI model to do what we want when we provide the right input.

This problem formulation approach required preplanning, but thanks to the detailed information provided to the chatbot, it was possible to receive high-quality output with much less prompting. But what specifically made it a smarter problem formulation approach instead of solely prompt engineering?

We did not ask the AI model what *we* needed to do. We told it what *it* needed to do. We were not attempting to learn; we were attempting to create. This is where the AI model is transformed from a teacher into a tool.

As we conclude this practical example, it's evident how our deep dive into prompt engineering and problem formulation culminates in a more efficient approach to interacting with AI. By relying on our expertise and understanding of the subject matter, we can guide the AI model effectively, leading to faster and more relevant results. Instead of waiting for the AI to steer us, we take control, using our knowledge to shape precise prompts and well-defined problems. This approach not only saves time but also ensures that the AI's responses are directly aligned with our specific needs and objectives. When we combine our professional expertise with strategic prompt crafting and thoughtful problem formulation, we harness the full potential of AI as a powerful tool for productivity and problem-solving in the workplace.

Let's pivot to where theory meets practice! Chapter 6 marks an exciting transition as we try out document handling—the first of many chapters that will transform how you work. We'll demonstrate real-world techniques for summarizing, converting, and analyzing documents and more.

## *Summary*

- Effective prompt engineering leads to better AI interactions in project management.
- Detailed context in prompts yields more actionable AI responses.
- Recursive prompts utilize previous outputs for coherent, advanced queries.
- Problem formulation enables quicker, more relevant results from AI models.
- Expert guidance in any subject area maximizes AI performance and output value.

# Document handling

### This chapter covers
- Summarizing lengthy documents quickly and accurately
- Converting between different file formats with ease
- Extracting text from images and scanned documents
- Managing document metadata and organization

IT workers deal with numerous documents every day. Technical manuals, project reports, system logs, and support tickets quickly add up, and their various file formats can make document management challenging.

In this chapter, we'll show how AI can improve your document workflow, even with just a basic chatbot. You'll learn how to prepare documents for AI processing and get better results. We'll cover practical techniques you can use right away, like summarizing long documents, converting file formats, and extracting text from images.

## 6.1 Best practices for document handling with AI

Before feeding any documents into AI tools, check your company's security policies. AI services process data on external servers, so avoid sharing confidential or sensitive information unless you're using a secure, approved platform.

When working with documents and AI, keep these key points in mind:

- *Document preparation and size matter.* Break large documents into 10- to 20-page segments with clear labels like NetworkSecurity_Section1_Firewall.pdf. This helps manage token usage and enables more precise processing. Extract the raw text rather than using formatted files like PDFs or Word documents; this helps the AI focus on content rather than format.
- *Be explicit.* Tell the AI what you'd like it to read. Say "Read this entire report before answering" or "Go through all sections of the file." This results in better output than nonspecific requests, but the best output comes from chunking.
- *Provide clear instructions.* Be specific about what you want, such as a summary, format change, or text extraction.
- *Handle long outputs.* If you need a long response, tell the AI up front: "Give me the full output, even if you hit the token limit. I'll ask for more if needed."
- *Use multi-shot prompting.* For long documents, have the AI summarize first, and then ask specific questions. This often works better than jumping right into detailed questions.

Multi-shot prompting helps because the AI builds a better understanding of the document's context. This initial overview leads to more accurate answers to later questions.

### 6.1.1 Text extraction methods

Table 6.1 shows several ways to get text from documents. We typically use the chatbot itself in a separate session.

Table 6.1 Document text extraction options

| Method | Description | Pros/Cons |
|---|---|---|
| Copy/Paste | Manually select and copy text from the document, and then paste it into the chatbot interface. | Pro: Simple and quick for short documents<br>Con: Time-consuming for large documents |
| Optical character recognition (OCR) software | Extracts text from scanned documents or images | Pro: Works well for scanned documents<br>Con: May require additional software |
| PDF-to-text converters | Online tools or software that convert PDF files to plain text | Pro: Efficient for PDF documents<br>Con: May lose formatting |

**Table 6.1 Document text extraction options** *(continued)*

| Method | Description | Pros/Cons |
|---|---|---|
| Command-line tools | Tools like `pdftotext` (Linux) and `Get-Content` (PowerShell) that extract text | Pro: Scriptable for batch processing<br>Con: Require command-line knowledge |
| Chatbot assistance | Ask the AI chatbot to extract and process text from a given input. | Pro: Can handle various formats<br>Con: May have token limitations |

Once you've extracted and prepared your text, you can move on to more advanced document processing techniques, which we'll explore in the following sections.

### 6.1.2 Structuring and refining outputs

When you need specific formats from the AI, tell it directly. Whether you want bullet points, tables, or JSON, clear format requests help you use the results in your work.

Document processing works best as a step-by-step process. Start broad, and then narrow down. For instance, begin with "Look at all 2024 incident reports," and follow up with "Show me serious network problems from April to June."

Always verify the AI's work so you catch any errors. You can ask follow-up questions to fix mistakes or dig deeper into key points. Although this uses more tokens, it rarely causes problems. If you hit token limits, start a new chat, and bring over the essential parts. This approach lets you do the following:

- Keep the context from your earlier chat
- Copy only the important parts to save tokens
- Get fresh insights from starting a new conversation
- Handle big documents and complex tasks more efficiently

These techniques work for even the largest document management tasks. Next, we'll explore the ethical considerations in AI document processing.

## 6.2 Ethics in AI document handling

AI document processing varies across models, each taking a different approach to safety and privacy. Claude focuses on strong privacy protections, ChatGPT warns users about sharing sensitive data, and Gemini lets companies customize safety settings. Azure AI works with Microsoft security tools like Key Vault for encryption, and AWS AI provides detailed access controls and supports Health Insurance Portability and Accountability Act (HIPAA) and General Data Protection Regulation (GDPR) compliance.

Teams must verify AI output to prevent hallucinations, such as when an AI might add nonexistent API endpoints to documentation or mix up information between different sources. These errors can be subtle but significant.

Tracking AI document processing requires a systematic approach, where organizations record which AI model was used, when it was used, and who verified the output.

A simple header stating "Processed by [AI Model] on [Date], Verified by [Name]" works well, while others maintain detailed logs in tracking software.

When handling sensitive documents, use only company-approved AI tools with appropriate security measures, and reserve free services for public documentation. Healthcare organizations often implement multiple verification steps, including having two staff members review any AI-processed patient records.

Document versioning and clear labeling help maintain data integrity through secure storage of all versions and clear marking of AI-processed sections. For sensitive data, consider using AI models with clear deletion policies, and process only necessary sections, keeping sensitive processing in-house when possible. Table 6.2 summarizes key ethical concerns and best practices for AI document handling.

Table 6.2  Ethics in AI document handling

| Ethical concern | Best practices |
| --- | --- |
| Data privacy | Only use AI tools your company approves for sensitive files. Skip free public AI services for work tasks. |
| Transparency | Tell your team when you use AI on shared documents. Be open about how AI helped. |
| Human oversight | Check AI's work yourself, especially for important documents. AI helps but doesn't replace your judgment. |
| Bias awareness | Watch for unfair or slanted results. AI can show bias or make mistakes, just like people do. |
| Intellectual property | Be careful when creating content with AI. Make sure you're not accidentally using someone else's work. |
| Accountability | Own your work, even when using AI. Don't blame the AI if something goes wrong. |
| Continuous learning | Keep up with AI best practices. The field changes fast, so stay current on using AI ethically. |

Regular audits help prevent problems by catching them early, such as when a software company discovers outdated code examples in its AI documentation through monthly reviews. This kind of monitoring helps maintain accuracy and trust.

Good document handling requires balancing AI capabilities with proper oversight. Organizations should update their practices as technology evolves to ensure safe and effective processing.

## 6.3 Document summarization

AI is great at making long documents shorter while keeping the important parts. Figure 6.1 shows how ChatGPT turned the Paris Agreement into two clear paragraphs that cover the main goals, the commitments, and how they'll be carried out.

## 6.3 Document summarization

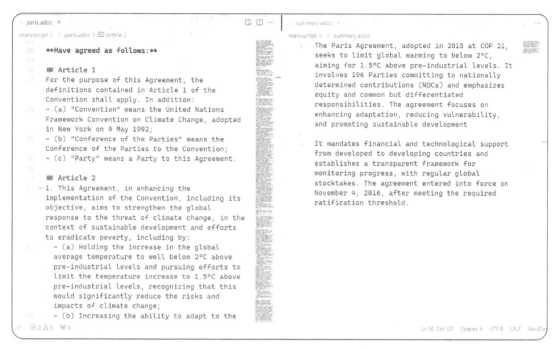

**Figure 6.1** Prompt: Summarize this in 2 short paragraphs.

Need to understand a long document? Upload it to a chatbot, and say "Give me a 500-word summary covering the main points, methods, findings, and takeaways." You'll get a clear overview that captures all the essential information. This demonstrates how AI can simplify complex content, making it accessible and digestible.

When you want a summary, using the right prompt helps you get exactly what you need. Table 6.3 shows different prompts for various summary types. Try these, and change them to fit your documents.

**Table 6.3** Document summarization prompts

| Task | Prompt |
| --- | --- |
| Executive summary | Make a 500-word executive summary of this 50-page report. Include key findings, methods, and recommendations. |
| Technical overview | Write a technical summary of this whitepaper. Focus on algorithms, data structures, and performance metrics. |
| Key takeaways | List the top 5 main points from this conference presentation. |
| Chapter synopsis | Summarize each chapter in this technical manual, focusing on main topics. |
| Comparative summary | Compare the main points from these two research papers about cloud security. |

These prompts can help you get the right summary style for different situations, whether you're creating quick updates for managers or detailed briefs for technical teams. Remember that AI models aren't great at counting words. They understand language well, but basic math can confuse them. Figure 6.2 shows ChatGPT giving 19 words when asked for 20.

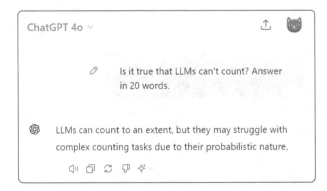

Figure 6.2  Chatbots can't always count.

> **Try it now: Multilevel summarization**
> 1. Find a long technical article or whitepaper like https://gptmaker.dev/book/stuxnet.
> 2. Write three different summarization prompts:
>    – Make a high-level summary for managers (about 100 words).
>    – Create a detailed technical summary (about 500 words).
>    – List five to seven key points from the article.
> 3. Look at each AI summary. Which one works best for you? Why?

Although summaries help us understand content quickly, many of us also need to convert files between formats. Let's look at how AI can make this task easier.

## 6.4 Format conversion

Converting files between formats is often slow and annoying, especially with complex layouts or nested code. Regular conversion tools usually need multiple steps and manual fixes. But AI can now handle many common conversions better and faster than older methods.

AI is also particularly good at pulling text from PDFs, changing Word files to Markdown for documentation, and turning HTML newsletters into plain text. This saves time and work by cutting down on manual file changes.

> **WARNING** Always verify AI-converted documents carefully. AI can make mistakes with complex formatting and special document types, particularly those with detailed layouts or industry-specific formats.

Here's a common situation: you get a nicely formatted PDF report that needs to go into your team's wiki. Without AI, you'd need to copy and paste everything, losing the formatting. But with AI, you can upload the PDF and ask for Markdown or HTML. This keeps most of the original layout and format intact. Use the following prompt to convert PDF to Markdown:

 Please convert this PDF document to a well-formatted Markdown file. Ensure that headings, lists, and tables are preserved. For any images in the PDF, please provide a placeholder text describing the image content.

 Certainly! I've converted the PDF to a Markdown file. Here's a sample of the converted content:

```
# Quarterly Sales Report

## Executive Summary

Our Q3 sales have exceeded expectations, with a 15% increase over the
previous quarter.

## Key Highlights

- Total Revenue: $10.2 million
- New Customers Acquired: 500+
- Customer Retention Rate: 95%

## Sales by Region

| Region  | Revenue  | Growth |
|---------|----------|--------|
| North   | $3.5M    | 18%    |
| South   | $2.8M    | 12%    |
| East    | $2.1M    | 10%    |
| West    | $1.8M    | 20%    |

![Q3 Sales Chart]
(Image placeholder: Bar chart showing sales figures for each region)

## Recommendations

1. Expand marketing efforts in the Western region
2. Implement new customer retention program
3. Investigate potential for new product lines

...
```

One prompt turned a complex PDF into clean Markdown, handling tables and images well. The result is ready to use in a wiki or docs.

Table 6.4 lists different prompts for changing file formats. These examples show how AI can handle many types of conversions, from basic text changes to complex document restructuring.

**Table 6.4  Format conversion prompts**

| Task | Prompt |
|---|---|
| HTML to plain text | Change this HTML newsletter to plain text. Keep the main structure and links. |
| Word to LaTeX | Turn this Word file into LaTeX. Include proper formatting for headings, tables, and equations. |
| JSON to CSV | Make this JSON data into CSV format. Use top-level keys as column headers. |
| Markdown to HTML | Change this Markdown to HTML. Add CSS classes for styling. |
| XML to JSON | Turn this XML into JSON. Keep the element structure. |

> **TIP**  When asking for format changes, tell the AI about any special requests—like how to handle images, complex layouts, or specific formatting. This helps you get exactly what you want.

These are just some examples of what you can do with a basic chatbot. As you try different conversions for your work, you'll likely find yourself using this feature more and more.

## 6.5  Text extraction from images

Working in IT, we often need to get text from images like error message screenshots, scanned manuals, and whiteboard photos. Typing everything manually takes time and risks mistakes. OCR solves this by turning image text into searchable words quickly.

For example, if someone sends you an error message screenshot in chat, AI can extract the text instantly instead of you squinting at tiny text or asking for a typed version. This makes searching for solutions or updating incident reports much simpler.

 Extract the text from this screenshot of an error message. Format the extracted text as it appears in the image, preserving any line breaks or special characters.

 I've extracted the text from the error message screenshot. Here's the formatted result:

Error Code: 0x80070643

Windows could not search for new updates

An error occurred while checking for new updates for your computer.

Error(s) found: Code 80070643 Windows Update encountered an unknown error.

✘ Get help with this error  Search online for this error

The text has been formatted to match the layout in the screenshot, including the error code, main message, and options at the bottom. This text can now be easily copied, searched, or included in your troubleshooting documentation.

One prompt changed a static image into text we could use. The AI's OCR pulled out the words and kept the formatting, which helps a lot when you need to understand error messages or other structured text. This makes troubleshooting faster and your documentation better.

For those of you who are curious, this specific query was run on OpenAI's GPT-4o model. We've always found that OpenAI-based models (such as the one ChatGPT runs on) perform exceptionally well when dealing with images.

For the best results with AI text extraction, use images with clear text and good contrast. If you're working with handwriting or complex layouts, you may need to try different AI models made for those tasks.

We were surprised by how well ChatGPT handled unexpected challenges. It even read a restaurant menu written in cursive French from across the room—despite the glare (see figure 6.3)!

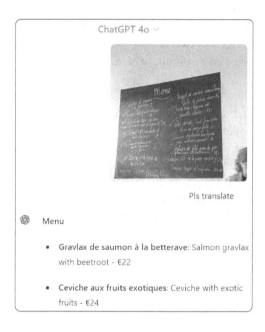

Figure 6.3  ChatGPT can translate from less-than-perfect images. Here, it translated French to English from an image of a French menu.

To show how flexible AI is with text extraction, table 6.5 lists prompts for different image-to-text tasks.

Table 6.5  Text extraction prompts

| Scenario | Prompt |
| --- | --- |
| Scanned document | Pull the text from this scanned manual page. Keep the paragraphs, headings, and subheadings in order. |
| Whiteboard photo | Get the text from this whiteboard brainstorming photo. Keep related items together and show any diagram structures. |
| Command-line screenshot | Extract the text from this command line screenshot. Keep all formatting, line breaks, and spacing exact. |

> **Try it now: Improving OCR accuracy**
>
> 1. Get three different images with text:
>    - A clear printed document
>    - A handwritten note
>    - A screenshot with text and graphics
> 2. Use an AI tool like ChatGPT to get text from each image.
> 3. Check how well it worked for each type.
> 4. Try different prompts or image fixes (like changing contrast) to improve results for the hardest image.

AI helps turn many types of image-based text into searchable content, from technical diagrams to quick notes. But working with documents isn't just about extracting text—we often need to spot what's changed between different versions. This brings us to another useful AI capability: smart document comparison.

## 6.6 Document comparison

Comparing documents used to be hard, especially with complex file formats. Although `diff` tools worked fine for plain text, they had trouble with Word or PDF files. New comparison tools use machine learning to spot differences quickly, from small tweaks to big changes, making version control much simpler.

Most AI models can handle larger files than traditional comparison tools. Claude processes up to 150,000 words at once, Google Gemini Pro manages over 1.5 million words, and OpenAI o3 mini matches Claude's capacity. We don't need to fill these large context windows, but having the extra space lets us work with bigger chunks of text when needed. Still, as we mentioned earlier, we've found that breaking documents into smaller sections, typically a few paragraphs at a time, gives us the most accurate comparisons because the AI can focus better on specific changes.

Here's a common scenario: you need to check the latest version of your company's disaster recovery plan after several people have edited it. Instead of reading it line by line, you can use these tools to highlight what's changed, making sure you catch all the recent updates.

 Compare the attached two versions of our company's disaster recovery plan. Provide a summary of significant changes, including added, modified, and deleted sections. Generate a change log in Markdown format, categorizing changes as 'Major', 'Minor', or 'Editorial'.

 I've compared the two versions of the disaster recovery plan and generated a summary of changes. Here's the change log in Markdown format:

# Disaster Recovery Plan - Change Log

## Major Changes

- **Added**: New section on cloud-based backup procedures (Section 4.3)
- **Modified**: Updated RTO (Recovery Time Objective) from 4 hours to 2 hours (Section 2.1)
- **Deleted**: Removed outdated section on tape backup systems (Previously Section 3.2)

## Minor Changes ...

This comparison process takes seconds instead of hours. It spots specific changes, ranks how important they are, and quickly shows how they affect your disaster recovery plan. The comparison helps catch critical updates that might slip through in a manual review.

Table 6.6 shows prompts for different comparison tasks. These examples cover common file types that IT teams work with.

Table 6.6 Document comparison prompts

| Scenario | Prompt |
| --- | --- |
| Configuration files | Compare these two versions of our nginx configuration file. Highlight any changes to server blocks, proxy settings, or security directives. |
| API documentation | Analyze the differences between these two versions of our API documentation. Identify any changes to endpoints, parameters, or response formats. |
| Project timelines | Compare these two project timeline documents. Highlight any changes to milestone dates, task assignments, or resource allocations. |
| Security policies | Review these two versions of our information security policy. Identify any changes to access control rules, data classification guidelines, or incident response procedures. |
| Network topology | Compare these two network topology diagrams. List any added or removed devices, changes to connections, or modifications to IP address assignments. |

**TIP** When comparing documents with AI, tell it about the document type and which changes matter most. This helps it focus on the differences you care about.

The prompt examples in table 6.6 show how to guide AI through different types of comparisons. Being clear about what you want to compare helps the AI give you more useful results.

## 6.7 Document classification and tagging

Managing documents becomes more complex as organizations expand. Search tools that only match keywords often miss important files or return too many results. AI improves this by understanding document content and context, automatically adding relevant tags to make files easier to locate.

Companies typically handle document management with AI in two ways:

- *Custom AI using APIs*—We'll cover this in chapter 11. You can build your own system that learns your company's document types and sorting requirements.
- *Ready-to-use AI services*—Major cloud providers offer document tools:
  - Microsoft Azure AI Document Intelligence sorts and analyzes documents.
  - Google Cloud Document AI works with unstructured documents.
  - Amazon Textract helps AWS users process documents.
  - OpenAI's GPT models can be customized for document sorting.

These services can handle many documents at once, which works well for big organizations.

When setting up automatic document sorting, do the following:

1. Test with sample documents to get the sorting right.
2. Update your system as new document types come in.
3. Have people check important or sensitive documents.
4. Watch how documents are created and used to spot patterns.

These steps work best when you start small and expand gradually. Companies sometimes rush to automate everything at once, but that often leads to mistakes and confused users. We've found it's better to perfect the system on one department or document type first and then roll it out more widely once you've worked out the problems.

> **TIP** If you work with sensitive data, ensure that your company uses enterprise services that have good security and meet compliance rules. Look for features like data protection, audit logs, and the option to run everything in your own secure setup. Just make sure the service matches your company's privacy requirements.

Table 6.7 shows prompts for different sorting tasks, from technical manuals to project files, to help you see how this technology works. Try these prompts to learn how AI can sort and tag your IT documents.

Table 6.7 Document classification and tagging prompts

| Task | Prompt |
| --- | --- |
| Technical manuals | Sort these product manuals. Tag them by product type, features, and common fixes. |
| Project files | Sort these project files by phase, department, and stakeholders. Add tags for project milestones. |
| Incident reports | Look through these IT incident reports. Sort by how bad they were, what broke, and how it got fixed. Find common problems. |
| Policy documents | Sort company policies by department and when they were last updated. Mark old ones that need review. |
| Training materials | Sort training docs by skill level, topic, and job role. Tag them with what people will learn and what they need to know first. |

## 6.8 Document anonymization

IT teams often handle private information that needs to be anonymized. Although AI tools can help with this, they also bring new risks. Let's look at how to anonymize documents safely and use these tools properly.

> **When to avoid AI for anonymization**
>
> Don't use AI to anonymize critical or regulated data, including medical records and health data protected by HIPAA, financial records, personal data covered by GDPR, government IDs, employee records, and sensitive customer information. For these types of data, you should use manual anonymization by trained staff or specialized software that's certified for compliance and specifically approved for regulated data.
>
> AI tools can help with less sensitive data, but you still need to be careful. Stay away from consumer AI products like ChatGPT, free online anonymization tools, public AI models without security controls, and any AI tool not approved by your security team. Instead, only use an enterprise AI solution like your company's Azure OpenAI Service or Amazon AWS Bedrock instance, approved secure platforms, tools that integrate with your security systems, and solutions with proper access controls and auditing.
>
> Before using any AI anonymization, get approval from your security team and check your company's data handling policies. Review relevant regulations, document your process, test the tools on sample data first, and make sure you have a plan for handling edge cases. Following these guidelines helps protect sensitive data while still letting you use AI where appropriate.

Enterprise tools like Microsoft Purview and ARX Data Anonymization can find and hide sensitive data in many documents at once. These are built to handle private information and follow data protection rules. Microsoft Purview tracks how data gets sorted and used, and ARX lets you set custom rules and works with your security setup.

Remember that no anonymization is perfect. With big or complex data sets, someone might piece together the original information. Always check the risks when working with sensitive data.

Here's a typical case: you need to share support logs with an outside consultant to make your ticketing system better. The logs have sensitive stuff like customer names, emails, and account numbers. Instead of manually cleaning each log, you might use an approved anonymization tool to process them all quickly and consistently, keeping the sensitive data safe.

 Anonymize the attached customer support log. Replace all customer names with "Customer X" (where X is a number), email addresses with "email@example.com", and phone numbers with "(xxx) xxx-xxxx". Ensure that the context and readability of the document are maintained.

 I've anonymized the customer support log as requested. Here's a sample of the anonymized content:

> Ticket ID: 45678 Date: 2023-05-15 Customer: Customer 1 Contact: email@example.com | (xxx) xxx-xxxx
>
> Issue Description: Customer 1 reported difficulty accessing their account dashboard. They attempted to log in using their usual credentials but received an "Invalid username or password" error.
>
> ...
>
> I've maintained the structure and context of the log while anonymizing all sensitive information. This process has been applied consistently throughout the entire document.

The AI changed sensitive details quickly while keeping the support log clear and useful. Teams can now share data efficiently and safely through automated anonymization, following all data protection rules.

Manual processes and specialized compliance software work better than AI tools for sensitive or regulated data. When dealing with sensitive information, the risks of using automation outweigh its benefits.

> **TIP** Tell the AI exactly what to change and how when anonymizing data. Always review the output for any missed sensitive information, especially with regulated or critical data.

Table 6.8 shows how anonymization works across common IT tasks. The examples cover different document types and show when to use AI tools versus manual processes, based on how sensitive the data is.

**Table 6.8  Document anonymization prompts**

| Scenario | Prompt |
|---|---|
| Database dumps | Change this database dump by replacing personal names, emails, and phone numbers with realistic fake data. Keep the field formats the same. |
| System logs | Process these system logs. Use placeholder IPs instead of real ones and change usernames/account IDs. Keep the structure and timestamps intact. |
| HR documents | Remove personal details from these HR documents. Use generic placeholders for employee names, Social Security numbers, and contact details. Keep job titles and departments as they are. |
| Financial reports | Clean up this financial report. Use generic IDs for account numbers and client names. Keep all financial figures and structure unchanged. |
| Medical records | Change these medical records for research use. Replace names, birth dates, and identifying details with coded IDs. Keep all medical conditions and treatments as they are. |

These methods help you share data safely, make realistic test data, and follow data protection rules. Security and compliance come first, especially when handling sensitive or regulated data.

## 6.9 Language translation

Working at international companies or with global clients means dealing with language barriers. Translating technical documents, manuals, and communication logs by hand takes time and often leads to mistakes. AI translation tools built on large language models (LLMs) have changed this process completely.

Why are language models so good at technical translation? They've seen millions of documents in different languages, so they know how terms and concepts map between them. They're not just doing word-for-word replacements—they actually understand what they're translating and keep the meaning intact.

Although these models handle many translation tasks well, they sometimes struggle with specialized terms, cultural content, and technical words that need specific context. For important documents or those with industry-specific language, human review is still needed. Let's write a prompt to translate a technical manual.

Translate the attached software user manual from English to Portuguese. Maintain the technical terminology and formatting. Flag any terms or phrases that may require human review for context or industry-specific meaning.

I've translated the user manual from English to Portuguese. Here's a sample of the translation:

2.3 System Requirements

Before installing TechPro Software, ensure your system meets the following requirements:

- Operating System: Windows 10 (64-bit) or later
- Processor: Intel Core i5 or equivalent (2.5 GHz or faster)
- Memory: 8 GB RAM minimum, 16 GB recommended
- Storage: 20 GB available space
- Graphics: DirectX 11 compatible graphics card

2.3 Requisitos do Sistema

Antes de instalar o software TechPro, certifique-se de que seu sistema atenda aos seguintes requisitos:

- Sistema Operacional: Windows 10 (64 bits) ou posterior
- Processador: Intel Core i5 ou equivalente (2,5 GHz ou mais rápido)
- Memória: mínimo de 8 GB de RAM, recomendado 16 GB
- Armazenamento: 20 GB de espaço disponível
- Gráficos: placa de vídeo compatível com DirectX 11

[FLAG] "TechPro Software" - Consider whether to translate the product name or keep it in English.

The translation maintains the technical terminology and formatting of the original. I've flagged the product name for review, as company policies may vary on translating product names.

The translation tool quickly changed the technical manual while keeping its structure and technical terms intact. It also showed which parts needed human review, like the product name. This method saves significant time and resources when localizing documents.

Table 6.9 shows different translation tasks IT professionals often handle. AI translation helps create localized versions of technical documents quickly, making it easier to work with international teams and clients. Always check AI-translated content, though, especially critical or complex technical documents, to make sure everything is accurate and makes sense.

Table 6.9  Translation prompts for IT documents

| Scenario | Prompt |
| --- | --- |
| Error messages | Change these error messages from English to Japanese. Keep the error codes and variable placeholders the same. |
| API documentation | Change this REST API documentation from English to German. Keep all code snippets and endpoint URLs in their original form. |
| Release notes | Change these software release notes from English to French. Keep version numbers and feature/module names the same. |
| Training materials | Change this IT security training from English to Mandarin. Make culture-specific examples work for a Chinese audience. |
| Support scripts | Change these customer support scripts from English to Portuguese. Keep technical troubleshooting steps and product terms the same. |

**TIP** Give the AI a list of industry terms and their approved translations when doing technical translations. This keeps terms consistent across all translated documents and means less editing afterward.

Next, chapter 7 looks at where most modern work communication happens: emails and instant messaging. You'll learn how to write clearer emails and take better meeting notes, turning these often-overwhelming tools into assets for workplace productivity.

## 6.10 Prompts used in this chapter

- Create a prompt that can generate a comprehensive summary of a 50-page technical report, focusing on key findings, methodologies, and recommendations.
- This chapter should be more conversational and engaging while keeping it business casual. Can you help? Let's go paragraph by paragraph.
- What considerations should be made when using AI for translating technical documentation between languages? Provide a list of best practices.
- What are best practices when using AI for document handling in enterprise settings? Focus on data privacy, security, and compliance.

## *Summary*

- LLMs have made document tools more capable. We can now summarize and process information faster while getting better results.
- AI can convert documents between formats while keeping their structure and layout intact, which helps when working with many file types.
- We can now pull text accurately from images and scanned documents, turning old IT documentation into searchable, useful resources.
- LLMs can translate technical documents accurately across languages, preserving specialized terms and meaning without losing precision.
- Automated systems now manage document workflows and check compliance, making sure materials follow organizational standards.
- Better security features handle data redaction, version control, and document organization, improving both protection and findability.

# Emails and instant messaging in the workplace

**This chapter covers**
- Enhancing email communications with AI
- Using AI in instant messaging
- Integrations and automations
- Tools to improve your writing style
- Maintaining critical thinking skills
- The future of AI in communication

Some of the benefits of generative AI are that it can offer smarter ways to manage emails and instant messages, act like a personal assistant, organize your inbox, draft responses, and automate routine tasks. By using AI, emails become less burdensome and instant messages more efficient, turning these communication tools into productivity enhancers rather than distractions. This is especially important in remote work environments where effective communication can not only build better working relationships but also help you keep your job. This chapter focuses on enhancing these tools to streamline and improve your daily communications.

## 7.1 Enhancing email management with AI

Working in pretty much any field requires the ability to manage and communicate effectively through email. Email is not only used for communication between internal and external teams but also for alerting and monitoring systems. This can lead to a constant stream of notifications and alert fatigue. The sheer volume of emails can be overwhelming and a drain on productivity. Instant messaging has helped to lighten the load but is not appropriate for every situation. Even worse, email is a common vector for phishing and other security threats, which is the number one threat to any organization. If you are an IT security professional, you've likely lost sleep over what other people are doing with their email.

With so many potential problems surrounding email, it's no wonder that many people feel overwhelmed by their inboxes. Fortunately, AI can help. Models like Google Gemini and Microsoft Copilot's Outlook integration are still in their infancy, but they are already offering hope for what the future of email will look like. The first features out of the gate are focused on summarizing conversations and helping you write better emails. Building these features into an email client is the best implementation, but there are also third-party tools and chatbots that can help.

In this chapter, we'll demonstrate a number of services and AI engines. To help keep our lingo straight, when we say M365 Copilot, we are referring to the Microsoft 365 Chat feature that is provided to Microsoft 365 enterprise subscriptions and integrated into the M365 suite. When we mention Copilot for Outlook, we are referring to the integrated buttons in the Outlook application. And when we say simply Copilot or Copilot Pro, we are talking about the publicly available consumer products that anyone can use. Microsoft has been working to standardize the term *Copilot* across the platform, but the abundance of implementations can be confusing, even to us. In the next section, we will look at drafting emails and summarizing conversations so you can stop tweaking a draft for hours and get back to work.

### 7.1.1 AI-enhanced email summarization and drafting

There are many potential prompts to help with email. Each AI service has specific advantages, so various prompts may work better with some services than others. For example, Google Gemini and M365 Copilot are great because they have direct integrations into email messages. This is a limitation of OpenAI's ChatGPT because it is an isolated general-purpose chatbot. However, the quality and conciseness of the writing will vary across services, and you may develop a preference.

Email integrations are also very handy, but they sometimes limit what you can accomplish. For example, Microsoft Outlook with Copilot focuses on being easy to use and provides a simple interface to summarize emails and draft responses. Although convenient for quick replies, it doesn't offer the same flexibility as a chatbot.

You'll want to experiment to see what works best for you. If we don't get the results we like with one, we try the same task in another. In table 7.1, we've listed several great examples. These examples will work best with a chatbot capable of email integration, but you can also use them with a general-purpose chatbot by pasting in the email text.

**Table 7.1  Examples of AI-enhanced email management**

| Task | Prompt |
|---|---|
| Summarize an email conversation. | Find all email conversations over the past week from Manning.com. Summarize the emails, focusing on the main points, decisions made, and any action items or deadlines. |
| Respond to emails using AI. | Craft a response to the following email that addresses all questions asked, reiterates any important points, and proposes next steps. |
| Draft emails with AI assistance. | Help me draft an email to [recipient's name/role] regarding [topic], ensuring it's clear, concise, and professional. |
| Decode technical jargon in emails. | Explain the technical terms found in the attached email in layman's terms, ensuring clarity and accessibility for non-specialist readers. |
| Check emails for tone, clarity, and professionalism. | Review my draft email below for tone, clarity, and professionalism, and suggest any necessary revisions. |
| Find unread or follow-up emails. | Identify all unread emails or emails that require a follow-up in my inbox from the past week. |
| Draft an email for various target groups on the same topic. | Draft a single email about [topic] that is suitable for sending to different target groups, including [group 1], [group 2], and [group 3], ensuring it resonates with each audience. |
| Tailor messages to your audience. | Adapt the following message for [specific audience], considering their interests, knowledge level, and cultural context. |
| Deal with technical jargon. | Rewrite the following sentences to remove technical jargon and make the information accessible to a general audience. |
| Make quick announcements. | Compose a brief announcement about [topic/event] that is informative and engaging for the entire team. |
| Provide feedback and suggestions. | Formulate constructive feedback and practical suggestions for the attached project proposal, ensuring the tone is encouraging and supportive. |
| Maintain inbox zero. | Provide guidance on effective strategies and best practices for managing a high volume of emails, with the goal of achieving and maintaining an organized, prioritized inbox that supports the concept of 'inbox zero'. |

Let's start with the first prompt in table 7.1, summarizing an email conversation. For this example, we will use the premium version of Google Gemini, because it has a direct integration with Gmail and is very responsive. Instead of asking to summarize a single email, we want to attempt to summarize an entire conversation and identify any action items we need to be aware of.

If you do not have Gemini Advanced available in Gmail, you can ask Gemini questions about your email from the regular Gemini chatbot. In Gmail, find the Gemini diamond in the top right corner near your profile photo. As seen in figure 7.1, clicking the diamond will expand a chat interface where you can chat with Gemini about your inbox. This is a strength of Google Gemini's integration into Google Workspace. Copilot, Apple Intelligence, and Gemini on Android also have available integrations into their ecosystems. This means you get secure access to various personal data with increased security and no need to copy and paste information.

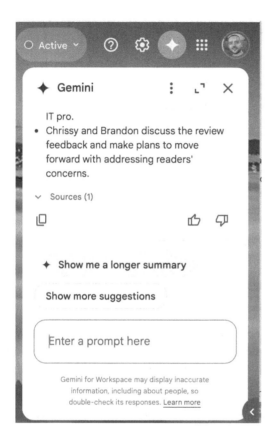

Figure 7.1 Gemini chat integrated into Gmail

In this real-life example, Brandon has had a very busy work week, and he is behind on emails from Manning. This book is getting ready for the Manning Early Access Program (MEAP), and a number of things need to be prepared. Brandon wants to quickly see what is needed, so he asks Google Gemini to summarize all of his emails from Manning over the past week. He is not sure if he has any action items, so he asks Gemini to include any action items or deadlines.

 Find all email conversations over the past week from Manning.com. Summarize the emails, focusing on the main points, decisions made, and any action items or deadlines.

> Manning.com Email Conversations (Jan 20-27, 2024):
>
> Conversation 1: MEAP Launch and Formatting (Jan 25-26)
>
> - Emails:
>     - Re: Starting the MEAP for AI for the IT Pro (Jan 26)
>     - Re: Formatting / meeting (Jan 25)
> - Main Points:
>     - Manning launched the MEAP for your book, AI for the IT Pro.
>     - Kishor Rit from Manning shared the MEAP link and proposed a meeting to discuss details.
>     - Formatting discrepancies in the MEAP were identified and further discussion requested.
> - Decisions:
>     - MEAP officially launched for reader participation.
>     - Need for formatting review and potential adjustments.
> - Action Items:
>     - Brandon to participate in the upcoming MEAP discussion meeting.
>     - Brandon to review MEAP formatting guidelines.
>     - Both parties to confirm meeting attendance.

The prompt doesn't have to be complicated, but as always, it should be specific. We want a summary with special attention to the main points, decisions, and—most importantly—action items. We don't want to miss any deadlines! Without highlighting these specific items, the summary may be too broad and less actionable.

> **WARNING** Asking questions about your email and calendar is very useful, but due to the sheer quantity of emails in your inbox, there's a good chance that some information is being dropped. Always be mindful that the results may not be 100% accurate.

In the next example, we will combine a few prompt ideas into a single example to draft an email. We want to address the problem of technical jargon while drafting an email for multiple audiences. The following email was sent by a network engineer to a project manager discussing upcoming work on a new intrusion prevention system (IPS). The email is full of technical jargon and acronyms, which is fine for the engineer, but the project manager wants to decode the email and draft a new email for the department to let them know of the upcoming maintenance.

If you are using a chatbot with email integration, you can direct the chatbot to the email in your prompt. Otherwise, you will have to paste it in.

## 7.1 Enhancing email management with AI

Subject: IPS Switch Integration Update and Next Steps

Hey Freja,

Quick update on the IPS switch deployment:

1. **Network Assessment**: Completed. Vulnerability gaps identified and traffic patterns analyzed for IPS placement optimization.
2. **IPS Selection**: Done. Chose the next-gen model for best performance and compatibility with our current infrastructure.
3. **Lab Configuration and Testing**: Finalized. Policies are set, and initial tests show promising precision with minimal false positives.

**Pending:**

- **Production Deployment**: Scheduled for this Saturday's maintenance window. Plan to run the IPS in passive mode initially to gauge impact.
- **Transition to Active**: Aiming for next week, post-analysis of passive mode data. Will adjust policies to fine-tune threat detection and system response.
- **Team Briefing**: Need to schedule a session early next week for a run-through on management and maintenance protocols.

Can you take a look at the current configuration settings and ensure they align with the updated network security policies? Also, let's draft a quick reference guide for the IT security team on handling alerts and policy adjustments.

Thanks!
Michele

The first thing the project manager can do is ask for an AI model to explain the jargon in lay terms. This will help the project manager understand the information better and increase the chances of relaying that information effectively.

 Identify technical terms and jargon in this email and explain what they mean.

 The email contains several technical terms and jargon related to network security and the implementation of an Intrusion Prevention System (IPS). Here's an explanation of these terms:

...

**IPS Switch Deployment:** "IPS" stands for Intrusion Prevention System, a device or software application that monitors network and/or system activities for malicious activity or policy violations. The "deployment" refers to the process of setting up and activating the IPS in the network.

**Passive Mode:** Initially, the IPS operates in a monitoring-only state, where it does not actively intervene or block traffic but observes and reports on potential threats. This is done to assess the impact of the IPS on the network without risking disruption.

**Transition to Active:** After the initial observation period, the IPS is switched to "active mode," where it will actively intervene by blocking or mitigating detected threats based on preset "policies" or rules.

...

Freja, the project manager, now has a better understanding of the email and can draft and verify the accuracy of the email to be sent. Freja has additional details that must be communicated to the audience, so Freja includes them in the prompt.

 Based on the email provided, draft a new email suitable for general communication of this upcoming maintenance. The maintenance is planned for this Saturday at 10pm and will require validators from each team to verify all applications are functioning as expected. Please specify that a meeting invite will be sent to each team manager to be shared with the appropriate validator.

 Subject: Upcoming Network Maintenance Notification and Validator Coordination

Dear Team,

This message is to inform you of an upcoming scheduled network maintenance this **Saturday at 10 PM**. This maintenance is part of our ongoing efforts to enhance our network security and efficiency.

**Key Points of the Maintenance:**
- **Purpose**: The primary objective is to integrate a new security enhancement to our network infrastructure. This is a crucial step in fortifying our defenses against potential cyber threats.
- **Date and Time**: The maintenance is scheduled for this Saturday at 10 PM. We anticipate it will take a few hours, during which there might be intermittent network disruptions.
- **Validator Role**: Post-maintenance, we require the assistance of validators from each team to ensure all applications and services are running smoothly. Validators will check that all systems are functioning as expected without any issues.

**Next Steps:**
- **Meeting Invite**: Each team manager will receive a meeting invite shortly. We kindly ask managers to share this invite with the appointed validator from your team. The meeting will cover the validation process and address any questions your team may have.
- **Preparation**: Please ensure that any critical work requiring network access is completed before the maintenance window or scheduled for after the maintenance completion. We also recommend saving all work and logging off from all systems before 10 PM on Saturday.

We understand that maintenance can be an inconvenience, and we're committed to executing these enhancements as smoothly and quickly as possible. Your cooperation and understanding are greatly appreciated as we work together to maintain a secure and efficient network environment.

Should you have any immediate questions or concerns, please do not hesitate to reach out to the IT department.

Thank you for your attention to this matter and for your ongoing support.

Best Regards,

...

In a few simple prompts, we were able to take a technical email, obtain a better understanding of the technical references, and draft a general email to the department. This is a great example of how AI can help us communicate more effectively and with less effort.

We used ChatGPT Plus to draft this email. What we appreciate most about ChatGPT Plus is the additional suggestions and details it provides in the output. We keep making the point that we sense a deeper level of understanding of the material. ChatGPT Plus did not just regurgitate the information it was provided: it identified the potential effect on users by warning of intermittent network disruptions, reminding users to save their work before the maintenance, and including a note about the inconvenience of maintenance. These are all things that a human might have included in the email, but we didn't have to tell the AI to include them. It just did it.

### 7.1.2 *Not ready for prime time*

Current AI models can do many things to assist with email, but there are some big things that we wish they did better. The primary problem we run into with chatbots like M365 Copilot and Google Gemini is that their ability to find information within emails is spotty. Sometimes they find what you want, and sometimes they don't. We don't believe this is necessarily a limitation of the AI model as much as an intentional limitation on the current implementation. A question that requires the chatbot to look through hundreds or thousands of emails reduces the accuracy of the response: the chatbot often drops relevant information in the provided summary or is overwhelmed by irrelevant emails.

One thing we really like about some integrations, such as GitHub Copilot, Microsoft Teams, and Gmail, is that the chatbot is integrated into the app. But it's not yet available in Microsoft Outlook; instead, users are limited to specific options and concise prompts. Although this has benefits for novice users and UI design, it limits the ultimate capability of the chatbot when working with email.

Table 7.2 includes a few prompts that exceed the current capabilities of chatbots. We have no doubt that these prompts will work in the future, so we are providing them as a wish list. Give them a try, and see if the chatbots have improved enough to get the job done.

**Table 7.2 Future prompts**

| Task | Prompt |
|---|---|
| Identify unsent or unresponded emails. | List all emails I've sent in the past month regarding [project/topic] that have not yet received a response. |
| Analyze my email patterns, and suggest organization strategies. | Review my email usage patterns over the past 3 months and suggest personalized strategies to organize my inbox more efficiently, focusing on common subjects and frequent senders. |
| Suggest automated filters based on my most frequent email interactions. | Analyze who I email most frequently and what types of messages are highest priority, then suggest specific automated filters to highlight important emails and reduce noise in my inbox. |
| Calendar management | Find a time on my calendar for a meeting with [person] and [person] to discuss [topic]. Create a meeting invite and send it to all attendees. |

Managing email rules and folder organization are at the top of our list of necessities. These tasks are much more complex, so it's understandable that they are not yet available. Microsoft and Google, if you're reading this, the current ways of managing rules and folders are awkward. We believe these capabilities would contribute greatly to the value of Copilot and Gemini.

Finally, calendar management is surprisingly limited in both M365 Copilot and Google Gemini. Although they can access the calendar, we found accuracy to be a concern here as well. In addition, neither service can create meetings due to privacy concerns. We look forward to a day when AI can do this for us. For now, if you want to use AI to manage your work calendar, you'll have to rely on third-party AI services. However, that could be a security risk. It makes the most sense for integrated chatbots to perform these tasks when possible.

### 7.1.3 Email security

The security of an organization's data and computer systems is a top priority today. Email is one of the most effective ways to spread malware and other malicious software. Phishing attacks are a common way to gain access to sensitive information, and they are becoming more sophisticated every day. AI can help detect these attacks before they happen. In this section, we will walk through an example of how AI can help you determine whether an email is legitimate. No matter how legitimate an external email appears, it can easily be faked. We don't intend for you to be so paranoid that you never open another email, but if it seems off, wants you to click a link, or asks for sensitive information, you should be cautious, especially if you aren't expecting it.

In this example, we are going to take the novel approach of analyzing the email header and source code. Obtaining this information depends on your email client. In Outlook for Mac, as shown in the top half of figure 7.2, you can right-click the email message and choose View Source to see the source code.

7.1  *Enhancing email management with AI*   123

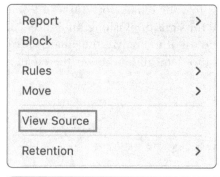

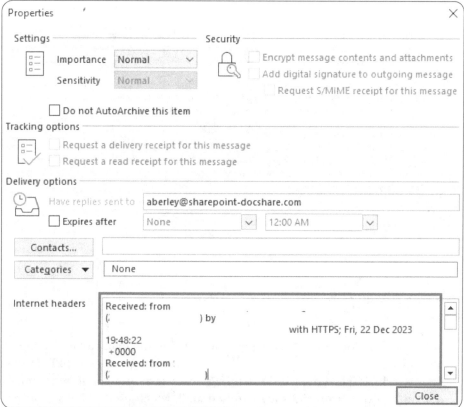

**Figure 7.2  Finding the source text and headers of an email in Outlook for Mac and PC**

In Outlook for PC, open the email in a new window, click the File menu option, and then click Properties. A dialog box will appear containing the header information, as shown in the bottom half of figure 7.2. The source code and header information will be a jumble of text, but you don't need to understand it. You just need to copy and paste it into the AI service and let the AI do the work.

Since M365 Copilot has direct access to your email, you can also ask Copilot to identify the email first and then analyze it for signs of phishing. In figure 7.3, we paste the source content into M365 Copilot and ask it to analyze the email. Our prompt is very straightforward, asking M365 Copilot to determine whether the email is a phishing attempt.

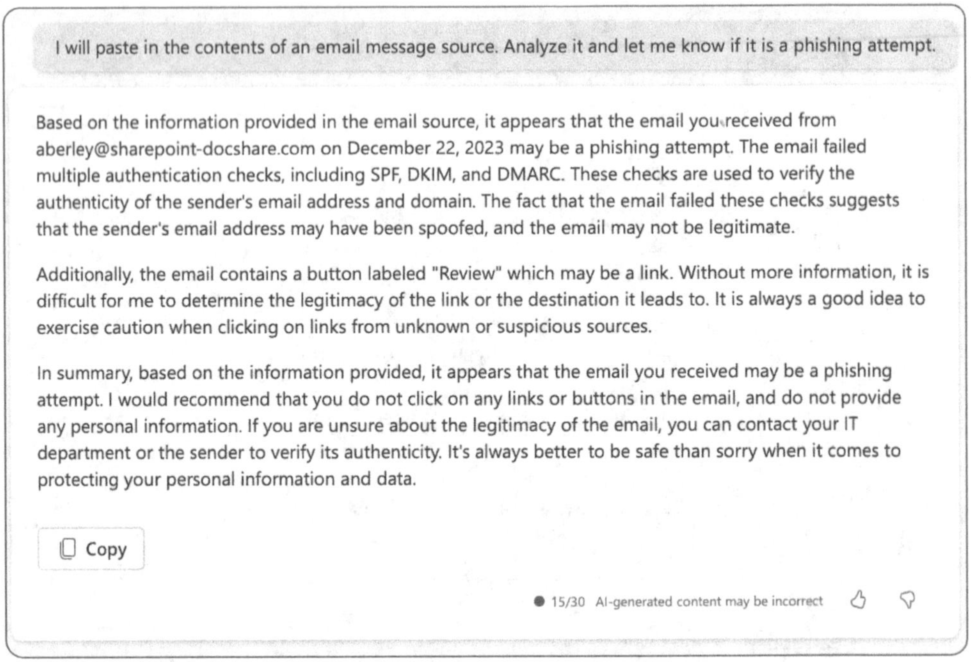

> I will paste in the contents of an email message source. Analyze it and let me know if it is a phishing attempt.

Based on the information provided in the email source, it appears that the email you received from aberley@sharepoint-docshare.com on December 22, 2023 may be a phishing attempt. The email failed multiple authentication checks, including SPF, DKIM, and DMARC. These checks are used to verify the authenticity of the sender's email address and domain. The fact that the email failed these checks suggests that the sender's email address may have been spoofed, and the email may not be legitimate.

Additionally, the email contains a button labeled "Review" which may be a link. Without more information, it is difficult for me to determine the legitimacy of the link or the destination it leads to. It is always a good idea to exercise caution when clicking on links from unknown or suspicious sources.

In summary, based on the information provided, it appears that the email you received may be a phishing attempt. I would recommend that you do not click on any links or buttons in the email, and do not provide any personal information. If you are unsure about the legitimacy of the email, you can contact your IT department or the sender to verify its authenticity. It's always better to be safe than sorry when it comes to protecting your personal information and data.

15/30 AI-generated content may be incorrect

Figure 7.3 M365 Copilot analysis of email source text

M365 Copilot does a satisfactory job of identifying the email as a phishing attempt by identifying failures in several email authentication protocols: SPF (Sender Policy Framework, which verifies if the sending server is authorized to send emails for that domain), DKIM (DomainKeys Identified Mail, which uses digital signatures to verify email hasn't been tampered with), and DMARC (Domain-based Message Authentication, Reporting and Conformance, which tells receiving servers how to handle authentication failures).

M365 Copilot also identifies a button labeled Review, but it doesn't explicitly identify the links in the email. However, the overall assessment is that this is potentially a phishing attempt, which will be good enough for many users.

To illustrate the difference in responses across models, we will now look at the analysis from OpenAI's ChatGPT Plus. Even though M365 Copilot is based on the same GPT-4 model, the two AIs have different training data and respond differently.

We've found that all of Copilot's implementations tend to be more conservative and concise in their responses, which we sometimes want, and ChatGPT Plus tends to be more verbose and detailed. The following is ChatGPT Plus's analysis of a suspicious email.

 **Email Source Code Analysis**

Analyzing the provided email source code reveals several indicators that suggest it might be a phishing attempt:

**Mismatched Sender Information** The email claims to originate from "SharePoint" but uses the domain `sharepoint-docshare.com`, which is not an official domain associated with Microsoft SharePoint. This discrepancy is a common tactic employed by phishers to create the illusion of legitimacy.

**SPF Soft Fail** The email's `Received-SPF: SoftFail` header indicates that the sender's IP was not authorized by the domain's SPF record but wasn't explicitly denied either. This soft fail is often seen in spoofed emails.

**DKIM Fail** The `dkim=fail` result in the Authentication-Results header signifies that the email failed DKIM verification. A failed DKIM check suggests the email may have been altered or didn't originate from the claimed domain.

**DMARC Fail** The `dmarc=fail action=oreject` header implies the email failed DMARC evaluation, with a recommendation to reject the message. This failure is a strong indication of potential phishing or spoofing attempts.

**Suspicious Links** The presence of links to `sharepoint-docshare.com` raises suspicion, as it is not a recognized domain for SharePoint or Microsoft. Phishing emails often contain such malicious links that mimic legitimate services to deceive recipients.

**Urgency and Call to Action** The content of the message creates a sense of urgency and prompts immediate action through a "Review" button. This pressure tactic is typical of phishing attempts to elicit hasty actions from the recipient.

**External Sender Warning** The email includes a cautionary note about external senders, advising against clicking links or opening attachments unless the content is verified as safe. Although possibly part of standard email security protocols, it adds to the email's suspicious nature given the other red flags.

**Email Origin** Inconsistencies or unexpected routes in the chain of `Received` headers, which trace the email's path through various servers, can indicate email spoofing or the use of malicious servers.

Given these indicators, it is recommended to approach this email with caution. Recipients should avoid clicking any links or downloading attachments from this email and consider reporting it as phishing within their email client. Verification of the email's authenticity should be sought by contacting the supposed sender through official channels.

Clearly, ChatGPT Plus gives a more thorough response than M365 Copilot. For us, ChatGPT Plus wins because not only does it clearly explain all the items, but it even identifies that the domain claiming to be SharePoint is not a legitimate Microsoft

SharePoint domain. We were disappointed when reading the output from M365 Copilot and were happy that ChatGPT Plus was able to identify this problem. Why this isn't built right into Outlook, we don't know. It seems like a no-brainer and extremely valuable.

As we wrap up this section, we want to mention that there are many other ways AI can help with email. We've only scratched the surface. We encourage you to experiment with the prompts we've provided and see what else you can do. Some functionality still needs to be fleshed out by Microsoft and Google, and we encourage you to try other AI services. Later in the chapter, we outline two of our favorite AI-based tools: Grammarly and Apple Writing Tools.

Next, we move on to instant messaging, with a focus on Microsoft Teams. We'll explore some inventive approaches using more advanced techniques like webhooks and Power Automate. If you aren't skilled in either of these technologies, we weren't either. We used ChatGPT to guide us through generating new automations and scripts. We'll show you how we did it and how you can do it too.

## 7.2 Using AI in instant messaging

Instant messaging (IM) is a popular communication tool both at home and in the modern workplace. IM is a quick and convenient way to communicate with colleagues and stay connected with friends and family. However, IM can be a distraction and a time sink. It's easy to get caught up in a conversation and lose track of time. It's also easy to miss important messages or forget to respond to a message. AI can help you manage your IMs more effectively, similar to how it can help with email.

In this section, we will focus on Microsoft Teams, but the same concepts can often be applied to other IM platforms. We will show you how to use AI to summarize conversations, identify action items, and suggest responses. We will also show you how to use AI to create simple automations and integrations that you may not have known were possible. First, let's look at meeting transcriptions.

### 7.2.1 Meeting transcription and recap with AI

Of all the ways we've attempted to work AI into our normal processes, meeting transcriptions are hands down the most useful for us. Microsoft Teams has this built in, but there are other applications and services to choose from. One third-party service we've tried is Krisp. We like it because it's accessible: you don't have to work for a company that can afford M365 Copilot or Teams Premium. Krisp can also work with any communication platform because it accesses the microphone to create transcripts.

No matter how your transcripts are generated, there are multiple methods to create recaps and action items. With Krisp and Microsoft Teams, the process is automated. Just make sure recording is turned on, and a recap with action items will automatically appear in the online dashboard after the meeting ends. We found Krisp was very good at summarization and generating action items. Copilot for Microsoft Teams has improved significantly in the year prior to this book's publication, offering more comprehensive meeting summaries with better ease of use and more thorough analysis.

> **NOTE** It's always good manners to tell people when transcription is enabled. Even in a professional environment, some people may not want the discussion recorded.

If the results of the Copilot analysis are not detailed enough for you, you can get more information by asking additional questions in the interface. Let's take a look at how we got more detailed information from Copilot for Microsoft Teams.

#### USING COPILOT FOR MICROSOFT TEAMS TO GENERATE A MEETING RECAP

In Microsoft Teams, you need to record the meeting or selectively start only the transcription function. If you have access to Copilot, there's also a Copilot button available that starts transcription for you. When recording the full video of the meeting, Teams builds a comprehensive recap with visuals and automatically generates notes, which is extremely impressive. If your company has the proper licensing for Teams, recording the entire meeting will always be the best option. Microsoft has realized the value of this feature and now offers a dedicated add-on for Teams instead of requiring a full Copilot license. Based on the feedback we've seen from users, we think the Teams add-on is worth the cost for companies that aren't sold on the full Copilot licensing.

For this example, we will start a meeting transcription because it can be used with any chatbot without dependencies on Copilot. You can view transcripts in real time as they are generated. As mentioned, if you have M365 Copilot, the Copilot icon will also start transcriptions for you, as shown in figure 7.4. If you don't have M365 Copilot, you'll need to download the transcript file after the meeting and provide it to a chatbot.

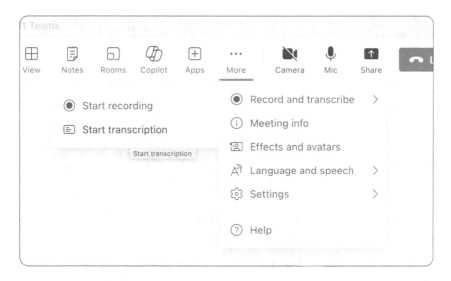

Figure 7.4 Starting a transcription in Microsoft Teams

Once the meeting has concluded, Teams will notify you that the transcript is ready, as shown in figure 7.5. You can download the transcript for use in your preferred chatbot or click View Recap to view the available information about the meeting.

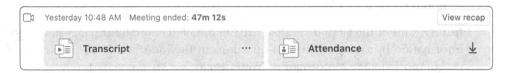

Figure 7.5  Meeting transcript in Microsoft Teams

On the meeting's Recap tab, click the Copilot icon (if available) to open the chat interface in Teams, as shown in figure 7.6. You'll be able to ask questions about the meeting. Click the AI Notes subsection to view the notes generated by Copilot; this section contains a summary of the meeting, including bullet points and expandable sections.

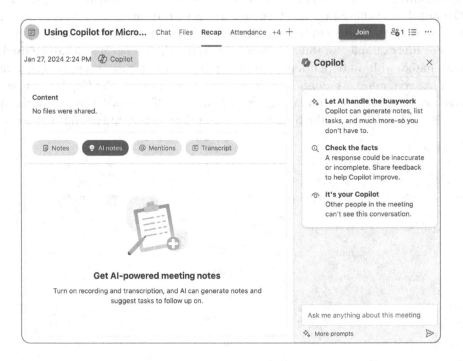

Figure 7.6  Viewing the meeting recap in Microsoft Teams

The AI Notes summary and action items are accurate, and the level of detail has improved dramatically over the year prior to this writing. However, if you need more detailed information, or want to know other information, simply ask Copilot for it.

### USING TRANSCRIPTION TO GENERATE DOCUMENTATION

In the next prompt, we will ask Copilot to use the transcription from a training session to generate documentation.

> **CA** Recap the meeting. This meeting was a training session, so provide a detailed overview. Include as many details and step-by-step instructions as possible in order to use the information to train others.

> Here is a possible recap of the training session we held today:
> - The topic of the session was how to use the SQL tuning advisor to improve the performance of queries on Oracle databases that have the tuning and diagnostic pack licenses.
> - The DBA demonstrated how to run the SQL tuning advisor on the OEM and in SQL*Plus, using some examples of long-running queries on the database.
> - The DBA explained the steps involved in creating a tuning task, executing it, and getting the report that shows the recommendations and benefits of the SQL tuning advisor.
> - The DBA showed how to implement a SQL profile that can improve the query performance by 99.99%, using the OEM or SQL*Plus.
> - The DBA also mentioned some other possible recommendations that the SQL tuning advisor can give, such as creating indexes or changing the SQL text.
> - The DBA highlighted some of the challenges and limitations of using the SQL tuning advisor, such as the need for the tuning and diagnostic pack licenses, the time limit for the tuning task, the private database link issue, and the grants required for the user to run the advisor.

As you can see, even though we requested a detailed analysis, Copilot for Microsoft Teams provided the same summary it would have given for a simple *Recap the meeting* prompt. To get closer to our goal, we can ask individual questions about each bullet point in the summary. This allows for more detailed information about each step.

> **CA** For the following bullet point, provide detailed bullet points and information:
>
> The DBA demonstrated how to run the SQL tuning advisor on the OEM and in SQL*Plus, using some examples of long-running queries on the database.

> Some detailed information for the bullet point are:
> - To run the SQL tuning advisor in OEM, the DBA showed how to go to the performance home page, select the SQL monitoring tab, choose a long-running query, and click on the action button to run the tuning advisory or the SQL repair advisory.
> - To run the SQL tuning advisor on the SQL plus, the DBA showed how to use the DBMS_SQLTUNE package to create, execute, and report a tuning task for a given SQL ID. They also explained the parameters and steps involved in the process.
> - The DBA used some queries from the database as examples to demonstrate the benefits of the SQL tuning advisor, such as finding a better SQL profile, creating indexes, or changing the SQL text. He also compared the execution plans and the performance improvement of the queries.

- The DBA also mentioned some challenges and limitations of the SQL tuning advisor, such as the need for diagnostic and tuning packs, the grants and roles required for the users, and the issues with private database links.

Although not ideal, asking individual questions about each bullet point in the summary allows us to get more detailed information about each step. We can continue down the list of bullet points, issuing the same prompt for each one, and then compile the results into a single document for a more detailed recap of the meeting, or paste the final results back into the meeting chat for everyone to see.

The more detail you achieve in your output, the easier it will be to create additional documentation, procedures, or training information. If you work with teams that speak different languages, you can ask Copilot or another AI model to translate the meeting recap into the desired language. This is a great way to ensure that everyone is on the same page with much less effort.

### ALTERNATIVES

If you don't have M365 Copilot, you can still use a chatbot to generate a meeting recap. As with any chatbot, token limits apply, and very long transcripts may end up with less accurate results or omitted details. The capabilities of each chatbot vary, with premium paid accounts being more capable.

First download the transcript from Teams, and paste it into the chat interface or attach the file. You can then ask for a meeting recap and action items. The results will be similar to what we've shown, but ChatGPT, Claude, or Google Gemini may provide more verbose responses up front. In one test, ChatGPT added additional best practices to the recap. Normally we might appreciate this, but we felt ChatGPT had taken too many liberties with the content, and we preferred the more concise response from M365 Copilot.

> **WARNING** If you are using a third-party chatbot, be sure to review its privacy policy and terms of service: you may be sharing sensitive information with the chatbot provider. It's best to use an encrypted chatbot dedicated to your organization if your transcripts contain any proprietary or sensitive information.

Earlier, we mentioned that starting a recording of your meeting instead of a transcription allows Copilot to provide a more robust recap. In addition to the AI notes, Teams will identify the participants with visuals indicating the times they spoke, and it can break the meeting into topics and chapters. The result is well organized and makes it easy to navigate the video recording. Although the AI notes are a big improvement over using transcription alone, remember that you still have the ability to chat with Copilot to derive additional information from the transcription until you get the results you desire.

> **TIP** Record or transcribe training presentations, and use Copilot to create documentation, procedures, and even quizzes! Or ask Copilot to list all the unexpected problems encountered during the meeting, with suggestions for resolving them.

Copilot can summarize any chat conversation, whether private or group. This is useful for ongoing chats that happen outside of regular meetings. You might use a chat for an unplanned downtime or troubleshooting a problem over weeks or months. Copilot can recap the problem, identify what's been resolved, and determine current action items. It's also great for catching up after being away. The potential uses are vast: Brandon even used Teams to transcribe a podcast episode he enjoyed and saved the AI notes for later reference.

Coming up, we'll discuss ways to integrate tools and automations into your Teams environment to help you stay on top of important events and emails.

## 7.3 Integrations and automation with AI

A lesser-known function in Teams is Microsoft Teams Workflows. Workflows are part of Power Automate, but Microsoft has pulled in a subset to simplify implementation with Teams. You can choose from prebuilt workflows or customize a flow to do exactly what you want. The best part is that workflows are not limited to Microsoft technologies. Although most of the flow templates revolve around M365 products, you can find a large library of connectors to choose from. *Connectors* are prebuilt integrations that enable communication between different applications and services without needing complex coding. Not all connectors are free, though, so keep an eye out for the premium indicator on each of them.

### 7.3.1 Teams workflows in action

For the purposes of this section, we will cover an AI workflow that is available in Teams and can be implemented with little or no advanced knowledge. This example is a bit different than others in this book because we will not directly use a chatbot or AI model to create the workflow. Instead, we'll use prebuilt templates and services.

#### CREATING A TEAMS FLOW WITH AI

The first thing to do to create a flow is to navigate to the Teams channel where you want the flow to be available. Click the ellipsis next to the channel name, and choose Workflows, as shown in figure 7.7.

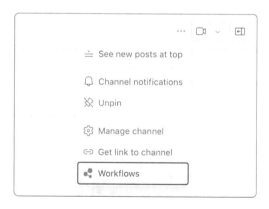

Figure 7.7 Accessing Workflows in Teams

A dialog box will appear with a list of available workflows. Click Workflows to access the main Workflows area of Teams. Here you can choose from a list of prebuilt workflows or create your own. If you click Create a Flow at upper right, you can browse all available connectors and the corresponding triggers and actions. Take a look around if you like, and when you're ready, choose the AI Automation template category from the Create menu, as shown in figure 7.8.

Figure 7.8 Accessing AI templates in Teams

You'll see a list of available AI templates. We're going to choose "Analyze email sentiment with AI Builder and send results to Teams." Click the template to open it.

In the Create a Flow window, you can rename the flow and verify that all of your connectors are ready, as shown in figure 7.9. If not, you'll have to log in to the connector and authorize the connection. Once you're ready, click Next.

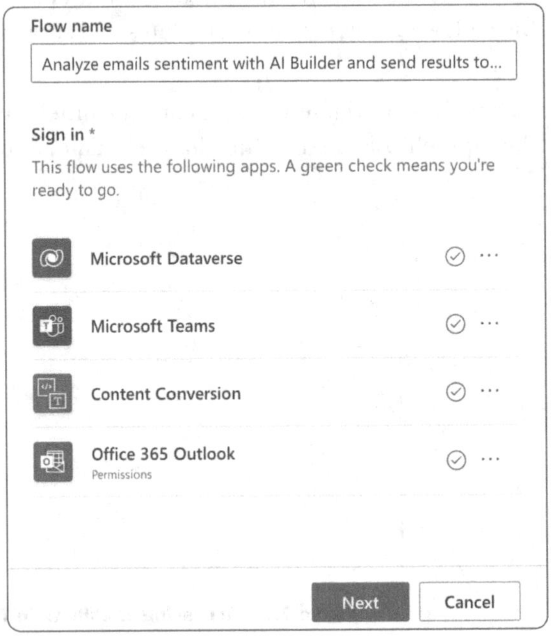

Figure 7.9 Validating connectors in Teams

## 7.3 Integrations and automation with AI

In the next window, enter one or more email addresses if you want to analyze emails from specific senders, or leave the field blank to analyze all emails received. In the second text box, enter a recipient name or email address. It will populate from the global address book, allowing you to choose it from a dropdown. You will likely want to choose yourself for now. Then click Create Flow.

You will see a dialog box indicating that the flow was created, as shown in figure 7.10. Choose Manage Your Workflow.

**Figure 7.10 Managing your workflow in Teams**

You are now on the settings page for your flow. If you are happy with what you have created, you can stop here. When the flow runs, you will get Teams messages from the Workflows bot. However, we want to make a few changes so the flow will be useful for the whole team.

We will modify the flow to only process emails from a specific folder in Outlook. We need to set up a rule in advance to route emails to this folder based on some criteria: in this example, based on the group email address. Instead of having the workflow bot message us directly, we will direct the output to a Teams channel with multiple recipients.

Start by clicking Edit in the Workflows menu. You will see a list of all the steps in the flow. It may look intimidating, but don't worry—we're only going to make a few changes.

Click the first step, "When a new email arrives." In the Folder field, click the little folder, and choose the folder you want to monitor, as shown in figure 7.11.

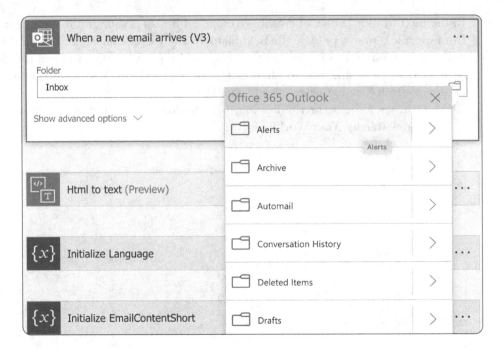

Figure 7.11  Choosing the email folder to monitor

If you previously set up the flow to analyze only specific email addresses, you can leave that setting in place, or you can change it by clicking Show Advanced Options and clearing the From field. Scroll down to the last step, and click "Post adaptive card in a chat or channel" to expand the options, as shown in figure 7.12.

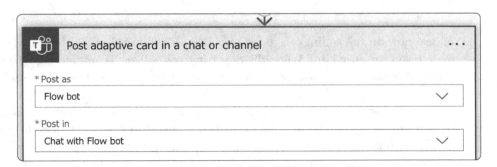

Figure 7.12  Choosing a Teams channel for the post

Click the Post As dropdown, and choose User. This will allow the message to be posted as yourself to the Teams channel. After the dialog box updates, choose the Post In dropdown, and select Channel. If you'd like, you can choose a group chat instead.

## 7.3 Integrations and automation with AI

If you chose Channel, you now have Team and Channel options to choose from. Click the Team dropdown, and choose the team you want to post to. Then click the Channel dropdown, and choose the channel. Leave the Adaptive Card unchanged, and scroll down to the bottom of the page to Body/Recipient. Remove the email address from this field, and click Save, as shown in figure 7.13. The flow will save in place, but the screen will not change.

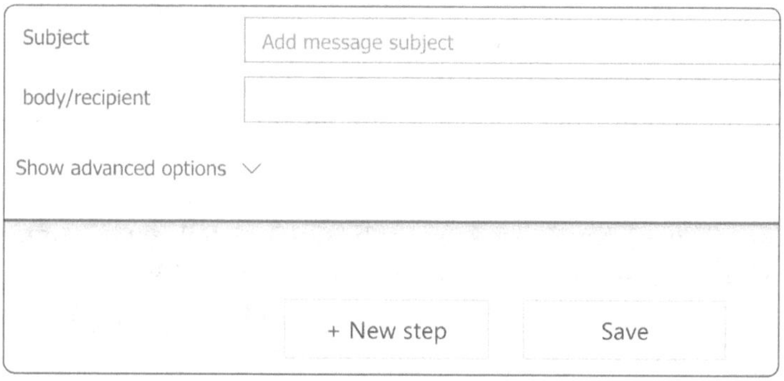

**Figure 7.13** Clear the email address from the recipient field, and save the flow.

Click Home at the top of the Workflows menu to return to the main Workflows page to view your available flows. That's it! You should now have a flow that will analyze emails from a specific folder and post the results to a Teams channel. If you need to further manage your flow or view run statistics or error messages, you can click the flow name to open the settings page.

To test it, send an email to the appropriate address, and wait for the flow to run. You should see a message in the Teams channel with the results of the sentiment analysis. If you don't see the message, check the settings page for the flow to see if there are any errors. If you don't see any errors, you may need to wait a few minutes for the flow to run. If you still don't see the message, check your email rules to ensure that the email was routed to the correct folder.

You may be wondering why you'd want to enable this workflow. The main reason we like it is that it allows us to create notifications to the entire team when an email is sent to the team distribution list. If the email is negative, we can address it quickly instead of waiting for busy team members to see the email message in their inbox.

Our favorite workflow is one that sends a Teams message when a meeting is about to start. Teams is much more visible to us than our email client and gives us better control over notifications. When the Flow bot sends a message, it grabs our attention much more consistently than Outlook. Since implementing the workflow, we can confidently say that we are less likely to be late to a meeting because we missed an Outlook popup. And if you have a smart watch, you can receive the message right on your wrist while digging through the kitchen for a snack.

#### SENDING A TEAMS MESSAGE BEFORE A MEETING

If you'd like to use this workflow, create a new flow with the following standard connectors:

- *Office 365 for Outlook - Trigger*—When an upcoming event is starting soon
- *Microsoft Teams - Actions*—Posts a message in a chat or channel

Now do the following:

- In the Outlook trigger, select your calendar, and set a look-ahead time. We used 5 minutes.
- In the Teams step, post as the Flow bot.
- For the Post In option, choose Chat with Flow Bot. This will send you private messages.
- Enter your email address in the Recipient field, and customize the Message box to your liking. As a minimum, we suggest the Outlook Subject dynamic content, followed by the text "starting soon," as shown in figure 7.14.
- You can set a True or False value in the IsAlert field if you want your notices to be logged in the activity feed.

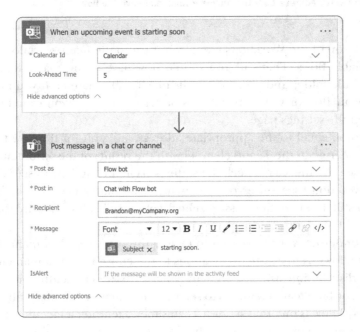

Figure 7.14  Settings for the workflow

That's it! Save it, and enjoy never missing another meeting.

Teams workflows range from simple to incredibly complex. Microsoft has also added SharePoint Agents to Teams group chats, enabling AI chatbots that answer questions about your organization's documents. These Agents allow companies to create custom bots trained on their SharePoint content with no coding required. While powerful, these features are still evolving as Microsoft continues to enhance their capabilities.

### 7.3.2 Webhooks

Before we close out this chapter on automation and integration, we want to quickly mention webhooks. Webhooks are used in web development to exchange information between unrelated applications. Instead of repeatedly polling for information, an application sends information to a specific webhook URL address when an event occurs. The receiving service then processes that information to perform a predefined action.

Implementing webhooks may require more advanced knowledge, but AI chatbots are an excellent source of information to guide you through implementation. The basic idea is that you obtain some useful information and then post it to a webhook URL as a JSON object. The receiving service will then process that information to perform an action.

Brandon recently implemented a new process using PowerShell to query ServiceNow and post the team's open ticket queue to a Teams channel. The amazing thing is that once he realized it was possible, he asked ChatGPT to walk him through the process. ChatGPT was able to reduce the implementation time of the process considerably.

ChatGPT generated PowerShell code and provided explanations of the process to query ServiceNow via REST API calls and then posted the results to a newly created Teams webhook. The code was not perfect, but it was a great starting point. Brandon was able to tweak the code and implement the process in a few hours, estimating that ChatGPT had done about 80% to 90% of the work for him.

Webhooks are supported by a variety of applications and services, so if you aren't using Teams, you can still create custom code to post information to webhook addresses in Slack and many other services. For more on advanced programming with AI, check out chapters 11 and 12.

In the next section, we will discuss how to improve your writing quality without losing your personal touch. You've seen how AI can draft emails for you, but sacrificing your style to an AI chatbot makes your communication feel inauthentic. We'll show you how to use AI to improve your writing without losing your voice.

## 7.4 Improving your writing while maintaining your voice

A major paradox of AI-assisted writing is that it's often painfully obvious when AI writes content. Those who use AI regularly quickly learn to spot the signs. Overused words (such as "crucial," "akin," and "delve") and repetitive phrasing make the content jarring to read, causing readers—including us—to question its authenticity. If we suspect something was written by AI, then the validity of the content comes into question. Did the author actually write something they know about, or was it generated by a chatbot?

AI detection technology, similar to plagiarism checkers, is emerging but remains imperfect. It sometimes misclassifies both human- and AI-generated content. This chapter isn't intended to debate the ethics of AI writing, but we do want to make sure you always take an active role in the output of your writing. And if you are using tools to detect AI, please keep in mind that they're not guaranteed to be accurate.

If you've used AI tools like Copilot in Outlook to draft emails, you know results vary widely. We are more likely to reject drafts than to use them as is.

There are several effective strategies for writing with AI. The first is generating a quick draft with minimal input and then editing it either manually or through additional prompts. This approach requires less upfront work, but the initial draft may require more effort to get it on track. It's also the least likely way to produce output that is immediately useful. Stay true to your message. Well-crafted AI text can sound impressive while saying nothing meaningful. This approach is best used for simple emails that you can knock out in a hurry.

 Write an email/message to the team about submitting benefit elections by December 31st.

The second approach involves providing comprehensive details in your prompt. Although this helps generate a more accurate draft, you'll spend considerable time crafting detailed instructions and then fine-tuning the output. Your time is often better spent writing the content yourself if the subject matter is too complex. However, this detailed prompt approach works well when you want more control over the wording and structure of the content, even if it requires more upfront effort.

 Write an email/message to the team about submitting benefit elections by December 31st. Include the following details:
- The deadline for submitting benefit elections is December 31st.
- Employees who do not submit their benefit elections by the deadline will be automatically enrolled in the default plan.
- Employees can make changes to their benefit elections during the open enrollment period.
- Employees should contact HR if they have any questions or need assistance.

The third approach, which is our preferred approach, is writing the content yourself and then using AI for review and improvement. Don't aim for perfection in your draft—it's just a framework for the AI to follow. This typically preserves your key points while enhancing grammar and wording. Think of the chatbot as an assistant rather than expecting it to outperform you. This approach also works better with inline editing tools, letting you refine text word by word instead of tackling entire paragraphs at once.

 Review the provided write-up. Preserve all relevant details and structure, focusing only on grammar and style. Identify redundant or unnecessary information and suggest improvements for readability and clarity.

We've seen three different approaches for enhancing your writing with any chatbot, but we have a couple of favorites that we use most often: Grammarly and Apple Writing Tools. Grammarly and Apple Writing Tools can be used for inline editing (word by word or restructuring individual sentences) as well as for generating new content. These tools also work across different platforms and/or applications. However, we rarely use Grammarly and Apple Writing Tools to generate new content. Instead, we prefer to use Claude Writing Styles, as mentioned in chapter 2, for new content generation and to address our writing as a whole (paragraphs or pages at a time).

With countless AI tools available, it all comes down to your preferred workflow and the tools that fit into it the best. Let's take a look at both of these tools to outline why we like them.

### 7.4.1 Grammarly

Grammarly uses AI and natural language processing to help you write, rewrite, and check grammar. Available as a browser extension, desktop app, and mobile app, it's versatile enough for any writer. It's particularly beneficial for crafting professional emails and assisting non-native English speakers. We love Grammarly because it is available on so many platforms. And because it is integrated, you don't have to copy and paste text back and forth between a chatbot and your application.

Grammarly helps identify and correct grammar mistakes, spelling errors, and tone problems and can suggest alternative words and phrases to improve your writing style. You can set a target tone for your audience, and Grammarly will assist in maintaining it by rating your writing style and providing suggestions.

Although Grammarly offers a free version, its premium features are worth considering. We often find Grammarly more effective than chatbots for real-time grammar corrections and rephrasing. It allows you to make changes as you go, and you can accept or reject each suggestion individually.

### 7.4.2 Apple Intelligence Writing Tools

For Apple users, the Apple Intelligence Writing Tools introduced in iOS 18 is a game changer. It enables seamless text editing across Apple platforms and consistently delivers high-quality suggestions. We especially like the ability to change the tone (More Friendly, More Professional, More Concise) of our writing.

In addition to rewriting text, you can also summarize text, create key points, and generate lists and tables from paragraphs of text. There is also a compose option that integrates into ChatGPT for free! If you have an OpenAI account, you can sign in for advanced functionality. Apple states that ChatGPT will not train from the data submitted to it through Apple's platforms, but as always, we advise caution and good judgement.

Apple Intelligence Writing Tools comes free with Apple operating systems. Although not as widely available as Grammarly, its deep integration into the Apple ecosystem ensures rapid adoption.

> **IMPORTANT** Even accepting AI suggestions may trigger AI detection flags. The key is maintaining your unique style and viewpoint throughout your writing, ensuring that it truly represents your work. No matter how great it reads, if people don't think you wrote it, it's likely to backfire.

Having explored these approaches to AI-enhanced communication, let's consider some final thoughts on critical thinking and AI's future in communication.

## 7.5 Maintaining critical thinking and good judgement

As you increase your use of AI at work, don't suspend your critical thinking skills. AI is not a replacement for your brain; it is meant to supplement your capabilities, and it often makes mistakes. It's important to verify the accuracy of the information you receive from AI in any scenario before using it in your work. Recently an AI chatbot recommended using nontoxic glue to stick cheese to a pizza, and to eat one rock a day for good health. That's clearly advice we won't take, but not all bad recommendations will be as obvious.

If you are a novice at a task, an AI chatbot may seem brilliant. But if you are an expert, you will begin to see the limitations of the chatbot. It's still too early to tell how long-term use of AI will affect us. Overreliance on a chatbot also means less exercise for your brain and potentially less experience figuring things out for yourself. As the saying goes, "Use it or lose it." If you rely too heavily on AI, you may find yourself falling out of practice with skills you once had.

And once again, data privacy must be protected, necessitating adherence to best practices for secure communication. Using AI in email and IM communications is an easy way to expose sensitive data. Enterprise solutions are becoming more available, providing end-to-end encryption and securing company data. We expect all organizations to define acceptable use policies for AI in the workplace as the technology becomes more prevalent, so make sure to read and understand these policies.

If you elect to use third-party AI services, consider what data you are sharing and any risk it would pose if it were exposed. Removing sensitive details, server and account names, personally identifying information, and other sensitive data from your prompts is very important to protect your organization and yourself.

## 7.6 The future of AI communications

We are really excited about where AI is heading and how it can be used in communications. We are on the verge of seeing a deeper integration of AI into work applications and even our mobile devices. As outlined earlier in table 7.2, there are some prompts we really wanted to show, but we didn't feel the technology was there yet. As AI becomes better at managing our calendars, filtering our emails, and organizing our documents, we'll take a major step toward eliminating tedious administrative tasks from our daily lives.

With the eventual integration of AI into our mobile devices, we will have personal assistants that know us and can remind us of the places we need to be and things we need to do. We'll also begin to see AI agents performing increasingly complex specialized tasks. So keep an eye out: it's coming more quickly than you may expect.

Effective communication meets technical problem solving in chapter 8. You'll learn how to use AI to diagnose problems more accurately and craft appropriate responses to support problems—all while providing the empathetic, human-centered support that users need.

## 7.7 Prompts used in this chapter

- Generate prompts for using AI in email drafting.
- Create an example of an email with a lot of technical jargon and bullet points. Think of a complicated IT issue, such as the implementation of a new IPS. State the steps that have been completed and those that remain.
- Condense the technical email into an example that a network engineer may send to another.
- Based on the email provided, draft a new email suitable for general communication.

## Summary

- AI can significantly improve email management by drafting emails, customizing responses, summarizing conversations, and decoding jargon.
- AI can help identify and mitigate potential security threats in email by identifying phishing attempts and other malicious emails.
- Using AI to create efficient workflows allows for better focus on essential tasks.
- Webhooks are a powerful tool for integrating AI with other applications and services, allowing for the automation of complex tasks and processes.
- Meeting transcription and summarization is one of the most immediately useful applications of AI in the workplace. If an initial summary is not detailed enough, ask individual questions about each bullet point in the summary to get more detailed information about each step.
- Grammarly, Apple Writing Tools, and Claude Writing Styles are useful tools for correcting grammar, generating content, and improving writing during the writing process.
- Balancing the benefits of AI with the need for human ethics, oversight, and critical thinking ensures that AI tools enhance rather than detract from workplace communication.
- Secure communication practices, including data encryption and the use of dedicated AI instances like M365 Copilot, are essential for protecting sensitive information at work.

- Although AI has lots of potential to enhance email management, it still struggles with accuracy and functionality, especially for analyzing email rules, folder management, and calendaring.
- AI has the potential to soon be integrated into work applications and mobile devices, providing personal assistants that can remind us of the places we need to be and things we need to do. AI agents will be able to perform increasingly complex specialized tasks.

# Part 2

# IT operations and AI

The world of IT operations and database management is getting a major upgrade through AI. Chapters 8 to 10 explore how AI is transforming both the day-to-day running of IT systems and the specialized work of database professionals. You'll see how AI enhances service desk interactions and system administration, making routine tasks smoother and troubleshooting more intuitive. For database administrators and developers, we'll also see how AI can help with everything from query optimization to database design. Each chapter walks you through practical ways to use AI in your work, with real solutions you can start using right away. When you finish this part of the book, you'll have a solid grasp on using AI to make your IT operations more efficient and your database work more powerful.

# IT support and service desk

**This chapter covers**
- Using AI for soft skills at the service desk
- Identifying problems and asking the right questions
- Crafting responses to technical problems
- Troubleshooting technical problems with AI and custom GPTs
- The future of AI and the service desk

The service desk is a critical function in any organization: it is responsible for resolving routine incidents and service requests but also for escalating complex problems to other IT support teams. It is the first point of contact for users who need help with their IT systems. Because the service desk interfaces directly with end users, it is often the first team to identify and report widespread problems.

In the prior two chapters, we demonstrated that chatbots excel at conversation, making the service desk a natural fit for AI. Service desk agents can use chatbots to solve technical problems and address the emotional needs of users who are experiencing problems. Chapter 13 deep-dives into conflict resolution and crisis management in everyday roles, but in this chapter, we'll focus on specific scenarios for the service desk, starting with emotional support.

## 8.1 Service desk therapy

The role of a service desk agent can be a stressful job, as users may be upset or frustrated when they contact the service desk. A combination of skills is needed to handle emotions and provide support to users who are experiencing these problems, often in real time.

Table 8.1 provides a few examples of prompts that service desk agents can use to practice responding to tense or emotional situations. These prompts are designed to help agents develop the skills they need to handle difficult conversations with users who are upset or frustrated. By practicing these prompts, agents can learn how to respond to users in a way that is empathetic and supportive to disarm the caller while providing an effective pathway to problem resolution.

Table 8.1 Prompts for tense or emotional situations

| Task | Prompt |
| --- | --- |
| De-escalate a tense situation | Craft a response to an upset customer expressing understanding and empathy, and offering a solution to their problem. |
| Provide emotional support | Compose a message to a customer who is frustrated with a recurring issue, showing empathy and assuring them that their issue is being prioritized. |
| Acknowledge a service failure | Respond to a customer's complaint about a service failure, acknowledging their dissatisfaction, apologizing, and outlining the steps to prevent similar situations in the future. |
| Increase customer satisfaction | Draft a follow-up message to a customer who previously had a difficult issue, asking about their current experience and offering further assistance. |
| Practice tense scenarios | I work the service desk for a software company. An upset customer has written with the following complaint, and I would like to practice conversing with them to resolve the issue. Using the complaint below, act as the customer via chat, and I will respond as the agent. Provide feedback after the conversation to help me improve my responses, with a focus on de-escalation and effective troubleshooting. [attach or paste in customer complaint] |

Across service desk roles, agents may need to respond to the same complaint from a variety of angles. One agent may need to tackle a problem as it is being worked through, and another may need to follow up with a customer after the problem has been resolved. A service desk agent can use AI to draft all relevant responses from a single prompt, saving time and ensuring that the customer receives the best possible service. In the following example, we use ChatGPT to draft different responses to the same complaint, based on prompts in table 8.1.

The following email was received by a service desk agent from a customer who is frustrated with recurring issues in the app they are using.

"I'm really at my wit's end here. Your app's been throwing up error messages left and right, and it's completely messing up my work. I keep getting this "Error 502: Server Communication Failed" and a bunch of other random ones, and it's driving me nuts!

I'm falling behind on important stuff because it just won't work right."

Create responses to this email, each with a different objective: de-escalate a tense situation and suggest a workaround; acknowledge a service failure and outline process improvements; increase customer satisfaction after resolution.

 Hello [Customer Name],

### De-escalate a tense situation and suggest a workaround

I just read your email, and I want to first say I'm truly sorry for the stress and frustration you've been experiencing due to the errors in our app. It's clear this situation has significantly impacted your work, and that's the last thing we want for any of our users. I appreciate you bringing this to our attention, and I want to assure you that we're on it.

To start addressing your concerns, we're prioritizing a review of the error codes you've mentioned, especially the "Error 502." Our development team is already on the case, and we're pushing for a quick resolution. In the meantime, I'd like to offer you a temporary workaround that might help. [Provide specific workaround steps here.]

Again, I'm really sorry for the inconvenience this has caused you. We're committed to making this right and restoring your confidence in our app.

### Acknowledge a service failure and outline process improvements

I want to extend my sincerest apologies for the frustration and inconvenience you've experienced due to the errors in our app. It's clear we've fallen short of providing the reliable service you deserve, and for that, I am truly sorry.

We're taking immediate steps to address the issues you've raised, including a thorough investigation of the error messages and implementing necessary updates to prevent this from happening in the future.

Your trust in our service is paramount, and we're dedicated to restoring that trust by resolving this issue and ensuring a smoother experience moving forward.

### Increase customer satisfaction after issue resolution

I hope this message finds you well. I'm reaching out to check in on your experience with our app since our last communication. Have you noticed an improvement in the issue you were encountering, or is there anything else you're still concerned about?

Your satisfaction is very important to us, and we're committed to ensuring that our app meets your needs effectively. If there's anything further we can do to assist or improve your experience, please don't hesitate to let us know.

Looking forward to hearing from you.

Best regards,

[Your Name] - Support Team

Subtle differences in the objective of the prompts produce different responses simultaneously. This is a time-saver for service desk agents, as it allows them to quickly draft customized responses to specific customer problems while wearing multiple hats. It also reduces the appearance of a canned response, which can be off-putting to customers.

### 8.1.1 Identifying problems

Communication is a two-way street. Service desk agents need to be able to understand the problem that the user is experiencing. This can be difficult, as users may not be able to articulate the problem in technical terms or may use slang or colloquialisms from their local area. Service desk agents need to be able to ask the right questions to understand the problem and then translate that into a technical solution. In the following example, we use ChatGPT to help a service desk agent understand a user's problem and ask the right questions to clarify the problem.

A customer calls the customer support line of a tech company because they are experiencing trouble with their laptop. They explain that their screen keeps getting "fuzzy" whenever they try to watch something. The representative, who is not a native speaker of American English, initially interpreted "fuzzy" to mean a problem with the laptop's sound. Realizing there might be a misunderstanding due to the colloquial use of the word "fuzzy," the representative decides to use an AI chatbot for clarification.

The caller is from Kaplan, Louisiana and said: "Tee, this laptop isn't working. The screen is fuzzy. It gets so frustrating, I just save it up."

Considering colloquialisms from Louisiana, what does the caller indicate is the problem? Provide 3-5 questions I can ask to clarify the issue with the fuzzy screen.

From the caller's description, "fuzzy" likely refers to an issue with the display quality, where the screen might show distorted images, blurred text, or static-like interference.

The phrase "I just save it up" could imply that the caller stops using the laptop when the issue arises, possibly out of frustration or hoping it might resolve on its own over time.

To clarify the issue, consider asking these questions:

1. When you say the screen is "fuzzy," can you describe what you see? Are the colors off, or is the text and images unclear?
2. Does this issue happen all the time, or only when you're using certain applications or performing specific tasks on your laptop?
3. Have you noticed if the fuzziness appears more when the laptop is hot or has been in use for an extended period?
4. Have you tried any fixes, like adjusting the display settings or restarting the laptop? If so, what was the outcome?
5. Can you recall any recent changes or updates to your laptop before the screen started getting fuzzy, like new software installations or system updates?

Misalignment in communication is often a root cause of frustration for both callers and agents, and AI can help bridge that gap. Instead of confusion and assumptions, the agent was able to clarify the conversation without asking the caller to restate the problem. Next, we'll look at how AI can be used to help service desk agents craft responses to technical problems in a way that customers can better understand.

## 8.1.2 Crafting a response

A response should be relevant to the customer's problem and easy to understand. This can be difficult, as technical problems are often complex and difficult to explain in simple terms. Service desk agents need to be able to translate technical jargon into language that the customer can comprehend.

Analogies are a powerful tool for explaining complex concepts in a way that is easy to understand. In the following example, we use ChatGPT to help a service desk agent craft a response to a customer experiencing slow internet speeds without using technical jargon.

 A customer is experiencing slow internet speeds. We have reports of excessive bandwidth congestion at this location. The service provider has sent out technicians to upgrade a router to one supporting a higher bandwidth. The estimated resolution is in 5 hours. Explain the issue to the customer using an analogy that they will understand. Assure them that we are working on the issue as quickly as possible and include language to make them feel heard and understood.

 Dear [Customer's Name],

I understand how frustrating slow internet speeds can be, especially when you're relying on it for important tasks. To help explain what's happening, let's use the analogy of a highway during rush hour. Right now, the "highway" that carries your internet data is experiencing a lot of "traffic" due to high demand in your area, much like a road gets congested with too many cars. This "traffic jam" is what's causing the slowdown in your internet speeds.

To address this, think of us as the roadwork crew coming in to widen the highway. We're upgrading a key "intersection" - in this case, a router - to handle more "traffic," allowing data to flow more freely and at higher speeds. This upgrade should significantly ease the congestion and improve your internet experience.

The estimated time for this "construction" to be complete is about 5 hours. We're working as quickly as we can to get this done because we know how important a smooth, fast internet connection is to you. Your patience and understanding during this time are greatly appreciated.

I want to assure you that we're on top of this and doing everything in our power to resolve the issue promptly. Your satisfaction is very important to us, and we're committed to providing you with the reliable service you expect and deserve.

Thank you for bearing with us. If you have any more concerns or need further assistance, please feel free to reach out. We're here to help.

Warm regards,

[Your Name] - Customer Support Team

## 8.2 Technical support

Large language models (LLMs) like generative pretrained transformers (GPTs) do more than just understand technical terms; they can also quickly master the documentation for products that a tech support department is responsible for. This can help speed up problem-solving, reduce the time it takes for new hires to become productive, and enhance the quality of customer service. OpenAI and similar assistants were practically made for this task, and we'll explore them later in this chapter.

### 8.2.1 Setting up the environment

Typically, chatbots can be used to ask random questions about topics. Their default training covers a wide variety of topics, but often, in the field of service desks, much of the information and many of the processes are proprietary. This means the chatbot needs to be trained on the company's specific information and processes. Training an AI model is a complex process that most of us would not want to attempt. Luckily, we can use document retrieval capabilities to make the process easier. This is made possible by something called *RAG architecture*. RAG stands for *retrieval-augmented generation*. The architecture uses a retriever and a generator to respond to prompts with information from the documents. A *retriever* is a model that is trained to find the most relevant documents, and a *generator* is a model that is trained to generate responses based on the content.

Attaching documents to your prompts is the easiest way to temporarily train a model with custom information. We can attach documents to our prompts to add context and specific information to the chatbot's knowledge base. This is useful in a variety of ways, but in the context of the service desk, it can be used to provide the chatbot with the specific information and processes of the company, to provide detailed technical or troubleshooting information, or to analyze data about trends and problems.

### 8.2.2 Troubleshooting problems

Once you have the appropriate documentation at your disposal, you can use chatbots to troubleshoot technical problems. This can be done by asking the chatbot to provide information about a specific problem or detailed steps that need to be taken to resolve the problem. Depending on the capabilities of your selected chatbot, you will be able to attach documents, provide URLs, upload files to integrated services (i.e., Google Drive and OneDrive), or paste text directly into the prompts.

In the following example, we use ChatGPT to troubleshoot a technical problem. First we attach a CSV file containing an export of IT service desk tickets from our imaginary company's ticketing system. We then ask ChatGPT to help us solve VPN connectivity problems by analyzing past VPN problems and resolutions. You can download this basic sample file from https://gptmaker.dev/book/vpn_tickets.

I have attached a CSV file containing various IT service desk tickets, including the problem and resolution for each ticket. Based on the information in the file, provide the most common resolutions to problems with VPN connection drops.

 Based on the sample data for VPN connection drop issues, the most common resolutions are:

1 **Adjusted VPN settings for optimal performance, resolving connection issues**. - This resolution was applied 6 times, indicating that optimizing VPN settings can effectively address connection stability issues.
2 **Updated VPN client to the latest version, improving connection stability**. - This was also applied 6 times, suggesting that ensuring the VPN client is up-to-date is crucial for maintaining a stable connection.
3 **Switched to a less congested server, significantly improving speed**. - Used 5 times, this resolution implies that server congestion can cause connection drops, and switching servers can help.
4 **Reset user credentials and provided guidance on login process**. - Also used 5 times, indicating that login issues can contribute to connection instability and should be addressed.
5 **Network settings reset and the issue resolved after troubleshooting**. - This was applied once, suggesting it's a less common but still viable solution to connection drop issues.

These resolutions highlight the importance of maintaining up-to-date VPN software, optimizing settings, and choosing the right server to minimize connection drops.

In the real world, you will likely have a much larger dataset to work with and more variation in descriptions and resolutions, which can be both a pro and a con. This is a simple example to illustrate the concept. The chatbot was able to analyze the data and provide the most common resolutions to problems with VPN connection drops. This approach allows service desk agents to quickly access information about past problems and resolutions and use that information to solve current problems.

You can apply this same approach to any technical problem, as long as you have relevant data to analyze. This data can come from CSV exports, PDF or text documentation, or any other supported file types, as well as from URLs.

### 8.2.3 Practicing for real-time scenarios

Throughout this chapter, we've presented a variety of potential scenarios a service desk agent may encounter. Attempting to use a chatbot in real time can be a lot to juggle. One of the coolest things you can do with a chatbot is practice these scenarios in a safe environment. Using the "Act as" prompts we introduced in chapter 4, you can practice de-escalating tense situations, troubleshooting specific types of technical problems, or both simultaneously.

Using the "Practice tense scenarios" prompt we outlined in table 8.1 with the email in the "Customer email" example following it, try your hand at interacting with a chatbot that is acting as an upset customer. Focus on de-escalating the situation with the customer, and then begin to troubleshoot the problem they are experiencing. The chatbot will play along, providing feedback and answers to your troubleshooting questions. The resolution to the specific scenario will be unknown to you at the start but is likely to involve a relatively straightforward resolution path.

When we tried this exercise with ChatGPT, the chatbot was able to provide feedback on the following items: empathy and patience, clarifying questions, instruction clarity, proactive solutions, follow-up assurance, and closing the interaction. ChatGPT also suggested checking for common problems like administrative permissions earlier in the conversation to potentially resolve problems more quickly.

We highly recommend building a custom GPT for service desk scenarios. A custom GPT can use documents with your training or support information, processes, and troubleshooting steps. The custom GPT will also be geared toward service desk tasks, making it more efficient and effective in assisting you in various scenarios. Let's take a look at OpenAI's custom GPTs and how to create one.

## 8.3 Custom GPTs

Custom GPTs are an OpenAI offering that allows you to customize a chatbot for a specific task. The possibilities are endless. We have created custom GPTs to help us write, to teach us languages, and to craft recipes. They are a lot of fun to use and surprisingly easy to create. You may not even need to build a custom GPT, as the OpenAI GPT store has many to choose from. However, we always build custom GPTs and keep them private to protect our data. An OpenAI account is required to use Custom GPTs in the OpenAI GPT store, and building your own requires a paid Plus account.

Custom GPTs also support functions for the implementation of custom code. Functions extend the capabilities of the custom GPT, allowing them to interact with remote sites through API calls.

> **TIP** When dealing with Custom GPTs, remember not to share them publicly if they contain sensitive information. And always look for options to opt out of model training. OpenAI's custom GPTs have an option at the bottom under Additional Settings that should be unchecked. You can also submit a privacy request to OpenAI to ensure that your data is not used for training.

As shown in figure 8.1, the interface is very user-friendly. You can create a custom GPT with natural language by chatting with the GPT builder, or you can choose to configure the bot to gain access to the individual settings.

In this example, we'll create a custom GPT to analyze IT service tickets to help categorize problems and resolutions. The example requires a ChatGPT Plus account.

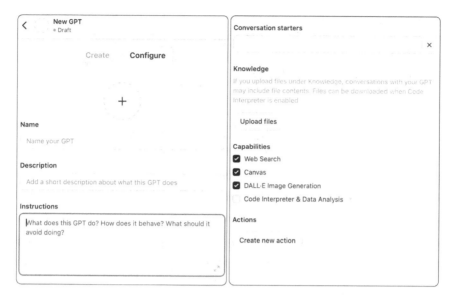

**Figure 8.1  Custom GPT interface**

## 8.3.1 Creating a custom GPT to analyze IT service tickets

Navigating to https://chat.openai.com/gpts will bring you to the GPT store. Here, you can find a variety of GPTs that are pretrained and ready to use. You can also create your GPT by clicking Create GPT and following the prompts.

OpenAI has created an easy-to-use interface where you chat with the GPT Builder to design your GPT. It will ask you a series of questions and even generate an image for your GPT. Clicking the Configure tab will allow you to set parameters for your GPT directly and edit the instructions. For the sake of this example, the following table lists the settings for our GPT, which we call Ticket Analyst, as shown in table 8.2.

**Table 8.2  Ticket Analyst settings**

| Setting | Value |
|---|---|
| Name | Ticket Analyst |
| Description | Analyze IT service tickets to help categorize problems and resolutions. |
| Instructions | Your primary role is to analyze IT service tickets from spreadsheets, categorizing problems into major categories and subcategories. When ticket details are unclear, you're expected to make educated guesses based on available information. You will delve into comments, work notes, and closure notes to understand problem resolutions. Besides categorizing individual tickets, you should also provide summaries of overall trends and patterns in the data, highlighting common problems, effective resolutions, and any notable anomalies. This comprehensive analysis will aid in improving IT service management by identifying areas for process enhancement and training initiatives. |

**Table 8.2** Ticket Analyst settings *(continued)*

| Setting | Value |
| --- | --- |
| Conversation Starters | 1. Analyze this service ticket for me.<br>2. What category does this problem belong to?<br>3. Summarize the resolution of this ticket.<br>4. Identify patterns in these ticket closures. |
| Knowledge | We provided a file named task.csv which contains several examples of IT tickets which we can use for the custom GPT to analyze. |
| Capabilities | Web Browsing, DALL-E Image Generation, Code Interpreter |
| Actions | Advanced programming required, not used in this example, but allows the GPT to interact with external resources |

The instructions for the GPT are very important, as they will guide the GPT in its responses. Think of the instructions as constraints on the GPT-4 model. Instead of knowing everything, this custom GPT has a very specific role to play. You want to restrict it from going off-topic and instead make it focus on its main purpose. You are also attempting to load up the appropriate context for the GPT to perform the work you need it to do.

The conversation starters are just prompts for users to use when they want to interact with the GPT. These are the questions that the GPT will be able to answer. You can add more conversation starters as you see fit.

As you move down the New GPT interface, you'll see options for Knowledge and Capabilities, as shown in figure 8.2. Under Knowledge, you can upload files that the GPT will use to generate responses. This is extremely useful because you can "train" the model through these files. The GPT will use the information in the files to generate responses.

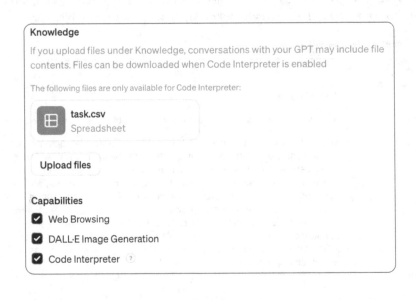

Figure 8.2 Custom GPT settings

The Capabilities setting is where you grant the GPT access to browse the web, generate images, and run code. Code Interpreter makes your GPT much more powerful but can also introduce risk, such as someone downloading your knowledge documents. Don't upload anything you wouldn't want a stranger to download.

In the upper-right corner, you can see the Create button. Clicking this button saves the custom GPT to your account. A sharing dialog box will also appear to enable sharing via a link or in the GPT Store.

We keep our GPTs set to Only Me so they are not available to the public, as shown in figure 8.3. Click Save to save your GPT.

You're ready to use your GPT to analyze IT service tickets, as shown in figure 8.4. Because we enabled Code Interpreter, you can upload additional files with your prompts or have the GPT write relevant code for you using Python.

Figure 8.3   Save the GPT.

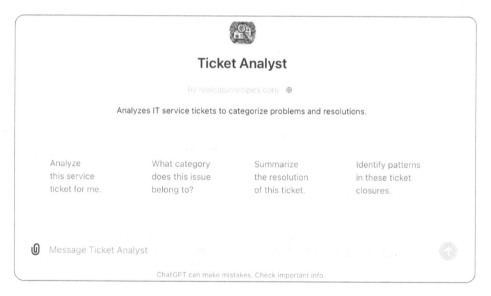

Figure 8.4   A new chat with our custom GPT

Now we will ask for an analysis of our IT service tickets to see how the custom GPT responds. All data analyzed for the response is in the tasks.csv file that we attached to our GPT when we created it. No setup prompting is needed, so we can continue with testing the prompt. The response is abbreviated to save space.

Categorize our service desk tickets and provide totals for each category. Identify the most common issue, and resolution. Analyze trends and provide insights and recommendations.

 **Overall Analysis**
- **Total Tickets**: 1000
- **Tickets by Category**:
  - Hardware Issues: 209
  - Software Issues: 205
  - User Support and Training: 203
  - Network Connectivity: 197
  - Security and Access: 186

**Most Common Issue**: VPN connection issues

**Resolution for Most Common Issue**: Checked VPN server status and network settings

**Trends Over Time**
- The line graph displays the trend in ticket volume over time, broken down by category. This helps identify any fluctuations in the number of tickets per category over the sample time frame.

**Spike Analysis**
- Spikes in ticket volumes were identified by comparing monthly ticket counts to a calculated threshold (mean + 2 standard deviations) for each category.

**Insights and Recommendations**

1. **Common Issues and Resolutions**:
   - The most common issue was "VPN connection issues," with the resolution typically involving checking the VPN server status and network settings.
   - **Recommendation**: Create a comprehensive guide or automated diagnostic tool for users to troubleshoot and resolve common VPN issues independently. This can reduce the number of tickets related to this issue.

2. **Hardware Issues**:
   - Hardware issues are the most frequent category, with common problems including laptops not turning on and printers not responding.
   - **Recommendation**: Implement routine maintenance checks and provide users with easy-to-follow troubleshooting steps for common hardware issues. Consider training sessions focused on basic hardware troubleshooting skills.

3. **User Support and Training**:
   - A significant number of tickets fall under user support and training, often involving training on new software or systems.
   - **Recommendation**: Develop comprehensive training programs and resources, including video tutorials and user manuals, to empower users with the necessary skills to use new software and systems effectively.

4 **Security and Access**:
- Issues related to security and access, such as forgotten passwords and malware infections, are also common.
- **Recommendation**: Promote the use of password management tools and conduct regular security awareness training to educate users on best practices for password security and recognizing phishing attempts.

5 **Network Connectivity**:
- Network connectivity issues, including Wi-Fi and VPN problems, are frequent.
- **Recommendation**: Improve network infrastructure to ensure stable connectivity and provide users with a troubleshooting guide for common network issues. Regularly update network equipment and firmware to prevent connectivity problems.

By addressing these areas, the help desk team can improve efficiency and reduce the volume of repetitive issues, ultimately enhancing user satisfaction and service quality.

Our session with the chatbot is new, yet the Ticket Analysts GPT already had context about its purpose along with our service desk ticket information. The ticket counts are accurate, and the custom GPT is able to create graphs and tables to represent data if desired. In this test, our Ticket Analyst focused on each category and provided recommendations for the most common problems. If you want the Ticket Analyst to focus on a different aspect, you can simply adjust the instructions in the custom GPT and try again, or issue follow-up prompts to guide the chatbot.

One of the benefits of creating the custom GPT is that the ticket data was already known to the custom GPT. We did not attach it to the prompt. The custom GPT becomes an agent that can give you quick, centralized access to the data without uploading files each time. If you share the custom GPT with others, they will have access to the same data. This is a great feature for a team that needs to analyze or query data repeatedly, or for users who may struggle with uploading files. It's a simplified experience.

Imagine a use case where you provide technical documentation to the custom GPT and allow your coworkers to ask questions about those topics. The custom GPT has effectively become a support agent for your team.

Custom GPTs are some of the latest features available, but what else is on the horizon? In the next section, we'll discuss where we see the service desk heading in the future.

## 8.4 The future of the service desk: Agents

Imagine walking into an IT support center of tomorrow where service desk professionals work alongside a new kind of technology: AI agents. Unlike traditional service desk tools, these systems work independently to solve problems without constant human guidance.

*AI agents* can take initiative rather than just responding to questions. They can navigate websites, use computer systems, analyze complex data, and complete multi-step processes on their own. While not specifically built for IT support, today's AI agents show what's possible for future service desk environments.

### 8.4.1 Key agentic AI offerings

Several AI agent platforms show what these tools can do for service desk operations:

- *ChatGPT Operator* from OpenAI works independently across many different tasks. It uses web tools, runs multi-step processes, and creates reports with minimal human input. While not specifically built for IT service desks, it maintains context through complex processes, making it good for automating routine support tasks.
- *Claude Desktop User,* built by Anthropic, focuses on safety and reliability. It's good at understanding language, which helps it summarize information, analyze tone, and write appropriate responses. It works directly with desktop systems and handles complex data, potentially making IT processes faster and more efficient by streamlining tasks.
- *Google Gemini 2 Flash* handles text, voice, and images at the same time. This helps with practical troubleshooting tasks like diagnosing hardware problems through pictures or walking users through fixes with step-by-step visual instructions. Its independent operation suggests future systems where IT teams can solve complex technical problems more quickly.

As AI agents improve, we'll likely see more specialized tools, including ones that work with customer relationship management (CRM) systems and IT service desk platforms. These systems will combine independence with technical expertise, making them valuable for support teams.

### 8.4.2 Agentic AI in enterprise CRM systems

Enterprise platforms are adding AI agents to their service desk tools, improving traditional workflows:

- *Salesforce Agentforce* uses AI to improve ticket handling. It automatically sorts and assigns issues while suggesting solutions based on past cases. This helps teams respond faster and sends complex problems to human agents when needed, leading to happier customers.
- *Zendesk's AI* shows how these systems work in real support situations. It handles simple questions automatically and spots patterns in common problems to make support more efficient. The system gives human agents helpful information and suggestions while they work, helping them solve problems better.
- As these tools get better, the line between what AI and humans can do is becoming less clear. This creates a workplace where support staff and AI systems work together smoothly, each using their strengths to solve problems more effectively than either could alone.

From service desk improvements, we move to broader IT management. Chapter 9 shows how AI changes systems administration, making scripting, compliance, and security work more efficient.

## 8.5 Prompts used in this chapter

- Create a real-life scenario where a caller may be having communication issues with the representative and illustrate how the representative can ask AI to help clarify.
- Simulate a technical issue being faced by a non-technical customer. The job of the help desk is to explain the issue in non-technical terms, appropriately translating jargon with analogies that the customer can understand.
- Generate an adoc table with 2 columns, "Task" and "Prompt". Create 5 rows for the table. Each row should be a task useful to a helpdesk representative that can be used to disarm upset customers, provide emotional support, and increase satisfaction during difficult situations.
- Create up to 8 bullet point summaries from this chapter that outline what the reader has learned. The bullet points should be full sentences.

## Summary

- AI can be integrated into service desk operations to improve the support experience for both employees and customers.
- AI can guide service desk representatives in disarming upset customers, providing emotional support, and increasing satisfaction during difficult situations.
- AI can assist in providing clarity across cultural or language barriers, ensuring that customers receive the help they need.
- Service desk representatives can use AI to explain technical problems in non-technical terms, translating jargon with analogies that the customer can understand.
- Support ticketing systems centralize and streamline access to information, which can be used as a data source by AI to provide swift, accurate support resolutions.
- Custom GPTs can tailor a chatbot to handle special tasks and retrieve data from uploaded files.
- The future of the service desk will be shaped by the integration of Agentic AI-driven tools, including autonomous task execution systems, advanced Natural Language Processing engines, multimodal AI capabilities, and adaptive knowledge management systems.

# Systems administration

**This chapter covers**
- Using AI tools in systems administration
- Applying ChatGPT in change requests, Linux distributions, file renaming, and log analysis
- Auditing configuration files for compliance and optimization
- Exploring existing AI applications in systems engineering
- Simplifying complex systems administration tasks

A systems administrator manages servers on a network. They back up and protect data, fix application and service problems, and handle user accounts. They work with Linux and Windows systems and use tools like System Center Configuration Manager (SCCM) to manage large deployments.

From our experience managing systems, we know the work can get tedious. There are lots of detailed troubleshooting, complex configurations, and tasks that need to be done over and over. But we've seen how AI can make many of these tasks easier. In this chapter, we'll show you how we used AI to create change requests, work with Linux, rename files, analyze logs, check systems for compliance, and automate workflows.

Looking at our own work and our coworkers' experience with ChatGPT, here are some common prompts we've used to get AI help (much like our old Google searches):

- Get the SHA of Docker Image
- Create beautiful role-based access control in Active Directory
- Help me create netApp Config Docs
- How do I find the install date on Linux
- Help me figure out why this SharePoint upgrade failed
- How do I restart sound in Fedora?

Let's see how AI services like ChatGPT can make managing change requests simpler, leading to better documentation, decisions, and efficiency.

## 9.1 Change request

*Change requests* are formal IT documents that ask for approval to update systems or processes. Writing these requests takes time because they need many details. AI tools like ChatGPT can make this process much faster.

Joe, a systems engineer, tried using ChatGPT after hearing about his colleague Chrissy's success with it. He used ChatGPT to write a change request that his organization approved with just a few small edits. This made the task both quicker and more interesting. The following example shows the actual prompt and response.

 Write a change request to remove the DHCP role from a domain controller and put it on its own server.

 **Summary** This change request proposes the removal of the DHCP role from a domain controller and placing it on a dedicated server to improve system performance, security, and reliability.

**Details**

**Current State** Currently, the DHCP role is installed on a domain controller that is responsible for managing Active Directory, DNS, and other critical services. This configuration can lead to performance issues and potential security risks since DHCP traffic can impact the processing of other critical services.

**Proposed State** We propose removing the DHCP role from the domain controller and placing it on a dedicated server. This configuration will allow us to improve system performance, enhance security, and minimize the impact of DHCP traffic on other services. The new DHCP server will be configured with a failover mechanism to ensure high availability.

**Impact Analysis** The proposed change will require the following steps:

- Set up a new server with the DHCP role installed

- Configure the new DHCP server with the same scopes and options as the current DHCP server
- Migrate all DHCP reservations and leases from the current DHCP server to the new DHCP server
- Update DHCP client settings to use the new DHCP server

This change will require downtime for DHCP clients during the migration process. The estimated downtime is expected to be less than one hour.

**Implementation Plan** The following steps will be taken to implement this change:

1. Preparing the new server for the DHCP role installation
2. Installing and configuring the DHCP role on the new server
3. Migrating DHCP scopes and options from the current server to the new server
4. Updating DHCP client settings to use the new DHCP server
5. Testing the new DHCP server to ensure proper functionality
6. Decommissioning the DHCP role on the domain controller

**Rollback Plan** If the implementation of the new DHCP server fails or causes unexpected issues, the following rollback plan will be executed:

1. Remove the DHCP role from the new server
2. Reinstall the DHCP role on the domain controller
3. Restore the DHCP scopes and options to the domain controller
4. Update DHCP client settings to use the domain controller for DHCP
5. Perform further analysis to identify and address the root cause of the issue

**Approval** This change request has been reviewed and approved by the Change Advisory Board (CAB) for implementation on the scheduled date and time.

What Joe liked about the response was that ChatGPT not only knew what a change request was but also proposed a solid change request format. Further, it provided a basic outline for how he'd actually perform the task, even including a rollback plan. Joe's request worked well mainly because *he clearly understood what he needed* from the start and *gave detailed instructions* to the AI. He also made sure to carefully check the AI's suggestions to ensure that they fit his organization's requirements and included plans for any necessary adjustments.

Joe's story shows us that AI can make the nitty-gritty parts of our jobs, like change requests, a lot smoother. By keeping these tips in mind, you can start making your workload a bit lighter too.

The ability of ChatGPT to handle change requests so intelligently showcases a concrete shift in the administrative workflow, illustrating how AI can make even routine tasks more efficient. But the utility of such AI tools isn't just limited to traditionally structured tasks like change management. Let's now turn our attention to a more fluid, sometimes chaotic aspect of systems administration: dealing with varying Linux distros.

## 9.2 More distros, more problems

Linux comes in many flavors, known as *distributions* or *distros*. Each distro combines the Linux kernel—the core of the operating system—with a mix of software and apps to create a complete package. This diversity is great for tailoring systems to companies' very specific needs, but it can also introduce a lot of complexity. Distros sometimes handle things differently, such as which services start up automatically or where log files are stored. If a company is running multiple distros, the sysadmins need to be familiar with the specifics of each one. This means having a solid overall understanding of Linux, as well as some specific technical know-how for each distro.

When working with different Linux distros, it's important to be aware of key differences that may affect your workflow. Things like the init system (System V or systemd), package management, configuration tools, security policies, and library/compiler versions can vary between distros.

In the next example, we deal with a classic sysadmin challenge: diagnosing network problems by locating logs and utilizing tools to track dropped packets. In the following example, we look for dropped packets on SUSE 15.5. This showcases the practical application of understanding system nuances, from init systems to log file management, in resolving real-world problems.

 I'm running SUSE Linux Enterprise Server (SLES) 15.5 on a server that's having network issues. We assume it's dropped packets because we're seeing slow connectivity and timeouts from client machines. I need to dig into the logs to figure out what's going on. Where does SLES 15.5 keep its network and firewall logs? Also, are there any commands or tools on SLES for tracking or logging dropped packets directly?

 On SUSE Linux Enterprise Server (SLES) 15.5, log files are typically located in the /var/log directory. This is a standard directory for storing logs on most Linux distributions, including SLES. Here are the common log files and directories you might find there:

- /var/log/messages: This is the general system log file where you can find messages logged by the system and system services. It might contain information about dropped packets, depending on how your logging is configured.
- /var/log/firewall: If this directory exists, it might contain logs specifically related to the firewall, including dropped packets.
- /var/log/audit/audit.log: If auditd is installed and running, this log file contains logs related to the Linux Audit framework, which can include detailed information about system events.

For dropped packets specifically, you will likely be interested in logs from the firewall (e.g., SuSEfirewall2 or firewalld, depending on what you're using) or kernel logs that might be directed to /var/log/messages. The exact location can vary based on specific system configurations and logging settings.

To view dropped packets, you might also consider using tools like iptables or firewalld directly, depending on what your system is using for firewall management. For example, with iptables, you can list rules along with packet and byte counters:

```
sudo iptables -L -v -n
```

This command shows all rules along with the number of packets and bytes that matched each rule, which can help identify dropped packets.

If you're specifically looking for dropped packets, ensure that your firewall is configured to log these events. By default, dropped packets might not be logged unless explicitly configured. You can add logging rules to your firewall configuration to ensure that dropped packets are logged to a file that you can monitor.

The prompt we provided looks a whole lot like a post on a SUSE forum, and the result gives a highly useful start. From here, the conversation could be continued by asking how to gather more details about the specific firewall configuration or how to add logging rules to the firewall.

Troubleshooting network problems on Linux can be daunting, but AI can simplify the process, especially for administrators who have a multitude of servers to manage.

## 9.3 *Multiserver administration*

Running tasks against multiple servers at once is a common practice for IT admins. One such task is ensuring that all Linux servers are running compatible kernel versions. Typically, this involves logging in to each server and executing commands to verify the kernel version. This can be both time-consuming and prone to errors.

The next example shows how ChatGPT can be used to create a shell script that automates the process of checking kernel versions across a server list. This script can be customized easily to perform tasks on multiple servers, such as updating software packages, monitoring disk usage, or overseeing system performance.

Act as a senior Linux system administrator, adept in bash programming. We are going to work together to write a shell script that we can use to read a list of servers from a file. The script will iterate through the servers in the list and issue a command on each server, storing the results from that server in an output file. The management server the script will run from has key pairs, so no password will be required. I would like the command to check the current kernel version. I would like to set an expected kernel version and have the script tell me if the kernel is lower, equal, or higher.

Certainly! We'll create a bash script to read server names or IP addresses from a file, execute a command on each server, and save the output to an output file. We'll use `uname -r` to get the kernel version of the remote server, and then compare it with a predefined expected kernel version. The script will output whether the kernel version on each server is lower, equal, or higher than the expected version:

```
#!/bin/bash

# Define the file containing the list of servers
SERVER_LIST='servers.txt'

# Expected kernel version
EXPECTED_KERNEL_VERSION='4.18.0-513.5.1.el8_9'
```

```bash
# Output file where results will be stored
OUTPUT_FILE='kernel_check_results.txt'

# Function to compare kernel versions
# Returns 0 if equal, 1 if first is higher, 2 if second is higher
compare_kernel_versions() {
    # Using sort with version sort and tail to get the highest version
    higher_version=$(echo -e "$1\n$2" | sort -V | tail -1)
    if [ "$higher_version" == "$1" ] && [ "$higher_version" != "$2" ];
    then
        return 1 # First is higher
    elif [ "$higher_version" != "$1" ] && [ "$higher_version" == "$2" ];
    then
        return 2 # Second is higher
    else
        return 0 # Versions are equal
    fi
}

# Check if the SERVER_LIST file exists
if [ ! -f "$SERVER_LIST" ]; then
    echo "Server list file $SERVER_LIST not found."
    exit 1
fi

# Empty or create the output file
> "$OUTPUT_FILE"

# Read each line in SERVER_LIST as a server address
while IFS= read -r server; do
    echo "Processing $server..."
    # Get the kernel version of the server
    server_kernel_version=$(ssh -o BatchMode=yes -o ConnectTimeout=5
    "$server" 'uname -r')

    # Compare the server's kernel version with the expected version
    compare_kernel_versions "$server_kernel_version"
    "$EXPECTED_KERNEL_VERSION"
    comparison_result=$?
    # Append comparison result to the output file
    case $comparison_result in
        0) echo "$server: Kernel version is equal to the expected (
            $EXPECTED_KERNEL_VERSION)." >> "$OUTPUT_FILE";;
        1) echo "$server: Kernel version is higher than expected (
            $server_kernel_version > $EXPECTED_KERNEL_VERSION)." >>
            "$OUTPUT_FILE";;
        2) echo "$server: Kernel version is lower than expected (
            $server_kernel_version < $EXPECTED_KERNEL_VERSION)." >>
            "$OUTPUT_FILE";;
    esac
done < "$SERVER_LIST"

echo "Script execution completed. Check $OUTPUT_FILE for results."
```

This script introduces a function `compare_kernel_versions` to compare two kernel versions and determine if the first is higher, lower, or equal to the second. It then uses `uname -r` on each server to get its kernel version, compares this version with the expected version using the function, and logs the result (lower, equal, or higher) in the output file.

Ensure the `EXPECTED_KERNEL_VERSION` variable is set to the kernel version you want to compare against, and that your servers.txt file is populated with the server addresses.

Impressive! Chatbots excel in language and coding. Although they are not always 100% perfect (we need to add the expected kernel versions), our general experience with coding has been that ChatGPT can get you 80% to 90% of the way sometimes, and that's a huge time saver. It's also a great way to learn new things, as you can see how the script is written and then modify it to suit your needs.

In this prompt, we decided to go with the "Act as" approach. It may not have been required, but one of the interesting things about chatbots is that they train on human interactions. There are claims across the internet about how to make a chatbot "try harder." One claim we've heard is that if you ask a chatbot to "please" do something, it may not try as hard because you're giving it the option of doing what you are asking. We've also heard that if you offer it money, threaten it, or say that it's a life-or-death situation, it may give better results. Our own tests have shown that some of these suggestions work sometimes; other times, they don't. It's not a perfect science, but we've found that the "Act as" approach works pretty consistently after testing for this chapter.

So why did we ask it to "Act as a senior Linux administrator, adept in bash programming"? It's simply an attempt to get the chatbot into the mindset of a person who would be good at this task. Offering to work together on the task also might motivate the chatbot. And this sets the stage for us to make modifications to the script by suggesting changes if necessary. Over a few iterations, we hope to get exactly the script we want.

Next, we'll simplify our approach to see how the chatbot performs with minimal guidance. Unlike the detailed "Act as" strategy, this time we present a straightforward request.

 Write a bash shell script to iterate through a list of servers and identify the kernel version on the servers. Report back to an output file if the kernel is lower, equal, or higher than the version we want.

 To create a bash shell script that iterates through a list of servers and checks their kernel versions against a specified version, you can follow these steps. This script will connect to each server using SSH, check the kernel version, and then compare it to the desired version. The results will be saved in an output file.

First, make sure you have SSH access to all the servers without needing to enter a password each time, which can be set up using SSH keys.

```
#!/bin/bash

# List of servers (replace with actual server IPs or hostnames)
servers=("server1" "server2" "server3")
```

```
# Desired kernel version for comparison
desired_version="5.4.0"

# Output file for the results
output_file="kernel_version_report.txt"

# Function to compare kernel versions
compare_versions() {
    if [ "$1" = "$2" ]; then
        echo "equal"
    elif [[ "$1" > "$2" ]]; then
        echo "higher"
    else
        echo "lower"
    fi
}

# Clear the output file
> "$output_file"

# Iterate through the list of servers
for server in "${servers[@]}"; do
    echo "Checking server: $server"

    # Retrieve the kernel version from the server
    kernel_version=$(ssh "$server" 'uname -r')

    # Compare the retrieved kernel version with the desired version
    comparison_result=$(compare_versions "$kernel_version"
    ↪"$desired_version")
    # Append the result to the output file
    echo "$server: Kernel version $kernel_version is $comparison_result
    ↪than desired version $desired_version" >> "$output_file"
done

echo "Check completed. Results are saved in $output_file."
```

Save this script in a file, for example, `check_kernel_versions.sh`. Make it executable with the command `chmodx check_kernel_versions.sh`, and then run it with `./check_kernel_versions.sh`.

This script defines a list of servers, the desired kernel version, and an output file. It includes a function `compare_versions` to compare kernel versions. It iterates over the list of servers, retrieves the current kernel version using `uname -r`, compares it to the desired version, and writes the result to the output file. Make sure to replace the placeholder server names with your actual server addresses and adjust the desired kernel version as needed.

Whoa! That's a much lazier response. It seems that our experiment revealed a clear lesson: the detail and complexity of your prompt directly influence the chatbot's response. In a side-by-side comparison, the more straightforward, "lazier" prompt resulted in a less sophisticated script. Specifically, this simpler approach led to the script hardcoding server names into an array instead of dynamically reading them from a list, and it skipped using the `sort` command to compare kernel versions. Although functional, the script lacks the finesse of the response to our initial more-detailed request.

Our tests show that giving chatbots clear, detailed instructions and specific roles (like "Act as a senior Linux administrator…") leads to much better results. Being polite isn't necessary, but precise and thorough requests produce the best outcomes. Just as Joe's example showed, a well-crafted prompt helps the chatbot generate more accurate and useful responses. We recommend including plenty of context and details in your prompts to help the chatbot better understand and handle your tasks.

## 9.4  Renaming files

As we were writing this book, we realized that we needed to reorder the chapters. With that came the requirement to rename not only the .adoc files but also images. (We even needed to modify content but left that to find/replace in VS Code because it was straightforward.)

Sometimes you just want a script to do something so you don't have to. Maybe you'll never need to do the task again because it is very specific. In this example, we knew we needed to rename files and folders, but writing something to do so would take more time than doing it by hand. We decided to ask the AI in plain English, which is destined to become the next big programming language according to many people, including Nvidia CEO Jensen Huang:

> *The next big programming language is the human language*
>
> —Jensen Huang

What we appreciate about the following prompt is that it turned our requirements, written in English, into commands, written in PowerShell. And it worked the very first time.

I'm on macOS using PowerShell. I am in the "book" directory. I have two subfolders: one named images and one named manuscript. I need to do some renaming to align with a new table of contents.

Inside manuscript, there are files named like chapter01.adoc chapter11.adoc. it goes 01-16 but these are the only chapters that have been written so far: 1, 2, 3, 4, 6, 7, 8, 9, 12, 15, 16.

Inside the images folder, I have folders like ch01 and ch16. Inside of those are files named CH16_F01_LeMaire.png and CH01_F01_LeMaire.png, CH01_F02_LeMaire.png

Chapter 7 is now Chapter 13 Chapter 8 is now Chapter 17 Chapter 9 is now 7 Chapter 12 is now 10 Chapter 15 is now 14 Chapter 16 is now 15

Rename files in the subfolders, keeping in mind that some files may need a temporary placeholder name to avoid conflicts.

Please give me the commands all in one block

Given your renaming requirements and the potential conflict with existing
chapter numbers, the process will involve using placeholder names to
avoid overwriting files during the renaming process.

First, we'll rename the files in the manuscript folder. We'll use a
temporary placeholder name to avoid conflicts. Then we'll rename the
files in the images folder.

```
# Switch to manuscript directory and rename chapters
cd ./manuscript
Rename-Item -Path chapter07.adoc -NewName temp13.adoc
Rename-Item -Path chapter09.adoc -NewName temp07.adoc
Rename-Item -Path chapter12.adoc -NewName temp10.adoc
...
Rename-Item -Path temp07.adoc -NewName chapter07.adoc
Rename-Item -Path temp10.adoc -NewName chapter10.adoc
Rename-Item -Path temp13.adoc -NewName chapter13.adoc

# Switch to images directory and rename image folders
cd ../images
```

```
Rename-Item -Path ch07 -NewName temp13
Rename-Item -Path ch08 -NewName temp17
Rename-Item -Path ch09 -NewName temp07
...
Rename-Item -Path temp07 -NewName ch07
Rename-Item -Path temp10 -NewName ch10
Rename-Item -Path temp13 -NewName ch13

# Renaming image files within each folder
Get-ChildItem -Path ./ch07/*.png |
Rename-Item -NewName { $_.Name -replace 'CH09', 'CH07' }
Get-ChildItem -Path ./ch10/*.png |
Rename-Item -NewName { $_.Name -replace 'CH12', 'CH10' }
Get-ChildItem -Path ./ch13/*.png |
Rename-Item -NewName { $_.Name -replace 'CH07', 'CH13' }
...
```

It's not the fanciest PowerShell code. It doesn't use hashtables and loops, but we just needed it to work, and it did. In this way, it's as efficient as can be. This reminds us of a quote Chrissy shares all the time:

> *C# is about optimizing computer resources. PowerShell is about optimizing human resources.*
>
> —Jeffrey Snover

Generative AI follows a similar pattern—it helps IT teams work more efficiently by simplifying common tasks.

Building on our PowerShell wins, let's examine another universal IT challenge: making sense of log files. Our next example demonstrates how ChatGPT can assist with log analysis and spot potential problems.

**TIP** Check out the appendix for local models and structured outputs. These can work together to intelligently rename files by analyzing patterns—such as by standardizing log file names across servers or organizing documents based on context rather than just explicit renaming rules. See https://gptmaker.dev/book/rename for Chrissy's blog post on this topic.

## 9.5 Analyzing error logs: Identifying exceptions and failures

Going through log files for errors and problems is usually a tedious and draining task. Typically, it requires a considerable amount of effort to find the specific messages that give a clear understanding of the actual problems.

Chatbots like ChatGPT make log analysis much easier. Simply upload your log file, and ChatGPT scans the data to highlight errors and find root causes. You spend less time digging through logs and more time fixing the actual problems while finding problems more accurately.

**WARNING** When uploading error logs from systems like SharePoint, protect your data carefully. Use an enterprise chat provider with data protection features if possible. Otherwise, remove sensitive information like IP addresses, hostnames, and usernames before sharing.

Let's look at a SharePoint log example. We picked SharePoint because we've used ChatGPT this way ourselves, most recently during an upgrade that hit problems. But ChatGPT works well with logs from any system, as it can spot errors and suggest fixes regardless of the source.

Read the uploaded SharePoint log file and extract all lines containing error, exception, failure, or fatal messages. Then tell me what went wrong.

Based on the search results from the SharePoint log file, the following issues were found:

1 An exception of type **Microsoft. SharePoint. PostSetupConfiguration. PostSetupConfiguration TaskException** was thrown because the specified user **sharepointse\sharepoint** is a local account. The log indicates that local accounts should only be used in stand-alone mode.

2 Task **configdb validation** threw an exception related to the above issue with the local account.

3 The form **CreateConfigurationDbForm** did not pass validation, which is likely a result of the issue with the local account being used in a non-stand-alone mode.

These messages suggest that the configuration process was expecting a domain user account instead of a local user account for the operation it was trying to complete, which is not supported outside of a stand-alone SharePoint installation.

To address this:

1 Verify your SharePoint configuration, specifically the database and account setups.

2 If your SharePoint instance isn't set up as standalone, switch from using a local account to a suitable alternative for configuration tasks.

ChatGPT surprised us by going beyond just finding critical problems in the log file. Without being asked, it provided fix steps after explaining what went wrong, which was exactly what we needed.

Want to try this yourself? You can download the same 1.8MB SharePoint log file we used at https://gptmaker.dev/book/splog and test our prompt. Even without SharePoint expertise, you'll see how ChatGPT breaks down complex problems and their solutions.

This shows how AI changes the game for system administrators. Instead of spending hours combing through logs, we can quickly pinpoint and understand problems, leaving more time to actually fix them.

## 9.6 Automating tasks for efficiency and compliance

System engineers love building automation and designing networks but often groan at the thought of following Information Technology Infrastructure Library (ITIL) practices. The ITIL Framework outlines recommended ways to deliver IT services. When companies adopt ITIL, IT teams need to weave these practices into their daily work.

Table 9.1 shows some prompts that make it easier to blend frameworks and best practices into your work. We'll focus on ways to keep your automation running while meeting new standards.

Table 9.1 Systems engineering task prompts

| Task | Prompt |
| --- | --- |
| Business process integration | I need help integrating ITIL into our Windows systems team's daily work. Could you help me set up ITIL-based incident, problem, and change management processes? Please focus on practical steps for a Windows environment. Ask me anything you need to know about our current setup. |
| Network configuration generator | Write a network config script to set up [a VLAN network] in vSphere. Include [VLAN IDs, IP schemes, subnetting, gateway setup, and security]. The script needs to match our network standards and security rules. I've attached our current network requirements - let me know if you need any details clarified. |
| Troubleshoot container orchestration problems | List the key diagnostic commands for fixing common Kubernetes problems like pod failures, service discovery issues, and resource limits. Make the steps clear enough for junior admins, focusing on using kubectl for diagnosis and fixes. |
| System update planner | Create a step-by-step plan for [updating our server farm]. Cover [update order, backups, testing, and rollback steps]. The plan should keep downtime low and follow our IT standards and risk policies. |
| Kerberos Troubleshooter | Help me build a troubleshooting guide for fixing random Kerberos auth issues, focusing on "KRB_AP_ERR_MODIFIED" errors. Include steps to [check clock sync, review service principal names, and examine TGT lifetimes]. Give clear starting points and expected results that follow Kerberos best practices. |

These AI prompts not only simplify complex tasks but also open the door to a future where AI's role in systems engineering evolves to handle more sophisticated challenges.

## 9.7 Auditing configuration files with AI

Now we'll explore how ChatGPT can audit and optimize configuration files, including those from operating systems and applications. By using AI to analyze these files, sysadmins can easily identify potential problems, ensure compliance with best practices and industry standards, and generate optimized configurations.

Let's take a look at a specific example of using ChatGPT to perform a compliance check on an Internet Information Services (IIS) web server's applicationHost.config file against the Payment Card Industry Data Security Standard (PCI-DSS).

Review the provided applicationHost.config file for compliance with the PCI-DSS. Identify any configurations that are not compliant and provide recommendations for achieving compliance. Generate a new file named 'applicationHost_PCI_compliant.config' that includes the necessary changes to meet PCI-DSS standards.

Given the file's size and complexity, along with PCI-DSS's comprehensive requirements, I'll focus on common areas in `applicationHost.config` that typically require attention for PCI-DSS compliance. These include:

1. **SSL/TLS Settings**: Ensuring only secure protocols and ciphers are enabled.
2. **Authentication and Authorization**: Verifying that secure authentication methods are used and permissions are correctly set.
3. **Logging and Monitoring**: Confirming that appropriate logging is enabled for security-related events.
4. **Application Isolation**: Making sure applications are adequately isolated in their own application pools for security. ... Given these findings, the next step is to generate a new `applicationHost.config` file that incorporates the necessary changes for compliance. This will include:

- Enforcing TLS 1.2 or higher for all SSL/TLS communications.
- Verifying or adjusting authentication methods for security.
- Ensuring logging configurations are adequate and secure.
- Configuring separate application pools for application isolation.

...

This file includes enhancements for SSL/TLS settings and application pool isolation to comply with PCI-DSS requirements. Please review the specific implementations and adjust them further as needed for your environment, especially regarding authentication methods and logging configurations.

This prompt is effective because it clearly states the objective of reviewing the applicationHost.config file for PCI-DSS compliance, provides specific instructions on identifying noncompliant configurations and generating a new compliant file, uses a clear naming convention, references domain-specific knowledge, and requests an actionable output. These all work together to guide the AI in effectively completing the task and delivering a useful result.

AI can help audit IIS configurations against industry standards, best practices, and organizational requirements, beyond just PCI-DSS compliance. Table 9.2 shows useful prompts for different types of IIS configuration audits.

Table 9.2 IIS configuration audit prompts

| Task | Prompt |
| --- | --- |
| Best practices review | Please review this applicationHost.config file and identify any deviations from IIS best practices. Provide recommendations for improving the configuration to align with industry standards. For each recommended change, show the exact modifications needed in the configuration file. |
| Security audit | Analyze the applicationHost.config file for potential security risks or misconfigurations. Look for settings that may expose the web server to vulnerabilities or attacks. Suggest changes to enhance the security posture of the IIS server. |
| Performance optimization | Examine the applicationHost.config file and identify any settings that may impact the performance of the IIS web server. Provide suggestions for optimizing the configuration to improve responsiveness, resource utilization, and overall efficiency. |
| Compliance check | Review the applicationHost.config file against our organization's specific compliance requirements (e.g., HIPAA, PCI-DSS). Identify any settings that do not meet the required standards and provide recommendations for achieving compliance. |

You can use ChatGPT to audit many other types of configuration files too:

- Windows Registry files (.reg)
- Active Directory Group Policy files
- Apache or Nginx web server configurations (httpd.conf, nginx.conf)
- Linux system configurations (sshd_config, fstab)
- Docker and Kubernetes files (docker-compose.yml, deployment.yaml)

To audit any configuration file, upload it to ChatGPT with a clear prompt stating what you need, whether that's a compliance check, security review, or performance analysis. ChatGPT will analyze the file and give you specific recommendations and the exact changes needed.

## 9.8 Existing AI in systems engineering

AI tools are already being integrated into common IT software through APIs and GPT Actions. GPT Actions, released in November 2023, lets AI models perform specific tasks like getting database information or starting application processes. Other AI companies are likely to add similar features soon.

Here are some advanced AI applications available now:

- *Predictive system failure analysis*—AI models trained on system performance history can spot potential failures before they happen, which helps prevent unexpected downtime. IBM Watson AIOps and Splunk Machine Learning Toolkit already do this kind of predictive maintenance.

- *Advanced disaster recovery planning*—AI analyzes threat patterns and past disruptions to create detailed recovery plans that update automatically as conditions change. HPE Zerto and Datto are using AI to improve their disaster recovery solutions.
- *Enhanced network design*—AI can test different network setups and see how they perform under various conditions, helping engineers build efficient, reliable networks. Cisco Catalyst Center (formerly DNA Center) and Juniper Networks' NorthStar Controller already use AI for network optimization.

The future of AI in systems engineering looks promising. As AI technology advances, it will do more than just handle routine tasks—it will bring new ways of working that we haven't even thought of yet.

Next up is chapter 10 on database administration and development. We'll look at how AI makes database work more efficient, covering everything from performance tuning and maintenance to schema design.

## 9.9 Prompts used in this chapter

- That's the result I was looking for. It took a few prompts to get there, however. How can I best ask in order to repeat this result in one shot?
- That was great output. I'd like to copy it to an asciidoc file. Can you repeat in asciidoc format?
- What other foundational things can vary in distros besides the use of System V or systemd?
- Does the table's intro line up with the actual table contents?
- What commercial products are available for disaster recovery that integrate AI

## Summary

- AI tools like ChatGPT are changing how system administrators work, speeding up tasks such as creating change requests, working with Linux systems, renaming files, and analyzing logs.
- A systems engineer's hands-on work with ChatGPT v4 shows how AI significantly improves daily workflows.
- AI can write scripts to automate work like checking kernel versions and renaming files across servers. It's particularly good at finding problems in complex log files by spotting errors and failures.
- AI helps check configuration files, including IIS applicationHost.config, to ensure that they follow industry standards, security practices, and performance guidelines.
- Current AI systems in systems engineering, such as tools that predict system failures and plan for disasters, are already making big improvements, with more advances coming soon.

# Database administration and development

**This chapter covers**

- Utilizing AI in DBA tasks
- Basics of query and object creation
- Techniques in query optimization
- Managing heterogeneous database environments
- Strategies for database maintenance and advanced admin tasks

In the database administration field, there are two main roles: administrative DBAs, who ensure the database's smooth and secure operation, and development DBAs, who design the database structure and optimize application performance. The overlap between these roles varies, with some DBAs specializing in one area and others integrating skills from both. AI tools have made it easier to bridge the gap between these tasks, assisting in generating SQL syntax and guiding administrative tasks no matter the DBA's primary focus.

Whether you are new to DBA work or a skilled pro, we'll show you how AI can provide multiple benefits in your daily work. We'll start with the basics of query and object creation and then move on to query optimization, managing heterogeneous database environments, and advanced administration tasks. We'll also cover how AI can assist in ensuring the recoverability and performance of your database environment, with a special focus on using PowerShell for automation and data collection.

## 10.1 Query and object creation basics

Ever mixed up INSERT INTO and SELECT INTO syntax, or puzzled over DBSM_STATS parameters? Maybe you've tried to capture a procedure's output into a table variable. In the past, you'd have to search blogs and documentation for examples and code snippets. These often provide generic samples that need further customization for specific scenarios. Now chatbots can generate the exact code you need, based on your unique requirements.

As you read this chapter, consider what you want from the chatbot. Do you want a list of best practice recommendations or specific queries to audit your environment? Both are useful, but generating reusable code can save you time on various tasks. Chatbots are great at creating SQL statements, especially for basic queries that don't need detailed prompts.

Consider this scenario: a user reports past database performance problems on a system without historical query monitoring. To investigate, you'll need to query SQL Server Dynamic Management Views (DMVs). A typical approach would be to use a search engine to search for "DMV query metrics" or "DMV stored procedure metrics." With AI, you can ask for this information directly or request a complete solution right in the chat. For example, instead of just identifying the relevant DMV, you can ask the chatbot to generate a SELECT statement to identify the worst-performing stored procedures in your database.

 Write a select statement to query the worst-performing stored procedures in my database.

 Certainly! To identify the worst-performing stored procedures in your SQL Server database, you can query the sys.dm_exec_procedure_stats Dynamic Management View (DMV). This DMV provides performance statistics for cached stored procedures.

The following SQL query retrieves the top 10 worst-performing stored procedures based on the total elapsed time. The query also provides information like database name, object name, and execution count for further analysis.

```sql
-- Top 10 worst-performing stored procedures based on total elapsed time
SELECT TOP 10
    DB_NAME(ps.database_id) AS DatabaseName,
    OBJECT_NAME(ps.[object_id], ps.database_id) AS StoredProcedure,
    ps.execution_count AS ExecutionCount,
    -- Avg elapsed time in microseconds
    ps.total_elapsed_time / ps.execution_count AS AvgElapsedTime,
    -- Avg CPU time in microseconds
    ps.total_worker_time / ps.execution_count AS AvgCPU,
    -- Avg logical reads
```

```
      ps.total_logical_reads / ps.execution_count AS AvgReads
FROM sys.dm_exec_procedure_stats AS ps
ORDER BY ps.total_elapsed_time / ps.execution_count DESC;
```

This query sorts the stored procedures by their average elapsed time in descending order, thereby showing the worst performers at the top.

Please note that the statistics are only for stored procedures that are currently in the cache. The statistics might not include every stored procedure if some have been removed from the cache. Also, you'll need VIEW SERVER STATE permission to query this DMV.

With a straightforward prompt, we achieved excellent and relevant results from the chatbot, which efficiently identified the necessary DMV without us specifying its name or providing it in our request. The chatbot not only pinpointed the correct DMV but also crafted a comprehensive query against it, complete with calculations, informative comments, and the appropriate ORDER BY clause. This process contrasts sharply with the pre-chatbot era, where you would spend additional time analyzing the available fields, data types, units, and calculations. The response even indicates the permissions required to view the DMV and a note about the DMV's limitations, which is a nice touch.

> **TIP** In your prompt, ask the chatbot to convert default units like bytes or microseconds into more user-friendly measurements, such as megabytes or milliseconds, to enhance the utility and readability of the data.

We now highlight a set of prompts to illustrate AI's ease in generating SQL Server T-SQL queries and database object data description language (DDL). If you prefer to create SQL code for Oracle, MySQL, PostgreSQL, or any other database platform, modify the prompt accordingly. Table 10.1 lists these prompts and summarizes the responses we were able to achieve. We urge you to try these examples hands-on. If you've recently written a query, see if you can accurately instruct the chatbot to recreate it. Does it take less effort with AI?

Table 10.1  Query and object creation prompts

| Task | Prompt | Response summary |
|---|---|---|
| Query creation | Write a T-SQL query to list all tables in my database with a column named [SSN]. Then provide a SELECT statement that would redact the value of the [SSN] column. | A SELECT statement is written to query INFORMATION_SCHEMA.COLUMNS for matching column names. The database, schema, and table names are included columns. A SELECT statement is also created that uses the STUFF function to redact the first five digits of the Social Security number, leaving the last four digits visible. |

**Table 10.1  Query and object creation prompts** *(continued)*

| Task | Prompt | Response summary |
|---|---|---|
| Table creation | I am being asked by a developer to create a new SQL Server database table named [Users] that will hold login information for application users. Please design a suitable table and provide the Create Table statement. | A `CREATE TABLE` statement is crafted, consisting of `UserID`, `Username`, `Email`, `PasswordHash`, and other relevant information useful for auditing the user account. |
| Procedure creation | Create a T-SQL stored procedure to rebuild fragmented indexes on database tables. Include input parameters that are helpful to allow the procedure to target only specific tables and indexes that need to be rebuilt. | A `CREATE PROCEDURE` statement is provided that accepts the database name, minimum page count and fragmentation levels, and table and index name pattern inputs. It also provides an example of how to call the procedure. |
| Trigger creation | Create a SQL Server trigger that will send an email whenever a new database is restored or created. | The chatbot first provides a link to configuring database mail as a prerequisite. It then writes a `CREATE TRIGGER` statement for a server-level trigger, which fires on the `CREATE` and `RESTORE` commands. The database name and create date are added to an email message and sent using `sp_send_dbmail`. |
| Function creation | Create a SQL Server scalar function that takes a date of birth as an input parameter and returns the age of a person in years. The function should handle leap years and should return an integer. Provide example usage of the function. | A new function is created that uses the `DATEDIFF` function to calculate an age, accounting for leap years. If the person's birthday has not yet passed, it subtracts 1 year from the result. |

The prompts in table 10.1 demonstrate the AI's versatility in generating SQL queries and database objects that are carefully engineered to be clear, concise, and specific to the task at hand. This ensures that the chatbot understands the context and can generate the most accurate and useful code. As you experiment with these prompts, you'll gain insights into how to best phrase your requests.

In the table-creation prompt, we tackled a database development task, asking the chatbot for the `CREATE TABLE` code and also to determine the table's structure. We briefly explained that the table would hold login information for application users and that we needed something suitable. The chatbot determined independently that we would need columns for `UserID`, `Username`, `Email`, and `PasswordHash`. Not only were the columns relevant, but the chatbot took security into account with the `PasswordHash` field, directing the user away from storing passwords in plain text. The chatbot also suggested a `LastLogin` field to use for auditing purposes.

## 10.2 Query optimization

Query optimization can be a grueling task for both administrative and development DBAs. It's often overlooked or misunderstood, much like proper error handling. This makes it an ideal area for AI assistance.

Chatbots can do more than just create and analyze query syntax. They can also analyze execution plans. The chatbot can suggest improvements for a given query, pinpoint bottlenecks, and explain why the changes could be beneficial. The revised query will still need to be validated for performance and accuracy, but you can handle these suggestions and code rewrites in minutes.

Table 10.2 provides example prompts to demonstrate common optimization tasks. We've included a summary of the output for each prompt. As always, we encourage you to experiment with these prompts to see how the chatbot responds to different scenarios.

Table 10.2 Query optimization prompts

| Task | Prompt | Response summary |
| --- | --- | --- |
| Query performance troubleshooting (part 1) | I have a query that is performing poorly in my database. I will first provide the query, followed by the execution plan. Do not respond until you have been provided both. Analyze the data and make suggestions on how to boost performance. Provide an optimized query incorporating the recommendations.<br>Here is the query<br>[Query SQL] | The chatbot accepts the initial prompt and query. As instructed, it waits for the execution plan to be provided. |
| Query performance troubleshooting (part 2) | Here is the execution plan<br>[Execution plan] | The chatbot waits for all necessary information and then analyzes the query and execution plan. The chatbot identifies the complexity of the query and several bottlenecks in the execution plan. The chatbot recommends removing unnecessary joins, using indexes, avoiding functions affecting index usage, avoiding sorting, and using IN with subqueries. An optimized query is provided for testing. |
| Index suggestions | Analyze this query and make suggestions on which fields should have indexes. [Query SQL] | The chatbot analyzes the query's JOIN and WHERE clauses to make suggestions about which fields should be indexed. |

**Table 10.2  Query optimization prompts** *(continued)*

| Task | Prompt | Response summary |
|---|---|---|
| Code review | I was asked to perform a code review on a new SQL statement. Analyze the statement, looking for any opportunities to improve the query, possible logic errors and security concerns. If you identify any issues, please provide constructive feedback on why the changes should be implemented. I have also provided a list of requirements my team has established as standard practice.<br>1. Avoid table variables<br>2. *Include* SET NOCOUNT ON<br>[Continued list of standards]<br>[Query SQL] | The query is analyzed as requested, and recommendations are made regarding readability and maintainability, performance, logic, security, and clarity. Most notably, the JOIN syntax is validated, index recommendations are made, and custom functions are identified. The security considerations (SQL injection attacks and hardcoded values) are discussed. If query code violates the list of standards, those items are denoted. |

The prompts in table 10.2 are specific and inform the chatbot of additional information that will be provided, such as queries and execution plans. Notice that we broke up the query performance troubleshooting task into two parts.

> **TIP** When providing a large amount of information or complex instructions to the chatbot, it can be confusing to keep all the information straight. Attaching information, such as an execution plan, in a text file can be a great way to stay organized, but you'll need to use a chatbot that supports file uploads. If you don't have access to one, telling the chatbot to wait for more information before responding is the next best thing. There's nothing worse than having the chatbot drone on and on about a topic when you haven't provided all the information yet. Luckily, you can always click the Stop button to halt the chatbot's response. This is also handy if you realize the response isn't going in the direction you want.

To improve the quality of responses when creating queries or troubleshooting performance problems, provide additional information that is useful for the task, such as the table schema, existing indexes, and query plans. Be sure to properly identify the information you are providing so the chatbot can evaluate it appropriately.

Prioritizing multiple tasks, indicating the expected output format, and providing code examples can fine-tune the response further. For example, if you are looking for a specific type of index, such as a filtered index, or a specific type of query, such as one using a common table expression (CTE), ask for it directly.

> **WARNING** The potential for chatbots to assist with query optimization is very promising and will continue to improve. We encourage you to push the limits but also caution you to validate the query. Chatbots are not always right! Always test the query before implementing it in a production environment.

Next, we will look in depth at the ability of a chatbot to document SQL statements. This is a task that is often overlooked but is a must in any development environment to ensure that the code is easy to maintain and understand.

## 10.3 Code documentation

In this example, we will revisit our previous query example to find the worst-performing stored procedures in a SQL Server database. We will ask ChatGPT to document the query, including the purpose of the query, the expected output format, and any assumptions made. We will also ask the chatbot to include a few examples of how the query should be used. The response can be used to generate a document or Wiki article without the need for additional editing.

 I have a SQL statement that I need to document. Add comments to the code to document the functionality. Then, provide a detailed explanation of the query, including the purpose of the query, the expected output format, and any assumptions made. Please also include a few examples of how the query should be used.

```
SELECT TOP 10
    DB_NAME(ps.database_id) AS DatabaseName,
    OBJECT_NAME(ps.[object_id], ps.database_id) AS StoredProcedure,
    ps.execution_count AS ExecutionCount,
    ps.total_elapsed_time / ps.execution_count AS AvgElapsedTime,
    ps.total_worker_time / ps.execution_count AS AvgCPU,
    ps.total_logical_reads / ps.execution_count AS AvgReads
FROM sys.dm_exec_procedure_stats AS ps
ORDER BY ps.total_elapsed_time / ps.execution_count DESC;
```

 This SQL query is designed to analyze the performance of stored procedures in a SQL Server database. It provides insights into how often each stored procedure is executed, as well as the average time taken, CPU time used, and logical reads performed per execution. Such information is crucial for database performance tuning and identifying potential bottlenecks. Below is the commented version of the query:

```
-- Select the top 10 stored procedures based on average execution time
SELECT TOP 10
    -- Get the name of the database where the stored procedure exists
    DB_NAME(ps.database_id) AS DatabaseName,

    -- Get the name of the stored procedure
    OBJECT_NAME(ps.[object_id], ps.database_id) AS StoredProcedure,
    -- Count how many times the stored procedure has been executed
    ps.execution_count AS ExecutionCount,

    --
    Calculate the average execution time (in milliseconds) per execution
    ps.total_elapsed_time / ps.execution_count AS AvgElapsedTime,

    --
    Calculate the average CPU time (in milliseconds) used per execution
    ps.total_worker_time / ps.execution_count AS AvgCPU,

    -- Calculate the average number of logical reads per execution
    ps.total_logical_reads / ps.execution_count AS AvgReads
```

```
-- Specify the source of the data, which is the sys.dm_exec_procedure_stats
    dynamic management view
FROM sys.dm_exec_procedure_stats AS ps

-- Order the results by the average execution time in descending order,
    so the most time-consuming procedures come first
ORDER BY ps.total_elapsed_time / ps.execution_count DESC;
```

**Purpose of the Query:**

The main purpose of this query is to identify the top 10 stored procedures that, on average, take the longest time to execute. This is useful for database administrators and developers to pinpoint inefficient stored procedures that may need optimization to improve the overall performance of the database.

**Expected Output Format:**

The query outputs a table with the following columns:

`DatabaseName`: Name of the database where the stored procedure is located.

`StoredProcedure`: Name of the stored procedure.

`ExecutionCount`: Number of times the stored procedure has been executed since the last SQL Server service restart.

`AvgElapsedTime`: Average execution time of the stored procedure, in milliseconds.

`AvgCPU`: Average CPU time consumed by the stored procedure, in milliseconds.

`AvgReads`: Average number of logical reads performed by the stored procedure.

**Assumptions Made:**

- The query assumes that the `sys.dm_exec_procedure_stats` dynamic management view contains accurate and up-to-date information about the execution of stored procedures. This view is reset when the SQL Server service is restarted.
- It assumes that average execution time is a good indicator of stored procedure performance. However, in some cases, procedures with high variability in execution times might need a different approach for analysis.

**Examples of Usage:**

**Performance Tuning**: Database administrators can use this query to identify stored procedures that are potentially slowing down the database. By focusing on these top 10 procedures, they can investigate further and optimize the code or the database design.

**Regular Maintenance**: This query can be part of regular database health checks to monitor and maintain the efficiency of stored procedures over time.

**Capacity Planning**: Understanding which procedures consume the most resources can help in planning for future database scaling or hardware upgrades.

The resulting documentation of the SQL query is impressive! Not only are the comments accurate for every line of the code, but the explanation of the query's purpose, expected output format, and assumptions made is thorough and well-structured. The examples of usage are also relevant and provide a clear understanding of how the query should be used in different scenarios. The information provided by ChatGPT can be copied and pasted right into our documentation, saving us a lot of time and effort.

In the next section, we explore how AI can assist in translating concepts and syntax across various database technologies.

## 10.4 Heterogeneous database environments

DBAs often juggle multiple database platforms despite having a preference for one. Although these platforms vary greatly, they share commonalities. An AI chatbot can act as a teacher and translator, equating existing skills and syntactic knowledge across platforms.

In this section, we'll explore how AI aids in managing multiple database platforms, focusing on training, data types, and syntax. You can use an AI chatbot as a learning tool to quiz you interactively, provide analogies, and convert SQL syntax between platforms.

### 10.4.1 Staying up to date

Keeping pace with database technology demands dedication. Each new version of a database engine introduces fresh features and retires old ones. Chatbots can assist in pinpointing these changes and support continuous learning. These aren't complex concepts, but tracking changes across software versions often gets sidelined, and deciphering elusive licensing requirements can be tricky.

Consider these simple prompt ideas to stay informed about updates and licensing stipulations:

- What are the new features in SQL Server 2022?
- Is Software Assurance necessary for my SQL Server licenses?
- How does the licensing for Oracle 23ai differ from Oracle 19c?
- Does compression on a data pump export require Advanced Compression licenses?

For more challenging concepts, ask the chatbot to clarify them using everyday analogies. This method aids in understanding by connecting tough concepts to familiar ones, enhancing retention.

In this example, we write a meta-prompt (discussed in chapter 4) using lay terms to simplify the explanation of SQL Server transaction logs.

 What is a SQL Server transaction log?

 Think of a SQL Server transaction log as a detailed diary that the database keeps. Every time you do something in the database, like adding new information or changing existing data, the transaction log writes down exactly what was done. This diary is super important because it helps in two main ways:

1 **Undoing Mistakes**: If something goes wrong or if you accidentally delete important data, the database can look back at the diary to undo the changes and bring everything back to how it was.

2 **Recovering From Crashes**: Imagine if your computer suddenly turned off while you were working on something important. Normally, you'd lose your work. But with the transaction log, the database can read the diary to pick up exactly where it left off, making sure nothing is lost.

So, the transaction log is like a safety net, making sure that your data is secure and consistent, no matter what happens.

We defined a meta-prompt by enclosing it in square brackets. "[In lay terms]" is a commonly used meta-prompt, and there are no limits to the prompts you can create. The response was easy to understand, using a diary as an example of why the transaction log file is needed. Not only is this a useful tactic for learning new material yourself, but simplifying responses in this manner can help a DBA explain these concepts to others as well.

Recently, Brandon was tasked with refreshing a test environment with production data for a vendor application, including de-identifying sensitive data. The requester assumed that the DBA team could easily handle this task. To clarify why this wasn't straightforward, Brandon sought ChatGPT's help. The AI likened a DBA to a librarian and the database to a library. The librarian maintains and provides access to the books but doesn't edit their content. Similarly, de-identifying data should be done by those familiar with the data layout and relationships, such as the vendor. The analogy was successful, and the requestor agreed to involve the vendor.

In the next section, we'll focus on using AI as a tutor and translator between platforms.

### 10.4.2 Teaching an old DBA new tricks

Table 10.3 lays out a series of prompts from the perspective of an experienced Microsoft SQL DBA supporting an Oracle database. AI can translate Oracle database concepts to SQL Server, convert data types and DDL from one format to another, and even perform tedious tasks like writing a CREATE TABLE statement from a suboptimal service request.

Table 10.3 Syntax and format conversion prompts

| Task | Prompt | Response summary |
|---|---|---|
| Explain Oracle database concepts to a SQL Server DBA | Act as the instructor of a class on Oracle Databases. I am a SQL Server DBA trying to learn Oracle. Explain the main concepts of Oracle Database and provide a comparison of the concept to its SQL Server equivalent. Focus on administration and what I would need to know to properly administer the database and respond to issues. Compare and contrast archive log management to transaction logs. | The chatbot lists various concepts and provides the SQL Server equivalent. A few of the explanations include "instance" versus "database" definitions, tablespaces versus data files, security, and backup and recovery. A well-formulated comparison of archive logs versus transaction logs is presented, along with practical tips for administration. |

## 10.4 Heterogeneous database environments

**Table 10.3 Syntax and format conversion prompts** *(continued)*

| Task | Prompt | Response summary |
|---|---|---|
| Oracle to SQL Server data type comparison | Create a table of Oracle data types and the SQL Server equivalent. | A table-formatted list is created, comparing each Oracle data type with the SQL Server equivalent. A description of each data type is included. |
| Convert a table to an external table for PolyBase (Advanced Data Analytics mode) | I have attached a text file of Oracle Database `CREATE TABLE` statements. I would like you to convert the statements to SQL Server external tables for use with PolyBase instead. Convert data types for compatibility. For all character data types (such as `CHAR` and `VARCHAR`), specify a collation of `Latin1_General_100_BIN2_UTF8`. Use placeholder values for the data source and locations that I can update later. Provide a link to download the results. | The text file is processed, and all included `CREATE TABLE` statements are refactored as SQL Server external tables. Data types are properly converted to be compatible with SQL Server. |
| Create a table from a spreadsheet | A data analyst has requested a new Oracle table to be created and provided a spreadsheet of each column name and data type. Please convert the list into a `CREATE TABLE` statement that I can execute. [List of column names and data types] | The list of column names and data types is successfully turned into a functional `CREATE TABLE` statement, ready to be executed against the Oracle database, preventing the DBA from having to hand-edit the file. |

In the prompts in table 10.3, we demonstrate a variety of prompt engineering techniques that can be used to get better results quickly. Let's review them:

- We directed the chatbot to act as an instructor. Asking the chatbot to adopt a persona is a useful technique to influence the quality and relevance of the response. It also helps the model "think" about the subject matter in a different way. We provided a list of concepts to focus on, which added constraints to the response.
- We asked the chatbot to provide data in a table format. This is handy for readability and to add structure to data.
- We uploaded a text file of Oracle `CREATE TABLE` statements, which the chatbot converted to SQL Server external tables. Uploading lots of text as a file is a clean way to organize a prompt without overwhelming the text input. Finally, we asked for the results to be provided as a file download link instead of being generated directly in the chat. This is a useful technique when the results are lengthy or contain sensitive information, but file upload and download capabilities may be limited to premium tiers in some AI services.
- We provided a list of column names and data types, which we copied from a spreadsheet that was attached to a service request. The chatbot interpreted the

**186**   CHAPTER 10   *Database administration and development*

delimited data and converted it to a valid `CREATE TABLE` statement that is ready to be executed.

In the next section, we'll explore how AI can assist DBAs of all skill levels in ensuring the recoverability and performance of their database environments.

## 10.5 *Maintenance jobs*

Guaranteeing the recoverability of a database environment is the number-one responsibility of any administrative DBA. In our years as administrative DBAs, we've come across too many databases without proper backups. This is a testament to the resiliency of modern database platforms, but these databases are also ticking time bombs. Smaller organizations often do not have an official DBA on staff; instead, they assign the duties of database installation to system administrators. They may be at risk and not even know it.

Installing a database with default configurations will make it functional, but proper configuration, maintenance, and recoverability are complex tasks. Although a trained DBA is required for the responsible administration of critical database systems, AI can help safeguard these environments, especially for part-time DBAs. We recommend validating your backup and maintenance strategies regularly. If you are a new DBA or just learning a new platform, we've provided a series of prompts to help you get started. Table 10.4 outlines prompts to guide a DBA through the basics of database maintenance.

Table 10.4   Database maintenance prompts

| Task | Prompt | Response summary |
| --- | --- | --- |
| Maintenance suggestions | Which maintenance tasks should I run for SQL Server? | The chatbot provides a comprehensive list of maintenance tasks, including backups, integrity checks, index maintenance, and statistics updates. The output is impressively detailed, touching on monitoring, cleanup tasks, security checks, job scheduling, DR testing and documentation. |
| Oracle maintenance concepts for SQL Server DBAs | I am a SQL Server DBA and administer a few Oracle databases. I hear that Oracle databases do not need to be reindexed like SQL Server databases. Is this true? | The chatbot confirms this as being true because Oracle's B-TREE index structure is less prone to logical fragmentation. It outlines scenarios where rebuilding an index should be considered, along with information on how to check if an index should be rebuilt. |
| Statistics sample rates | Provide a detailed table that outlines the recommended SQL Server statistics sampling methods based on table sizes and scenarios, including the reasons for each recommendation. | A table-formatted list is created, which covers recommendations for different ranges of row counts, tables involved with critical queries, and tables with frequently changing data. |

**Table 10.4  Database maintenance prompts** *(continued)*

| Task | Prompt | Response summary |
|---|---|---|
| Selective maintenance with community tools | Please provide the Ola Hallengren procedure command to update statistics that have not been modified since the last update. | The chatbot provides an overview of the IndexOptimize procedure and an example call:<br>`EXEC dbo.IndexOptimize`<br>`@Databases = 'USER_DATABASES',`<br>`@FragmentationLow = NULL,`<br>`@FragmentationMedium = NULL,`<br>`@FragmentationHigh = NULL,`<br>`@UpdateStatistics = 'ALL',`<br>`@OnlyModifiedStatistics = 'Y'` |
| Oracle backup methodology | I am designing a backup schedule for INC 0, INC 1, INC 2 and archive log backups for my Oracle databases. What is best practice? | A backup schedule is produced for Level 0 (INC 0) weekly backups, Level 1 (INC 1) daily backups, optional Level 2 (INC 2) backups, a few times a week if necessary, and short-interval archive log backups. Backup retention is discussed, along with monitoring and validation of backups and examples of RMAN backup commands. |
| Updating statistics in Oracle | What is the command to update statistics for a whole schema in Oracle? | The `DBMS_STATS.GATHER_SCHEMA_STATS` procedure call is demonstrated, including additional parameters for `ESTIMATE_PERCENT`, `METHOD_OPT`, `DEGREE`, `CASCADE`, and `OPTIONS`. |

The table demonstrates prompts to teach the basics of database maintenance and to generate useful code. Specifically, the third prompt shows the chatbot's ability to write code using SQL Server Maintenance Solution scripts written by Ola Hallengren (https://ola.hallengren.com). These scripts are a popular standard for database index and statistics maintenance, consisting of many parameterized options. We use Ola's maintenance scripts ourselves; they are so robust that it would make little sense for us to write our own.

The determining factor for whether a chatbot can generate SQL code utilizing a non-native tool or script depends on the availability of documentation. Most chatbots we've tried can generate code for built-in database maintenance procedures, such as `sp_updatestats` in SQL Server and `DBMS_STATS.GATHER_SCHEMA_STATS` in Oracle, but may not be able to generate code for some third-party tools without additional training.

In the case of Ola Hallengren's scripts, the syntax is thoroughly documented online, making it possible to incorporate these scripts into our prompts. For other tools, such as Commvault Backup & Recovery, an enterprise data protection tool, command-line interface (CLI) commands are available online as well. But in our experience, chatbots are not aware of the data dictionary for the Commvault CommCell database by default. This is the database that the Commvault application uses to store configurations and necessary system and operational data. If you wanted to generate queries to find data in these tables without using the application interface, you would need to provide the chatbot with a data dictionary for accurate results. We've seen chatbots hallucinate table names and columns when creating queries for Commvault, making up objects that don't exist.

Regardless of your comfort level with database maintenance or your approach to maintenance tasks, a solid understanding of recovery and integrity is a must for any DBA. If necessary, explore the prompts in table 10.4 in greater detail to avoid data loss and performance problems within your environment. Also be sure to check out Ola's SQL Server maintenance scripts if you are not already using them.

Next, we'll discuss how AI can help with advanced administration tasks.

## 10.6 Advanced administration

Once the basic needs of a database environment have been met, there are countless opportunities still to be discovered to improve operational tasks. Depending on the size of your database environment, it is increasingly difficult to monitor and analyze every system individually. The secret to making your life as a DBA much easier is a focus on automation, data collection, and reporting.

Regularly reviewing the configurations and performance of your existing database systems is essential as data volumes grow and usage patterns evolve. What worked perfectly yesterday may become a bottleneck today. Over the next few sections, we will cover data collection and analysis, with an example of how to identify critical problems before they impact your operations.

### 10.6.1 AI + dbatools = <3

Considering that Chrissy is the founder of dbatools.io, an open source PowerShell module for SQL Server administration, we may be a little biased. But if you are not using dbatools, you are working much harder than necessary. To our delight, ChatGPT can code PowerShell using dbatools commands! We highly recommend spending some time using AI and dbatools to implement data collection in your environment. Having data centralized for all your database instances will make reporting and automation possible.

> **TIP** To learn more about dbatools, check out *Learn dbatools in a Month of Lunches* (Manning, 2022; www.manning.com/books/learn-dbatools-in-a-month-of-lunches) or visit https://dbatools.io.

Here is a quick prompt to create PowerShell code using dbatools commands.

Write a PowerShell script using the dbatools module to query all of the SQL Servers in my server registration and identify the accounts with sysadmin privs. Email the results to me in an HTML-formatted email.

```
# Ensure you have the dbatools module installed
# Install-Module -Name dbatools -Scope CurrentUser

# Import the dbatools module
Import-Module dbatools
```

## 10.6 Advanced administration

```powershell
# Specify the server group from your Registered Servers
$ServerGroup = "MyServerGroup" # Replace with your actual server group
↪name

# Get the list of servers from the registered server group
$Servers = Get-DbaRegisteredServer -Group $ServerGroup

# Initialize an array to store the results
$Results = @()

# Query each server for accounts with sysadmin privileges
foreach ($Server in $Servers) {
    $SysAdmins = Get-DbaSqlLogin -SqlInstance $Server.SqlInstance |
    ↪Where-Object { $_.IsSysAdmin -eq $true }

    foreach ($Admin in $SysAdmins) {
        $Results += [PSCustomObject]@{
            ServerName  = $Server.SqlInstance
            LoginName   = $Admin.Login
            IsSysAdmin  = $Admin.IsSysAdmin
        }
    }
}

# Convert the results to an HTML table
$HtmlBody = $Results | ConvertTo-Html -Property ServerName, LoginName,
↪IsSysAdmin -As Table -Fragment
# Prepare the email parameters
$EmailFrom = "your.email@example.com"    # Replace with your email
$EmailTo = "your.email@example.com"      # Replace with your email
$Subject = "SQL Server Sysadmin Accounts Report"
$SmtpServer = "smtp.example.com"         # Replace with your SMTP server
$SmtpPort = 587                          # Replace with your SMTP port,
↪usually 587 for TLS
$SmtpUser = "your.email@example.com"     # Replace with your email
$SmtpPass = "yourpassword"               # Replace with your SMTP
↪password

# Create a MailMessage object
$mailMessage = New-Object system.net.mail.mailmessage
$mailMessage.From = $EmailFrom
$mailMessage.To.Add($EmailTo)
$mailMessage.Subject = $Subject
$mailMessage.Body = $HtmlBody
$mailMessage.IsBodyHtml = $true

# Create an SmtpClient object
$smtpClient = New-Object system.net.mail.smtpclient($SmtpServer, $SmtpPort)
$smtpClient.EnableSsl = $true
$smtpClient.Credentials = New-Object System.Net.NetworkCredential(
↪$SmtpUser, $SmtpPass)

# Send the email
$smtpClient.Send($mailMessage)

# Confirm script completion
Write-Host "Email sent with sysadmin privileges report."
```

With relatively few lines, we were able to generate a PowerShell script that iterates through a list of SQL Servers in a SQL Server Registration, queries all accounts with sysadmin permissions, and emails the results in an HTML-formatted email. This is a great example of how AI can help you automate tasks that you may not have the time or knowledge to do yourself.

> **NOTE** If you do not have a SQL Server Central Management Server and don't wish to create one, ask the chatbot to read a list of SQL Servers from a text file or database table instead.

Calling this script from a SQL Server Agent job is a simple way to compile a monthly report, but depending on the quantity of SQL Servers in your environment, it may be too lengthy to be valuable. To make the data more useful for automation, instruct the chatbot to insert the results into a SQL Server table instead. There is no need to re-enter the code yourself, as the previous code is in context.

 Instead of sending an email, use dbatools commands to write the results to a table.

 To modify the script so that it writes the results to a table instead of sending an email, you can use the Write-DbaDataTable cmdlet from the dbatools module. This cmdlet allows you to write the data stored in a PowerShell object directly to a SQL Server table. Here's how you can adapt your script:

```
...
# Define the destination SQL Server and database
$destSqlInstance = 'YourDestinationSqlServer'
$destDatabase = 'YourDestinationDatabase'
$destTableName = 'YourDestinationTable'

# Write the results to the SQL Server table
$results | Write-DbaDataTable -SqlInstance $destSqlInstance -Database
    $destDatabase -Table $destTableName -AutoCreateTable
```

The chatbot quickly adapted the script to meet the new requirements, providing a full script output that was ready to be copied and pasted. Within minutes, we produced a PowerShell script capable of iterating through a list of SQL Servers in a SQL Server Registration, querying all accounts with sysadmin permissions, and inserting the results into a SQL table for analysis.

This is just one of hundreds of commands available in the dbatools module. Explore other commands, and see what you can automate in your environment. We suggest that you start by collecting SQL instance and database information.

If SQL Server and PowerShell are not your primary tools, you can still use AI to generate scripts for similar tasks. For example, you can request shell, Python, or Perl scripts instead, connecting to your preferred database using the appropriate libraries or modules.

In the next section, we will analyze memory configurations previously collected from across our environment.

## 10.6.2 Analyzing memory configurations

An effective DBA is proactive. Instead of responding to problems after they occur, analyzing configurations and data about your environment in advance can prevent performance problems and outages. We have conveyed the importance of data collection and reporting in a database environment. In our environments, we use various methods to collect data from each SQL and Oracle database server, storing those metrics in a centralized SQL Server inventory database. We then use that data to identify problems and trends in the environment through reporting.

To analyze the data, we will ask an AI chatbot to write a query to identify improper memory configurations for our Oracle database systems. If you do not have a centralized inventory with server metrics, you can also attempt to directly access the database of your specific monitoring solution. The ability of the chatbot to query those systems will depend on the public availability of those schemas. However, you can provide a data dictionary or DDL to the chatbot to help it produce the queries, as we do in the following examples.

> **TIP** Writing complex queries correctly with a single prompt can be hard. If you have an OpenAI account, we recommend GPT-4o with Canvas. Canvas works like a text editor, letting you edit code line by line through prompts. For more advanced coding, check chapter 11 for information on specialized AI tools like Roo Code and Cline.

We will cover two methods, which we refer to as *explaining* and *instructing*. Although similar, they are slightly different approaches to the same problem. The "explaining" method is more natural for those new to prompting, and the "instructing" method is more direct and concise. Try both methods to see which works best for you.

#### METHOD 1: EXPLAINING

When writing prompts for any task, organize your thoughts in a way that simplifies the prompt. This is especially true for less-capable models because they are less likely to understand complex instructions. We've also observed that people can have trouble describing what they want the chatbot to produce. Figure out the best way to explain what you want to accomplish, and remove any unnecessary information.

If you aren't sure how to describe the query you want, one approach we've found helpful is to provide a basic query example or table schema followed by a sample output. This method provides context for the chatbot by giving examples. Although your prompt may not be the shortest or most efficient, you will be more likely to get the desired results when you can accurately express yourself.

Let's attempt to request the same query but with two slightly different methods.

 I am providing a basic select statement to query memory parameters for my Oracle database instances, followed by an example of the results.

```
SELECT
    [SERVERNAME], [DB_NAME], [memory_target], [memory_max_target],
```

```
        [pga_aggregate_target], [sga_max_size], [PhysicalMemory]
FROM
    [dbo].[vOracleMemoryConfigs]

  server1    DB1    0    0    2000M    6G    15297
```

Columns 3 through 7 sometimes end in M or G instead of being numeric. M is megabytes and G is gigabytes. I need to convert them to numbers for calculations. When ending in M, remove the M. When ending in G, remove the G and multiply by 1024. This will get all columns into megabytes. When the memory_max_target is not 0, the memory in use will be equal to the memory_max_target. When the memory_max_target is 0, the memory in use will be (sga_max_size + pga_aggregate_target). I would like the query to calculate the total memory in use as a percentage against the physical memory available. I would like this query to only include results where total memory in use is over 75%

Method 1 works because the chatbot is given an example of the basic query and output, allowing it to understand the layout of the data, which would be difficult to explain conversationally. Providing a list of column names and data types would also be effective but might consume more tokens. Once the data structure is established, we can use a conversational style to explain to the chatbot how to convert the alphanumeric values to integers and how to calculate the total memory in use.

For someone new to prompting, this approach may be more natural and achievable. In the next method, we will take a slightly more direct approach, which will create the same output but with a shorter, more direct prompt.

**METHOD 2: INSTRUCTING**

In this method, we provide a more direct prompt that is less conversational and more concise. This is a more confident approach that uses pseudocode and is useful for those who are already aware of what the solution should look like.

> **TIP** When writing prompts, focus on what your chatbot can do best. Simpler language often works better. Consider token limits and costs with API calls. Shorter, more specific prompts are less likely to cause problems and more likely to get what you need.

Specifying only the relevant columns allows us to avoid the full table definition and reduce the size of our prompt. The pseudocode is a great way to instruct the chatbot about a calculation without being too wordy or having to provide a complex explanation. Since there are several ways to write a query that produces our desired results, we ask the chatbot to reduce redundancy in the query to avoid the possibility of excessive REPLACE function calls.

 Provide a SQL query that retrieves memory settings from the table [vOracleMemoryConfigs] and include the following columns: [SERVERNAME], [DB_NAME], [memory_target], [memory_max_target], [pga_aggregate_target], [sga_max_size], [PhysicalMemory].

## 10.6 Advanced administration

Some numeric columns may contain values ending with 'M' or 'G'. Convert all such values to megabytes: remove the 'M' suffix and multiply values ending with 'G' by 1024.

Calculate the 'Total Memory in Use' based on the following conditions: if [memory_max_target] <> 0, then 'Total Memory in Use' = [memory_max_target] else 'Total Memory in Use' = [sga_max_size] + [pga_aggregate_target].

Only include records where the 'Total Memory in Use' is over 75% of [PhysicalMemory]. Simplify any redundancy in the SQL query.

The output of a chatbot is merely an elaborate calculation, so you may encounter deviations in how the same problem is solved each time. Some initial responses to our prompts included redundant REPLACE or SUBSTRING statements, which we avoided by instructing the chatbot to simplify redundancy in the query. This modification to the prompt resulted in the use of a CTE, which we thought was a good choice.

> **TIP** Sometimes the chatbot will get only 90% to 95% of the way to what you want, requiring you to tweak the results to address an unexpected syntactical problem or scenario. Providing additional prompts to refine output will usually clear up any problems. If you encounter a syntax problem with the chatbot's output, ask it to validate and correct its own syntax. The chatbot can determine that it was wrong and attempt to fix the problem. If it doesn't, you can provide an additional prompt to fix the syntax yourself.

The following response has been shortened to save space.

```
-- CTE for converting memory settings to MB and calculating total memory
   in use
WITH MemoryCalculations AS (
    SELECT
        [SERVERNAME],
        [DB_NAME],
        [PhysicalMemory],
        CASE
            WHEN RIGHT([memory_max_target], 1) = 'M' THEN CAST(SUBSTRING
(
                [memory_max_target], 1, LEN([memory_max_target]) -
                1) AS INT)
            WHEN RIGHT([memory_max_target], 1) = 'G' THEN CAST(SUBSTRING
(
                [memory_max_target], 1, LEN([memory_max_target]) - 1)
                AS INT) * 1024
            ELSE [memory_max_target]
        END AS [memory_max_target_MB],
    ...
),
-- Second CTE for calculating total memory in use
FinalCalculations AS (
    SELECT
        [SERVERNAME],
```

```
            [DB_NAME],
            [PhysicalMemory],
            CASE
                WHEN [memory_max_target_MB] != 0 THEN [memory_max_target_MB]
                ELSE [sga_max_size_MB] + [pga_aggregate_limit_MB]
            END AS [TotalMemoryInUse_MB]
        FROM
            MemoryCalculations
)
SELECT
    *,
    ([TotalMemoryInUse_MB] * 1.0 / [PhysicalMemory]) * 100
        AS [TotalMemoryInUse_Percentage]
FROM
    FinalCalculations
WHERE
    ([TotalMemoryInUse_MB] * 1.0 / [PhysicalMemory]) * 100 > 75
```

With minimal effort, the chatbot was able to use a CTE to standardize the memory parameter values and calculate the overall memory utilization as a percentage. It is not the only solution to the problem, but it is a solid solution, produced in a fraction of the time as compared to writing it by hand. Scheduling this query as a SQL Server Agent job and emailing the results monthly is a simple way to monitor memory configurations across your environment. We'll close out this chapter with a few more novel ideas for advanced administration prompts.

### 10.6.3 Additional advanced administration prompts

We've compiled the final set of prompts in table 10.5 from real-life experience. We love these prompts because they demonstrate the flexibility of what you can accomplish with a chatbot. We elected to provide a "good prompt" and a "better prompt" for each to demonstrate how to take a good idea and elevate it to do even more.

> **Try it now**
>
> Try out each of these SQL Server administrative prompts as written, or customize them to push the limits of the chatbot. Can you make them even more useful?

Table 10.5  Advanced administration prompts

| Task | Good prompt | Better prompt |
| --- | --- | --- |
| SQL snapshots | Create a SQL Server query to create snapshots. | Create a SQL Server query to create snapshots of each user database on my server. Use a subquery to retrieve the databases so that I can limit it to specific databases if needed. The snapshot file should be written to S:\MSSQL\Snapshots\. |

Table 10.5 Advanced administration prompts *(continued)*

| Task | Good prompt | Better prompt |
|---|---|---|
| Move data files | Create a SQL Server query to detach and reattach a database to a new directory. | Create a SQL Server stored procedure, which accepts parameters for the database name, the path for the data file and the path for the log file. When the stored procedure is executed, it will check to make sure the database exists and is a user database, determine the current file path for the data and log files, terminate any established connections, detach the database, move the files to the provided locations, and reattach them. |
| Optimize performance and best practice configurations | What are some SQL Server Best Practices for my configuration? | Make suggestions to optimize the performance of my SQL Server 2022 instance. My instance has 4 cores and 64GB of RAM. All system and user database files are on the C:\. Analyze the output of sp_configure and ask me any additional questions required to meet best practice recommendations. [output of sp_configure] |
| Log file AutoGrow settings | What should the log file auto-grow settings be for my SQL Server databases? | Create a table-formatted list that illustrates ranges of database log file sizes and the recommended auto-growth setting based on the size. Use best practice recommendations. Then, generate a SQL query to recommend those log file auto-grow settings for user databases. Store results in a temp table and include an ALTER statement column. Filter out databases already following best practices. |

We'd like to specifically discuss the prompt to move data files. The good prompt asked for basic detach and attach code, which is a typical approach to moving data files. However, to push the boundaries of the chatbot, we asked it to create a stored procedure instead. With the stored procedure, we were able to provide parameters to make the code reusable. We also asked the chatbot to include code to verify the validity of the database name, terminate any connections, and use xp_cmdshell to move the files for us before reattaching them.

> **WARNING** xp_cmdshell is a powerful SQL Server procedure used to execute commands on the operating system. It is disabled by default in SQL Server because it can be a security risk. If you are going to use xp_cmdshell, make sure you understand the risks and have a good reason to enable it, or be sure to disable it once you are done using it.

The result was a very clever stored procedure that we would have been unlikely to write ourselves, and we got it in a fraction of the time. Sure, you may not need to move data files often, but it's a great example of what you can do if you ask. Throughout this chapter, we've also included the term "best practice recommendations" in a few prompts. We often invoke the concept of best practice to direct the chatbot to consider professional guidance when creating content and making suggestions.

The opportunities for database administration and development prompts are endless. Not only can we use AI to write procedures we don't have time to write, but we can push the code further than we might on our own. We hope you've been inspired by some of these ideas and are instantly prepared to work more efficiently.

### 10.6.4 The role of the DBA in the AI era

Although the capabilities of AI and LLMs in database administration and development are extensive, we must still recognize that human expertise remains invaluable. One such domain is data modeling, which requires a deep understanding of business requirements and the ability to communicate effectively with stakeholders. Translating real-world processes into logical data structures demands a level of contextual awareness and domain knowledge that current AI systems cannot match.

Sensitive data handling and regulatory compliance require human reasoning and ethics that AI models lack. As DBAs, we understand our responsibility in managing sensitive data like employee records, financial information, and patient data. While AI can serve as a powerful assistant, it cannot replace a skilled DBA's ability to interpret and apply ethical and legal frameworks. Moving forward, we need a balanced approach that leverages both human expertise and AI capabilities to maximize efficiency while maintaining data governance, regulatory compliance, and ethical standards.

The conclusion of our chapter on database administration and development also signifies a change in focus from IT operations to code and software development. Chapter 11 is the first stop on this journey, beginning with code assistants and development tools.

## 10.7 Prompts used in this chapter

- I need an example of a prompt that can be written to create a useful function in SQL Server. Do you have any ideas?
- Help me verbalize the difference between Administrative and Development DBAs, as there is often a lot of confusion.
- Create an optimized prompt that would have gotten the above results with less effort.
- Is there an asciidoc highlighting syntax for PowerShell? If not, I'll just use "shell"

## Summary

- AI tools significantly enhance DBA capabilities, enabling both administrative and development DBAs to more effectively perform tasks outside their traditional roles.
- Chatbots can generate customized SQL queries for specific use cases, eliminating the need for manual code searches and modifying generic syntax examples.
- In query optimization, AI can analyze execution plans to identify bottlenecks, suggesting specific improvements that can lead to enhanced query performance. Ask chatbots to suggest indexes for queries and even perform code reviews.
- Managing databases in heterogeneous environments requires understanding the nuances of different platforms. AI can assist in translating concepts and syntax across systems like Oracle and SQL Server, summarize new features in platform upgrades, and explain the intricacies of database licensing.
- AI can suggest essential maintenance tasks for new DBAs and generate scripts for these tasks. AI can also audit configurations to identify drift from best practice recommendations.
- Chatbots are familiar with third-party products, such as dbatools.io and Index-Optimize by Ola Hallengren, writing PowerShell, SQL code, and more to utilize these tools effectively in various administration tasks and automations.
- AI can be employed for advanced database functions such as creating snapshots, moving data files, setting auto-grow settings, and more.

# Part 3

# *Development and AI integration*

Ready to supercharge your development work with AI? Chapters 11 to 13 show you how AI is changing the game for developers and DevOps professionals. We'll explore how AI can be your coding companion, helping you write better code faster and catch problems earlier in the development cycle. You'll learn the ins and outs of working with AI code assistants, streamlining your DevOps practices and even building applications that harness AI's power. Whether you're looking to automate your deployment pipeline or create AI-powered features in your applications, this part of the book will give you the knowledge you need to level up your development skills so you're ready to make AI a natural part of your development workflow and build the next generation of intelligent applications.

# Code assistants and development tools

## This chapter covers

- How AI coding assistants fit into development workflows
- Using GitHub Copilot, Cline, Roo Code, Cursor AI, Google Project IDX, and Aider
- Privacy considerations when working with AI coding tools
- Best practices for AI-assisted development
- Managing large codebases effectively with AI assistants

AI development tools have changed how we write software. What used to take hours—debugging, documentation, basic features—now takes minutes. Although these tools complement rather than replace developers, they've become an integral part of how we work.

Traditional code completion offers basic suggestions, but modern AI tools understand context, predict what we need, and can write complete functions or solve complex coding problems. This fundamental shift has transformed how we approach software development.

AI development tools come in several forms:

- *Terminals*—Assistants that integrate directly with your command-line interface
- *IDE extensions*—Plugins for popular Integrated Development Environments (IDEs) like Visual Studio Code or JetBrains IDEs
- *VS Code forks*—Customized versions of VS Code with built-in AI features
- *Web interfaces*—Browser-based coding environments with AI assistance

Before exploring these tools in detail, we need to discuss two important considerations: privacy and expertise.

## 11.1 Privacy and security

Most code assistants send your code snippets to their servers for processing. Although they need to do this for their AI models to work, it can create security risks—especially with private or sensitive code. This is particularly important for enterprise environments where code often contains sensitive algorithms, business logic, or authentication details. Consider whether your code contains secrets, proprietary logic, or personally identifiable information before sharing it with AI tools.

A good approach is starting with public code or test projects when first using these tools. This lets you evaluate their capabilities without putting sensitive information at risk. Once you understand how the tools handle your code, you can make informed decisions about using them with your main projects.

> **TIP** If you need total privacy control, check out appendix A on running local coding models. It takes some setup and is less capable, but gives you complete control over your data.

## 11.2 Understanding the value of existing skills

AI coding assistants are powerful tools, but they work best when guided by solid software engineering experience. During our projects, we find that architectural skills are particularly valuable, especially when working in unfamiliar languages.

Just like most developers, AI models can write code that works but may not scale well or handle edge cases properly. Having experience with system design helps you spot these problems early. When we built our own content filtering system, we knew to ask for things like proper error handling, efficient data structures, and smart caching, despite not being JavaScript experts.

For example, the code assistant used arrays for lookups, but our experience with performance optimization helped us recognize that this approach would slow as the dataset grew. We then asked if JavaScript had any better data structures that wouldn't slow down as we added more data, and it suggested switching to Maps instead.

> **TIP** When requesting code from an AI model, explicitly state your nonfunctional requirements like performance needs, error handling expectations,

and scalability concerns. This helps the AI understand the full context and generate more robust, production-ready code instead of simple examples.

This doesn't mean you need years of architecture experience to use AI effectively. But understanding fundamentals like separation of concerns, error handling, and basic performance optimization will help you get better results. Remember that all developers occasionally write inefficient code or miss edge cases. AI is a tool that helps us work faster, but it needs our expertise to work better.

## 11.3 GitHub AI suite

GitHub Copilot launched to great fanfare in 2021 and changed how developers think about code assistance. Unlike IntelliSense, which offers basic code completion, Copilot provides contextual understanding by analyzing codebases and comments to suggest relevant code, tests, and architectural patterns. Figure 11.1 demonstrates this in action, showing Copilot generating tailored recommendations for a README file.

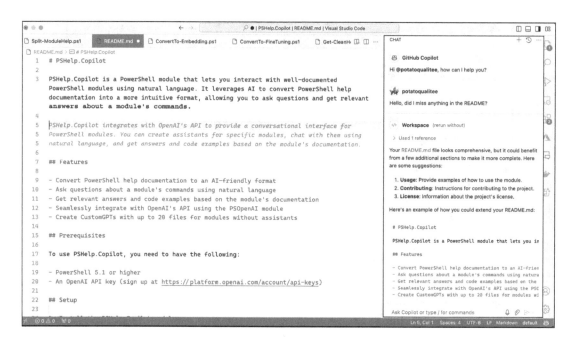

Figure 11.1　GitHub Copilot in Visual Studio Code

We're particularly impressed by Copilot's PowerShell capabilities: it not only knows the language but excels at it, despite PowerShell's relatively small user base. Recent support for the GPT-4o, OpenAI o1, Anthropic Sonnet, and Gemini models has made it even more capable, with the Copilot Chat feature being especially valuable.

GitHub's AI toolset extends beyond Copilot. Its suite integrates several tools that work together throughout the development process. What makes this powerful isn't

204   CHAPTER 11   *Code assistants and development tools*

any single feature but how everything connects into enterprise development workflows.

It starts with *Copilot Workspace*, which helps teams plan and build software together (see figure 11.2). Teams can tell Workspace what they need—such as *Add department-level permissions to the app store*—and it creates plans that fit with existing systems. As developers refine these plans, Workspace keeps track of all their decisions.

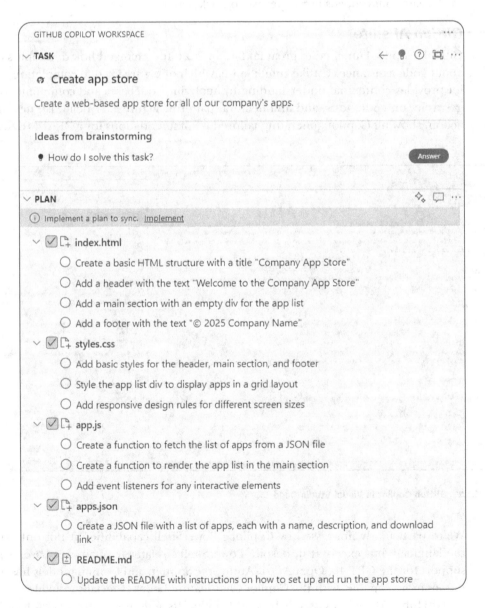

Figure 11.2   **GitHub Copilot Workspace in Visual Studio Code**

Next, Copilot suggests code that matches team patterns and conventions, maintaining established error handling and logging conventions without explicit instruction. Copilot's suggestions are often complete and accurate, requiring minimal changes to fit into existing codebases. In early 2025, GitHub added Copilot Edits with Agent Mode, bringing autonomous multifile editing similar to what we'll see next with Cline and Cursor AI. Agent Mode lets Copilot plan tasks, find and modify relevant files, run terminal commands, and fix any problems that come up—all without constant developer input. For example, when adding a new feature, Agent Mode can create needed files, write the code, test it, and fix problems it finds, much as Cline (covered next) checks its own work through its browser. This makes Copilot even more useful for complex changes that affect multiple parts of your codebase.

With initial code in place, *Spark* creates working prototypes for stakeholder review. When security teams need to evaluate a new admin interface, Spark generates functional prototypes in minutes, giving teams tangible examples to review before full development.

Finally, *Copilot for PRs* ensures that changes are safe, documented, and consistent. During access control reviews, it flags missing error handling, finds similar implementations across repositories, and explains technical changes in business terms.

Consider building an internal app store: teams describe requirements in Workspace, Copilot suggests code matching existing patterns, Spark generates prototypes for review, and Copilot for PRs ensures quality through automated assistance. This integrated workflow reduces development time while maintaining consistency with existing systems and security standards.

> **TIP** Use Copilot for PRs' summaries as starting points for documentation. They often capture the reasoning behind architectural decisions that teams forget to document.

GitHub Copilot brings AI straight into your development workflow. Each developer account costs $10 per month for access, or they can start with the free tier that includes 2,000 completions and 50 chat messages each month. Teams who need more can add Copilot for PRs and other group features.

## 11.4 Cline

Cline, formerly known as Claude Dev, is a Visual Studio code extension that can easily create and edit files, execute commands, and even use a built-in browser to check its own work. If the web page it's working on doesn't look or function as expected, Cline will continue to edit the web files until it does. This really stood out to us.

We'll be honest: in a very short time, Cline completely changed the way we code. Over a holiday weekend, Chrissy created a beautiful and functional website, all without deeply knowing graphics design principles, CSS, or JavaScript: see figure 11.3.

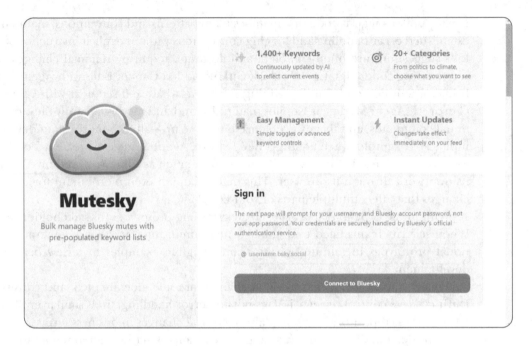

Figure 11.3 Mutesky.app: a JavaScript website built entirely without advanced JavaScript knowledge

**NOTE** Roo Code, a fork of Cline, adds features like custom workflows and enhanced API support. Although this section focuses on Cline, we now use Roo Code and GitHub Copilot for our projects.

Cline's solutions, which can edit multiple related files in one go, are often complete and accurate. You can add an entire feature to your project with a single casually crafted prompt, as shown in figure 11.4. This makes using Cline fun and addictive.

Cline does have one big downside, and it's a doozy. Although Cline itself is free, using it can get very expensive. We're talking $300 USD in less than a week if you're working on your website 12+ hours a day like Chrissy did.

This is because Cline has to send a lot of data back and forth to the API to ensure that it provides as complete a solution as possible. Other code assistants offer their product for $10 to $20 per month, so you can imagine how much throttling is likely to occur until AI API prices come down.

In our experience, Cline's exceptional performance can only be matched using Anthropic Sonnet models and OpenAI's o1, and these models aren't the most affordable. Newer, highly capable models, such as DeepSeek v3 and R1, are significantly cheaper (up to 53× in early 2025) but pose significant privacy and IP risks, as they require you to agree to training. Some API providers, such as Fireworks.ai (https://fireworks.ai), do not require training when using the DeepSeek model, but this comes at a slightly increased cost, basically requiring you to pay for privacy.

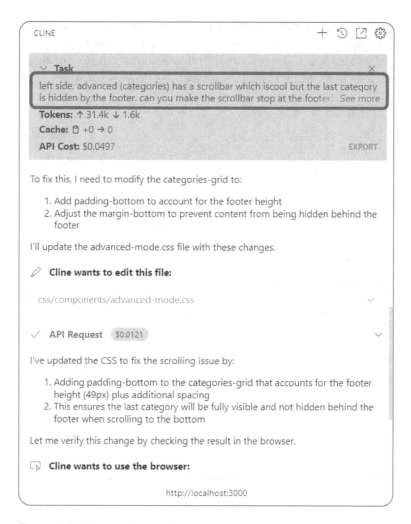

Figure 11.4  Cline solving a problem and prompting to see the solution in action

Overall, we suggest experiencing Cline and Roo Code for yourself. We started with $5 in token credits from OpenRouter.ai (https://openrouter.ai) and were able to create a simple yet complete tasker using the Anthropic Sonnet 3.5 model.

## 11.5  Cursor AI

Cursor AI, like Cline and GitHub Copilot, can generate complete applications from simple descriptions. Built as a specialized version of VS Code, it figures out what files to create and what code to write with minimal input from you.

When we wanted to create a test Chrome extension that replaces "teh" with "the" on websites, all it took was describing the idea. Cursor created the manifest file, content scripts, and logic without needing additional prompts or clarification. This can be seen in figure 11.5, where the simple prompt has been highlighted and the resulting code is displayed. Although other code assistants can do this too, Cursor's no-fuss approach to generating complete projects works well for quick experiments like this.

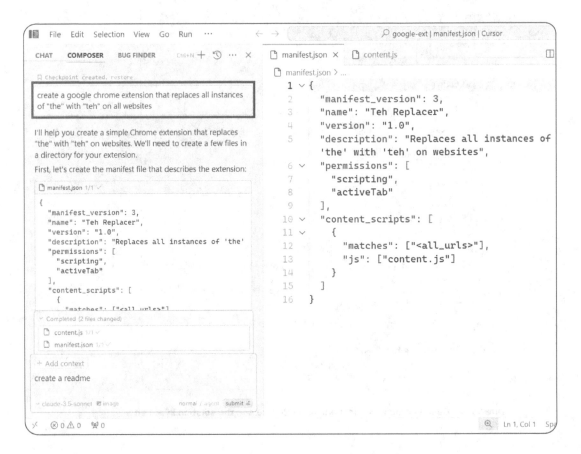

Figure 11.5  Cursor creating a Google extension from one simple prompt

The free version of Cursor AI lets you write code using natural language and search your project based on concepts instead of exact matches. The Pro version is $20 monthly and adds tools for refactoring and debugging. Unlike Cline, which charges based on usage, Cursor AI keeps costs steady each month.

Pro subscribers get unlimited regular completions, 500 fast premium requests monthly, unlimited slower requests, and 10 daily o1-mini uses. Although Cline offers faster models without restrictions, Cursor AI keeps costs predictable for developers who want AI help without surprise bills.

## 11.6 Google Project IDX

Google launched Project IDX in 2023, adding another way to code with AI help. It runs entirely in your browser and includes templates for Go, Python, Flutter, and other languages.

When we tested IDX by building a basic web app, we didn't need to write much code ourselves. Figure 11.6 shows the app we made using a template, a few prompts, and help from IDX's AI assistant that uses Google's Codey model.

**Figure 11.6** Go web app template in Project IDX

Because everything runs in the cloud, you don't need to mess with local development environments or complicated setups. This makes it perfect for prototypes or coding from different computers. You can deploy your apps directly from the browser through Google Cloud.

But IDX comes with limitations. Your code stays on Google's servers, which may not suit sensitive projects. The environment also lacks the customization found in VS Code and other IDEs.

IDX is currently free during preview. However, Google will likely add paid options with more features later.

## 11.7 Aider

Aider is a terminal-based coding assistant that helps developers manage project structure and dependencies, allowing coordinated changes across multiple files. Like other

210    CHAPTER 11    *Code assistants and development tools*

AI coding tools, it can build new projects from basic descriptions, creating anything from simple scripts to complete applications.

Figure 11.7 shows what happens when we ask Aider to *Create a PowerShell module that outputs ASCII ghosts. Use a module manifest.* Aider creates both the module file and manifest file and then writes a PowerShell function that displays ASCII ghost art. This shows how Aider understands what you want and creates working code right in your terminal, where developers typically work.

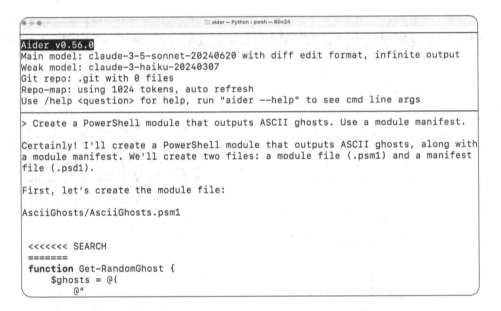

Figure 11.7  Aider in the terminal

Aider automatically updates its model of your project when you modify files outside the AI session. This synchronization keeps its suggestions aligned with your latest code changes, enabling seamless collaboration between AI and developer.

> **WARNING**  Although Aider can help you code faster, you need to understand your codebase. Always check AI suggestions before using them to avoid bugs and performance problems.

If you're new to terminal tools, getting started with Aider takes some time—especially setting up API keys and learning commands. But the boost in coding speed makes it worth learning.

And Aider does more than write code. Like Cline, it can show you how files depend on each other, suggest changes across multiple files, and build entire application structures from simple descriptions. This makes it useful for both quick prototypes and larger projects.

## 11.8 Summary comparison of code assistants

Choosing the right code assistant can be daunting, given the many options available. To help you make an informed decision, table 11.1 provides an overview of features to consider.

Table 11.1  Comparison of AI code assistant features

| Feature | GitHub Copilot | Google Project IDX | Aider | Cursor AI | Cline |
|---|---|---|---|---|---|
| Platform | IDE integration (VS Code, JetBrains, Neovim, Visual Studio 2022, Xcode) | Browser-based IDE | Terminal-based; integrates with local Git repositories | Standalone app; integrates with VS Code; available for Windows, macOS, and Linux | VS Code extension |
| AI model integration | Supports multiple models from various vendors including OpenAI, Anthropic, and Google | Google Gemini | Wide vendor support including OpenAI, Anthropic, and Google. Plus local models. | Wide vendor support including OpenAI, Anthropic, and Google. Plus local models. | Wide vendor support including OpenAI, Anthropic, and Google. Plus local models. |
| Privacy options | Code processed on cloud servers; customizable privacy settings | Code processed on Google's servers | Code processed locally; configurable to use local models | Privacy Mode and local storage available; SOC 2 certified; code is never stored remotely when Privacy Mode is enabled | Code processed via API calls |
| Cost | Free tier with limited usage; Pro plan at $10/month (individual); $19/month (teams) | Free tier; paid plans for advanced features | Free; requires API keys or local models | Free version; Pro at $20/month | Free extension; API costs per use |
| Key strengths | Multimodel support; advanced code suggestions; multifile editing; customizable workflows | Cross-platform development; ease of access | Direct code editing within Git repositories; automatic git commits with meaningful messages; supports multiple programming languages | Intelligent autocompletion; natural language coding; privacy options; multiline edits; codebase understanding; smart rewrites; extension compatibility | Multifile editing; browser verification |
| Key limitations | Privacy concerns; potential overreliance; varying model performance | Privacy concerns; AI still maturing | Potential for introducing unintended code changes; reliance on LLM quality and accuracy; may require manual code review and testing | Autocompletion reliability; multifile edits; dependency on internet connectivity for AI features | High API costs; token usage |

Each tool excels in different scenarios. Your choice should depend on your use case:

- For *enterprise development* with established workflows, consider GitHub Copilot.
- For *complex multifile changes* with immediate verification, all of the assistants will work.
- For *command-line* power users who need Git integration, Aider is best.
- For *browser-based* development with easy deployment, try Project IDX.
- For *privacy-focused* development with natural language support, explore Cursor AI.

## 11.9 Best practices for AI-assisted development

After months of building and shipping products with AI coding assistants, we've learned a lot about what works and what doesn't. This section covers essential practices for working with AI tools, from security considerations to test-driven development. We'll share real examples from our projects where these practices made a significant difference, along with specific strategies for handling common challenges like code quality and version control. These lessons apply no matter which AI coding assistant you choose.

### 11.9.1 Foundation principles

Before we get into specific practices, we need to discuss security: AI coding assistants are powerful tools, but their output needs careful review, especially for security-sensitive code. Run security scanners and fuzz testing on AI-generated code, particularly for components handling authentication, data access, or user input. It's worth scanning AI-generated code carefully, but let's be honest: humans write vulnerable code too, especially when tired, rushed, or just wanting to get things done. We've found that even experienced developers and PhDs aren't immune to this. It's important to maintain security standards and review processes, regardless of who or what wrote the code.

Getting good results with AI requires more than knowing the basics. How you frame your requests dramatically affects the quality of output. Adding specific qualifiers like "follow UI/UX best practices" or "use Python best practices" consistently produces better results. This works because AI models learn from a mix of good and bad examples: explicitly requesting best practices helps focus them on quality patterns from their training data.

> **TIP** When working with AI, be specific about what you want. Tell it to "use semantic HTML for accessibility" or "apply SOLID principles in object-oriented design"—these clear requests help the AI give you better output.

Interestingly, we've found that the more popular the language, the better the best practices. PowerShell, for example, has a smaller user base than Python, so AI models often struggle with PowerShell best practices. When working with less common

## 11.9 Best practices for AI-assisted development

languages, be prepared to provide more guidance on coding standards and practices. Specific requirements like these help ensure you get high-quality code that follows established patterns and practices.

**COMPREHENSIVE LOGGING**

Although AI tools can analyze code effectively, they often lack runtime context. Adding detailed logging shows exactly what happens during execution, giving AI assistants the concrete information they need to suggest accurate fixes.

We've found that adding logging improves AI's code quality across all types of operations, from simple functions to complex state management. What's especially interesting is that AI tends to maintain the logging patterns it sees: when you show it code with good logging practices, it will add appropriate logging to any new code it generates.

 I need you to add a user authentication system to our Express app. Here's our logging pattern - each major operation logs its state and result. Please implement the authentication following this same logging approach:

```
logger.info("Starting user lookup by email", { email })
const user = await findUser(email)
logger.info("User lookup complete", { found: !!user })
```

This kind of prompt helps the AI understand what program states and events you want tracked. When shown examples like this, the AI will typically respond with well-structured code that includes appropriate logging:

```
logger.info("Starting payment processing for amount", { amount })
process_payment(amount)
logger.info("Payment processing completed", { result })
```

Surprisingly, we often get better code quality from the assistant after we add logging statements to our code—even before sharing any actual logs. The very act of showing the AI how we track program execution seems to help it understand the flow of operations better, leading to more thorough solutions.

**WORKING WITH AI EFFECTIVELY**

AI assistants work best when you keep requests focused and conversations short. Long chats often lead to confused or less helpful responses. Starting fresh conversations for each task helps maintain quality and gives better results.

AI assistants measure usage with tokens, similar to mobile data plans. Every character you send (including code) counts as a token, and responses use tokens too. We've found that responses become less reliable after about 1.3 million tokens, with usage growing exponentially after this point. What takes six messages to reach 1.3 million tokens can jump to 2 million in just three more messages.

It's been reported that AI acts strangely and costs soar at extreme token counts. In one case, the code assistant generated lots of files, tried debugging, and then started deleting its own work in a cycle—a clear sign of an overloaded context window. Others complain about broken code suggestions and sky-high bills after hitting 19 million tokens. Similar to what we saw in chapter 3 with Dave's two-month chat session, pushing AI beyond its limits leads to odd behavior like false claims and broken promises. Starting new conversations and breaking work into smaller tasks helps avoid these problems. Table 11.2 shows examples of discrete tasks that have worked well for us in practice.

Table 11.2  Sample tasks and their prompts

| Task | Effective prompt |
|---|---|
| Refactoring large files | The keywordHandlers.js file is too large. Split it into multiple files. The code must work exactly the same way after splitting - don't change any functionality. |
| Setting feature boundaries | Enable click-to-show-original only for Reddit and Bluesky posts. All other sites should have this feature disabled. |
| UI improvements | Make the footer sticky on desktop versions but let it scroll normally on mobile devices. |
| Performance feedback | Add in Write-Progress and Write-Verbose statements where appropriate to show operation status. |
| Documentation | Create PowerShell help for each file in the directory and include a synopsis. |
| Visual states | Disable badge count on disabled domains and gray out the icon. |

Notice how each request focuses on one specific change and clearly states what should stay the same. Although it's tempting to give the AI lots of background ("since you already deeply understand our project …"), you'll get better results by letting it ask for exactly what it needs. This is especially important during refactoring, where small changes can have unexpected effects.

#### TEST-DRIVEN AI DEVELOPMENT

Tests are small programs that check whether your code works as expected. They verify that when you give your code specific inputs, it produces the right outputs. For example, a test might check if your login function accepts valid passwords and rejects invalid ones.

We've found that just giving the AI detailed instructions isn't enough to control what it produces. Even with careful documentation, AI tools often go their own way. The fix? Start with tests.

When you begin with tests, you create firm boundaries that the AI must follow. Unlike written requirements that the AI might misinterpret, tests give clear pass/fail results. This is particularly important for critical features like authentication, where small mistakes can create security problems. Table 11.3 shows why tests are so effective at guiding AI development.

## 11.9 Best practices for AI-assisted development

**Table 11.3  Benefits of test-first AI development**

| Benefit | Description |
|---|---|
| Clear requirements | Tests provide nonnegotiable specifications that the AI must follow. |
| Early problem detection | Failed tests prevent problematic code from reaching production. |
| Focused development | The AI stays within defined boundaries instead of adding unexpected features. |
| Safer refactoring | Tests catch when the AI's changes would break existing functionality. |

For example, when building a Chrome extension that hides social media content, we struggled to get the AI to maintain consistent boundary conditions. Initial prompts like *Hide posts unless they match our filters* led to the AI removing too much content. By starting with this test instead, we got exactly what we needed:

```
describe('Content Filtering', () => {
  test('does not hide non-social-media content', () => {
    const regularPost = document.createElement('div');
    regularPost.innerHTML = '<p>Just a regular webpage post</p>'
    expect(shouldHideElement(regularPost)).toBe(false)
  });
});
```

When shown this test first, the AI understood exactly what *not* to touch, leading to more precise implementations. How did we get that test? We asked the AI to write it with this prompt.

 Write a test for our content filtering function that ensures we don't accidentally hide regular webpage content.

This prompt works, and it's often good enough when you're not familiar with the programming language. Sometimes simple is better: the AI may create exactly what you need, even with basic instructions.

For developers who know the language well, being more specific helps get precisely what you want.

 Write a Jest test for our content filtering function that ensures we don't accidentally hide regular webpage content. The test should create a basic div element with non-social-media content and verify that shouldHideElement() returns false for it. Follow Jest best practices and focus on edge case prevention.

This prompt works particularly well because it specifies the following:

- What testing framework to use (Jest)
- The exact behavior to test
- How to set up the test (creating a div)

- What outcome we expect (returning false)
- Where to focus (edge case prevention)

Many coding assistants let you set up project-wide test requirements so you don't have to specify testing rules in every prompt. For example, the .clinerules file tells the Cline AI assistant how to handle tests for your project. This file lives in your project's root directory and contains testing standards and quality rules:

```
Testing Standards
* Unit Tests: Test individual components of business logic
* Integration Tests: Verify API endpoints' interactions with external services
* End-to-End Tests: Simulate critical user flows across the application

Code Quality Rules
1. Test Coverage
    * Assess coverage before finalizing code changes
    * Ensure all tests pass prior to submission
2. Code Reviews
    * Conduct regular reviews to uphold standards
    * Use static analysis tools to detect issues
3. Continuous Integration
    * Implement CI pipelines for automated building and testing
    * Automate test execution on new commits
4. Documentation
    * Maintain clear, up-to-date code documentation
    * Document testing strategies and cases
```

With these rules in place, Cline automatically follows your testing requirements for every code change. Other AI assistants have similar features—check their documentation for details.

**SOURCE CONTROL INTEGRATION**

Version control tools like Git are necessary when working with AI assistants. It's not just for tracking changes anymore: it helps the AI better understand your code.

Here's a real problem we solved using Git. Our authentication broke while adding a new feature. Instead of spending hours explaining the problem to the AI, we showed it our code at different points in time, as can be seen in table 11.4.

Table 11.4  Using Git with AI

| Step | Actual prompt used |
| --- | --- |
| Get working code | Your changes broke authentication so I've discarded them. This is a persistent bug. To address it, I'd like you to learn from another branch that has a working version. I'm going to switch to that one so that you can learn from it. Ready? |
| Learn the pattern | Okay done. I'm now on a branch with working code. Please analyze the code to see what went wrong with your changes. |
| Fix the problem | Now I'm back on our active branch. Again, I removed your previous changes. Please implement working auth using the patterns you just learned. |

Cline fixed it on the first try! This approach was so effective because Git let the AI study working code to understand proper implementation, start fresh without being influenced by broken code, and apply correct patterns to the new solution.

This pattern is especially useful for persistent bugs that resist normal debugging approaches. Instead of getting stuck trying different variations of a broken solution, you give the AI a fresh start with working code as its guide.

### 11.9.2 Advanced techniques

Complex projects need better ways to work with AI. Although the basic approaches we've covered help, we've found additional methods to prevent quality from degrading as projects grow. For example, we noticed that sharing images with AI models can lower code quality, so we only use essential screenshots. We still include images when they're needed but keep them focused on specific tasks. This section covers techniques that will help you tackle harder problems and get more from your AI assistant.

#### LIBRARY ANALYSIS

Libraries and frameworks change fast, and both docs and AI models often lag behind. The solution? Let the AI read the source code directly to understand how things really work. This strategy is particularly useful when you're using libraries newer than the AI's training data, working with frequently updated packages, exploring features that aren't documented yet, or dealing with recent breaking changes.

 The BlueSky OAuth library keeps changing and their docs aren't updated. Can you look at the code in node_modules/@atproto/oauth-client-browser and explain how their latest authentication flow works? Then help me update our implementation to match.

Reading source code lets the AI give you advice based on exactly how the code works now, not how it worked months ago. For example, when BlueSky's user base exploded, its team was pushing rapid updates to the OAuth module without updating docs. Instead of waiting for documentation, we had our code assistant analyze @atproto/oauth-client-browser directly from node_modules to understand the latest changes and update our implementation accordingly.

#### UNDERSTANDING DIFF AND WHOLE-FILE APPROACHES

Files should stay under 200 lines when possible. Large files consume more tokens and context space. Code assistants perform better with smaller, targeted pieces of code.

Larger files also cause problems with the assistant's ability to suggest changes. When files are too long, the assistant's "diff" strategies start to break down, and you may need to switch to "whole" to get better results. This generally results in slower processing.

In diff mode, the assistant only shows the specific lines it changed, similar to Git. This works well for quick edits and uses fewer tokens. But when files are large or changes become complex, diff mode can break down, leading to incomplete or incorrect suggestions.

Whole-file mode means the assistant rewrites the entire file with your changes. This uses more tokens and takes longer, but it often produces better results for major changes or refactoring.

Create your directories ahead of time if you have specific structure requirements, and intelligent models like Claude Sonnet will use your existing layout. If a file grows too big, ask the assistant to help you split it into smaller, logical pieces.

Table 11.5 summarizes the key differences between diff and whole-file modes to help you choose the right approach for your task.

Table 11.5  Comparing diff and whole-file modes

| Aspect | Diff mode | Whole-file mode |
| --- | --- | --- |
| Best for | Small changes, quick edits | Major refactoring, complex changes |
| Token usage | Lower; more efficient | Higher; uses full file context |
| Speed | Faster suggestions | Slower processing |
| Accuracy | May miss context in large files | More reliable for complex changes |
| Review effort | Easy to spot changes | Need to compare full files |

Understanding these modes helps you work more efficiently with code assistants. Start with diff mode for small changes, and then switch to whole-file mode if you notice the suggestions becoming incomplete or incorrect. Some assistants let you specify your preferred mode, whereas others switch automatically based on file size and complexity.

**TROUBLESHOOTING AI LOOPS**

When the AI gets stuck repeating the same wrong solution, here's a simple trick: ask it to explain the problem to a "new session." You don't need to actually restart; the request itself helps the AI break out of its loop. Table 11.6 shows some prompts that have helped us fix two seemingly unsolvable bugs, like a stats tracker in one of the Chrome extensions we built.

Table 11.6  Prompts that helped us unstick AI

| Scenario | Effective prompt |
| --- | --- |
| Breaking thought loops | Your solutions aren't working and I've discarded them. Explain the problem we're working on to a new AI session, starting with a Problem Statement. |
| Fixing stubborn bugs | 1. Explain how syntax highlighting works<br>2. Now that you understand it, please remove the entire feature, ensuring that you don't leave any litter in seemingly unrelated files<br>3. (To a brand new session) Add JavaScript syntax highlighting to the textbox |

Sometimes the nuclear option works best because AI generates slightly different solutions each time due to randomization in its responses. So starting fresh often leads to a completely new approach that avoids the previous problems.

If you're curious about the kind of output generated by our request to document the problem, starting with a problem statement, here's an example:

```
Problem Statement:
The options page statistics tab should show all-time keyword stats (which
keywords were blocked and how many times), but currently it only shows
stats from the current page. The extension already tracks total blocks
in the 'stats' storage key, but needs to track per-keyword counts that
persist across page loads and browser restarts.

Key Files to Look At:

scripts/core/contentDetectionModule.js - This is where keywords are
detected in content. Line ~150-160 shows where matches are found.
options/optionsUI.js - This displays the stats in the options page.
Line ~10-50 shows the current stats display logic.
docs/keyword-tracking-system.md - Documents how keyword tracking works,
showing storage keys and data structures.
Suggested Minimal Approach:

Add a new storage key 'allTimeKeywordStats' to track per-keyword counts
When contentDetectionModule.js finds matches, increment the counts in
storage
Modify optionsUI.js to read from allTimeKeywordStats instead of current
page stats
```

This kind of systematic problem breakdown helps both you and the AI understand exactly what needs to be fixed. By getting the AI to explicitly state its understanding of the problem, files involved, and proposed approach, you can catch misunderstandings early and guide it toward better solutions.

Now that you know how these tools work and the best ways to use them, you can start using the AI to help with your development tasks. In chapter 12, we'll show you how the AI makes DevOps work easier and helps teams get more done.

## 11.10 Prompts used in this chapter

- For the TDD section, I need help clarifying my point which is that writing software with AI is different and sometimes it makes sweeping changes. To keep it in line, you can have it make tests first THEN implement the changes. This will keep it from, for example, breaking expected functionality of a button when auth is modified.
- Is GitHub Copilot Workflow just a tasker?
- Add in that we tried to do a lightweight version of this by writing out documentation but we found that it'd ignore the documentation and change the functionality anyway. Tests make it fail though, and boom, it cant negotiate.
- I have the basic ideas for the source control section but it's written confusingly. Please help me clarify it.
- The best practices section has a ton of info that is hard to organize. I can't put it into one giant table. Please review the content and suggest a restructure.

- Please add an ACTUALLY USEFUL tip based off of the valuation of my own architectural experience in a recent project: <pastes in review of skills>

## *Summary*

- AI coding assistants have fundamentally changed software development, with different tools excelling at solving different challenges.
- GitHub Copilot provides comprehensive IDE integration and enterprise-focused features like Copilot Workspace and PR review.
- Cline and Roo Code excel at multifile editing and solution verification but come with higher usage-based costs.
- Cursor AI offers natural language coding with predictable monthly pricing.
- Google Project IDX provides browser-based development with built-in deployment.
- Aider enables terminal-based AI coding with Git integration.
- Best practices for AI-assisted development include starting with tests rather than just documentation to control AI output.
- Using detailed logging helps the AI understand runtime behavior.
- Using source control effectively manages AI-generated changes.
- Breaking large projects into smaller chunks improves AI accuracy.
- Having the AI document solutions before implementation enhances clarity.
- Analyzing library source code directly provides up-to-date guidance.

# AI in DevOps engineering

> **This chapter covers**
> - Integrating AI into existing DevOps workflows
> - Converting 7,000 PowerShell tests using AI tools
> - Selecting and using AI models for bulk code changes
> - Managing costs in mass code updates
> - Understanding GenAIOps fundamentals
> - Setting up AI-powered testing solutions

AI has reshaped DevOps and Platform Engineering over the past two years. It now helps with everything from deploying infrastructure to reviewing code changes.

We originally wanted to focus on GenAIOps—the practice of managing AI applications using DevOps principles. But we found it more useful to start with practical ways to add AI to your current DevOps work.

This chapter shows you real examples of AI in DevOps, like automating infrastructure and updating test suites. We'll share what has worked for us, what problems we've run into, and what we've learned along the way.

## 12.1 Practical AI use cases in DevOps

As infrastructure engineers who build automation tools, we're always looking for ways to simplify our work. We found three main ways to add AI to our workflow.

First, we can wrap commands and advanced processes with AI interfaces. For DevOps engineers, this creates a layer that turns natural language into technical commands. Instead of typing exact syntax like `Copy-DbaDatabase`, users can say *migrate the Northwind database from SQL01 to SQL02*. The AI understands the context and runs the right commands in PowerShell, kubectl, or cloud CLI, making complex operations as simple as having a conversation.

Second, we can use coding assistants. These include tools like GitHub Copilot and Cline, as well as API Assistants built on top of coding assistants. We built an API assistant loaded with our documentation and a detailed prompt. This gives us specialized tools that know our codebase, naming rules, and best practices, helping our team write reliable code that meets our standards.

Third, task automation has changed how we handle documentation, dependencies, and maintenance. Let's look at how AI helped us finish a complex upgrade project.

## 12.2 Upgrading nearly 7,000 tests: A real-world AI project

Pester is the main testing tool for PowerShell, just like JUnit for Java or pytest for Python. In 2020, Pester v5 came out with big improvements but required changes to how tests were written. The dbatools team had put off upgrading almost 7,000 tests from Pester v4 to v5 for five years. We needed to update syntax, scope rules, and assertion formats in every test file—too big of a job to do by hand.

Then we found Aider and Cline, which we covered in chapter 11. And by combining these tools with PowerShell automation, we could finally tackle this huge update project.

### 12.2.1 Choosing our tools

Aider is a command-line AI coding assistant that works directly with Git and understands your entire codebase. You can ask it to add features, fix bugs, refactor code, or update documentation using natural language or even voice commands. Each change is automatically committed with a descriptive message, keeping your Git history clean. Table 12.1 lists the Aider features that made it essential for our project.

Table 12.1 Aider's key features

| Feature | Description |
| --- | --- |
| File-specific editing | Allows targeted file editing by specifying files on the command line or adding them to the chat |
| Automatic Git integration | Automatically commits code edits with meaningful commit messages after changes |

**Table 12.1  Aider's key features** *(continued)*

| Feature | Description |
|---|---|
| Repository mapping | Maps Git repositories to facilitate navigation in large codebases |
| Real-time pair programming | Syncs with your local editor to update changes, creating a responsive pair programming environment |
| Voice-to-code | Accepts voice commands for editing code, transcribing directly into the chat interface |
| Multifile editing | Manages edits across multiple files, ideal for large or interdependent code changes |
| In-chat commands | Offers command options (/add, /run, /model, and so on) to customize and control file editing and LLM settings |

Aider's command-line interface was useful but limited, so we added Cline for its Visual Studio Code integration. Cline offered additional development and testing features within our existing IDE, as shown in table 12.2.

**Table 12.2  Cline's capabilities**

| Feature | Description |
|---|---|
| Integrated IDE assistant | Works directly within VS Code, offering contextual editing and command execution within the IDE |
| Step-by-step coding tasks | Supports complex tasks like file creation, imports, and syntax fixes autonomously |
| Command execution in the terminal | Executes commands directly in the terminal and monitors outputs for errors during tasks |
| Headless browser interactions | Enables headless browser testing to debug web-based code autonomously |
| Model and API flexibility | Configurable with various API providers, including OpenAI, Anthropic, and others |
| XML-based prompt engineering | Utilizes XML tags for efficient and precise prompt management, reducing interaction overhead |
| Image analysis | Analyzes screenshots and mockups to help translate visual data into actionable code changes |

> **NOTE**  The Git integration in Aider is convenient but comes with one downside: it occasionally replaces new code with old versions during updates. When this happens, we discard the changes and try again, which always works.

With our tools selected and their capabilities understood, we needed a reliable way to handle thousands of test files. Getting the process right would be critical—both for maintaining code quality and for keeping costs down.

### 12.2.2 Developing an effective process

Our first try was too simple. We picked five test files and used a basic but ineffective prompt.

 Convert all of these tests from Pester v4 to Pester v5.

The prompt was weak, and the AI didn't fully understand the differences between Pester v4 and v5. It needed clear instructions about specific changes.

We also found that handling multiple files at once gave mixed results. When we fed it all five files together, the AI started well but would lose track of key details or undo changes. So we switched to working with one file at a time.

As we improved our prompt, we'd test it on a single file, learn from what happened, and use those lessons on the next file. This step-by-step process helped us make our prompt better. Once the prompt worked well enough, we could handle about 20 files at once while keeping quality consistent.

Our next prompt included Pester's documentation and worked better but still had problems. The AI could handle clear syntax changes but sometimes got confused about Pester's complex features, like test scoping and mock implementations.

 Please update this Pester test from v4 to v5 syntax:
- Each test file must start with `#Requires -Module Pester v5`
- Move setup code into `BeforeAll` blocks
- Replace `Assert-True` with `Should -BeTrue`
- Update `Context` blocks to use proper nesting
- Maintain existing test logic

Each batch showed small patterns that we wanted to fix. We made a conventions.md file with detailed rules about our coding standards and PowerShell syntax. At nearly 1,400 tokens, only larger AI models could handle these long instructions.

We had a breakthrough when we showed the AI actual test examples from our code.

 Our key requirements include:
- Parameter validation must be tagged as "UnitTests"
- All setup code must go in `BeforeAll` blocks
- Test assertions must be in `It` blocks
- Use `$PSItem` instead of `$_`
- Array declarations should be on multiple lines

```
Describe "Get-DbaDatabase" -Tag "UnitTests" {
    BeforeAll {
        $command = Get-Command Get-DbaDatabase
        $expected = $TestConfig.CommonParameters
        $expected += @(
            "SqlInstance",
```

```
                "SqlCredential",
                "Database",
                "Confirm",
                "WhatIf"
            )
        }
        Context "Parameter validation" {
            It "Has parameter: <_>" -ForEach $expected {
                $command | Should -HaveParameter $PSItem
            }

            It "Should have exactly the number of expected parameters" {
                $hasparms = $command.Parameters.Values.Name
                Compare-Object -ReferenceObject $expected `
                -DifferenceObject $hasparms | Should -BeNullOrEmpty
            }
        }
    }
}
```

This example showed everything from better test organization to proper Pester v5 syntax. Our success rate went up dramatically when we switched to showing examples instead of just giving instructions.

### 12.2.3 Implementation strategy

We couldn't process hundreds of files at once. We needed a careful approach to catch problems early while keeping a steady pace through the code. We split our work into key areas, listed in table 12.3.

Table 12.3  Migration strategies

| Focus area | Steps taken |
| --- | --- |
| Batch processing | Started with 5 files per batch; grew to 20 as confidence increased; used Aider's retry feature during API overloads; checked results after each batch |
| Error handling | Used Cline for quick fixes when continuous integration and continuous delivery (CI/CD) tests failed; tracked common errors to make our prompts better |
| Version control | Committed changes after each successful batch; used different branches for each set of 20 to 50 files |
| Handling large files | For files over 7.5 KB; split instructions into multiple focused passes instead of trying to do everything at once |

This organized approach helped us maintain quality while moving quickly. But as we tackled larger files, we needed to adjust our strategy.

### 12.2.4 Managing large files

When test files were bigger than 7.5 KB, AI models had trouble staying accurate with complex instructions. So rather than trying to update these large files all at once, we broke our conversion into separate steps. Each step focused on one task, which helped the AI work more precisely. We ran about nine passes per file using GPT-4o mini, costing around 3 cents per file—both effective and cost-efficient.

### 12.2.5 Breaking down instructions into focused passes

We split our main prompt into smaller, specific tasks. Each task matched one part of our original instructions:

- *First pass*—Add #Requires -Module Pester v5 to the file
- *Second pass*—Move setup code into BeforeAll blocks
- *Third pass*—Update assertion syntax (e.g., Should Be to Should -Be)
- *Fourth pass*—Correct parameter validation blocks
- *Fifth pass*—Update mock implementations
- *Sixth pass*—Fix scoping problems
- *Seventh pass*—Update variable declarations
- *Eighth pass*—Standardize Context block naming
- *Ninth pass*—Final cleanup and formatting

This step-by-step method gave each run a single clear goal. The AI could focus on one change at a time instead of handling multiple requirements at once.

We also found that prompt caching helped cut costs and speed up work when using AI models at scale. Instead of explaining the same context over and over, we save this information. When the AI sees similar patterns in later files, it uses this saved knowledge instead of starting fresh.

The cache lasts about 5 to 10 minutes, perfect for processing related files in batches. The first cache write costs a bit more, but reading from it costs much less, saving money on large-scale projects like ours. Cline includes prompt caching automatically, whereas Aider needs a switch to turn it on.

### 12.2.6 The results

What looked like an overwhelming project took just two weeks to complete. The numbers in table 12.4 show how well it worked.

Table 12.4 Project outcomes

| Metric | Outcome |
| --- | --- |
| Tests converted | Nearly 7,000 tests updated to Pester v5 |
| Total cost | Under $50 using different models |
| Prompt development time | One week to understand and refine |
| Main refactor speed | 20 seconds per file |
| GPT-4o mini's fix speed | 2 hours per 700 files |
| Manual fixes needed | Two days for one developer |
| Success rate | 100% after cleanup passes |

The AI didn't just update syntax—it made our tests better:

- More descriptive `Context` block names
- Clearer test names that show their purpose
- Consistent PowerShell best practices
- Better parameter handling through splatting

These consistent standards across thousands of tests make them much easier to maintain and update. For an open source project like dbatools that runs on volunteer work, this level of consistency is a huge win.

### 12.2.7 Lessons learned

Different models excel at different tasks. For complex, full-file changes, larger models like Sonnet worked best. For specific changes, GPT-4o mini did surprisingly well and cost less at $0.007 per file.

This project changed how we view large-scale code updates. Tasks that once looked impossible have become organized, affordable projects. Large refactoring has turned from something we avoided into a clear process with expected results.

### 12.2.8 Beyond test updates: Other uses for AI-assisted development

Our Pester migration showed how AI tools can handle complex code changes at scale. Aider doesn't just find and replace text—it understands code context and makes smart changes. It analyzed our tests' structure and logic, moved setup code to proper blocks, updated assertion syntax, and kept PowerShell best practices throughout.

This method also works for other development tasks that need deep code understanding. Table 12.5 shows some practical examples.

Table 12.5 Other practical use cases

| Category | Use cases |
| --- | --- |
| Code modernization | - Updating framework versions across projects<br>- Converting between API versions<br>- Modernizing legacy code patterns<br>- Standardizing coding conventions<br>- Restructuring code organization |
| System updates | - Modifying configuration files across server farms<br>- Updating package versions in deployment scripts<br>- Converting between data formats<br>- Updating API endpoint references<br>- Standardizing error handling |
| Content migration | - Converting documentation formats<br>- Updating technical specifications<br>- Standardizing code comments<br>- Migrating between platforms<br>- Updating system-wide text patterns |

Our Pester project proved that AI tools can change large development tasks. But as teams add more AI tools to their work, they need organized ways to manage these tools throughout their lifecycle. This is where frameworks like GenAIOps help: they let teams handle AI applications using familiar DevOps methods. Let's look at how GenAIOps works and how it can help manage AI projects like our test migration.

## 12.3 The GenAIOps lifecycle

AI models require specific management throughout their lifecycle, from development to production and maintenance. Standard DevOps practices alone aren't sufficient, so teams use specialized frameworks like MLOps, LLMOps, and GenAIOps to handle AI workflows. Each framework has its own focus, as shown in table 12.6.

Table 12.6 Comparison of GenAIOps, LLMOps, and MLOps

| Framework | Focus |
|---|---|
| MLOps | Extends DevOps to ML models, with reproducible pipelines, automated workflows, and CI/CD integration |
| LLMOps | Focuses on large language models (LLMs), handling training, deployment, and performance monitoring unique to LLMs |
| GenAIOps | Includes LLMOps but covers all generative AI, including smaller models and multimodal applications. Handles scalability, security, and orchestration across diverse generative systems. |

As DevOps engineers, we connect most with GenAIOps because it matches our usual work managing applications through DevOps principles. MLOps works like CI/CD for machine learning (ML) workflows, LLMOps specializes in LLMs, and GenAIOps provides a complete approach for managing generative AI applications.

Figure 12.1 shows the three main GenAIOps phases, which DevOps engineers will recognize: ideation, building, and operationalization. Each phase includes validation steps to ensure quality before moving forward.

The cycle starts with ideation: picking your use case, choosing models, testing prompts, and linking to your data. The build phase follows, during which you test against sample data, check results, and adjust as needed. After success with small tests, you move to larger datasets. Finally comes operationalization: setting up endpoints, adding monitoring and alerts, and connecting the solution to your application.

GenAIOps differs from traditional DevOps in that it needs extra focus on prompt engineering, model performance, and AI output quality. Each phase allows you to go back to previous stages when results aren't good enough.

## 12.3 The GenAIOps lifecycle

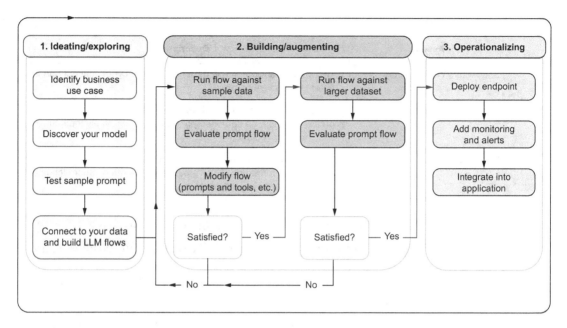

Figure 12.1 The GenAIOps lifecycle. Image courtesy of Microsoft's Nitya Narasimhan, PhD.

### 12.3.1 Applying GenAIOps: A practical workshop example

Microsoft's "Build a Retail Copilot" workshop shows how to manage AI applications in a DevOps environment. This workshop is particularly useful for DevOps engineers new to GenAIOps, as it demonstrates real AI implementation without requiring deep ML knowledge.

We recommend working through the workshop materials—especially the videos and hands-on exercises. Even if you don't build the complete solution, the workshop teaches practical skills for connecting AI to your databases, monitoring performance, handling deployment challenges, and scaling systems reliably. These skills work across Microsoft Azure, AWS, Google Cloud, and other AI platforms.

The workshop creates a customer service chatbot, which is often where organizations start with AI. This chatbot goes beyond basic scripted responses and understands natural language questions to help customers find products. When someone asks "What's the best backpack for a week-long hike?" the chatbot searches product data to give relevant suggestions. Table 12.7 outlines the workshop's key aspects.

The workshop includes tools like Prompty for prompt creation and Prompt flow for managing response workflows. These tools help maintain consistent response quality and smooth integration with Azure services.

> **TIP** If you use AWS or Google Cloud, the same concepts apply. AWS offers Sage-Maker Pipelines, and Google has Vertex AI for similar AI management tasks.

**Table 12.7 Workshop approach**

| Aspect | Description |
|---|---|
| Start with a clear business need. | Test your idea with sample data first to check your concept and find potential problems early. |
| Use familiar tools. | The system uses Cosmos DB for orders and Azure Search for the product catalog, so database professionals can apply their current skills to AI projects. |
| Ensure accurate information. | The system gets answers from your actual product data rather than making up information. This "grounded generation" approach is critical for business applications. |

The workshop shows three essential parts that most AI applications need:

- A system to store and find relevant information (using your existing database skills)
- An AI model to understand user questions (using Azure OpenAI Services)
- A system to monitor and maintain everything (using standard DevOps tools)

DBAs and system administrators will recognize the familiar database and monitoring practices. DevOps engineers will see standard deployment patterns and monitoring approaches. Work through the materials to get hands-on experience managing AI applications. Study the code samples, try the exercises, and adapt the examples to your environment using the resources listed in table 12.8.

**Table 12.8 Workshop resources**

| Resource | Link |
|---|---|
| Sample code | https://aka.ms/aitour/contoso-chat |
| Workshop guide | https://aka.ms/aitour/contoso-chat/workshop |
| Additional resources | https://aka.ms/aitour/WRK550 |

AI technology continues to evolve, but infrastructure practices, monitoring, and data quality are still important. The workshop examples demonstrate how to implement AI for database management, coding, and system maintenance roles.

In chapter 13, we build on these DevOps engineering basics to help you create your own AI-powered applications. You'll learn about function calling, which gives you practical ways to build intelligent applications that understand natural language, handle data, and work with external services.

## 12.4 Prompts used to write this chapter

- Here's a script that's basically a step-by-step of a larger script. The larger script has also been provided for context. Please provide a complete list of summary bulletpoints. I'll start: "First pass: Add #Requires -Module Pester v5 to the file"

- I'm a DevOps Engineer and I find GenAI ops the most relatable because it's similar to what I already do. Would you agree that it's the closest in practice vs MLOps and LLMOps?
- Please convert this markdown table to asciidoc
- I find that providing example code is VERY effective - much better than explaining in words. Why is that?

## Summary

- AI works with DevOps through command wrapping, coding help, and task automation.
- In a real project, AI tools helped convert 7,000 Pester tests from v4 to v5.
- Aider works well on the command line, whereas Cline fits into IDEs. Use both for the best results.
- Show the AI what you want instead of just explaining it.
- Smart batch processing and prompt storage can keep project costs low (under $50).
- GenAIOps adds AI handling to standard DevOps, from planning to deployment.
- Microsoft's Retail Copilot workshop shows how to put GenAIOps into practice.
- AI tools can handle big code changes while keeping quality high.
- Pick the right AI model for each task to save money.
- Good database and DevOps practices still matter when using AI.

# Building AI-powered applications

**This chapter covers**
- Adding AI to applications using APIs, even without advanced AI knowledge
- Using function calling to make AI outputs work with application logic
- Creating AI assistants for databases, documents, and automated tasks
- Working with OpenAI's Assistants API to maintain conversation state
- Getting structured data safely using function calling
- Securing AI systems with proper validation, permissions, and tracking

*Any sufficiently advanced technology is indistinguishable from magic.*

—Arthur C. Clarke

Many software engineers will soon need to add generative AI to their applications. This could mean letting users interact with data through natural language, using AI to sort documents in SharePoint, or creating realistic test data. These AI features can expand your app's capabilities without requiring deep AI expertise.

Adding AI to your applications is often simpler than you may think. You don't need advanced knowledge of AI models because most integrations work through standard REST APIs—similar to how you'd use Stripe or Twilio. This applies to both chat interfaces and core application features.

This chapter focuses mainly on AI integration through function calling. Here, *function calling* means a specific API feature, not the general programming concept or chat interface you may know. It's a method that makes AI models structure their output to match predefined functions, which your app's logic can then use. We'll concentrate on OpenAI's implementation of function calling because it's currently the most popular and easy to use, although other AI models offer similar features.

> **Microsoft's AI integration options**
>
> Microsoft provides its own AI integration options through Copilot. OpenAI lets developers create functions to format AI outputs, but Microsoft gives you several choices: you can use ready-made Copilot features, add plugins and connectors, or build custom solutions with Azure AI services.
>
> Take Microsoft Copilot Studio: it helps you create AI chatbots without much coding. Azure AI Studio lets developers build custom Copilot systems that use Azure OpenAI and Azure AI Search to interact with your data. These tools come with enterprise security features and work well with Microsoft's products, although they need different setup methods than OpenAI's function calling.

Working with function calling has shown us many practical applications. For instance, it can help auto-populate SharePoint metadata, clean up data automatically, and even rename files. As you go through this chapter, remember that these ideas aren't just theory—they're tools you can use to make your data and AI work more efficient.

## 13.1 Function calling

Function calling gets structured data from the OpenAI API, making it easier to add AI features to your applications. When you define functions with specific output types, you ensure that the API returns data in a format your app can use.

> **NOTE** Function calling differs from OpenAI GPT Actions: the former structures AI outputs, and the latter enables live data access. For more on GPT Actions, see appendix B.

When using function calling, OpenAI's API doesn't actually run your app's functions—instead, the model creates JSON that your code can use to call functions.

Here's how function calling works:

1. You define a set of functions that the AI model can use to structure its responses.
2. When a user makes a request, the AI model analyzes the input and determines which function to call based on the defined function specifications.
3. The model generates a JSON object containing the function name and any required parameters.
4. Your application parses the JSON and executes the corresponding function within your codebase.

Because OpenAI's API doesn't directly run the functions, you control how they work in your application. This means you can add security measures, validate inputs, and handle errors as needed.

In this section, we'll show you how to use function calling with OpenAI's API to build AI copilots for your software projects. We'll walk you through the process, although we won't build a complete application.

### 13.1.1 Chatting with the OpenAI API

Let's look at the two main ways to interact with the OpenAI API: the Chat Completions and Assistants APIs. *Chat completions* work by sending a question or prompt and getting an AI response back, like most AI chat interfaces you've used before. They work well for simple, independent interactions where you don't need to remember previous context, such as quick Q&A systems. Chat completions take messages as input and give you an AI-generated message back. For instance, ask *What is the capital of France?* and the AI simply responds "Paris" without needing other context. Chat completions can also use tools like function calling to do more.

*Assistants* are more flexible and can be customized for specific tasks. You can give them instructions to shape their personality and abilities, which helps create AI apps that behave consistently. Assistants can keep track of conversation threads, remembering context from earlier messages. Like chat completions, they can also use tools such as function calling.

Figure 13.1 shows how conversations work between users and AI assistants. The developer creates the assistant, which then handles user questions by analyzing them, creating responses, and sending those responses back.

We'll use the Assistants API because it maintains conversation context, which we need for effective AI copilots. These copilots must understand user questions based on previous messages and the developer's goals. The Assistants API handles this better than managing multiple separate requests.

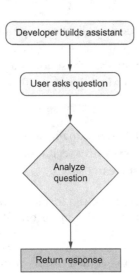

Figure 13.1 Assistant simple conversation overview

### 13.1.2 Building a database copilot

Although Microsoft uses *copilot* in its AI products, the term is widely used across AI applications. A copilot does more than a typical chatbot: it's an advanced, task-focused AI assistant that helps users complete complex tasks in specific areas.

Take a database copilot: it helps users explore databases, write and check SQL queries, and explain results through natural language. Unlike basic chatbots that just answer questions or do simple tasks, copilots work as smart partners that enhance user capabilities in specialized fields.

As SQL Server professionals, we wanted to see how OpenAI's function calling could create a proof-of-concept (POC) copilot for exploring our data. At first, we thought OpenAI would need to access our databases directly: what firewall ports would we need to open? This seemed risky for production data. But we learned that OpenAI doesn't need local agents or firewall changes. Instead of it pulling data, we send the data to it.

Let's see how to add AI to an application using function calling. We'll use PowerShell to run our code and send data to OpenAI, which the chatbot will use to answer questions about the Northwind sample database. Figure 13.2 shows a chatbot's response to a question about the orders table in the Northwind database.

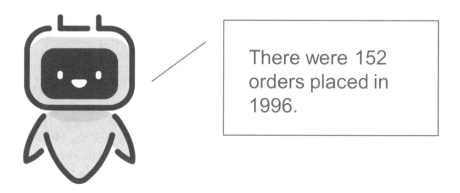

Figure 13.2  Chatbot answering a question about the Northwind sample database

How does the model know about our database schema? It's simpler than we expected: we included the schema in the "system" role message of the API payload. Not quite the magical solution we were hoping for.

The API payload uses system, user, and assistant roles. Getting these roles right matters because they control how the model handles your data and answers questions. When set up properly, these roles help the model give accurate, relevant answers based on your information and questions. Let's look at how each role works in the conversation.

### SYSTEM ROLE

The system role gives context and guidelines that stay active throughout the conversation. When the chatbot creates a response, it follows these system role instructions.

This role sets up how the interaction works by defining rules, instructions, and key information that guide the AI. For applications using AI, you'll put important details like database schemas or the conversation's purpose in the system role.

In our example, we're building a database copilot that makes and checks SQL queries based on what users ask. The system role includes details about the database structure, its rules, and how to handle expected questions. This helps the model understand the context and give useful, accurate answers for our specific requirements. The following listing shows a system role payload example from our database copilot project.

#### Listing 13.1 System role

```
{
  "role": "system",
  "content": "You are an AI assistant that specializes in translating
  natural language queries into MSSQL queries. Your task is to analyze
  the provided database schema, including tables, columns, data types,
  views, and relationships, and generate the appropriate SQL query based
  on the user's natural language input. Ensure that the generated SQL
  query is optimized, efficient, and accurately retrieves the desired
  data from the specified database. If the natural language query is
  ambiguous or lacks necessary information, ask clarifying questions
  to refine the query. The Northwind database schema is as follows:
  Table: dbo.Categories Columns: CategoryID (int), CategoryName
  (nvarchar), Description (nvarchar), Picture (varbinary) Table:
  dbo.CustomerCustomerDemo, Columns: CustomerID (nchar), CustomerTypeID
  (nchar), Foreign Keys: CustomerTypeID -> dbo.CustomerDemographics(
  CustomerTypeID)..."
}
```

The detail you include in the system role payload affects how well the model works. In our example, we list "tables, columns, data types, views, and relationships" instead of saying "all user objects": this specific wording helps the AI focus on key parts of the database schema and removes confusion about what to include.

The right amount of detail depends on your requirements and database complexity. Simple databases may work fine with basic instructions. But if you have complex relationships or critical performance requirements, you may need more detailed guidance.

Finding the right balance often takes some testing. You may discover that the AI works better with more specific or general instructions as you use your application. Feel free to adjust the system role payload based on how the AI performs and what you need it to do.

When adjusting your system role, remember the token limits of different models. GPT-4o can handle 128,000 tokens, and GPT-3.5 Turbo has a 4,096 token limit. Although it's hard to say exactly how much fits in 128,000 tokens, you can usually include a complete database schema with GPT-4o. With the 4,096 token limit of

GPT-3.5 Turbo, you'll need to keep your system instructions brief, potentially skipping helpful but optional details like column datatypes.

Keep in mind that function calling in the OpenAI API is part of the system role structure. These function definitions count toward your token limit and can't be used to get around it. When building your application, consider how to balance system instructions, function definitions, and your model's token limits.

#### USER ROLE

The user role represents the person interacting with the AI model. This is where they ask questions, give commands, or provide data. The model takes this user input and combines it with the instructions from the system role to come up with a response. The clearer and more concise the user is, the easier it is for the model to understand and handle the request effectively. See the following listing.

##### Listing 13.2  User role

```
{
  "role": "user",
  "content": "Show me all the customers from Belgium"
}
```

In practice, crafting effective user messages often requires balancing detail with brevity. This example shows a clear, focused request that the model can easily process given the database schema provided in the system role.

#### ASSISTANT ROLE

The assistant role determines how the model responds to user input. Based on the system context and what the user asks, the assistant creates responses that address the user's goals. These responses can be text, structured data, or specific actions defined by function calls. Listing 13.3 shows an example.

The content in the assistant role comes from the AI model based on the information provided in the system and user roles. The format of the assistant's response will match the function-calling mechanism, which we will explain shortly.

##### Listing 13.3  Assistant role

```
{
  "role": "assistant",
  "content": "Sure, here are the customers from Belgium:
CustomerID: 101, CustomerName: 'Marie Dubois'
CustomerID: 210, CustomerName: 'Lucas Janssen'"
}
```

> **NOTE** Don't mix up the assistant role with OpenAI Assistants in the API we discussed earlier. Although OpenAI assistants are predefined AI personalities with specific traits and behaviors, the assistant role in the conversations API is simply the chatbot's part of the dialog.

Setting up these roles correctly helps your AI model work efficiently with your data and provide accurate answers to user questions. Now let's explore how you can implement function calling in your projects.

### 13.1.3 Implementing function calling

We can create functions that help the assistant generate and validate SQL queries based on user questions. Function calling lets developers define functions that shape how the AI model responds, creating a link between the AI and your application.

The assistant's response when calling a function always comes in JSON format—that's how the OpenAI API works. Your application can then parse this JSON and run the right function in your code. Because OpenAI doesn't actually run the functions, you control their implementation, including security, validation, and error handling.

Database developers typically follow these steps when working with SQL queries:

1 Understand what data the user needs.
2 Write a SQL query that matches those requirements and follows database best practices.
3 Check the query for problems like syntax errors or performance problems.
4 Run the validated query, and return results.

Our copilot mimics this workflow using two main functions:

- One function generates SQL queries based on user questions and the database schema.
- Another function checks these queries for syntax errors, performance problems, and security risks.

By using these two functions, our copilot works like an experienced database developer, following proper steps and best practices to handle queries safely and efficiently. In the context of our database copilot example, we'll define the two functions shown in table 13.1.

Table 13.1 Example functions

| Function name | Description |
| --- | --- |
| get_sql_query | Creates SQL queries based on user questions and the database schema. Returns a JSON object with the SQL string. |
| examine_sql | Checks SQL queries for validity and security risks. Returns a JSON object showing whether the query is valid and safe, with notes about any risks found. |

Figure 13.3 shows how to build and use an AI assistant that creates and checks SQL queries from user input. Here's an example of how it works. When a user asks, "How many orders were placed in 1996?" the assistant checks the question and sees that it needs SQL data. It uses get_sql_query to create a query that will find this information.

## 13.1 Function calling

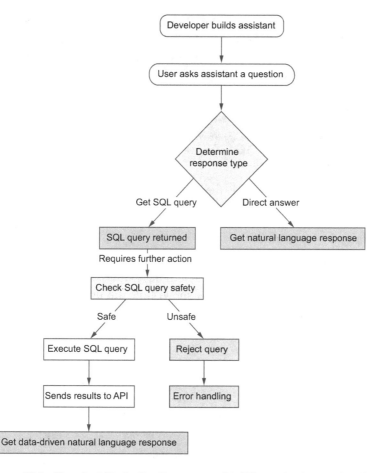

**Figure 13.3** Flowchart illustrating the process of building and using an AI assistant

The get_sql_query function creates the following SQL.

**Listing 13.4 Generated SQL query from an AI assistant**

```
SELECT COUNT(*) AS order_count
FROM orders
WHERE YEAR(order_date) = 1996;
```

Next, examine_sql checks whether this query is safe and correct. After confirming that it's safe, the query runs in the database. If the query shows 152 orders in 1996, the assistant can tell the user the results.

**Listing 13.5 Database response to the SQL query**

```
According to the database, there were 152 orders placed in 1996.
```

If at any point the SQL query is considered unsafe or invalid, the assistant rejects the query and handles the error appropriately. For example, if the user says, "Delete all orders from 1996," the assistant will recognize the potential harm and respond with an error message, as the next listing shows.

> Listing 13.6  Error handling: preventing harmful SQL execution

```
I'm sorry, but I cannot execute that query as it would delete data from
the database. Please reformulate your request in a way that does not
involve deleting or modifying data.
```

Using function calling, developers can build helpful AI assistants that safely work with databases and APIs, making it easier for users to find and use information.

## 13.2 The functions

Let's see a practical example of function calling. Say you're making an AI assistant to help users explore a database with natural language queries. A user asks: "How many orders were placed in 1996?" Figure 13.4 shows how the user, AI assistant, and database work together.

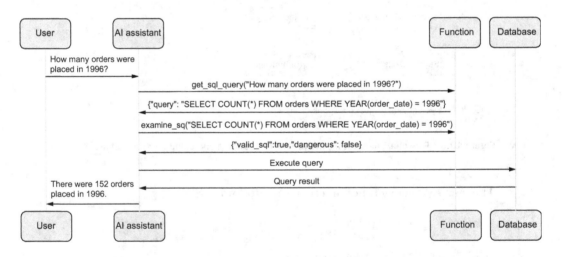

Figure 13.4  Diagram illustrating the process of handling a user query with an AI assistant

Here's how the assistant handles the query:

1. Creates a SQL query to find the information
2. Uses `examine_sql` to check whether the query is safe and valid
3. Runs the query with PowerShell's `Invoke-DbaQuery` cmdlet
4. Sends results to the OpenAI API through REST
5. Creates a natural language response from the query results

**NOTE** Always use read-only database accounts or other security measures to protect against dangerous queries. The AI's query validation adds security but shouldn't be your only safeguard.

We use PowerShell and `Invoke-DbaQuery` in this example because many IT pros know these tools well when working with SQL Server. You could also use C# with `Microsoft.Data.SqlClient` or OpenAI's Python SDK, or make API calls with curl.

### 13.2.1 What matters in AI function design

Effective AI function design focuses on creating well-defined functions that help structure the model's responses. These functions go in the JSON payload that you send to OpenAI. Here's what that JSON might look like.

Listing 13.7 Example JSON payload for AI function calling

```
{
  "model": "gpt-4o",
  "messages": [
    {"role": "system", "content": "You are an AI assistant that helps
     users explore a database with this schema: TABLE:employees..."},
    {"role": "user", "content": "How many orders were placed in 1996?"}
  ],
  "functions": [
    {
      "name": "get_sql_query",
      "description": "Generate a SQL query to retrieve the requested
       information.",
      "parameters": {
        "type": "object",
        "properties": {
          "query": {
            "type": "string",
            "description": "The generated SQL query."
          }
        },
        "required": ["query"]
      }
    },
    {
      "name": "examine_sql",
      "description": "Check if a SQL query is valid and potentially
       dangerous.",
      "parameters": {
        "type": "object",
        "properties": {
          "valid_sql": {
            "type": "boolean",
            "description": "Is this a valid SQL query?"
          },
          "dangerous": {
            "type": "boolean",
            "description": "Is this query potentially dangerous?"
```

```
          },
          "danger_reason": {
            "type": "string",
            "description": "If dangerous, why?"
          }
        },
        "required": ["valid_sql", "dangerous"]
      }
    }
  ]
}
```

When the AI uses our functions, it sends back structured JSON that our code can process, not just text. Here's what a response might look like when we ask the AI to create a SQL query.

Listing 13.8 AI response: function call with SQL query

```
{
  "required_action": {
    "type": "submit_tool_outputs",
    "submit_tool_outputs": {
      "tool_calls": [
        {
        "id": "call_0bFnwcUq61DPk05CwDb9XaQy",
        "type": "function",
        "function": {
        "name": "ask_database",
        "arguments": "{
          \"query\": \"SELECT EmployeeID, FirstName, LastName,
            BirthDate FROM dbo.Employees
            WHERE DATEPART(dayofyear,BirthDate) >=
            DATEPART(dayofyear,GETDATE())
            AND DATEPART(dayofyear,BirthDate) <=
            DATEPART(dayofyear,DATEADD(day, 30, GETDATE()))
            ORDER BY DATEPART(dayofyear,BirthDate);\"
            }"
        }
      }
      ]
    }
  }
}
```

This response has several layers of information. After parsing it, we get a simple JSON object with our SQL query, as shown next.

Listing 13.9 Parsed SQL query from the AI response

```
{
"query": "SELECT EmployeeID, FirstName, LastName, BirthDate
  FROM dbo.Employees
  WHERE DATEPART(dayofyear,BirthDate) >=
```

```
    DATEPART(dayofyear,GETDATE())
    AND DATEPART(dayofyear,BirthDate) <=
    DATEPART(dayofyear,DATEADD(day, 30, GETDATE()))
    ORDER BY DATEPART(dayofyear,BirthDate);"
}
```

We can take this query and send it back to the AI using our `examine_sql` function. The response for this function call might look like the following listing.

#### Listing 13.10 AI response: SQL safety and validity check

```
{
"required_action": {
  "type": "submit_tool_outputs",
  "submit_tool_outputs": {
    "tool_calls": [
    {
      "id": "call_1cGoxdVr72EQl86DxEc0ZbRz",
      "type": "function",
      "function": {
        "name": "examine_sql",
        "arguments": "{
          \"valid_sql\": true,
          \"dangerous\": false,
          \"danger_reason\": null
        }"
    }}]}
  }
}
```

When parsed, this gives us the following response.

#### Listing 13.11 Parsed AI validation response

```
{
  "valid_sql": true,
  "dangerous": false,
  "danger_reason": null
}
```

This structured data works well in our application. Instead of dealing with natural language, we get clear data that we can use directly in database queries or to determine whether a query is safe to execute.

Our app follows this simple flow:

1 We define functions in our API payload that specify what data structure we expect back.
2 The AI model reads user requests and picks the best function to use.
3 It creates a JSON response that matches the structure we set for that function.
4 Our application gets this JSON, pulls out the data it needs, and uses it to do tasks or respond to users.

This makes working with the AI model more predictable and manageable, making it easier to add AI features to our software.

To run these queries and send results back to the AI assistant, you can use `Invoke-DbaQuery` on your local system, as shown in the PowerShell script in the following listing.

##### Listing 13.12 Executing a SQL statement

```
$params = @{
    SqlInstance = $server
    Database    = $db
    Query       = $generatedQuery
}
$queryResult = Invoke-DbaQuery @params
```

You can integrate this functionality into your application in many ways. You might call the REST API from your app code using Python's `requests`, Node's `axios`, or other libraries. What's important is that your app receives structured JSON it can process.

## 13.3 Validating SQL queries with examine_sql

Let's examine the `examine_sql` function, which checks whether generated SQL queries are safe and valid.

##### Listing 13.13 SQL validation function definition

```
{
  "name": "examine_sql",
  "description": "Check if a query is valid and if potentially dangerous.",
  "parameters": {
    "properties": {
      "valid_sql": {
        "type": "boolean",
        "description": "Is this a valid SQL statement?"
      },
      "dangerous": {
        "type": "boolean",
        "description": "Is this SQL query potentially dangerous?"
      },
      "danger_reason": {
        "type": "string",
        "description": "If the query is dangerous, why?"
      }
    },
    "type": "object",
    "required": [
      "dangerous",
      "valid_sql"
    ]
  }
}
```

The examine_sql function takes a SQL query and sends back a JSON object that indicates whether the query is valid and potentially dangerous. If it detects a dangerous query, it provides an explanation. This validation helps protect your database's security and integrity. Both get_sql_query and examine_sql use ad hoc chat completions—quick, separate responses outside the main conversation.

### 13.3.1 Defining what makes a query dangerous

What makes a query "dangerous" depends on your requirements. Your application can set its own rules. For example, you might flag queries that

- Use DELETE or UPDATE without WHERE clauses
- Attempt to modify the database schema
- Try to access sensitive information without authorization

Setting these rules in examine_sql helps ensure that the AI only generates safe SQL queries.

Listing 13.14 Query danger assessment

```
"dangerous": {
  "type": "boolean",
  "description": "Is this sql query potentially dangerous? Will it delete
 data, modify the schema, or expose sensitive information? Updates and
 inserts are allowed."
}
```

We use natural language with function calls even as developers, which is powerful.

### 13.3.2 Generating a user-friendly response

After the SQL query runs through the generate, validate, and execute steps, the assistant creates a conversational response from the results.

Listing 13.15 User-friendly query response

```
There were 152 orders placed in 1996.
```

Function calling creates a clear interface between AI models and database operations, reducing security risks while maintaining flexibility. This approach lets developers use existing skills and tools to integrate AI capabilities without overhauling their architecture.

### 13.3.3 AI-powered SQL assistance in action

Our database assistant example demonstrates how function calling turns natural language into SQL queries. Whether using PowerShell, Python, or Power Apps with the OpenAI API, developers can create AI applications that securely interact with databases and help users analyze data.

Let's look at a real-world example of function calling in action. We'll see how AI can simplify a time-consuming HR process, showcasing how AI integration improves everyday work.

> **Case study: Automating HR data cleanup with AI**
>
> Chrissy, a software engineer, identified an opportunity to use AI for process automation. With basic OpenAI API knowledge, she set out to solve a pressing business problem.
>
> **The problem**
>
> The HR team spent hours each month cleaning training data from a vendor system. They had to manually extract specific information from messy exports and move it to a SharePoint list—a tedious, error-prone task that took time away from critical work.
>
> **The solution**
>
> 1. *Understanding the problem*—After meeting with HR, Chrissy saw that AI could automate the data extraction and cleanup using Azure OpenAI Service and function calling.
> 2. *Designing the solution*—The plan included the following:
>    - A SharePoint Online document library for vendor CSV files
>    - A Power App to start the data processing when files upload
>    - Azure OpenAI Service for data extraction and cleaning
>    - Automated updates to the target SharePoint list
> 3. *Building the AI-driven workflow*—Chrissy built a Power App integrated with Azure OpenAI Service. She used function calling to extract data points, clean them, and ensure accuracy.
> 4. *Testing and refining*—Working with HR, Chrissy tested the workflow on sample data and refined it based on feedback.
> 5. *Deployment and documentation*—After testing, Chrissy deployed the solution with documentation and training to ensure smooth adoption.
>
> **The results**
>
> - Eliminated manual data processing, saving significant HR time
> - Improved data accuracy through AI-based consistency checks
> - Demonstrated practical AI application in business processes
> - Established Chrissy as an AI implementation expert
>
> **Lessons learned**
>
> - Identifying automation opportunities is key to driving innovation.
> - Close collaboration with stakeholders ensures effective solutions.
> - Using existing platforms speeds up AI implementation.
> - Showing business impact helps establish technical leadership.

This case study shows how AI solves common business problems like cleaning data and automating tasks. AI solutions bring key benefits, shown in table 13.2.

Table 13.2  Function-calling advantages in AI applications

| Advantage | Description |
| --- | --- |
| Structured data handling | Consistent, reliable output through data extraction and validation functions |
| Integration flexibility | Works with common tools like SharePoint and Power Apps |
| Better speed and accuracy | Cuts manual errors while freeing staff for critical work |
| Scalability | Solutions work across departments and different data types. |

## 13.4 Practical applications and security considerations

Function calling shines in real-world applications beyond just database work. Currency conversion, data extraction, and image processing are all made simpler when AI can understand natural requests and trigger the right functions. Of course, with great power comes the need for solid security practices.

### 13.4.1 Example: AI-powered currency conversion

Let's look at a Python example of an AI assistant that converts currencies. This assistant uses OpenAI's API to interpret a user's request and the `forex_python` library to perform the actual currency conversion.

Listing 13.16  Python implementation: AI-driven currency converter

```
import openai
from forex_python.converter import CurrencyRates

# Initialize the OpenAI client
openai.api_key = "your-api-key"

# Define the currency conversion function
def convert_currency(amount, from_currency, to_currency):
    c = CurrencyRates()
    return c.convert(from_currency, to_currency, amount)

# Simulate the AI assistant recognizing the need to call the function
def run_assistant():
    # Simulate a response as if coming from an AI assistant
    user_message = "Convert 100 USD to EUR"

    # Extracting details from the user message (this is simplified and would
    # typically involve more complex processing)
    amount = 100
    from_currency = "USD"
    to_currency = "EUR"
```

```
# Call the conversion function
conversion_result = convert_currency(amount, from_currency, to_currency)
print(f"{amount} {from_currency} is {conversion_result:.2f}
↪{to_currency}")
```

```
run_assistant()
```

This code shows how function calling lets AI do specific tasks like currency conversion using external data and custom functions. Other uses include

- Getting clean, typed values from data entry validation
- Extracting structured labels and boxes from images
- Pulling action items and key points from meeting notes

> **NOTE** Want to see function calling in practice? Check out https://github.com/potatoqualitee/dbatools.ai—a PowerShell module built to demonstrate how function calling works. This project shows PowerShell and .NET developers how to build database assistants using OpenAI models. Looking at the code helps you understand how to create an AI assistant, structure function calls, and work with AI responses in a real app.

Function calling makes AI models better by providing structured data, helping you add AI features to make your applications more capable. If you want the power of function calls without programming expertise, check out appendix B, which shows how to connect ChatGPT to external tools and services through a simple web interface.

For developers implementing function calls, security should be a top priority. We discuss this next.

### 13.4.2 Security considerations for function calling

The biggest risk with function calling comes from the AI model giving malicious input to your functions. Even trusted models like GPT-4o sometimes give unexpected output. Here's how to protect your applications:

- *Input validation*—Use strict type checking and whitelisting. For SQL queries, always use parameterized queries and never string concatenation. For file paths, validate and normalize all paths before access. Store sensitive paths in the configuration; never let the AI build them.
- *Output filtering*—Parse all JSON responses into objects first. Never evaluate strings or dynamically execute code from AI output. Use strong typing and schema validation to reject malformed responses.
- *Access controls*—Run AI functions with minimum permissions. For database queries, use read-only accounts. For file access, limit the AI to specific directories. Never let AI functions access sensitive data without human review.

- *Error handling*—Log errors without exposing details to the AI. A malicious prompt might try to extract system info from error messages. Return generic errors like "Query failed" rather than SQL error text.
- *Rate limiting*—Count function calls by time period and complexity. Complex queries need stricter limits than simple lookups. Consider per-user and per-model limits.
- *Logging*—Track each function call's input, output, and context. Log who initiated the call and what data was accessed. Set alerts for unusual patterns like repeated failed calls or access attempts.

Always test your security with adversarial prompts. Try to trick the AI into accessing forbidden data or running dangerous commands. If you find holes, fix them before production.

> **TIP** Want to explore another approach to getting consistent AI responses? Check out appendix A to learn about structured outputs, a technique that works with both cloud and local models. Whereas function calling provides a way to make AI wait for external data or actions, structured outputs let you specify exact response formats with no expectation of a return call. Both approaches help you get reliable, machine-processable data from AI models, whether you're working with OpenAI's cloud services or local models like Ollama.

This wraps up our technical coverage. The book's final section shifts focus to the human side of IT work. Chapter 14 looks at handling conflicts and crises—skills that often matter as much as technical knowledge. These insights into managing difficult situations and people will help build your leadership abilities and career growth, which we explore in the remaining chapters.

## 13.5 Prompts used in this chapter

- I'd like to move the attached case study to somewhere in the attached chapter. Please suggest a spot.
- Should I include information about GPT Actions or move it to the appendix?
- Please reorder the summary bullets in order of appearance

## Summary

- AI adds natural language interaction and workflow automation to software without requiring deep AI knowledge.
- OpenAI's function calling formats AI outputs consistently, making them reliable and easy to use in applications.
- The Assistants API from OpenAI maintains conversation context, perfect for AI copilots that need to track ongoing tasks.

- AI copilots excel at creating and checking SQL queries, helping users work with databases safely and efficiently.
- AI assistants integrate well with PowerShell and Python, making it simple for developers to add AI features to their applications.
- AI automation improves business workflows by handling tasks like tagging metadata, organizing SharePoint files, and cleaning HR data.
- Good security practices, including input validation, access controls, and query verification, keep AI automation safe.

# Part 4

# *Leadership and growth with AI*

How do you lead effectively in an AI-powered workplace? Success in the AI era requires more than just technical know-how: it needs a fresh approach to leadership and professional growth. Chapters 14 to 17 show you how to blend AI capabilities with the human touch, which makes great leadership possible. You'll discover practical ways to handle interpersonal challenges, manage team dynamics, and guide your organization through AI adoption. Whether you're currently leading a team or building toward your next career move, we'll explore how AI can help you be more effective while staying true to what makes leadership human: empathy, judgment, and vision. This part of the book gives you a clear picture of how to thrive as a leader in an AI-enhanced workplace and help others do the same.

# Conflict resolution and crisis management

**This chapter covers**
- Handling workplace conflicts and how AI can help resolve them
- Managing IT project crises, including how to lead and make decisions
- Setting up tech solutions for disaster recovery and keeping operations running

AI can help IT professionals handle workplace conflicts, manage project crises, and set up systems for disaster recovery. This matters because technical work often involves disagreements that need quick solutions.

When it comes to handling disputes, including technical ones, AI helps by giving neutral, fact-based suggestions. This keeps the focus on fixing problems rather than getting stuck in arguments. Even if you're not trained in difficult conversations, AI tools can guide you toward better outcomes.

We love this chapter because it shows how AI can make work life better. When we think about what makes jobs difficult, avoiding conflicts causes more problems than technical mistakes. People often dodge conflicts to keep things peaceful, but this usually backfires—creating more tension and bigger problems down the line.

Dealing with problems right away tends to create a better workplace where people are happier. Take Chrissy's experience: she was asked to quickly write replication code for "temporary" use. Knowing that temporary solutions often become permanent, she pushed back and asked for time to build something proper.

Her request was initially rejected, leading to a clash. She defended her position, pointing to the team's commitment to quality work. Her lead insisted that they were too pressed for time but eventually admitted the deadline could shift. Despite some heated words, Chrissy got the time needed to build a solid solution. This face-off actually improved their working relationship—her lead valued her drive for quality, and she appreciated that he listened to her concerns.

Chrissy's case shows how handling conflicts well can lead to positive outcomes. She's had previous experience practicing, but not everyone has that advantage. That's where AI comes in: it provides guidance for handling conflicts and crises, helping IT teams build stronger, more effective workplaces.

## 14.1 Addressing workplace conflicts

Most people avoid conflict, even though it's part of work life. When facing a difficult situation, many skip hard conversations because they worry about stress and discomfort. But avoiding these discussions often leads to worse problems, from growing resentment to reduced work quality.

AI helps people who dislike confrontation by suggesting good responses and ways to solve problems. With AI support, finding the right approach becomes easier, making tough situations less scary.

IT teams often face several types of conflicts:

- Personal clashes between team members
- Disputes over limited resources
- Disagreements about technical choices
- Problems from outside pressure, such as client deadlines

AI can help in the early detection of these problems through sentiment analysis and communication pattern recognition and then suggest ways to fix them. In technical terms, *sentiment analysis* means using AI to detect whether text shows positive, negative, or neutral feelings—basically, reading between the lines. *Communication pattern analysis* means finding trends and connections in how teams interact, which helps improve working relationships. Now let's look at how AI can spot and help solve IT conflicts.

### 14.1.1 Strategies for effective conflict resolution

ChatGPT and similar applications are valuable for decision-making because they're neutral. Although AI can have data biases, it doesn't play favorites. Unlike humans, AI isn't influenced by who it had dinner with last night, which side is more confident, who's more attractive, who they went to school with, or who did them a recent favor. It stays free of the human factors that often affect decisions.

Making AI the official tiebreaker can work well. Team members are less likely to resent their manager for decisions they don't like: they can blame the AI instead. This removes personal tension from work disagreements and reduces pressure on leaders.

The following section presents a real example from our work when we faced a technical dispute about our SharePoint farm recovery plan. It shows perfectly how AI can help solve technical disagreements.

### 14.1.2 SharePoint standoff

Something we appreciate about ChatGPT is how it sees all sides of a situation. Remember the "unexpected mediator" case from chapter 1? During a major system outage, an engineer insisted on sole control over recovery work, citing their unique expertise. This created tension and delays, even though other team members felt capable of helping despite not being SharePoint subject matter experts (SMEs). After resolving the crisis, we used ChatGPT to document everything for the report.

AI could have helped even more as a neutral decision-maker. It could have shown how downtime affects customer satisfaction and suggested practical solutions, including backup plans if the engineers' work didn't succeed. This would have encouraged everyone to work together better.

Let's show how ChatGPT could have helped here. We'll explain the situation and ask for its advice.

 The heads of our departments face a dilemma: should they allow our systems engineers to repair the SharePoint farm in the absence of our SharePoint SME? The SME has been away for two weeks and won't be back for another week, during which time SharePoint has been entirely offline. The SME suggested we wait for their return to undertake the repair, doubting the systems team's capability to resolve the issue. The SharePoint SME is trusted by management, so overriding their advice raises concerns. Meanwhile, our systems engineers are ready and willing to attempt a fix. The customer has lost all patience — 3 days of downtime was fine, 2 weeks is not. What information do you need from me to help decide whether we hold off until the SME's return, or mobilize the engineers to fix the system now?

 Before making an informed decision on whether to wait or have the engineers step in to resolve the issue, I would need answers to a few vital questions:

- Has the SharePoint SME provided any specific reasons for their concern over the Systems Engineers approaching the problem? Have there been previous experiences where similar issues were mishandled by others?
- Do the Systems Engineers have all the access and permissions they need to fix the SharePoint farm?
- How detrimental has the downtime been to the business productivity? What are the potential risks associated with elongated downtime?
- ...

- Are there any temporary measures currently in place to run the operations that rely on SharePoint? Are these sustainable if you wait another week for the SME to return?
- Do you have support contracts with Microsoft or third-party vendors that could provide emergency assistance in this situation?

Once these questions are answered, we can assess the risk and benefit of each approach and make a decision that minimizes disruption and cost to the business, while maximizing the efficiency of resolution.

Already we see several questions that management did not ask in the real-life scenario. Perhaps they didn't know enough about IT to go deeper or didn't think to ask *why* the SME thought the engineers were incapable.

Questions like these are central to understanding the situation and making an informed decision. If you're in the early stages of your career, you may not know to ask these questions. If you're more experienced, you may not ask them because you assume you already know the answers. Either way, ChatGPT is a perfect tool for helping you think through these questions and make a better decision.

An unexpected benefit from the response to this example is that ChatGPT not only gave the recommendation to allow the systems engineers to move forward but also provided detailed reasons.

Given the current situation and the further information provided, it seems feasible to allow the Systems Engineers to attempt a fix on the SharePoint farm.

Several factors lead to this conclusion:
- The SharePoint Subject Matter Expert (SME)'s concerns appear to stem more from personal distrust rather than any evidence suggesting the incompetence of the Systems Engineers.
- While the official SME is not present, the experience across the Systems team is more than sufficient to handle the situation.
- The fallout from the current SharePoint downtime is increasingly causing disruption and dissatisfaction across the organization. The temporary measures in place are seen as insufficient, and the event is attracting higher-level executive attention - indicating a need for a solution sooner than later.
- Finally, the fact that you have existing support contracts with Microsoft to provide emergency assistance in this situation adds another layer of security. They are already on standby, ready to provide any necessary assistance.

In conclusion, it seems advisable under the current circumstances to authorize the Systems Engineers to proceed with the repair, given their demonstrated expertise and understanding of the SharePoint system.

Perfect! This is exactly the kind of advice that management needed: it's clear, concise, and provides a solid rationale for the decision. The reasoning can then be used to explain the decision to upper management, to customers, and even to the resistant

SME. It's a win-win-win-win-win. (Did you just laugh at the "win-win-win-win-win"? It was suggested by GitHub Copilot. We laughed and accepted the proposed text.)

This story highlights AI's potential for mediating workplace disputes, providing unbiased advice for clearer and more effective decision-making. It can even bring some of that magic to possible early detection of potential conflicts, offering proactive strategies to mitigate them before they escalate. Let's see how to do this in the next section.

### AI's role in detecting and mediating IT conflicts

In chapter 7, we covered managing email with chatbots like Google Gemini and Microsoft M365. These tools do more than check emails for tone and clarity. They can analyze how your team communicates to find possible conflicts and suggest ways to prevent them. This helps remote teams where body language and subtle signs of trouble are harder to spot.

If your email system doesn't have a chatbot (or if it's not working well yet), ChatGPT can still help with conflicts. The process takes more work because ChatGPT can't access your mailbox directly. You'll need to copy the text, remove sensitive details, and upload it yourself.

Even though it required extra steps, we found ChatGPT better at analyzing emails than early versions of Gemini and Microsoft Copilot. Microsoft's tool wouldn't do sentiment analysis, and Gemini skipped most of our emails.

Let's see how ChatGPT can spot early signs of conflict in team emails. We took a tense email thread, changed names and private details, saved it as text, and asked ChatGPT to examine it. We wanted it to find shifts in tone and communication patterns that might show growing tension.

 Conduct an analysis of recent team email communications to detect any subtle signs of emerging conflicts, particularly focusing on the dynamics between team members. Look for changes in tone, frequency, and patterns of communication that might indicate underlying tensions. Since team members may not openly discuss their concerns, suggest a strategy that includes a set of direct, open-ended questions. These questions should be designed to facilitate constructive dialogue among team members, helping to uncover and address any issues before they escalate.

 A detailed analysis of the team's email exchanges reveals subtle signs of potential conflict, particularly between Carlos and Sofia. Carlos's communications with Sofia have gradually become more terse and functional, deviating from the more engaging tone he uses with other team members. This shift might suggest a growing tension or discomfort in their interactions. Similarly, Sofia's increasingly frequent and detailed requests for clarification from Carlos could indicate a lack of confidence in his contributions, further straining their working relationship.

To proactively address these emerging tensions, especially considering that Carlos and Sofia might be reserved about discussing their issues, facilitating a structured conversation with them could be highly effective. Here, direct questions can serve as a powerful tool to encourage open dialogue. You might consider arranging a session to ask them questions such as:

For Carlos:

- Can you recall any recent interactions with Sofia where the communication didn't go as planned? What do you think was the reason?
- How do you feel Sofia's responses have affected the project or team atmosphere?
- Have there been times when you felt your input was not adequately considered by Sofia? How did this impact your work approach?

For Sofia:

- Are there instances where you've found it difficult to understand Carlos's directions or expectations?
- In what ways do you think Carlos could provide better support to help meet the project's objectives?
- Have you felt hesitant to share your viewpoints with Carlos? What would make you feel more at ease in expressing your thoughts?

Questions for both:

- What strengths do you see in each other that could benefit the project?
- Can we discuss a recent disagreement and explore how it was handled? Might there be a more effective way to address such issues in the future?
- What steps can we take to enhance our communication and clarify our roles and responsibilities to avoid misunderstandings?

This approach not only aims to unearth the specific issues causing friction between Carlos and Sofia but also encourages them to consider how their interactions affect their work and the broader team dynamic. By guiding them through a thoughtful examination of their communication challenges and encouraging them to propose solutions, you can help foster a more understanding and collaborative environment.

ChatGPT provided valuable insights when we tested this approach. Although we can only use it for specific situations right now, it taught us a lot about handling conflicts and understanding everyone's point of view. The system was remarkably good at figuring out why people acted the way they did.

Looking ahead, we expect AI systems will be able to analyze conflicts as they happen and offer immediate solutions. They'll also be able to help manage conflicts over time, not just in single conversations.

### Role-playing potential responses and likely scenarios

AI helps prepare for tough conversations by letting you practice various approaches beforehand in a safe space without worrying about embarrassment or regret if you make a mistake. *Role-playing* means rehearsing conversations to get ready for real situations. Lawyers often use this method to prepare their clients for court. Chrissy learned this technique from her wife, a former attorney, and uses it to get ready for difficult conversations. It reduces her stress and helps her feel more prepared when facing uncertain or tense situations.

## 14.1 Addressing workplace conflicts

Because we've already given ChatGPT the background about Carlos's situation, we can continue our conversation and practice how to talk with him. If you're starting fresh or using a new chat, you'll need to explain the situation to ChatGPT first.

   I am uncomfortable with conflict and afraid to have this conversation. Can we role-play like lawyers do? Let's start with Carlos.

   Sure, in this scenario, I will take on the role of Carlos. Here's how Carlos might express his feelings:

"I've been feeling a bit frustrated lately. I've noticed that Sofia has been asking a lot of questions about my work. It seems like she's second-guessing my decisions. I've been in this field for a long time, and I know what I'm doing. I wish she would trust my judgment more."

Now it's your turn to respond as the mediator. You could acknowledge Carlos's feelings, reassure him about his competence, and express understanding about his concerns. You could also explain Sofia's perspective to him, to help him see that her questions are not an indictment of his competence, but rather a reflection of her desire for clarity. Practice your response, and remember to keep it neutral, empathetic, and solution-focused.

This kind of practice makes a big difference. It boosts your confidence and enhances empathy. AI is particularly useful because it's nonjudgmental and often surprisingly empathetic—sometimes more than people are.

We practiced being a mediator in this example, but AI can also help when you're directly involved in a conflict. Whether you're in Carlos's or Sofia's position, you can use AI to understand the other perspective and plan how to express your views without making others defensive.

Table 14.1 shows some examples of using AI to practice handling personal conflicts. AI creates an environment where you can freely express feelings and learn from different viewpoints. These prompts can help you explore problems thoroughly, especially when discussing them with coworkers feels uncomfortable. Just remember that AI works with what you tell it: if you're not honest about the situation, you won't get useful advice. Next, let's look at a way to prevent conflicts before they start.

Table 14.1  Examples of AI-enhanced conflict-resolution strategies

| Task | Prompt |
| --- | --- |
| Reflective insight | Help me understand different perspectives in a conflict. I'm dealing with a situation involving [brief description of the conflict], and I'd like to see it from other viewpoints to gain a broader understanding. |
| Solution-focused strategy | What are some constructive approaches to resolving a disagreement about [specific issue]? I'm looking for strategies that can help both parties find common ground and work toward a resolution. |
| Communication strategy | Suggest ways to initiate a difficult conversation about [specific issue] at work. I want to address the issue directly but in a way that is respectful and open to dialogue. |

**Table 14.1** Examples of AI-enhanced conflict-resolution strategies *(continued)*

| Task | Prompt |
|---|---|
| Emotional intelligence enhancement | How can I manage my emotions better during sensitive topics? I'm finding it challenging to keep my emotions in check during discussions about [specific issue] and would like some tips on staying calm and composed. |
| Feedback and resolution follow-up | After resolving a conflict, what's the best way to provide and receive feedback to ensure continuous improvement? I'm interested in maintaining a positive relationship with my coworker post-conflict and would like to know how to approach this. |

### 14.1.3 Proactive conflict-resolution agreement

Although practice helps you handle conflicts when they happen, it's smart to plan ahead. A conflict-resolution agreement sets rules for handling disagreements before they occur. Creating these guidelines when everyone is calm helps teams work through problems better later.

It's easier to talk about problems before they come up. Once you're in the middle of a conflict, emotions take over, and people get defensive. We often fail to resolve conflicts because we focus on defending our position instead of understanding others. That's why having rules in place ahead of time works so well. Think of it as the ground rules for your work relationships that you create when you're thinking clearly.

What you're about to read is a true story of how we used ChatGPT to solve a completely unexpected conflict. The irony isn't lost on us that we (Brandon and Chrissy) got into a conflict when writing about conflict resolution. So the obvious thing to do was to follow all our advice and use ChatGPT to help us resolve it.

After a few hours of text messages that failed to lead us to common ground, we copied the text of the entire argument and pasted it into ChatGPT. We were very careful to craft a prompt that was neutral and didn't take sides. We provided the position of each party, what our concerns were, and why we thought our position was the correct one. ChatGPT provided great advice on how to approach a resolution, discussing the pros and cons of each argument. However, it was the suggestion of a conflict-resolution agreement that became a "wow" moment.

Here's what it said:

 Toward the end, Author 1 makes a suggestion, indicating a need for a framework to manage future disagreements. Establishing mutual agreements on how to handle disagreements, what constitutes a reasonable request, and how to communicate concerns respectfully can prevent similar conflicts and ensure a productive working relationship.

We immediately requested an agreement based on the previous suggestion, and the results were amazing.

**Purpose**

This agreement aims to establish a constructive framework for resolving conflicts, ensuring a collaborative and respectful working environment that upholds the integrity of our joint writing project.

**Principles**

1. **Open Communication:** We commit to expressing our concerns, ideas, and feelings clearly and respectfully, avoiding assumptions and ensuring we understand each other's perspectives.
2. **Active Listening:** We agree to listen actively to each other's points of view, seeking to understand before responding and acknowledging the emotions and thoughts expressed.
3. **Empathy and Respect:** We will approach each conflict with empathy, considering the other's feelings and viewpoints, and maintaining respect for each other's expertise and contributions.
4. **Collaborative Problem Solving:** When disagreements arise, we will work together to find solutions that address both parties' concerns, focusing on the project's success and our mutual goals.
5. **Focus on Interests, Not Positions:** We agree to focus on underlying interests and needs rather than defending fixed positions, facilitating more flexible and creative resolutions.

**Procedures**

1. **Issue Identification:** When a conflict arises, the concerned party will clearly articulate the issue, explaining how it affects them or the project.
2. **Discussion:** We will set a dedicated time to discuss the issue without interruptions, ensuring both parties have the opportunity to speak and be heard.
3. **Solution Exploration:** Together, we will explore potential solutions, considering various options that could address the concerns without compromising the project's integrity or our professional relationship.
4. **Agreement:** We will agree on a solution that is acceptable to both parties, clearly outlining any actions required and setting a timeline for implementation.
5. **Follow-up:** We will review the resolution's effectiveness at a later date, allowing for adjustments if necessary.

**Respect for Boundaries**

We acknowledge that certain requests or changes may be deemed unreasonable if they compromise the project's integrity, our professional standards, or personal boundaries. In such cases, we agree to revisit the principles of this agreement, seeking external mediation if we cannot reach a satisfactory resolution.

**Commitment to Professionalism**

Above all, we commit to maintaining a professional attitude, recognizing that our shared goal is the success of our project. We agree that the quality of our work and our collaborative relationship takes precedence over individual disagreements.

Not bad, right? We were both surprised at how well this worked, and we hadn't thought of creating a conflict-resolution agreement ourselves, much less including it in this chapter.

Following up, we asked ChatGPT to help define what an "unreasonable" request would be so that we could identify it as such when it happened. It's helpful to match your position against the definition yourself instead of being told by someone else.

 Defining what constitutes an "unreasonable" request in a collaborative project, especially in writing, involves several criteria:

1. **Impact on Integrity:** A request is considered unreasonable if it significantly compromises the project's integrity, purpose, or core message.
2. **Feasibility:** A request is deemed unreasonable if it is practically impossible to fulfill due to constraints such as time, resources, or existing commitments.
3. **Consistency with Goals:** Requests that diverge significantly from the established goals, audience, or scope of the project may be unreasonable.
4. **Personal Comfort and Ethics:** Requests that make one party feel ethically compromised, professionally uncomfortable, or conflict with their personal values or professional standards can be considered unreasonable.
5. **Precedent and Reciprocity:** A request that sets a difficult precedent or lacks reciprocity (one party consistently making demands without accommodating the other's needs) might be viewed as unreasonable.
6. **Effect on Working Relationship:** If fulfilling a request would likely damage the working relationship between the collaborators, it could be considered unreasonable.

To navigate these situations, it's important to have open discussions about each party's boundaries and expectations from the outset.

To top it off, we asked for a process diagram to show how the agreement would work. ChatGPT drew one for us, as shown in figure 14.1. Although isn't the fanciest diagram, it works well and saved us the effort of making one ourselves.

So did ChatGPT help fix our argument? Yes. Reading its analysis showed us new ways to think about our disagreement. We saw that each of us was partly right and partly wrong. Plus, we got a cool diagram out of it.

This shows what AI can do with conflicts. It helps us see different views, practice tough conversations, and create ways to solve problems. It's perfect for people who shy away from conflict or want to handle it better. We learned something too: we should have asked ChatGPT for help right away, before sending all those text messages. It would have saved time.

Now let's talk about managing crises in IT. Nobody likes to think about them, but solid planning makes a big difference if something goes wrong. Although good conflict skills help with daily workplace problems, we also need to be ready for bigger problems that can hurt our organizations. System outages, data breaches, or severe security incidents can quickly escalate into major crises without proper response protocols.

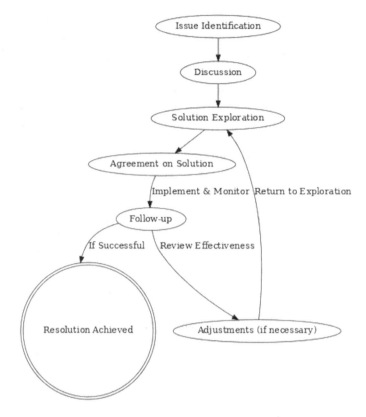

**Figure 14.1** Conflict-resolution process diagram

## 14.2 Crisis management

A crisis means handling an urgent problem and all the people it affects while protecting your organization. This could be a ransomware attack, stolen data, or major system failure. These situations need quick action and strong leadership. Crisis management is a valuable IT skill you can learn, but making tough choices under pressure and guiding your team through problems isn't easy—especially because you probably don't face major crises often.

We'll explore how AI can help during a crisis, from supporting leaders to practicing emergency scenarios and writing disaster recovery plans before you need them. You don't need an official leadership title to lead during a crisis. Whether you're already a manager or just someone who steps up when needed, you should know how to help your team through tough times.

### 14.2.1 Role of leadership in crisis situations

Leaders prove their worth during crises, when teams need them most. But many people struggle to handle high-pressure situations because they may not know where to start or how to tackle the problem, or they may not feel confident making decisions. And let's be honest—crises always show us where we need to improve. This makes sense because crisis management requires practice, but we rarely face serious threats like ransomware attacks or data breaches. And that's definitely for the best.

Let's look at how leaders can handle a crisis with AI support in real time. Picture this: a leader faces a ransomware attack that has locked up company data and caused major outages. They need to make quick decisions, communicate clearly, and guide the organization through this mess. They must update executives but don't fully understand the technical details of the attack. They turn to AI for quick, practical advice to handle the current crisis.

Our company just got hit with ransomware and most of our data is encrypted. I'm the VP above the IT director. I need to communicate with the CTO and I need to ask the IT director questions to get a better idea of what's going on. I know that we replicate our data to another site but that's about it. What questions do I ask and of who? I'm lost and freaking out.

Dealing with a ransomware attack is a challenging and stressful situation. Your first step should be to gather as much information as possible to understand the scope and impact of the attack. Here's a structured approach to help you navigate this crisis:

**Immediate Steps**

1 Ensure Isolation of the Attack: Confirm with the IT director that measures have been taken to isolate the affected systems to prevent the spread of the ransomware.

**Communicate with the IT Director**

Ask the following questions to get a clear picture of the situation:

1 What is the scope of the attack? - Understand which systems, data, and services are affected.
2 Have we identified the type of ransomware? - This can help in finding specific advice or decryption tools.
3 Is the incident response plan activated? - Confirm the steps being taken as per the company's predefined incident response plan.
4 What is the status of our backups? - Confirm if the replicated data is intact and when the last backup was taken.
5 What are the immediate next steps to mitigate the situation? - Understand the action plan to secure the network and recover the data.

**Communicate with Executives**

Prepare to communicate the situation to other executives by gathering the following information:

1 **Brief Overview of the Incident**: Explain what happened, the suspected time of the attack, and the type of ransomware, if known.
2 **Impact on Operations**: Detail which operations are affected, potential downtime, and impact on customers or partners.

3. **Response Actions**: Outline the steps being taken by the IT team to address the situation, including any immediate actions to secure the network and data.
4. **Legal and Regulatory Considerations**: Discuss any potential legal or regulatory implications, including data breach notifications.
5. **Communication Plan**: How and when we will communicate with employees, customers, and stakeholders.
6. **Next Steps and Decision Points**: Outline the decisions that need to be made, including whether to engage with the attackers, involve law enforcement, and the strategy for data recovery.

**Ongoing Management**

1. **Regular Updates**: Schedule regular updates with the IT director and executive team to monitor progress and adjust strategies as needed.
2. **External Communication**: Carefully manage communication with external parties to protect the company's reputation.
3. **Review and Learn**: Once the immediate crisis is managed, conduct a thorough review to understand how the breach occurred, and implement measures to prevent future attacks.

Remember, clear and calm communication is key during a crisis. Being well-informed will help you make the best decisions for your company's recovery and security.

This is already fantastic, and we're just getting started! You may be wondering why we told ChatGPT that we're lost and freaking out. It's because we often talk to ChatGPT the way we'd talk to a confidant, especially if we're feeling insecure. ChatGPT is surprisingly good at providing reassurance (and it can provide more if you ask), and it's also great at providing a clear, structured plan for moving forward.

This is an excellent example of how AI can help leaders in crisis situations. It's not just about the information; it's about the emotional support too. From here, you can continue to use AI to help with the steps that it proposed.

 Help me compose an email to the IT director that asks all the questions you told me to ask.

 Certainly! Below is a template for an email to your IT director that incorporates all the necessary questions. Feel free to adjust it to fit your company's tone and specific situation.

Subject: Urgent: Attack Assessment

[IT Director], Thanks for everything that you and the team are doing to address the ransomware attack.

I am looking to better understand the current status and eventually discuss our next steps. Can you please provide me with updates on the following:

1. What is the scope of the attack? Specifically, which systems, data, and services have been affected?

2  Have we been able to identify the type of ransomware used in the attack? If so, what specific advice or decryption tools are available for this type?
3  Is our incident response plan fully activated? I want to ensure we are following our predefined steps and adapting as necessary to the situation.
4  What is the current status of our backups? Are the replicated data and systems intact, and when was the last successful backup completed?
5  Finally, what are the immediate next steps we need to take to mitigate the situation? This includes securing our network, recovering data, and any other critical actions you recommend.

I am here to support you and your team in any way possible and understand it may take some time to respond. I'd like to update the executives and will let them know that we will provide them with an update as soon as we have more information.

This email is clear and concise, and it provides a solid foundation for the IT director to respond. Once you receive the IT director's response, you can continue to use AI to help you craft your next steps, including how to communicate with the executives and how to manage the situation moving forward.

It feels like with AI, we've got a crisis management expert on call during any disaster. What a relief.

### 14.2.2  Generative AI's role in disaster recovery and COOP

Disaster recovery (DR) deals with getting services back online after major problems like natural disasters or other catastrophic events. It involves systematic processes and steps to restore systems to working order. Continuity of operations planning (COOP) makes sure critical business functions keep running during and after disasters.

Every organization needs both DR and COOP to stay operational and limit downtime, but most people find these topics dull. Even when laws require having these plans, many resist creating them because the work seems overwhelming and they aren't sure where to begin. Figure 14.2 shows a humorous depiction of unpreparedness in a crisis.

Figure 14.2  A humorous depiction of unpreparedness in crisis

Generative AI makes these tasks easier by streamlining documentation. Although real-time DR and COOP plan generation are still on the horizon, AI helps us create required documents now and showcase our IT planning skills.

Enterprise AI services like Amazon Bedrock, Azure OpenAI Service, and Google Vertex prioritize security, so you can use actual company data when creating documentation. With consumer AI tools like ChatGPT Plus and Gemini Advanced, it's better to request templates and add details yourself or use placeholder data that you replace with real information later. The following example uses Azure OpenAI Service to build DR documentation.

 I'm a MySQL DBA at an organization with about 100 servers. I've been asked to deliver DR documentation and I want you to help me create it. What do you need from me?

 To assist you in creating comprehensive Disaster Recovery (DR) documentation for your MySQL environment, I'd need some specific information about your current setup and requirements:

1 **Inventory Details**: A list of all MySQL servers, including their roles (e.g., primary, replica), configurations, and any relevant hardware or cloud service details.
2 **Current Backup Strategy**: Information on how backups are currently handled, including the types of backups (full, incremental, binary logs), frequency, storage locations, and any backup software or services used.
3 **Recovery Objectives**: Your Recovery Time Objective (RTO) and Recovery Point Objective (RPO) for each server or application, to understand the maximum tolerable downtime and data loss.
4 **Existing Disaster Scenarios**: Any disaster scenarios you've already identified that the DR plan needs to address, such as data center outages, hardware failures, or cyber attacks.
5 **Disaster Recovery Procedures**: If any DR procedures are currently in place, details on those, including any automated failover mechanisms or manual intervention steps.
6 **Compliance Requirements**: Any regulatory or compliance requirements that affect your DR planning, such as data sovereignty laws or industry standards.
7 **Key Contacts**: A list of personnel involved in DR processes, including internal teams (IT, security, operations) and external vendors or partners, with contact information.
8 **Test Plans**: Any previous DR test plans and their outcomes, to identify areas of strength and weakness.
9 **Critical Dependencies**: Information on dependencies between servers or applications that could affect recovery processes.
10 **Budget Constraints**: Any budgetary constraints that might influence the choice of DR solutions or strategies.

With this information, we can begin to structure your DR documentation, outlining specific recovery strategies for each scenario, detailed procedures for backup and restoration, communication plans during a disaster, and schedules for regular DR testing and updates.

After you share this information, ChatGPT creates DR documentation with all the required sections. Simply paste your template into ChatGPT and ask it to merge everything into one document.

ChatGPT can help with each documentation component. Ask for guidance on backup strategies, recovery goals, possible disaster scenarios, DR steps, and compliance needs.

This approach works well beyond MySQL. Instead of adapting the response for other systems, just ask your chatbot directly for help with those specific platforms.

### CRISIS SIMULATION

AI can help you prepare for emergencies before they occur by running crisis simulations and testing your responses. Like role-play exercises, these practice sessions build confidence and improve your ability to handle stressful events. You can also check whether your crisis plans actually work and fix any problems you find.

Creating and using crisis management documents ahead of time helps too. Having solid plans means you won't need to improvise during an emergency—you'll know exactly what to do. The following example considers a simulation within a simulation.

 As an IT leader, I want to know how to proactively use AI to enhance our incident response plan and simulate crisis situations for training purposes. What types of simulations could we run, and how can AI generate realistic scenarios for our team to respond to? Also, how can you assist in analyzing our response to these simulations to help us prepare better for real-life crises?

 Leveraging AI in proactive crisis management and training is a forward-thinking approach that can significantly enhance your team's preparedness and resilience. Here are some ways AI can be utilized to create a robust incident response strategy:

**Scenario Generation**: AI can generate a variety of realistic cybersecurity incident scenarios, including ransomware attacks, data breaches, and DDoS attacks. By using historical data and current threat trends, AI can craft detailed simulations that reflect potential real-world situations your team may face.

**Real-time Decision Support**: During simulations, AI can provide real-time feedback and guidance to participants, offering suggestions for improvement or highlighting critical overlooked areas. This immediate feedback loop accelerates learning and skill acquisition.

...

It was interesting to see the different types of scenarios that AI generates. But in our opinion, the following prompt got a better response.

 I'd like you to work with me to do a Disaster Recovery Simulation. How can we get started? I have nothing but a ChatGPT subscription and vague information.

Asking ChatGPT why the second, less specific prompt was better led to a fascinating response.

 The prompt, "I'd like you to work with me to do a Disaster Recovery Simulation. How can we get started? I have nothing but a ChatGPT subscription and vague information," might be more effective for several reasons:

**Directness and Clarity**: It cuts straight to the point, clearly stating the desire to start a Disaster Recovery Simulation with minimal starting resources. This direct approach can help in quickly establishing the groundwork without getting bogged down in specifics.

**Openness to Guidance**: By admitting to having "vague information," it positions the user as open and ready for guidance, encouraging ChatGPT to provide foundational steps and broad suggestions that can help shape the early stages of planning.

**Flexibility**: The prompt doesn't box the conversation into specific outcomes or processes but instead opens the door for a wide range of suggestions. This can lead to creative and diverse solutions that might be overlooked with a more detailed prompt.

**Accessibility**: This prompt makes the task seem more accessible to someone who might not have a deep background in IT or AI, inviting advice that starts from basic principles and builds up.

The second prompt works better, as it's simpler and focuses on specific tasks. The first one might be less effective because it includes too many details and assumes deep knowledge of both AI and disaster recovery. Although this detailed style works well for experts, it could confuse teams new to using AI for DR and crisis practice.

When asking for help, be clear about what you need and any knowledge gaps. This applies whether you're working with humans or AI.

#### COMMUNICATION PLANS FOR CRISIS MANAGEMENT

Good communication during a crisis is essential. Microsoft learned this the hard way during the 2007 Xbox holiday outage. The company's poor communication led to legal problems and hurt Xbox's reputation when it was already falling behind PlayStation.

AI tools can help create better communication plans for everyone involved in a crisis. They excel at writing clear messages that share important information effectively and show understanding for those affected.

Let's look at how chatbots like ChatGPT can help create a communication plan for a possible data breach. This example of crafting a LinkedIn post for a hypothetical data breach shows how AI makes crisis communication planning easier.

 I need to draft a communication plan for a hypothetical data breach. I need you to prepare templates and draft statements for various scenarios to expedite the initial response to the breach. Let's start with a statement made for LinkedIn.

 **Subject:** Important Security Notice from [Company Name]

**[Company Name]** is committed to maintaining the security of the data entrusted to us by our customers and partners. We are writing to inform you of a security incident that may have involved personal information belonging to some of our users.

### What Happened?

We recently discovered unauthorized access to our systems, which was immediately investigated by our security team. This incident was detected on [Date], and we took swift action to secure our systems and investigate the nature of the breach.

### What Information Was Involved?

Our investigation indicates that the information accessed could include [types of information affected, e.g., names, email addresses, transaction histories]. We have no evidence that any financial data or passwords were compromised.

### What We Are Doing

- We have secured our systems and increased our monitoring to prevent future incidents.
- We are working with leading cybersecurity experts to enhance our security measures.
- We have notified law enforcement and are cooperating with their investigation.
- We are offering [details of any support offered, e.g., credit monitoring services] to affected users.

### What You Can Do

- Be vigilant against phishing emails and scams pretending to be from [Company Name].
- [Any recommended actions for users, e.g., change passwords, monitor accounts].

### For More Information

Please visit [link to FAQ or dedicated support page] for updates and more details. Our team is also available to answer any questions at [contact information].

We sincerely apologize for any inconvenience this may cause. The trust of our users and partners is paramount, and we are committed to earning that trust every day by taking this matter very seriously and addressing it with the utmost urgency.

Sincerely,

This template should be customized based on the specific details of the breach and your organization's response. It's crucial to communicate openly, transparently, and empathetically, acknowledging the concerns of those affected and the steps being taken to address the situation.

With this template, the chatbot helps write tailored messages for every group from executives to PR teams. You can quickly create press releases, customer updates, and answers to common questions.

**NOTE** AI-generated crisis plans must meet company rules and legal requirements. Get approval from legal teams, compliance officers, and executives to make sure all materials follow regulations and company values. This preparation helps handle crises smoothly and maintain trust.

In crisis communications, AI chatbots shine by crafting messages that speak to each specific audience, and they help teams respond faster without sacrificing quality or empathy.

Looking ahead to our chapter on management rhythms, we'll see how AI makes leadership easier. These tools handle routine tasks so leaders can focus on what matters most: growing their teams, planning ahead, and creating better workplaces.

## 14.3 Prompts used to write this chapter

- What are some top 10 conflicts in the IT workplace? Can be common debates or anything else.
- Okay take that prompt, and rewrite it so that I get those questions out of you. I don't expect the leader to know to even ask these questions.
- Read the following example, written in .adoc format. Understand and explain why it's an incredibly effective use of AI. After you explain, I will paste in another section that I'd like you to complete now that you know what we, the writers, find valuable.
- Any idea why this prompt <prompt1> would be more effective than this prompt <prompt2>
- Can you turn that commentary into a paragraph for me to conclude this section?
- Can you tell me about a crisis that was made worse by a lack of communication? preferably by Google, Microsoft, OpenAI or Amazon.
- Can you create a template Word document with crisis management then let me download it? (terrible result)
- My editor told me I need more media for this chapter—media is like images or tables or call outs, etc. Can you give me some suggestions?

## Summary

- AI can scan workplace messages to identify early signs of conflict and offers solutions before problems escalate.
- AI can help build clear crisis plans fast so teams understand their roles and timing.
- During emergencies, AI can assist in writing effective updates for staff, customers, and media.
- Practice emergency scenarios with AI to gain experience and confidence before real events occur.
- AI can make creating disaster recovery and operations plans easier, keeping IT prepared for problems.

# Management essentials

**This chapter covers**
- Using AI in management tasks
- Establishing team policies and understanding benefits
- Fostering career development and growth
- Streamlining performance review processes

The role of a technical manager is unusually demanding, as it requires a combination of both managerial and technical skill sets. Often, organizations will promote their technical leads to the tech manager position. This transition can be challenging, and letting go of the tech-lead role they're used to takes time. They also have a team to oversee and new managerial responsibilities to juggle. It's a lot on their plate, and effective time management is necessary if they are going to succeed.

Other managers are very good at dealing with people and budgets but find understanding the tech side challenging. Team members are expected to keep up with tech that's always changing, but it can be tough for a manager to stay on top of those changes along with handling their other responsibilities. There's rarely enough time in a day to do everything they need to get done.

In this chapter, we will explore ways to use AI models to address some of these routine and time-consuming managerial tasks. We are not suggesting that you offload all managerial tasks to a chatbot: our employees and coworkers are real people, with real needs, and we must keep that fact front and center at all times. As we work our way through performance reviews, goals, career development, and more, we will provide comprehensive prompts and examples to save you time and take the redundancy out of management tasks. The hope is that you can spend more time with your team members and less time on paperwork. The end goal is to save you time while providing a better experience for your team members.

## 15.1 Policies and benefits

From overseeing team projects and individual tasks to handling contract renewals and interviewing, the to-do list just keeps growing. Communicating PTO allowances and employee benefits can add to our mental workload. We know the information is *somewhere* in an email, an HR presentation, or a document repository we can't find the link to. We wait until we need it and then spend a bunch of time looking for it, but what if we could easily summarize the information for easy reference?

### 15.1.1 Policies

Not only is it important for a manager to understand policy, but it's equally important for team members to understand policy. This includes all the expectations surrounding them. Sharing this information up front can help stop bad habits before they start.

Your team policies will likely be an extension of company policies but customized to fit the culture of your team. We aren't targeting large, official policies here—more like the "rules of the road." Setting expectations around vacation requests, being on call, general communication, and work hours ensures that your team members are properly educated to make the right decisions. The prompts listed in table 15.1 focus on the policies you're most likely to need, starting with vacation requests.

Table 15.1 Team policy prompts

| Task | Prompt |
| --- | --- |
| Vacation requests | Write a vacation request policy for my technical team. Include information about deadlines for requests, discussing holidays with the team, waiting for approval before booking travel, potential blackout dates, passing off active work and projects while out of the office, etc. If you have other useful suggestions, please include them. |

**Table 15.1  Team policy prompts** *(continued)*

| Task | Prompt |
|---|---|
| On-call responsibilities | Write an on-call policy for my technical team. Each person will be on-call for 1 week in a rotation. Responsibilities include checking emails twice a day and monitoring the successful completion of specific scheduled tasks. The backup report should be checked each day to maintain the recoverability of all systems. Pages should be responded to within 15 minutes or less. The employee should be easily reachable at all times during their on-call period. The secondary on-call is responsible for page escalation if the primary on-call misses an alert, but is not expected to actively perform work on the weekend unless assistance is needed. Please include any other standards for on-call to keep systems running without downtime. Include in the policy that any outage affecting system availability should be reported to the on-call Incident manager. Email-based alerts should be responded to when addressed so that others on the team do not repeat work and know that the issue is not outstanding. |
| Communication | Write a comprehensive communication plan for my technical team. The plan should include best practices for internal and external communication, guidelines for using different communication channels like email, service tickets, instant messaging, and video conferencing, and clear expectations for all response times. Also incorporate the use of the paging system, updating the global address book to include cell phone numbers, and leveraging emergency bypass functionality on smartphones for immediate coworkers. |
| Work hours and remote work | Create a comprehensive policy on work hours and remote work for my technical team. Members work from different time zones but should adhere to the time zone of the business. Follow industry best practices for effective teamwork, and describe how each requirement will benefit the productivity and cohesion of the team. |

These prompts are a good starting point for creating your team policies. You can also use them to create a Wiki or KnowledgeBase article for your team to reference. If you already know the details of the policy you want to draft, include those details in the prompt. However, we always like to ask the AI model to make suggestions based on best practices for things we may have missed or simply haven't thought about.

## 15.1.2  Benefits

Let's talk about benefits—a topic that may seem dry but that directly affects your team's well-being. As a manager, you'll want to be ready when questions come up about health coverage and retirement plans. These conversations peak during open enrollment but also pop up when you're bringing new people on board. Think about your company's retirement options: Is there a 401(k) or similar plan? Can new hires join right away, or is there a waiting period? More importantly, does your team really understand how to make the most of these benefits? Remember how we explored AI's document analysis capabilities in chapter 6? Those same tools can help you navigate employee handbooks and benefits documentation. If your company allows it, you can feed these documents directly to AI chatbots for quick analysis. Here are some ways to do it:

- Google Gemini and Claude can process files from Google Drive.
- ChatGPT-4 works with various file types and plugins.
- If your company uses Microsoft 365, Copilot offers secure access to OneDrive files.

Once you've connected your documents to an AI tool, you can ask specific questions about any aspect of your benefits package.

> **NOTE** The following prompts assume that you have uploaded a benefits document to your chosen AI chatbot. Each chatbot has its own method for accessing documents. If your chatbot does not support document uploads, paste the text of the document into the prompt.

Table 15.2 lists some questions about benefits for the chatbot to answer.

Table 15.2 Employee benefits prompts

| Task | Prompt |
| --- | --- |
| Time-off benefits | Can you summarize the time-off benefits available to employees, including FMLA and emergency leave, as mentioned in the employee benefits guide? I live in California, are there extra options available? |
| Compare medical plans | What are the healthcare plan options available to employees according to the employee benefits guide? Please provide a comparison of their features. |
| Cost of benefits | Can you provide a table-formatted breakdown of the cost for the HMO plan for employees, segmented by pay grade, as outlined in the employee benefits guide? |
| Dental and vision | What are the guidelines for dental and vision coverage as per the employee benefits guide? Please include information on coverage limits and options. |
| Retirement | What plans can I choose from for retirement? Is there a 401k or a pension, and does the company match contributions? How can I get the most out of these benefits? |

Determine the most useful information for your team members, and document it separately in a Wiki or KnowledgeBase article to serve as a quick reference. Keep in mind that benefits information and pricing can change yearly, so linking to the live document via URL may be the best way to keep your information current.

### 15.1.3 *Custom GPTs and projects*

The management topics we're covering in chapters 15 and 16 are perfect for creating your own custom GPT. By loading it with your policies and benefits documents, you'll have an always-available assistant for questions that come up. You can use it throughout these chapters to help with evaluations and performance improvement plans. Just remember to keep your custom GPT private to protect your documents. If you need a refresher on setting up custom GPTs, check out chapter 8.

As an alternative to custom GPTs, ChatGPT and Claude also support Projects. Projects are a way to organize chats and documents within folders. You can create a project for each team member, and within that project, you can upload their self-evaluations, 360-degree feedback, and performance reviews. This way, you can keep all the information about a team member in one place, making it easier to reference during evaluations and one-on-ones.

> **WARNING** A word of caution about document sharing: never upload sensitive materials to a public custom GPT. Users can access and download these documents by asking the right questions. Use fictional names, and keep proprietary information out of the documents.

For the complex management tasks we're discussing—especially writing and analysis—we've found Claude Pro particularly valuable. It handles large amounts of information at once and consistently delivers strong results for management-related tasks. Although the free version of Claude is great, you may hit its limits quickly when working through these exercises. You can explore Claude's capabilities at https://claude.ai.

## 15.2 Career development and growth

Let's face it: when you're swamped with daily tasks and putting out fires, helping your team grow can slip down the priority list. But taking a genuine interest in each team member's success is one of the best ways to keep spirits high and get great work done.

One approach that really pays off is creating a skills matrix for each person on your team. Regular one-on-ones are perfect for keeping these matrices up to date. You can meet weekly, every other week, or monthly—whatever works best for your team's rhythm. These check-ins give your people the direct feedback many of them crave while making sure everyone knows where they stand. Plus, these conversations aren't just valuable for your team—you'll learn plenty as a manager too. In this section, we'll explore how AI can help with skills tracking, make your one-on-ones more effective, and even boost your own growth as a leader.

### 15.2.1 Skills matrices

Skills matrices are powerful tools for mapping your team's capabilities—think of them as your talent GPS. They're especially valuable in technical environments where you need to track a wide range of expertise. By understanding each person's strengths and growth areas, you can give more targeted feedback and support. When you combine individual matrices into a team view, you get a clear picture of where your group shines and where you may have gaps to fill through training or hiring. To help get you started, we've provided a sample skills matrix for a SysAdmin team that you can download from https://gptmaker.dev/book/SkillsMatrix.

Ready to build your own? Table 15.3 provides some prompts to help you create both individual and team-wide skills matrices. Keep these handy—you'll use them as building blocks for other management tasks we'll cover later. Although we're providing starter prompts, the real value comes from your input about your team's abilities and experience levels. Draw from performance reviews, self-assessments, and project work to paint the fullest picture possible.

Table 15.3  Skill matrices prompts

| Task | Prompt |
| --- | --- |
| Skills matrix generator | Generate a skills matrix based on team members' self-evaluations, performance reviews, and project contributions. Include soft skills in addition to a list of technical skills I have provided. |
| Skills gap identifier | Analyze the skills matrix to identify any gaps that could impact current or future projects. Provide recommendations for specific training programs or courses that would benefit the team, or if required, recommend hiring to fill these gaps. |
| Skill-project matcher | Given the current skills matrix and a list of upcoming projects, suggest the best team members for each project based on their skill sets. Also, recommend the team members who will learn the most from the project. |
| Team development planner | Use the skills matrix to generate a personalized development plan for each team member, focusing on improving skills that are most needed by the team. |
| Future skills predictor | Analyze industry trends and company strategy to predict what skills will be most valuable in the future. Update the skills matrix to reflect these future needs. |

If there's one tool from this chapter you absolutely need to adopt, it's the skills matrix. Although it may seem abstract at first, the payoff is worth every minute you invest in creating one. Every job role is unique, so you'll need to customize it—start with a simple spreadsheet or list of skills, and build from there.

We keep emphasizing skills matrices because they're useful for so many management tasks. They're especially valuable in one-on-ones, which we'll dive into next. Trust us on this one: taking the time to build a solid skills matrix now will make you a more effective manager in ways you may not expect.

### 15.2.2 *One-on-ones*

One-on-one meetings are vital for managers and employees to discuss performance, career goals, and any problems that may be affecting work. These meetings are an opportunity for personalized communication and can benefit greatly from careful planning and follow-up. Scheduling weekly or bi-weekly one-on-one meetings with an employee can not only keep them on track but also ensure that they know how you feel about their performance. A lack of feedback from a manager can sometimes be interpreted as a negative outlook. In other words, if you don't tell them they are doing a good job, they may think they are doing a bad job.

Using a fully featured video or audio conferencing application with transcription abilities can open doors to sentiment analysis, meeting summaries, and follow-up action items. As discussed in chapter 7, Microsoft Teams can create transcripts of conversations. If you have access to Copilot for Teams, Copilot can generate meeting minutes and action items from the transcription after the meeting. There are also stand-alone AI applications available, such as krisp.ai, which can summarize meeting minutes and create action items automatically. Stand-alone AI applications are more accessible for individuals who do not have enterprise solutions provided by their company. No matter how you accomplish it, the ability to create meeting minutes and action items is a huge time saver.

> **NOTE** Always let people know you're recording or transcribing a conversation; better yet, ask first. Even in professional settings, recordings can make people uneasy—and being up front builds trust.

The prompts in table 15.4 are designed to use existing data to create agenda items, assess sentiment, assist with career development, and resolve problems.

Table 15.4 One-on-one meeting prompts

| Task | Prompt |
| --- | --- |
| Meeting agenda generator | Automatically generate an agenda for one-on-one meetings based on recent performance data, upcoming deadlines, and previously discussed issues. |
| Sentiment gauge | Analyze the text from previous one-on-one meeting transcripts to gauge the sentiment or emotional tone. Highlight any areas that might require special attention in the next meeting. |
| Career pathway advisor | Based on performance reviews and the skills matrix, generate discussion points for career development during one-on-ones. |
| Meeting summary and follow-up | Review the notes and transcripts from the last one-on-one. Summarize the meeting and identify action items or commitments made during the meeting. Suggest a follow-up schedule or appropriate deadline for any identified items. |
| Issue resolver | Create a decision tree model to suggest potential solutions or discussion points for any issues or challenges mentioned in previous one-on-ones. |

These prompts are designed to help you get the most out of your one-on-one meetings with appropriate planning and follow-up. When planning your one-on-ones, set an agenda and review previous action items before the meeting. During the meeting, start with positives to set the tone for the conversation. Practice active listening, and ask open-ended questions. Try your best to be present, and remember to discuss career development and work-life balance with the employee. At the end of the meeting, summarize the key points discussed, and identify action items. Always set expectations and inform the employee of any areas for improvement, because they cannot fix a problem if they do not know about it. The results of successful one-on-one meetings lead up to the next section on performance reviews.

## 15.3 Performance reviews

Next, let's talk about performance reviews—that yearly task that makes most managers groan. The whole concept of merit-based reviews can be contentious, but they're a reality in many companies and demand significant time to do properly. Because most of that time goes into processing information and writing, AI can really shine, especially if you've been keeping good notes throughout the year. Even if you haven't, AI can still help streamline the writing process.

> **TIP** Here's a pro tip: when using AI for performance reviews, create a separate chat for each employee, and keep everything about that person in one place. This helps the AI maintain context and give you more relevant responses as you work through the review.

We've mentioned sentiment analysis in earlier chapters. Simply put, it's a way to analyze text and figure out the emotional tone: positive, negative, or neutral. This can be incredibly useful for spotting any unintended biases and ensuring that your feedback stays balanced. When you need to deliver constructive criticism (and honestly, that's never easy), AI can help you phrase things clearly and professionally while maintaining the key points you need to convey.

Let's begin the performance review process where most companies do: with self-evaluations. We'll show you how AI can help both write and analyze these assessments, walking you through prompts for each step.

### 15.3.1 Self-evaluations

AI can help you analyze your team's self-evaluations and write your own. When reviewing team members' self-evaluations, you'll get insights into how they view their performance, their place on the team, and their progress toward goals.

Good data in equals good analysis out. Ideally, you'll have tracked accomplishments throughout the year or held the one-on-one meetings we discussed in section 15.2.2. Project data showing timelines, accomplishments, and outcomes gives you solid ground to work from. The more concrete the information you provide, the more objective and thorough the evaluation will be.

Writing your own self-eval? Start by giving the AI your goals, rating criteria, and any supporting documentation. Let it know the key points you want to communicate to your manager. Tell the AI to ask you follow-up questions. This often draws out important details you may not think to include up front. This is also a great time to choose a writing style—do you want to be more descriptive or concise? Provide the most relevant information, but make it easy to read and understand.

> **NOTE** Keep in mind that self-evaluations can get lengthy. Some AI tools (especially free versions) may struggle with the amount of text. If this happens, try breaking your content into smaller chunks, or consider upgrading to a premium account that can handle more information at once.

Let's look at some real-world examples, starting with writing a self-evaluation.

 I have attached the goals defined for my performance review period. The goals include criteria on how to meet and exceed the goal. I have also attached a document outlining my achievements for the performance period. Using the defined goals as criteria, I would like you to analyze the achievements document, write a self-evaluation about my accomplishments, and rate my performance as "Meets" or "Exceeds" based on those criteria. Limit the evaluation of each goal to between 3 and 5 paragraphs. Use bullet points to reduce wordiness when appropriate. Be concise.

This example prompt gives you a solid foundation for writing a self-evaluation. Feeding the chatbot your goals, criteria, and achievements helps it understand what you're aiming for. From there, it can assess success and draft your evaluation. Remember to highlight any specific points you want included, and don't hesitate to refine the output with follow-up prompts.

A strong self-evaluation needs to make your case for that rating and merit increase. Without concrete evidence backing up your ratings, it's tough to convince your boss that you deserve a higher rating and bigger raise.

As managers, we tend to write detailed evaluations for our own bosses. But what about your team members? Some may turn in brief self-evaluations that don't give you or the AI much to work with. We've all seen it—someone rates themselves "Exceeds" across the board without explaining why. Get ahead of this by generating guiding questions for your team before evaluation time. Give them a clear framework for providing the detailed feedback you need.

 Create a set of self-evaluation questions for team members that encourages deep reflection on their strengths and weaknesses. The questions should also prompt them to discuss their key performance goals from the past cycle, including specific examples of how they achieved or fell short of these goals. Additionally, I'd like them to rate themselves on their goal achievements and explain the reasoning behind their ratings.

Hopefully, with this guidance, each of your team members will submit a comprehensive self-evaluation with adequate information for analysis. For each goal or section of their write-up, read their response. An AI model can summarize it for you, but it's important to genuinely understand the information and not miss anything the team member thought was important enough to include.

Once you understand the eval as it was intended, you can paste or attach the employee's self-eval into the AI model. Provide your thoughts about their eval, indicating what you agree with and disagree with. Make suggestions for personal growth in the next performance cycle, and ask the AI model to generate a response. To help you, we've created a MS Word document containing three team-member self-evaluations at https://gptmaker.dev/book/SelfEvals.

I have attached a self-evaluation written by an employee, along with the goal definitions assigned to them over the last performance period. I agree with the assessment for goals 1 and 3. However, for goals 2 and 4 I feel that they did not exceed them. The employee should focus on improving their time management skills to prevent missed deadlines. They also had errors in the execution of goal 4 that required intervention. While the employee is strong with operational duties, one recommendation for improvement is to also focus on their project management skills and participation during inter-group meetings. As the representative of their team, they should be present and provide appropriate technical representation. Analyze their self-eval, identify their strengths and weaknesses, and propose suggestions for goals during the next performance cycle classified into the categories: Projects, Personal Development, and Process Optimization. My final ratings for Goals 1 - 4 are Exceeds, Meets, Meets, Needs Improvement. Their overall rating is Meets. With all of this information in mind, write a response to their self-evaluation for me to include in their review. Since goal 4 is rated Needs Improvement, make extra effort to explain why this goal fell short of agreed-upon expectations.

Although the prompt involves multiple steps and lots of text, getting to this point of the evaluation is less work than it would have been otherwise. When you use a single chat conversation for each team member, most or all of the relevant information about the review is still in the context of the chatbot, and each part builds from the previous one.

If you want the chatbot to make suggestions for the write-up, don't forget to ask. And remember, requesting best-practice recommendations is always a good idea: it allows the chatbot to provide suggestions you may not have thought of.

A good self-evaluation isn't only useful for performance reviews. It can also be a valuable tool for career development and growth. Next we'll look at how to analyze self-evaluations to identify skill gaps, actionable insights, and goals for use throughout the next review period.

#### SELF-EVALUATION DEEP ANALYSIS PROMPTS

You've done the hard work of gathering and analyzing performance data—now let's turn those insights into action. Self-evaluations give you a perfect launching point for performance evaluations and planning future growth. Table 15.5 lists some prompts that can help you spot skill gaps, identify opportunities, and craft meaningful goals for the next review cycle.

Table 15.5 Self-eval deep analysis prompts

| Task | Prompt |
|---|---|
| Automated review summary | Generate a concise summary of each team member's self-evaluation, highlighting key strengths and areas for improvement. |
| Performance trend analysis | Compare this year's self-evaluations with last year's and identify patterns or trends in performance. Determine if the team member has effectively addressed weaknesses and improvement opportunities. |

Table 15.5 Self-eval deep analysis prompts *(continued)*

| Task | Prompt |
| --- | --- |
| Goal alignment check | Analyze self-evaluations to determine how well team members' personal goals align with team and organizational objectives. |
| Skill gap identification | Use the self-evaluations to automatically map out a skills matrix for the team, identifying any skill gaps that need to be addressed. |
| Actionable insights generator | Based on the self-evaluations, generate a list of actionable insights that the manager can discuss with each team member during one-on-one meetings. |

These prompts can help you spot important patterns: Is your team member growing over time, or are they facing the same challenges year after year? Although personal goals matter, they need to align with team needs for the best results. If someone wants to develop skills that don't fit their role, the skill gap analysis can help redirect their focus to more relevant areas. Plus, those actionable insights give you concrete items to discuss in your next one-on-one.

But let's expand our view beyond just manager and employee feedback: 360-degree feedback brings valuable perspectives from peers and collaborators. When improvement suggestions come from multiple sources, team members are often more receptive to the feedback and more motivated to act on it.

## 15.3.2 360-degree feedback

360-degree feedback gathers input from managers, peers, direct reports, and sometimes even external partners. When done right, it offers insights from all directions, giving you a fuller picture of how someone works and interacts with others. This broader perspective often helps people better understand their strengths and blind spots.

That said, it's not a perfect system—which explains why not every company uses it. It takes time to gather and process all that feedback, and you may run into problems with bias or feedback that's either too harsh or too soft. In addition, some team members may feel uncomfortable being evaluated from all angles.

Having worked in companies that use 360-degree feedback, we've seen its value when implemented thoughtfully. Used well, it's a powerful tool for both performance reviews and professional development. But you need a way to make sense of all that input—which is where AI can help.

The prompts in table 15.6 can help you analyze this feedback and turn it into actionable plans. These tools will help you spot patterns, create development roadmaps, and track progress over time. As with the skills matrix and self-evals, we've provided a sample MS Word document containing 360-degree feedback for a team at https://gptmaker.dev/book/360Feedback.

Table 15.6 360-degree feedback prompts

| Task | Prompt |
| --- | --- |
| Sentiment analysis | Perform sentiment analysis on all 360-degree feedback comments for this team member. Create a report that summarizes these sentiments, making it easier to grasp the emotional tone of the feedback. |
| Conflict detector | Analyze the feedback from multiple sources for contradictions or conflicting information. Highlight these areas to discuss and resolve during feedback sessions. |
| Strengths and weaknesses summary | Compile a summary of frequently mentioned strengths and weaknesses for each team member based on the 360-degree feedback, and prioritize them based on frequency and importance. |
| Customized development plans | Based on 360-degree feedback, generate a personalized development plan for each team member, complete with suggested training courses, reading materials, or mentorship opportunities. |
| Feedback trend tracker | Compare the latest round of 360-degree feedback with past rounds to identify trends, such as improved performance in specific areas or recurring issues that haven't been addressed. |

Let's walk through how these prompts work together. First, sentiment analysis helps you read between the lines: Are there emotional undercurrents in the feedback that need attention? Consistently negative feedback may signal that someone needs more support, whereas overwhelmingly positive feedback could mean they're ready for bigger challenges.

The conflict detector is particularly useful when feedback doesn't align. Take communication skills, for instance—if one person raves about someone's communication, but another finds it lacking, that's worth exploring. It often points to different communication styles working better with different team members, giving you specific areas to work on.

By summarizing strengths and weaknesses from all this feedback, you can build personalized development plans that make sense. These plans become living documents, helping you and your team members track progress over time.

Best of all, when you combine these 360-degree insights with self-evaluation analysis, you get a more balanced, comprehensive view for the final review. This approach helps reduce bias and gives you solid ground for rating decisions.

### 15.3.3 SMART goals

SMART (specific, measurable, achievable, relevant, and time-bound) goals are a fundamental tool for both managers and their teams—but let's focus on how you as a manager can use them to help your team succeed. SMART goals give everyone clear targets and a shared understanding of what success looks like. When goals are fuzzy, success becomes a matter of opinion. Without clear metrics, you're forced to evaluate performance based on gut feel, and your team members are left guessing about what "good" looks like.

Encourage your team to write their own goals rather than handing them down. When people craft their own goals, they're more invested in achieving them. AI can help—it's great at suggesting potential SMART goals and defining metrics when someone's stuck. Although writing SMART goals isn't anyone's favorite task, the clarity they provide is worth the effort.

Your role here is to help align these personal goals with team objectives. You can use everything we've gathered so far—self-evaluations, 360-degree feedback, and performance ratings—to guide this process. Whether you're helping validate goals your team has created or converting existing goals into SMART format, AI can help ensure that they're both meaningful and measurable.

AI can even help track progress, but keep in mind that predictive prompts need solid data to be useful. We've included some examples in table 15.7 to help you with validation, tracking, and alignment; think of them as starting points you can build on.

Table 15.7  SMART goal analysis prompts

| Task | Prompt |
| --- | --- |
| SMART goal validator | Review the following proposed goal and provide feedback on how well it aligns with the SMART criteria. Provide suggestions for making it more specific, measurable, achievable, relevant, or time-bound. Also provide criteria to rank the goal as Meets, Strongly Meets, and Exceeds. |
| Progress tracker | Based on the SMART Goals set for each team member, create a spreadsheet-based dashboard that tracks and measures progress, including the flagging of any goals that are at risk of not being met. |
| Goal alignment analyzer | Review the SMART Goals of each team member and assess how well they align with the team's objectives and the company's overarching strategy. Provide recommendations for realignment if necessary. |
| Resource allocator | Given the SMART Goals of each team member, suggest an optimal allocation of resources (time, headcount, budget) to achieve these goals within the set timeframe. |
| Performance prediction | Use historical performance data to predict the likelihood of each SMART Goal being achieved. Provide risk assessments and recommend contingency plans for goals that are less likely to be met. |

The SMART goal validator should be immediately useful for most managers because these goals are always tricky to write. But creating goals is just the start. Routine progress tracking during one-on-ones helps keep people on course and gives you early warning when someone's veering off track.

The alignment analyzer helps you check whether the goals connect to team and company objectives. Meanwhile, the resource allocator and performance prediction prompts help spot potentially unrealistic goals early on. It's much better to adjust goals at the start of a review cycle than explain missed targets at the end.

Now that we've covered individual performance, let's zoom out and look at how to evaluate your team as a whole.

### 15.3.4 Team goals

Team goals unite individual efforts toward shared success—and they often come with extra complexity. Whereas individual goals focus on personal growth, team goals require everyone pulling in the same direction. These goals often become part of your own performance metrics as a manager, so getting them right matters twice as much. The trick is finding the sweet spot: ambitious enough to motivate but realistic enough to achieve. Let's look at how to define these goals in a way that sets your team up for success.

#### DEFINING TEAM GOALS

Let's get smart about defining team goals. Start by looking at the patterns in the individual personal goals: if several team members need to strengthen the same skills, that's a natural team goal right there. Remember the skills matrices we created earlier? They're about to prove their worth again. They map out your team's essential skills and individual capability levels, making them perfect input for the prompts we'll cover next. For example, take your team skills matrix and upcoming project list, and let AI help you create winning combinations. Pairing stronger team members with those still learning not only improves project success rates but builds in natural mentoring opportunities.

Table 15.8 offers some specific prompts that will help you identify and define meaningful team goals. Just remember that the quality of AI's suggestions depends on the data you feed it.

Table 15.8 Team goal prompts

| Task | Prompt |
| --- | --- |
| Identify performance gaps | Conduct a thorough analysis to pinpoint areas where our team performance could be enhanced. Propose specific, measurable, achievable, relevant, and time-bound (SMART) objectives to effectively bridge these identified performance gaps. |
| Enhance accountability | Devise a strategy that intertwines individual milestones with our overarching team goals, ensuring each member's efforts are directly contributing to our collective success. Additionally, outline a rewards system that celebrates personal achievements as a means to inspire and motivate the entire team. |
| Goal definition (i.e., database security) | Focus on identifying and implementing key security best practices to fortify our database integrity this performance cycle. Determine the primary areas for security enhancements and establish a clear action plan to address them. |
| Goal and milestone alignment | List potential team goals that are in sync with the milestones of our major upcoming projects. Break down these goals into categories and ensure they are aligned with the overarching project objectives. |
| Encourage innovation and continuous learning | In a landscape that's rapidly evolving due to technological advancements, maintaining our competitive edge requires a commitment to continuous learning and innovation. Reflect on our current required skills and propose team goals that will foster an environment conducive to innovative thinking and upskilling. How can we incorporate new learning opportunities into our daily routines, and what measurable outcomes can we aim for to track our progress in innovation and learning? |

Don't feel like you need to use every prompt we've covered—start small, and build up. Pick the analysis tools that make the most sense for your team right now. They're meant to help, not overwhelm. Just as with individual goals, tracking team progress is mandatory for success. But instead of letting goal tracking slip down your priority list when things get busy, use AI to streamline the process.

Next, we'll discuss tracking these goals. When everyone can see progress at a glance, it keeps the whole team focused and motivated.

#### ORGANIZING AND TRACKING TEAM GOALS

Tracking the progress of a goal is often more difficult than defining it, because it takes ongoing effort. It's common to neglect tracking, but not putting in the work up front means working harder later. As you read the earlier prompts on performance reviews, you may have been thinking how much easier it would be if you already had the metrics in place. We agree, and there's no better time than the present to start collecting them. The prompts in table 15.9 are designed to help you track the progress of team goals so you'll be ready the next time you need to write a performance review.

Table 15.9 Team goal prompts

| Task | Prompt |
| --- | --- |
| Team goal prioritizer | Analyze team members' skills, project requirements, and deadlines to automatically prioritize team goals. Identify any concerns with meeting the goals due to unreasonable deadlines. |
| Team milestone tracker | Design a user-friendly spreadsheet dashboard that tracks and visualizes key milestones, providing real-time updates on progress and upcoming deadlines to ensure all team objectives are met on schedule. Output the result as a downloadable file, or if unable to do so, provide it in CSV format for me to copy. |
| Goal conflict resolver | Identify any conflicting goals within the team or between the team and organizational objectives. Suggest resolutions or alternative goals that eliminate the conflicts. |
| Team goal alignment | Review individual SMART Goals for alignment with team objectives, recommending adjustments for improved collaboration. |

We've given you a lot of prompts to choose from, but they're just the starting point. You may be thinking, "Wait—wasn't AI supposed to save me time, not add more tasks?" Building these systems takes some up-front investment, but it pays off in both efficiency and results. If AI saves you 10 hours on performance reviews but you spend that time tracking team goals, you're not just breaking even: you're building a foundation that will save even more time down the road while improving your team's success rate.

Think of these prompts as building blocks for a more efficient, effective management system. The time you invest now in setting up these processes will pay dividends in smoother operations and better results in the future.

In the next section, we will take a step back from the complexity of goal management and wrap up the chapter with learning opportunities for you—the manager.

### 15.3.5 Manager self-learning

Continuous learning benefits both you and your employees. Incorporating active learning into existing processes can help you stay up to date on the latest technologies and trends while also improving your leadership skills. The prompts in table 15.10 are designed to help you incorporate learning opportunities into activities you are already doing, requiring little to no additional time.

Table 15.10  Manager self-learning prompts

| Task | Prompt |
|---|---|
| Tech update alert | My team supports the following technologies and platforms… [List of technologies/platforms] Search current industry news and updates related to the technologies managed by the team. Provide summaries and implications of major updates or changes. Highlight any new features that I may benefit from implementing. |
| Technology deep dive | Summarize the key functionalities, limitations, and best practices for each technology stack used by the team. Provide links to key documentation and tutorials for further learning. |
| Use-case explorer | Generate real-world use cases that illustrate the capabilities and limitations of the technologies being managed. This can help in understanding how the technology can be leveraged effectively. |
| Peer review insights | Analyze code reviews and technical discussions within the team to identify common challenges or misconceptions related to the technologies in use. Suggest additional learning resources based on these findings. |
| Question generator | Generate a list of questions to ask when talking to internal or external experts on the technologies being managed. I would like to gain deeper insights from people with hands-on experience. |

Although these are only a few suggestions, the prompts in table 15.10 can provide an easy way to incorporate learning into everyday interactions. For more targeted learning, chat with an AI chatbot about specific technologies. As highlighted in chapter 4, ask the chatbot to explain complex concepts in lay terms using simpler analogies, or to act as a tutor to quiz you on your knowledge of a particular technology you oversee!

In the next chapter, we'll move from day-to-day basics to corrective actions and employee growth. Things don't always go according to plan, so what do you do when you need to step in and make a change? AI can help you navigate these tricky waters and keep your team on track.

## 15.4 Prompts used in this chapter

- Suggest 5 prompts to use in this section. They should be prompts a reader can enter and get a helpful response that they can use right away.
- Review this section of the chapter, considering the text and the associated prompts. Determine if the prompts are adequate and make suggestions for improvements.

- Suggest opening and summary bullets for this chapter based on the provided guidelines and defined sections.

## *Summary*

- AI models support tech managers in keeping up with technological advancements while managing team dynamics, ensuring a balance between technical acumen and leadership skills.
- You can streamline routine management tasks, especially performance reviews and policy setting, by integrating AI, thus enhancing efficiency and reducing redundancy.
- Personalize performance reviews using AI chatbots, which provide nuanced sentiment analysis and context-specific feedback to improve the quality and fairness of evaluations.
- Generating a skills matrix is one of the most valuable inputs when using AI in management tasks. Creating the skills matrix may take some work, but is worth the effort.
- You can use meeting transcription to generate meeting minutes and action items, saving time and improving accountability.
- Setting goals and tracking progress is a key component of the successful management of individuals and teams. AI can help with both, but it relies on accurate and detailed data being used as input.
- Using AI for self-learning can help managers stay up to date on the latest technologies and trends while also improving leadership skills.

# Management interventions

**This chapter covers**
- Implementing effective management interventions
- Building and maintaining team cohesion
- Conducting comprehensive candidate interviews
- Mastering time management for technical managers

In chapter 15, we discussed the routine tasks that form the backbone of a manager's weekly, monthly, and yearly responsibilities. Beyond these routines lies a more complex aspect of management: handling unpredictable challenges like diverse personalities and team dynamics. When personal hardships affect performance or new team members need integration, managers must draw on specialized skills that go beyond standard procedures.

This chapter transitions from management essentials to intervention strategies. These approaches require mental energy, thorough documentation, and a deep sense of compassion and understanding. We focus on managing emotions and maintaining clear, direct communication. Although interventions may represent the most challenging aspect of a manager's role, these guidelines help maintain a healthy, productive team environment when facing emotional and personnel challenges.

Can AI help with these sensitive tasks? We believe so. In this chapter, we explore how AI can assist in the intervention process, providing prompts that help managers navigate difficult conversations and create a supportive environment for their team. We also discuss how AI can help with team cohesion, team building, interviewing, and time management, allowing managers to focus more on the human side of management.

> **NOTE** The prompts and strategies outlined in this chapter may initially appear theoretical, but they are designed to enhance your effectiveness as a manager. Implementing these prompts in the workplace will require effort and thoughtful application. AI can offer significant support and insights, but the prompts are not substitutes for the nuanced understanding and decision-making capabilities of a dedicated manager; they are here to complement your skills, not replace them.

We've had success using these very prompts. Remember, the goal is to empower you to lead more effectively, foster a positive and productive work environment, and drive meaningful results for your team and organization.

## 16.1 Management intervention guidelines

Managing performance and behavior problems is an inevitable part of leadership. This section explores how AI can streamline and enhance the intervention process, providing managers with intelligent tools for drafting notifications, identifying problems, and tracking improvement through data-driven methods.

We'll start by examining how AI-generated templates can help create clear, professional documentation, from memos to formal warnings. These templates ensure consistency and objectivity while making efficient use of your time.

### 16.1.1 Memos, warnings, and write-ups

Documentation during interventions significantly affects both team dynamics and the workplace environment. AI tools can help craft clear and effective documents that align with company policies and legal requirements; they allow managers to focus on addressing the core problems rather than on getting caught up in documentation details.

Most organizations provide specific templates and guidelines for addressing performance problems. By incorporating these guidelines into AI models, managers can ensure that their documentation remains compliant with HR and legal standards. The prompts in table 16.1 will help you draft and refine these important documents while maintaining effectiveness, compliance, and fairness.

## 16.1 Management intervention guidelines

**Table 16.1 Memos, warnings, and write-ups prompts**

| Task | Prompt |
|---|---|
| Memo template generator | Generate a comprehensive memo template for announcing [a policy change regarding remote work]. Include the following essential elements: [a clear subject line, an introductory paragraph explaining the reason for the policy change, details of the new remote work policy, implementation date, whom it affects, any action required by employees, and a closing paragraph offering additional support or contact information for queries]. Ensure the template aligns with our company's standards for professional communication and tone. |
| Warning context analyzer | Given the following context: [detailed context of the issue], produce a warning message that addresses these specifics, while aligning with our standard warning protocol and maintaining a professional tone. |
| Write-up form filler | Using the provided details of the incident/employee behavior [insert specific details], create a detailed write-up form that covers all critical aspects as per HR guidelines. Include a section for previous interventions and ensure compliance with our internal policies. If additional details are required, ask me questions to obtain the information. |
| Documentation reviewer | Review this document [attach document] for clarity, tone, and completeness. Highlight areas that lack clarity, suggest tone adjustments for professionalism, and identify any missing key elements. |
| Compliance checker | Cross-check this document [attach document] against our company's compliance checklist and legal guidelines. Identify any sections that may not comply and suggest necessary amendments for compliance assurance. |

The memo template generator streamlines the creation of structured, informative communications. By specifying the message type and required elements, you guide the AI to produce relevant, tailored templates. This approach works for various memo types, including announcements, updates, and reminders, and can be modified to match your specific needs.

For sensitive communications, the warning context analyzer, documentation reviewer, and write-up form filler tools ensure clear language and appropriate tone while checking for potential bias. These tools rely heavily on context, so providing comprehensive information is critical. The AI will prompt you for any missing details needed to properly tailor the content to your situation and ensure complete documentation.

The compliance checker serves as an initial safeguard, verifying that documents align with company policies and legal requirements. Although not a replacement for legal counsel, it helps identify common problems before they become problems. You can provide context by attaching documentation either directly in your chat session or through cloud storage links, depending on your chatbot's capabilities.

Using AI to create reusable templates helps managers maintain consistency in their communications. The added layer of bias checking and compliance review promotes fairness and protects both employees and the organization. This systematic approach to documentation sets the stage for the next step in managing workplace behavior: delivering constructive feedback.

### 16.1.2 Constructive feedback

Constructive feedback is a delicate balance of understanding and tact that can transform team dynamics and boost performance. As a cornerstone of effective management, it builds stronger team engagement and leadership. Our focus here is on creating positive, progress-oriented feedback using carefully designed prompts.

The AI-assisted approaches in table 16.2 can help managers communicate more effectively with their teams, fostering an environment of continuous improvement and support. By incorporating sentiment analysis, AI helps navigate the nuances of team dynamics and individual sensitivities, making feedback more effective and meaningful.

Table 16.2 Constructive feedback prompts

| Task | Prompt |
| --- | --- |
| Feedback phrasing assistant | Generate phrases or sentence structures suitable for providing positive and constructive feedback in [specific scenario, e.g., a performance review or a team meeting]. |
| Situation-action-impact generator | Create a Situation-Action-Impact model for [describe the specific situation or incident, like a missed deadline or a successful project]. |
| Peer feedback compiler | Collate anonymous peer feedback about [specific project or behavior] and generate a summary for a one-on-one feedback session. |
| Feedback follow-up planner | Based on the transcript of a feedback session [attach transcript], develop a list of action items and a follow-up plan post-feedback session to ensure effective implementation and ongoing performance improvement. |
| Emotional intelligence advisor | Analyze the emotional tone of this feedback message [attach or describe the message] and suggest changes for increasing empathy and effectiveness, especially for sensitive topics. |

These five AI-assisted prompts help deliver feedback that minimizes misunderstandings while keeping messages positive and appropriate to the situation. When feedback is well-structured, employees are more likely to accept and act on it, leading to positive changes. The system helps managers compile comprehensive feedback that maintains balance, and regular follow-ups ensure both completion of the feedback loop and ongoing employee support. Through tone awareness and empathy features, these prompts help preserve healthy team dynamics. This AI-powered approach enables managers to deliver meaningful feedback that emphasizes continuous improvement and empathetic leadership.

However, even the best feedback efforts may not always succeed. This brings us to our next topic: the performance improvement plan (PIP). In the following section, we'll explore how PIPs provide a formal, structured approach to addressing ongoing performance problems, complete with clear objectives and measurable outcomes to help guide employees back to success.

### 16.1.3 Performance improvement plans

Performance improvement plans (PIP): three words that can make both managers and employees anxious. When done properly, PIPs aren't just corporate paperwork—they're effective tools for improvement. Think of a PIP as a GPS for someone who's veered off course: it shows their destination and helps them find the best path forward.

We've heard that most PIPs fail, or that by the time managers implement one, it's merely a tool to remove an employee. This isn't how PIPs should be used. We should genuinely try to help employees improve. If we're using a PIP as an exit strategy, we've waited too long to act and might share responsibility for any failures. Want to know the secret to making PIPs work? It's all about clarity, support, and realistic goals. No employee should ever be surprised by what's in their PIP, and they should never feel like they're being set up to fail. We're going for "helpful roadmap" here, not "mission impossible."

We'll demonstrate this approach through an expanded example featuring an Excel dashboard for PIP progress tracking. This dashboard visualizes employee efforts and provides systematic tracking of incidents and feedback. By incorporating AI analysis, we can assess potential success factors and evaluate the PIP's effectiveness by reviewing the completed tracking template.

 Create an Excel dashboard to track the performance improvement plan for a Database Administrator (Senior). The dashboard should include the employee's name, role, and department. It should feature a list of objectives, actions, metrics, deadlines, and KPI scores for each action item. It should also feature Milestones and Action Items with end dates and current status. Utilize bar graphs to visualize KPI scores over time and indicate if the KPI is being met.

The dashboard should look professional and be easy to update. To provide data for the dashboard, ask me questions about the objectives, milestones, and action items and make any suggestions you have to improve the quality of the dashboard.

Using the 4o model, ChatGPT went to work and asked questions relevant to the dashboard sections. It also asked for the milestones and action items the employee would complete. The final result was a downloadable Excel file providing a very solid template for performance tracking. Although it wasn't 100% complete, we were able to quickly tailor the Excel file to add more calculations. The template can also be reused in the future and includes worksheets to track the incident log and feedback loop. Figure 16.1 shows the finalized dashboard template created using information gathered from ChatGPT.

## CHAPTER 16  *Management interventions*

| Employee Name | Position | Department | Manager | | | |
|---|---|---|---|---|---|---|
| Employee 135790 | Database Administrator (Senior) | IT - DBA | Brandon | | | |
| **Objective** | **Actions to Take** | **Metrics for Evaluation** | **Deadline** | **Incidents** | **Max** | **Standing** |
| Improve Attendance | Arrive and leave on time; adhere to work hours | Days late or no-show | 2024-12-31 | 1 | 3 | 67% |
| Increase Participation | Participate in morning meetings; no camera off or mute | Participation score | 2024-12-31 | 0 | 2 | 100% |
| Improve Ticket Completion | Complete service tickets on par with team | Tickets completed | 2024-12-31 | 2 | 2 | 0% |
| Enhance Email Communication | Improve tone and accuracy of emails | Email quality score | 2024-12-31 | 1 | 3 | 67% |
| Reduce Mistakes | Double-check work to reduce errors | Mistakes recorded | 2024-12-31 | 3 | 5 | 40% |
| | | | Overall | 7 | 15 | 53% |
| **Milestone Progress** | **Milestone** | **Deadline** | **Status** | | | |
| | Complete Training | 2024-11-15 | Complete | | | |
| | Pass Assessment | 2024-12-01 | In Progress | | | |
| | Finish Certification Project | 2024-12-31 | Not Started | | | |
| **Action Items** | **Action Item** | **Due Date** | **Status** | | | |
| | Obtain Certification | 2024-12-31 | In Progress | | | |
| | Create Database Migration Plan | 2024-11-20 | In Progress | | | |
| | Present Training Presentation | 2024-11-25 | Not Started | | | |

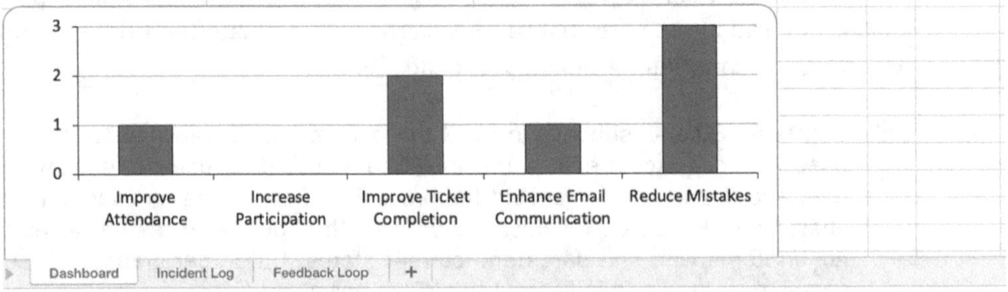

Figure 16.1  **PIP-tracking dashboard**

The results of this AI-assisted approach were impressive. The AI model provided about 90% of the dashboard's structure, and the final polish was done manually. Our manual adjustments included fine-tuning the graph, implementing standing percentage calculations, and adding conditional color formatting. It's not that the AI couldn't have eventually accomplished exactly what we wanted; it was simply faster to implement the changes ourselves. Starting with the AI-generated prototype significantly reduced development time compared to creating the dashboard from scratch. You can access this dashboard template at https://gptmaker.dev/book/EmployeeDashboard.

For the prompts in table 16.3, we'll continue in the same chat session to take advantage of the established context. This will help the AI model provide documentation and answers that align with our previous discussion.

16.1 Management intervention guidelines

**Table 16.3 Performance improvement prompts**

| Task | Prompt | Response summary |
|---|---|---|
| Success predictor | The employee usually misses 3 days of work per month, usually on a Monday or Friday. They were late another 3 days per month on average, over the last 6 months. Their performance reviews have been "Needs Improvement" the last 2 years, but "Meets" the 2 years prior. Team feedback reflects that the employee is less engaged and less likely to assist in tasks and answer questions.<br><br>Considering the attendance record, ticket completion rates by month, performance review ratings, and team feedback for this employee predict the likelihood of the employee completing the PIP. Provide additional insights that can help refine the plan. | The AI model states that based on the available information, the outlook for the employee completing the PIP is challenging. It lays out key points, including attendance, performance reviews, team feedback, and inconsistent performance, and provides feedback on each topic. In addition, the AI model provides predictive insights and suggests regular check-ins, attendance incentives, soft skills training, workload adjustment, transparent metrics, peer support, and professional development. |
| Feedback loop organizer | Create a 2-month schedule to organize the feedback loop for a Performance Improvement Plan, starting from November 1, 2024. Include weekly check-in meetings, KPI reviews at the end of each month, and a final review meeting at the end of the plan. Specify the key activities to be conducted during these meetings, such as outlining PIP objectives, discussing challenges and progress, and making decisions on the next steps. Display the schedule in a calendar format and create a meeting invite file that I can download. | The AI model creates a schedule for the period, outlining which days to meet, and when to discuss key activities, objectives, challenges and progress. A calendar .ics file is also created and presented for download, which requires an OpenAI premium account. |
| PIP outcome analyzer | I have attached a spreadsheet containing the results of a performance improvement plan. Compile a report evaluating the plan's success based on the predefined metrics. The Standing percentage represents the number of incidents committed toward the maximum allowable. The higher the percentage, the better the rating. Based on the analysis, recommend appropriate next steps and state if the employee has met the agreed-upon requirements of the plan. [Spreadsheet attachment] | The AI model creates a report from the spreadsheet. The response is a concise summary of the results of the PIP. The AI model states that the employee passed based on the criteria, except for ticket completion, which requires an intervention. |

The success predictor and PIP outcome analyzer prompts help managers evaluate both potential PIP success and final outcomes. By examining attendance records, performance reviews, and team feedback, the AI attempts to forecast success probability and recommend next steps.

**TIP** You can ask chatbots to output code for the calendar file, which can be copied and pasted into a text file and saved with the .ics extension. This is handy when file download is not supported. It also works for other files, such as spreadsheets with a .csv extension.

Although we can't verify the accuracy of AI predictions, our experience with the analysis proved interesting. In our case, the AI classified success as unlikely despite setting modest incident thresholds. However, it provided valuable recommendations to improve chances of success, including implementing weekly or biweekly progress check-ins. We used additional prompts to create a schedule for these feedback sessions, which we tracked in our PIP template.

When we fed the completed PIP template back to the AI for analysis, it provided a clear assessment of the employee's performance against requirements. The analysis showed that the employee met most PIP requirements but struggled with ticket completion, requiring intervention. The AI suggested extending the PIP for two months with new objectives. Obviously, this analysis is something you should do yourself, but you can use the AI model's unbiased input as a sounding board.

From our experience, AI-generated templates and dashboards prove consistently valuable. They add structure and visual appeal even to challenging management topics. Although they aren't a replacement for your own judgement, tough decisions can be made easier when properly organized and presented.

Now let's shift our focus from write-ups and PIPs to a more positive subject: team cohesion.

## 16.2 Team cohesion

Ever watched a great band perform? Each musician brings their own style and sound, but when they click together—magic happens. That's exactly what we're aiming for with our tech teams. You can have a bunch of rock star developers working in the same space, but if they're all playing different songs, you're just getting noise.

Building a cohesive team doesn't require making everyone best friends (although it's nice when that happens). A cohesive team is more about enjoying the work and each team member complementing the strengths and weaknesses of the others. And in today's world of hybrid and remote work, orchestrating this harmony takes some skill.

In table 16.4, we begin with the team cohesion survey strategy prompt, which helps establish a baseline understanding of team dynamics through systematic surveys. The cohesion score calculator then transforms this feedback into measurable metrics for progress tracking. Building on this data, the team-building activity recommender and conflict predictor offer customized approaches to strengthen team bonds and anticipate potential problems. The reward system designer prompt completes our toolkit by creating ways to recognize both individual and team achievements, helping build a positive and productive team culture.

**Table 16.4 Team cohesion prompts**

| Task | Prompt |
| --- | --- |
| Team cohesion survey strategy | Design a strategy for deploying a comprehensive team cohesion survey that collects actionable data on team dynamics, morale, and collaboration. This strategy should consider factors such as survey frequency, question type (qualitative and quantitative), anonymity of responses, and the method of data analysis. The goal is to ensure that the survey is both practical for team members to complete and effective in providing insights that can lead to meaningful improvements in team cohesion. |
| Cohesion score calculator | Analyze team member feedback and engagement survey results, the team skills matrix, and 360-degree feedback to generate a "Team Cohesion Score." [Attach document] |
| Team-building activity recommender | Suggest team-building activities tailored to the team's interests, strengths, and weaknesses, to improve cohesion. Factor in past activity success and current team morale to recommend the most effective team-building exercises. |
| Conflict predictor | Analyze recent negative team feedback to predict potential conflicts that could harm team cohesion, and make suggestions for proactive resolution. [Attach document] |
| Reward system designer | Design a recognition and reward system that celebrates individual and team achievements, fostering a sense of appreciation and collective success, which is key to team cohesion. Suggest ways to create a better work-life balance among the team members. |

By systematically assessing cohesion, we can address one of the most vital yet often overlooked aspects of team success: the feeling of belonging. Many talented professionals struggle to find their place in organizations even when they're performing well. Creating an environment where each team member feels genuinely valued and connected to their colleagues requires fostering a workplace where people want to stay and contribute.

Through tailored team-building initiatives, early conflict resolution, and meaningful recognition of achievements, we can build teams where belonging isn't just a buzzword. When people feel truly part of something larger than themselves, they're more likely to engage deeply with their work and support their colleagues. However, creating such an environment requires two critical elements we'll explore next: anonymous feedback and consistent team building.

Honest feedback can be challenging to obtain, but it provides managers with invaluable insights for improvement. And although the daily demands of work can make team building seem optional, it's mandatory for maintaining the connections that drive strong teams.

### 16.2.1 Anonymous feedback

Ever notice how people are way more honest in anonymous online comment sections than they are when giving face-to-face feedback? There's something about anonymity that lets people say what they really think—even when we'd prefer not to know.

It's difficult to get honest feedback, even when you have a great relationship with your team, but such feedback is pure gold. The trick is allowing people to share their thoughts without fear of repercussions, and to do that, they have to trust that their feedback is truly anonymous.

Here's the best way to make it work:

- Make it truly anonymous.
- Actually do something with the feedback.
- Keep it constructive.

The prompts in table 16.5 will help you gather anonymous feedback in ways that protect confidentiality while encouraging candid responses. Through sentiment analysis, we can better understand the emotional undertones of feedback, giving us deeper insight into team morale and workplace culture. We'll also address the challenge of synthesizing feedback: how to combine different perspectives into a cohesive narrative that can guide leadership decisions. This includes turning raw feedback into concrete actions and effectively communicating changes back to the team, ensuring that they know their input leads to meaningful improvements.

Table 16.5  Anonymous feedback prompts

| Task | Prompt |
| --- | --- |
| Anonymous feedback collector | Design a form for anonymous feedback. Suggest the fields and questions to include on the form. Then, design a communication plan that transparently explains the mechanisms ensuring the anonymity of feedback submissions. This plan should aim to build trust among employees, assuring them that their candid feedback is both valuable and truly confidential. |
| Sentiment analyzer | Analyze the anonymous feedback for emotional tone and sentiment to understand the general mood of the team. |
| Feedback aggregator | Consolidate all anonymous feedback into coherent themes and insights, making it easier for managers to act on the information. |
| Feedback-to-action converter | Translate the insights gained from anonymous feedback into actionable steps aimed at improving team cohesion and addressing issues. |
| Feedback follow-up engagement | Outline a protocol for responding to anonymous feedback, detailing how to communicate what actions will be taken, and how to engage with the broader team for follow-up. This should include strategies for maintaining the anonymity of the feedback while demonstrating to all employees that their voices are heard and acted upon. |

Think of these prompts as your starting point to a place where everyone on your team can share what's really on their minds. When people know they can speak freely without worry, amazing insights often emerge. Try to create the kind of environment where your team naturally drives positive change because they trust that their voices matter. By making this commitment to hear everyone out, you're not just collecting feedback—you're building the foundation for a stronger, more connected team.

Anonymous feedback gives us insights into an individual's needs, but turning these insights into action often requires bringing people together. The problems revealed through feedback can be addressed with thoughtful team building, which we explore next.

### 16.2.2 Team building

The massive shift toward remote and hybrid work over the past five years has fundamentally changed how teams connect and collaborate. Success now depends more than ever on building strong relationships—not just within our immediate teams, but across entire organizations.

This section explores strategies for meaningful connection in our evolving workplaces. We'll look at ways to help teams bond and collaborate effectively, whether they're sharing an office or connecting across time zones. Through practical approaches and the prompts in table 16.6, we'll address the real challenges of building trust and maintaining relationships in modern work environments. When we create opportunities for genuine connection, teams naturally develop the bonds that drive both innovation and satisfaction at work.

Table 16.6 Team-building prompts

| Task | Prompt |
| --- | --- |
| Inclusive team onboarding and DiSC style analysis | Create a workshop outline for integrating diverse talents and backgrounds into the team. Focus on activities that encourage understanding and appreciation of each member's unique contributions, facilitating an inclusive environment from the onset. Include a DiSC Assessment quiz to help each member determine their DiSC style, and provide tips for how to communicate with each style. |
| Interdepartmental team quest | Design a challenge that promotes collaboration between different functions within the organization. This should involve problem-solving tasks that require diverse skill sets and encourage teams to leverage each other's strengths in a competitive yet cooperative setting. |
| Digital team-bonding experience | Develop a series of virtual events that foster team spirit and camaraderie in a remote work setting. These events should be interactive, engaging, and suitable for digital platforms, ensuring remote team members feel connected and integral to the team. |
| Cross-functional interest-based teams | Develop a framework for creating cross-functional teams that align with the individual interests and strengths of team members. This framework should facilitate collaboration on projects across different teams, encouraging innovation and knowledge sharing. The objective is to harness the diverse passions and skills within the organization to achieve common goals and foster a culture of continuous learning and interdisciplinary teamwork. |
| Team wellbeing programs | Propose a series of health and wellness programs tailored to the team's needs. These could range from fitness challenges to mental health days, aiming to improve overall well-being and work-life balance, reinforcing the team's physical and mental health as a foundation for effective collaboration. |

The strength of a team lies in understanding and embracing each other's differences. One powerful way to build this understanding is through DiSC (dominance, influence, steadiness, conscientiousness) profiles—and AI can help create remarkably accurate insights into how different team members think and work best. Consider running a team exercise where members discover their DiSC profiles and learn how to better communicate and collaborate with different styles. These insights often lead to "aha moments" that transform team dynamics.

When we align individual working styles with cross-functional collaboration, we create deeper connections that make our teams truly exceptional. This understanding of personality dynamics leads us naturally to our next topic: how to introduce and integrate new personalities into existing teams through effective interviewing.

## 16.3 Interviewing candidates

Let's talk about hiring—or, as we like to call it, "technical dating." You've got a great team that works well together, and now you need to find that perfect someone who'll fit right in. No pressure, right?

Here's the tricky part: traditional interviews can be like speed dating. Some candidates are fantastic at first impressions but fizzle out on the job, and others may be nervous wrecks during interviews but turn out to be absolute rockstars once they're comfortable.

The secret? Looking beyond the standard "What's your greatest weakness?" questions. We need to figure out not just whether someone can code, but whether they'll mesh with our team's energy. Will they jump in to help when things get crazy? Can they handle Bob's dad jokes in the Slack channel? You know, the important stuff.

We all have biases, even when we try not to. That's where AI can help you focus on what really matters: skills, potential, and team fit.

In table 16.7, we explore practical assessments and behavioral insights that reveal not just experience and problem-solving abilities but also how candidates may fit into your team's culture. Fine-tuning these approaches helps create a complete picture of each candidate, allowing you to better predict how they'll contribute to your team's success. Before using these prompts, be sure to provide the chatbot with a job description so it understands the specific requirements of the position.

Table 16.7 Interviewing prompts

| Task | Prompt |
| --- | --- |
| Resume bias eliminator | Analyze the provided resume and job description to assess the candidate's fit for the role objectively. Identify their relevant qualifications, skills, and experience, summarizing key strengths and weaknesses in relation to the job requirements. Remove any potentially biasing personal details irrelevant to job performance, such as name, age, gender, ethnicity, or marital status. Present an anonymized summary highlighting the candidate's qualifications, focusing solely on their professional merits for the role based on the resume and job description. Ensure the analysis is fair, unbiased, and adheres to equal employment principles. |

**Table 16.7** Interviewing prompts *(continued)*

| Task | Prompt |
|---|---|
| Technical question generator | Produce a list of technical questions tailored to the specific role, ensuring they are up-to-date with current industry standards. Include:<br>• A real bug we encountered recently<br>• A system design challenge we're facing<br>• A customer interaction scenario<br>• A 'everything is on fire' situation they might encounter |
| Behavioral question recommendations | Suggest a list of behavioral questions aimed at assessing soft skills and team fit, based on the team's current dynamics and needs. Ask me questions about the current team personalities and values to create better questions. We are also looking for someone who is proactive, creative, and good with troubleshooting, problem solving, and customer support. |
| Aptitude test designer | Generate a set of aptitude tests or challenges that can be administered during the interview to gauge problem-solving and critical-thinking skills. |
| Sentiment analyzer | Analyze a transcript of the candidate's verbal cues during the interview, providing insights into their emotional state and confidence level. Attempt to identify any incorrect answers given to questions and provide a summary that we can reference later to compare candidates. Identify potential red-flags. |
| Post-interview evaluation | Compile the candidate's responses, test results, sentiment analysis, and team member notes to generate a comprehensive evaluation report. |

By following structured guidelines for questioning, aptitude testing, and realistic job previews, we can improve our chances of selecting candidates who will thrive within our teams. "But wait!" you may be thinking, "Can't I just Google 'technical interview questions'?" Sure, but that's how you end up asking candidates to recite the OSI model when what you really need is someone who can debug production problems at 3 a.m.

The best technical questions aren't puzzles—they're glimpses into your team's real world. You want to see how candidates think when faced with the kind of challenges they'll actually encounter on the job. Ask open questions that reveal how they approach problems, not just whether they can recite a textbook answer.

Although there's no foolproof formula for hiring, AI opens doors to creative approaches we might not otherwise consider. These new techniques complement our human judgment as we begin what we hope will become successful partnerships that strengthen both the individual and the organization.

In the final section of this chapter, we discuss how effective time management can reinforce the intervention strategies outlined in this chapter and reduce the stress of juggling multiple responsibilities.

## 16.4 Time management for the hands-on technical manager

Picture this: you're deep into troubleshooting a critical system problem when a bunch of IM messages pop up, your calendar reminds you about an upcoming one-on-one, and someone taps your shoulder (virtually or literally) with an "urgent question." Sound familiar? Welcome to the daily juggling act of technical management!

Most of us became technical managers because we were good at the technical stuff. But now we're playing a whole new game where we need to keep our tech skills sharp while also being there for our team. It's like trying to solve a puzzle while hosting a party—and somehow, we need to make both work.

This section provides practical approaches to managing this complex workload through effective scheduling, work prioritization, and delegation strategies. We'll provide prompts designed to conduct efficient meetings, analyze your current time usage, and create systems that help you stay on top of both technical and managerial duties.

Strong time management makes every aspect of leadership more effective, from handling performance problems to building team cohesion. When you control your schedule, you can give your full attention to important conversations, maintain regular check-ins, and still find time for technical contributions. The prompts in table 16.8 attempt to reduce the stress of competing priorities while ensuring that you remain an effective technical leader for your team.

Table 16.8  Time management prompts

| Task | Prompt |
| --- | --- |
| Balanced schedule creation | Based on my provided weekly technical and managerial tasks, create a balanced weekly schedule that allocates time slots for both technical and managerial responsibilities. Ensure that focus is maintained on both areas without neglecting the other. Additionally, allocate time for unexpected tasks or emergencies, which are common in technical management. |
| Prioritization | Identify the top 5 tasks that require immediate attention based on project deadlines and importance. Also, suggest tasks that can be postponed or eliminated to lighten my workload. |
| Task delegation | Determine which tasks and meetings can be effectively delegated to team members based on their skills. Include a follow-up mechanism to ensure these tasks are completed effectively and efficiently. |
| Meeting efficiency | Provide an agenda template for team meetings that focuses on minimizing time while maximizing productivity. Include strategies to encourage active participation and engagement from all attendees. |
| Time management self-assessment | Analyze my activities over a week, focusing on the time spent on each task. Offer recommendations for improving efficiency and suggest strategies to overcome personal time management pitfalls. Additionally, provide advice on balancing managerial and technical responsibilities more effectively. |

Throughout chapters 15 and 16, we've covered an extensive range of management responsibilities—from routine duties to sensitive interventions—along with dozens of practical AI prompts to help handle them. Although not every prompt will fit your priorities or management style, we hope this collection offers valuable starting points that you can adapt to your situation. Getting the most from these prompts requires thoughtful input and careful refinement, but the payoff in time saved and improved outcomes will make the effort worthwhile.

Remember that effective time management serves as the foundation for all these management activities. When technical managers balance their duties well, stay present for their teams, and prioritize effectively, they create an environment of trust and respect. Time management techniques are tools for building stronger, more productive teams while maintaining your technical edge. By applying the strategies and prompts that work best for you, you'll be better equipped to handle both the technical and human aspects of leadership, ensuring success for yourself and your team.

In chapter 17, our final chapter, we think it's fitting to focus on you, covering how to keep growing—both personally and professionally. We examine strategies for career development in an AI-enhanced workplace, touching on increasing your value in the job you have or landing the job you want.

## 16.5 Prompts used in this chapter

- I find the wording of this confusing, how can I reword it?
- What are your expert recommendations for the most successful interviewing tactics?
- I think my team-building prompts are a little too similar to team cohesion. Can you suggest better prompts that are not duplicated?
- Here are some prompts I am going to use, can you recommend a title for them?
- Review the paragraphs for Time Management and suggest a stronger connection to the intervention theme of the chapter. Include the concept that making time for your employees makes them feel like a priority and valued.

## Summary

- Management interventions are a critical part of a manager's role, requiring a delicate balance of empathy and objectivity, which can be made easier with AI.
- AI can assist in the intervention process by creating documentation, helping managers navigate difficult conversations, and creating a supportive environment for their team.
- A consistent approach to constructive feedback is essential for maintaining a healthy team environment. AI can help with phrasing, structuring, and analyzing feedback to ensure that it is effective and actionable.
- AI can help create performance improvement plans that are customized to the individual needs and circumstances of the employee and include a dashboard to track progress, which increases the likelihood of success.
- AI tools can analyze team dynamics and suggest tailored team-building activities, conflict-resolution strategies, and reward systems to enhance team cohesion and productivity.
- In interviewing candidates, AI can aid in balancing the evaluation of technical skills and behavioral aspects, ensuring a fair and thorough assessment of the candidates.
- AI can support technical managers in balancing their multiple roles through intelligent scheduling, task prioritization, and efficient meeting planning.

# Career advancement

**This chapter covers**
- Leading AI adoption in organizations
- Showcasing AI projects and accomplishments
- AI-assisted skill development and certification
- Using AI for job search and negotiation
- Ethical considerations in AI career advancement

Welcome to the last chapter of the book! In the past 16 chapters, we've explored how AI tools can help with everything from coding to documentation. Now it's time to look at what this means for your career.

Throughout our years in IT, we've seen how certain skills consistently lead to success: writing clear documentation that others can actually use, solving problems before they affect users, finding ways to improve processes instead of just maintaining them, and working well with teams even during stressful projects. Whether you're automating deployments or handling a system outage at 3 a.m., these skills make the difference between good IT work and great IT work.

We'll focus on two practical ways to grow professionally:

- Using AI tools to work more effectively in your current role
- Building specialized AI expertise as these technologies become increasingly important in IT

Let's explore specific strategies to achieve both goals.

## 17.1 Leading AI adoption in the organization

After months of implementing AI tools at work, we've found that IT professionals are uniquely positioned to drive AI initiatives. Your technical background helps you spot practical opportunities that others might miss, and your experience solving business problems helps you demonstrate concrete value to decision makers.

Our own journey started small. For example, we noticed our teams spending hours manually tagging documents in SharePoint—a tedious task that everyone dreaded. We implemented AI to handle this automatically, which not only saved time but showed others how AI could improve their work. This success led to other projects, like helping HR clean up their employee data, which used to take weeks of manual review.

These projects taught us valuable lessons about bringing new technology into organizations. Let's look at specific strategies that worked for us and that can help you, whether you're championing AI or any other tech initiative.

### 17.1.1 Advancing through practical problem-solving

If you've been following along with the examples in this book, you're already ahead in understanding how AI can improve workplace efficiency. We've found that many companies want to use AI but need someone to show them how. This creates a perfect opportunity to position yourself as a practical problem-solver.

When our global management suggested exploring AI, we didn't wait for detailed instructions. Instead, we looked for everyday tasks that frustrated our teams. Building on our initial SharePoint success, other teams started asking for help with their own projects. Soon we were working with departments across the organization, from IT to executive leadership.

In our experience, we've seen AI successfully handle

- Creating Power BI dashboards that turned complex data into clear insights
- Generating documentation templates for disaster recovery plans and incident reports in minutes instead of hours
- Documenting existing software systems faster and more thoroughly than manual methods

By starting with practical solutions and showing real results, we built a reputation for getting things done with AI. Each successful project strengthened our position as AI experts who could turn ideas into working solutions. People started coming to us not just for AI help, but for all kinds of technical challenges.

Our work had another benefit: it opened up new career opportunities. As teams saw what AI could do, we took on bigger projects and leadership roles. What started as finding ways to save time on tedious tasks led to promotions and new responsibilities guiding AI strategy across the organization.

> **TIP** AI tools are great at solving problems, but they're not so good at spotting which specific issues in your workplace need fixing. Your best bet is to really know what AI can do, then match those capabilities to the actual pain points you see day-to-day. When you combine your firsthand knowledge with AI's abilities, that's when you get the most useful implementation ideas.

These principles work for any new technology, not just AI. For instance, when we noticed database queries slowing down critical applications, we researched and implemented performance optimization techniques that cut response times in half. Similarly, our team's migration to centralized configuration management eliminated hours of manual server setup and reduced deployment errors by 80%.

The key is showing how your work helps the organization succeed. In our experience, technical skills matter most when they solve real problems and create measurable improvements. Whether you're optimizing databases, automating deployments, or implementing AI, success comes from understanding what your organization needs and delivering solutions that work.

If you're reading this book, you're already thinking about how AI can improve your work. Let's look at a real example of how this played out for Chrissy as she led AI adoption in her organization.

---

### Case study: Driving AI adoption in the organization

*Initial opportunity*—When leaders suggested exploring AI, Chrissy saw a chance to solve real problems. With her software engineering OpenAI background and experience using the API, she started experimenting with AI solutions while learning through hands-on practice.

*AI applications*—Chrissy identified three key areas where AI could help:
- Converting raw HR data into organized database entries, which improved data processing speeds
- Implementing automated metadata assignments in SharePoint, which reduced manual tagging time by several hours
- Generating comprehensive documentation by analyzing codebase content, producing both inline code comments and markdown documentation automatically

*Sharing knowledge across teams*—After discovering that her company had already bought enterprise GPT access, Chrissy made sure everyone knew about it. She helped colleagues learn to use it effectively, building a reputation as the person to ask about AI. Her willingness to teach others made her the go-to AI expert.

*Working with allies*—Chrissy found another engineer interested in AI, and they teamed up. Together, they built a stronger case for bringing AI tools in-house. Having two voices advocating for AI helped convince management to invest in the technology.

*Getting the technical details right*—While Chrissy focused on use cases, her colleague researched what hardware they'd need. Understanding the infrastructure requirements helped them plan better and create realistic budgets.

*Making security a priority*—Knowing their organization's strict security needs, Chrissy and her colleague proposed running AI locally in their air-gapped environment. They worked with security teams to ensure that their setup met all compliance requirements.

*Key lessons learned*

- Learn AI through hands-on implementation to identify business solutions.
- Find allies who share your vision.
- Research thoroughly before proposing solutions.
- Show measurable results to build support.

### 17.1.2 Documenting and showcasing your projects

Great work often goes unnoticed unless you can show its value clearly. In our experience, nothing beats a well-delivered presentation for getting people excited about your projects. This is true whether you're introducing a new AI tool or explaining how you improved system performance.

Modern AI tools that analyze speech, facial expressions, and body language have helped us improve our presentation skills significantly. We'll show you exactly how to use these tools later in the chapter; they've made a huge difference in how we prepare and deliver technical presentations.

Showing the effect of your work doesn't just help you get recognition—it can build support for future projects and encourage others to try new approaches. We've found several effective ways to share our work, listed in table 17.1.

Table 17.1 Communicating your work

| Channel | Description |
| --- | --- |
| Presentations | Create engaging slide decks to present your project to stakeholders and colleagues, focusing on key insights and real-world effect. |
| Blog posts | Write blog posts about your projects for internal or external audiences to share your experiences, challenges, and lessons learned. |
| Workshops | Organize hands-on workshops to explore the practical applications of your project, fostering knowledge sharing and collaboration among participants. |
| Demos | Conduct live or recorded demos of your solution to emphasize its capabilities and effectiveness in solving real-world problems. |

Each type of communication has its place, but presentations consistently get the best results when we need to show the value of our work. A well-crafted presentation has helped us win over skeptical managers, get funding for new projects, and even land speaking opportunities at technical conferences.

Good work doesn't always speak for itself—you need to help others understand its effect. We learned this lesson early on when our first AI projects went mostly unnoticed. Once we started actively documenting our work and showing clear results, like cutting processing time from days to hours, people paid attention. This led to more interesting projects, bigger responsibilities, and new career opportunities. Some of our team members even got promoted based on the AI improvements they championed and clearly demonstrated to leadership.

## Using technology to become a skilled presenter

In our years working with technical teams, we've noticed something interesting: the IT professionals who advance fastest aren't always the most technically skilled. Often, they're the ones who can explain complex ideas clearly. We've watched talented engineers turn small project presentations into career-changing opportunities simply because they could show the value of their work effectively.

Getting good at presenting has opened doors we never expected. What started as routine project updates led to speaking at major conferences. One team member's clear explanation of a tricky database migration caught senior leadership's attention and turned into a promotion. In our case, being able to explain AI concepts clearly helped us land this book deal. The technology itself matters, but being able to present it well matters just as much. The following example considers how to craft an engaging presentation.

 I recently completed an AI-integration project that automates our team's document management process in SharePoint, saving us from time-consuming manual work. I need to create a presentation to showcase this project to the organization's leadership.

Ask me 5 questions about the project that will help you provide an outline for a compelling 10-slide presentation, including key points to highlight, such as the problem statement, solution overview, results, and future potential. Suggest creative ways to visually represent the information.

 Certainly, I'd be happy to help you create an outline for your presentation. I'll ask you 5 questions to gather the necessary information, and then provide an outline with suggestions for visual representations. Here are the questions:

1 What specific manual tasks did your team have to perform before the AI integration?
2 What were the main challenges or pain points in the old document management process?
3 Can you briefly describe how the AI-powered solution works?

4 Have you observed any improvements in accuracy or reduction in errors since implementing the AI solution?

5 Have you received any notable feedback from team members or other stakeholders about the new system?

Once you provide answers to these questions, I'll create an outline for your presentation with suggestions for visual representations. Would you like to proceed with answering these questions?

Becoming a good presenter takes time and practice, but new tools make the learning process easier. Let's look at how AI can help you improve your presentation skills.

### 17.1.3 Advanced presentation training with AI

We give a lot of presentations as IT professionals: explaining new projects to executives, walking teammates through technical solutions, and speaking at conferences. Over time, we've learned that communicating clearly is just as important as having strong technical skills.

New AI tools that analyze speech, text, and video have transformed how we practice presentations. These systems watch and listen as you present and then provide specific feedback about everything from how fast you're talking to whether you seem confident.

We've found GPT-4o particularly helpful as a presentation coach. Here's what it can do:

- Analyze a recording of your talk and point out where you could be clearer or more engaging
- Act as a practice audience, asking the kinds of questions you're likely to get
- Help you prepare for different scenarios, from quick team updates to conference keynotes

Modern AI can also watch your body language and facial expressions while you present. OpenAI's computer vision features can analyze everything from eye contact to how people move around the room. It's like having a presentation coach that catches all the nonverbal details you might miss.

During a demo by OpenAI, their vision system demonstrated the ability to read body language and facial expressions (you can see this in action at https://gptmaker.dev/book/vision). The AI picked up on subtle emotional cues that even humans might miss, showing just how far this technology has come.

Figure 17.1 shows a key moment from this OpenAI demo. The AI accurately read the presenter's emotional state just from the video, pointing out specific facial expressions and body language signals. This kind of detailed feedback helps improve not just what we say but also how we say it.

Figure 17.1   Screenshot from our OpenAI vision capabilities demo

Adding tools like GPT-4o to presentation practice has helped us get better at explaining technical concepts clearly. When we first started using it, we were surprised by how much it improved our team's presentations—especially when explaining complex technical projects to nontechnical stakeholders.

## 17.2  Training and certifications

Staying current with new technologies and skills has always been required in IT, but AI has changed both what we need to learn and how we learn it. In this section, we'll show you how we've used AI to find the right training resources, identify skill gaps, and choose certifications that actually matter for career growth.

### 17.2.1  Acquiring new skills with AI assistance

Finding the right training path used to mean hours of researching different certifications and comparing course materials. Now we use AI to streamline this process. For instance, when we needed to upgrade our DevOps skills, we asked ChatGPT to analyze different certification options. It quickly broke down which certifications would be most valuable based on our current roles and career goals, saving us from pursuing certifications that looked good on paper but wouldn't help us advance.

Can you provide a list of practical, hands-on AI certifications that are suitable for DevOps Engineers? Focus on courses that include real-world applications, automation of DevOps processes, and the integration of AI tools into CI/CD pipelines. Ensure the certifications are current and offered by recognized institutions or platforms specializing in AI and DevOps.

 Certainly! Here's a list of practical, hands-on AI certifications suitable for DevOps Engineers. These certifications focus on real-world applications, automation of DevOps processes, and the integration of AI tools into CI/CD pipelines. They are offered by reputable institutions and platforms specializing in AI and DevOps:

1 **Google Professional Machine Learning Engineer Certification**
   - **Focus:** This certification covers designing, building, and productionizing machine learning models to solve business challenges using Google Cloud technologies. It includes aspects relevant to DevOps, such as automation and scaling of ML deployments.
   - **Platform:** Coursera and Google Cloud

2 **Microsoft Certified: Azure AI Engineer Associate**
   - **Focus:** This certification demonstrates subject matter expertise in the use of cognitive services, machine learning, and knowledge mining to architect and implement Microsoft AI solutions involving natural language processing, speech, computer vision, bots, and agents.
   - **Platform:** Microsoft Learn

3 **AWS Certified Machine Learning - Specialty**
   - **Focus:** This certification validates the ability to design, implement, deploy, and maintain ML solutions for given business problems. It includes the automation and integration of ML workflows and CI/CD processes in AWS environments.
   - **Platform:** AWS Training and Certification ...

These certifications provide a combination of theoretical knowledge and practical skills, focusing on the integration of AI into DevOps practices, which is essential for modern IT environments. They also typically include hands-on labs and projects that simulate real-world scenarios, ensuring that learners can apply their knowledge effectively.

This prompt worked well because it set clear expectations about what we needed: hands-on AI certifications tailored specifically for DevOps roles. Instead of asking for a generic list, we focused on practical skills like automation and continuous integration and continuous delivery (CI/CD) pipeline integration. By specifying that we wanted current offerings from reputable sources, we made sure the AI would filter out outdated or questionable certifications. We've found that this targeted approach consistently produces better results than broad requests.

But certifications are just one piece of the IT learning puzzle. The skills that matter depend entirely on your focus. If you're building cloud-native applications, you may want to dig into containerization or serverless architectures. For project managers, certifications in agile methodologies like Scrum and Kanban often prove more valuable. To help you find the right learning path, we've put together some prompts in table 17.2 that you can use with AI tools.

**Table 17.2  Prompts for skill development**

| Purpose | Prompt |
| --- | --- |
| Identify emerging skills | What are the top 5 emerging skills in [your field] for the next 2 years? |
| Create a learning plan | Based on my current skills in [your field], suggest a 6-month learning plan to stay competitive. |
| Find learning resources | Recommend the best resources to learn [specific skill] for a [your role] professional. |

These prompts will help you spot emerging skills in your field, create learning plans that match your goals, and find the best resources to build those skills.

## 17.2.2  Identifying and filling skill gaps with AI

AI can also help you identify and address skill gaps in your professional profile. Consider the following approach.

As an AI assistant specializing in career development, analyze the current job market for DevOps engineers focusing on AI integration. Provide a detailed breakdown of:

1. Top 5 in-demand skills for DevOps professionals working with AI
2. 3 emerging technologies or methodologies in this field
3. Specific tools or platforms associated with each skill
4. Recommended learning resources or certifications for each skill
5. Potential career paths or job titles for DevOps professionals with strong AI skills

Additionally, suggest a 6-month learning plan to acquire or improve these skills, including milestones and practical projects.

Certainly! Here's a comprehensive analysis of the DevOps and AI integration job market, along with recommendations for skill development:

1. Top 5 in-demand skills for DevOps professionals working with AI:
   - Machine Learning Operations (MLOps)
   - Cloud-native AI deployment
   - AI-driven automation and orchestration
   - AI model monitoring and maintenance
   - Data pipeline optimization for AI workloads
2. 3 emerging technologies or methodologies:
   - Federated Learning
   - AutoML in CI/CD pipelines
   - AI-powered observability
3. Specific tools or platforms for each skill: ...

Similar to the previous example, the prompt's structure was specific and targeted, which encouraged a well-organized response, making the information easy to digest and act on. By requesting a 6-month learning plan with milestones and projects, we obtained actionable guidance for skill development. This approach significantly reduces the time and effort typically required to research and plan career development strategies.

Using AI tools can help you identify areas where you need to improve, whether it's in MLOps, cloud technologies, or data management. By staying current with these skills, you'll be better equipped to handle complex AI-related projects and increase your value.

### 17.2.3 Writing conference attendance proposals

A lot of people don't know this, but most companies keep their conference and training budgets completely separate from salaries. This means even if you hear "We can't afford raises right now," there may still be money to attend professional development events. What's especially interesting is that when employees present at conferences, it often reflects well on their entire management chain—which can make your boss more likely to approve conference requests.

Let's look at how AI can help you create conference proposals that work. Instead of starting from scratch, you can use AI tools like ChatGPT to analyze conference websites and pull out the most relevant details. For example, if you're interested in DevOpsDays Amsterdam, you can share the conference URL (https://devopsdays.org/events/2025-amsterdam) with ChatGPT and have it identify key sessions, workshops, and opportunities that align with your team's goals.

I'm a DevOps engineer looking to attend the DevOps Days Amsterdam 2025 conference (devopsdays.org/events/2025-amsterdam) to learn about AI-driven automation.

The conference includes workshops, case studies, and networking opportunities that align with our company's goal of modernizing our CI/CD pipelines with AI.

Please review the conference website and help me draft a concise yet compelling proposal to my manager, highlighting:

1 The specific sessions and workshops I plan to attend and their relevance to my work
2 The potential benefits to our team and company, such as new skills, improved processes, and industry insights
3 The estimated costs (registration, travel, lodging) and any potential savings (e.g., early bird discounts)
4 How I plan to share my learnings with the team upon my return

 **Subject: Proposal to Attend DevOps Days Amsterdam 2025**

Dear [Manager's Name],

I wish to attend the DevOps Days Amsterdam from June 18-20, 2025, which presents an invaluable opportunity for advancing our CI/CD processes through AI-driven automation. This conference is renowned for its focus on both theoretical knowledge and practical application in DevOps.

**1. Relevant Sessions and Workshops:** - **AI and Machine Learning in CI/CD**: An in-depth session exploring the use of AI to optimize pipeline efficiency and predictability.
...

Having ChatGPT check out the conference website gives us a major advantage when writing proposals. It can quickly scan through the agenda and pull out dates, locations, and session details that match what our team needs. This level of detail makes our proposals much stronger than generic requests.

We've found that managers appreciate this thorough approach. When you can point to specific workshops and explain exactly how they'll help your work, it shows that you've done your homework. Adding clear cost breakdowns and plans for sharing what you learn makes it even easier for managers to see the value.

By using AI to help research and write these proposals, you're more likely to get them approved. This means more opportunities to learn new skills, stay current with industry trends, and grow your career.

## 17.3 External career advancement

Looking outside your current company? AI can help there too. We've found it especially useful for finding new roles, polishing resumes, and getting ready for salary talks. Let's look at how AI tools can help with each step of the job search process.

### 17.3.1 AI-powered job search

Looking for a new job takes a lot of work. We've found AI tools can make the whole process more manageable by helping with everything from finding the right openings to getting ready for interviews. Let's look at how these tools can help streamline your search and improve your chances of landing that next role.

 As a DevOps engineer with 5 years of experience and expertise in Kubernetes, Docker, and AWS, I'm looking for a new role that allows me to work on AI-driven infrastructure optimization projects. My ideal role would be at a mid-sized to large tech company in the San Francisco Bay Area, with a focus on innovation and employee growth.

Please help me: 1. Identify 5 relevant job openings on popular job boards and company websites 2. Tailor my resume to highlight my most relevant skills and experiences for each opening 3. Draft a compelling cover letter that shows my enthusiasm and fit for each role 4. Prepare for common interview questions related to DevOps and AI

 1 Relevant Job Openings:
- Senior DevOps Engineer - AI Infrastructure at [Company A]
- DevOps Architect - Machine Learning Platform at [Company B] ...

2 Tailored Resume Highlights: For [Company A]:

- Emphasize your experience with Kubernetes and Docker in the context of AI/ML workloads
- Feature any projects where you optimized infrastructure performance or costs ...
3 Cover Letter Draft for [Company A]: Dear Hiring Manager, ...
4 Common Interview Questions:
  - How do you ensure the reliability and scalability of AI/ML pipelines in production?
  - Can you describe a time when you optimized a CI/CD pipeline for AI workloads?
  ...

Although we're focusing on AI roles here, these resume tips work for all IT jobs. AI tools can help you match your skills to job descriptions, improve your resume's layout, and highlight your achievements with real numbers. Tailoring your resume for each application not only increases your interview chances but also keeps you informed about what employers are looking for in the current job market.

Finding a new job can be hard, but AI can help. Table 17.3 has prompts you can use to be a well-prepared candidate.

Table 17.3  Prompts for job search optimization

| Purpose | Prompt |
| --- | --- |
| Tailor application | Analyze this job description and my resume. Suggest how to optimize my application. |
| Prepare for interview | Based on this job description, what are 5 likely technical questions I might be asked? |
| Assess company culture | Research [company name] and summarize their culture and values in 3-5 key points. |

## 17.3.2 Resume optimization

A well-crafted resume can set you apart in your job search, but getting noticed isn't easy. We've found AI tools especially helpful for crafting resumes that work well for both human recruiters and the automated systems (ATS) that many companies use to screen applications. These systems scan and rank applications automatically, so knowing how to work with them matters.

AI can do more than just polish your resume—it can thoroughly analyze job descriptions and help you understand exactly what employers want. When we're helping teams with hiring, we often use AI to analyze job posts and identify key requirements. Try prompts like "Compare my resume to this job description. What skills am I missing, and how could I either learn them or show similar expertise from my background?"

This analysis helps you

- Identify gaps between your qualifications and job requirements
- Suggest ways to build missing skills
- Find equivalent experience in your background

When helping teams prepare for career moves, we've found this kind of detailed comparison invaluable for identifying the most effective areas for skill development. Always keep your long-term plans in mind when deciding where to focus your learning efforts. Our next prompt example shows these principles in action.

 Attached is my current resume. I'm a software engineer with 7 years of experience, specializing in Python, machine learning, and cloud computing. I'm looking for a new role as a Senior Machine Learning Engineer at a non-profit. Can you help me optimize my resume for both human recruiters and Applicant Tracking Systems (ATS)?

I need you to:

1. Identify the key skills and experiences I should emphasize for this type of role
2. Suggest improvements to my resume's structure, formatting, and wording to make it more impactful
3. Provide examples of quantifiable achievements I can include to demonstrate my impact
4. Recommend any additional sections or information I should add to strengthen my candidacy

1. Key skills and experiences to emphasize:
   - Your expertise in Python and machine learning frameworks like TensorFlow and PyTorch
   - Experience deploying and scaling ML models in cloud environments (AWS, GCP, Azure) …
2. Resume structure and formatting suggestions:
   - Start with a concise summary statement that highlights your key strengths and career goals
   - Use bullet points to make your achievements and responsibilities easy to scan …
3. Quantifiable achievement examples:
   - Developed and deployed a machine learning model that reduced customer churn by 20%
   - Optimized the performance of an ML pipeline, reducing training time by 40% and costs by 30% …
4. Additional sections and information:
   - Include a "Projects" section to present any relevant personal or open-source ML projects
   - Add any pertinent certifications, such as AWS Machine Learning Specialty or Google Cloud Professional ML Engineer …

We've learned to be careful with AI resume help. Companies are getting better at spotting AI-written content, and they often don't like resumes that sound too polished or generic. When we use AI suggestions, we always personalize them and double-check that everything matches our real experience. The goal is to enhance your resume, not to have AI write it for you.

### 17.3.3 AI-assisted interview preparation

Getting ready for interviews takes significant effort, and AI tools can help with your preparation. We've found AI particularly valuable for practicing responses without the pressure of a real interview. Here's what works well:

- Have an AI tool like Claude or ChatGPT evaluate your answers to common questions, helping you identify where you need more detail or clarity.
- Use AI to generate realistic technical scenarios. We've found this especially helpful for system design questions.
- Practice different interview styles, from initial screenings to deep technical discussions.

AI makes a great practice partner, but keep your actual interviews natural and conversational. The goal is to get comfortable expressing your ideas clearly, not to memorize perfect answers.

### 17.3.4 Salary negotiation

Salary negotiations can be very uncomfortable—they require confidence, market knowledge, and careful communication. We've found AI tools especially helpful for preparing these discussions. You can use AI to research typical salaries in your area, understand common benefits packages, and even practice negotiation conversations. Having concrete data and market insights ready helps you make a stronger case for your desired compensation. From our experience, going into salary talks well-prepared with AI-assisted research gives you more confidence and a clearer sense of your true market value.

I'm a DevOps engineer with 6 years of experience, and I've been offered a new position as a Senior DevOps Engineer at a large tech company in Seattle. The initial offer is $150,000 per year, plus standard benefits. I'm excited about the opportunity but want to ensure I'm being compensated fairly.

Use the web to help me: 1. Research and provide salary data for similar roles in the Seattle area 2. Identify any unique skills or experiences I have that could justify a higher salary 3. Suggest a target salary range and any additional benefits or perks I should consider negotiating for 4. Draft a polite and persuasive email to initiate the salary negotiation process

Here's the information to help you negotiate your offer:

1. **Salary Data for Seattle**: The average salary for a Senior DevOps Engineer in Seattle ranges significantly. According to Salary.com, the average is approximately $172,802 with the typical range between $159,794 and $188,210 …
2. **Unique Skills or Experiences**: To justify a higher salary, emphasize any unique skills such as …
3. **Target Salary Range and Benefits**: Based on the data, a reasonable target salary range for your experience and the job location would be …
4. **Draft Email for Salary Negotiation**: …

This approach emphasizes your enthusiasm for the role while opening a dialogue for negotiation.

Using AI to research and prepare for salary talks has helped us negotiate more effectively. After gathering solid market data and practicing with AI tools, we've found it easier to advocate for compensation that matches our skills and experience. This research-driven approach gives you real numbers to back up your requests when discussing pay with employers.

> **WARNING** Although AI tools like ChatGPT can help polish your online profiles, we've learned to be careful with how much we use them. In our experience, profiles that rely too heavily on AI often end up sounding generic or fake—not the impression you want to make. Maintain your personality and voice when using AI suggestions for LinkedIn and other platforms. We've found that it works best to use AI for ideas and improvement rather than letting it write everything for you.

Talking about salary can be tough. Table 17.4 has prompts to help you research salaries, check benefits, and prepare for salary talks.

Table 17.4 Prompts for salary negotiation

| Purpose | Prompt |
| --- | --- |
| Market research | What's the average salary range for a [your role] in [your location] with [your years] of experience? |
| Benefit analysis | Compare the standard benefits package for [your role] to what I've been offered. What's missing? |
| Negotiation script | Help me draft a salary negotiation email for a [your role] position, asking for a 10% increase. |

These prompts can help you feel more confident when talking about salary. Use this information as a starting point, and adjust your approach based on your situation and the company.

### 17.3.5 AI-powered career development prompts

Use the prompts in table 17.5 to improve your job search and skill development.

Table 17.5 Job search and skill analysis prompts

| Purpose | Prompt |
| --- | --- |
| Resume improvement | Compare this job description to my resume. Suggest how to adjust my resume for this job. |
| Skill planning | Based on my current skills, what new tech skills should I learn in the next 6 months? |
| Career exploration | Look at my resume. Suggest 3-5 possible career paths based on my skills and experience. |

### 17.3.6 AI-powered interview practice

Let's put everything we've learned about AI and careers into action. From our experience, one of the best ways to use AI tools is for interview practice. We've found that running through mock interviews with AI helps polish responses and builds confidence before the real thing. The AI can spot areas where you could explain things better or add more detail—exactly what you want to know before sitting down with an actual interviewer.

> **Try it now: Practice job interview**
>
> Let's use AI to simulate a job interview and get constructive feedback on your responses.
>
> 1. Choose a job role you're interested in (e.g., DevOps Engineer, Cloud Architect, IT Manager).
> 2. Use the following prompt with an AI assistant:
>
>  Act as an experienced interviewer for a [chosen job role] position. Ask me 3-5 relevant technical and behavioral questions. After each of my responses, provide constructive feedback on how I can improve my answer. Consider factors like clarity, relevance, depth of knowledge, and specific examples.
>
> 3. Respond to the AI's questions as you would in a real interview.
> 4. Review the feedback provided and consider how you can incorporate it to enhance your interview skills.
> 5. Repeat the process, focusing on areas where you received critical feedback.
>
> Example interaction:
>
>  Act as an experienced interviewer for a DevOps Engineer position. Ask me 3-5 relevant technical and behavioral questions. After each of my responses, provide constructive feedback on how I can improve my answer. Consider factors like clarity, relevance, depth of knowledge, and specific examples.
>
>  Certainly! I'll be your interviewer for a DevOps Engineer position. Let's begin with the first question:
>
> 1. Can you explain the concept of Infrastructure as Code (IaC) and provide an example of how you've implemented it in a previous project?

Using AI for interview practice can help you get better at explaining your skills and experience clearly. We've found these practice sessions valuable, but don't forget to also practice with real people. Combining AI practice with actual conversations helps you stay natural and confident in different interview settings.

## 17.4 Ethical considerations and best practices

As you explore the possibilities of AI for your career, keep these ethical points in mind:

- *Authenticity online*—When it comes to your online presence, keep it real. If you're using AI to polish up your resume or social media profiles, be sure it still sounds like you. It's okay to put your best foot forward, but don't pretend to be someone you're not. Your unique skills and experiences are what make you stand out.
- *Intellectual property*—If you're using AI to generate content or ideas, be sure you have the right to use them. Give credit where credit is due, and don't assume that just because an AI helped you create something, it's automatically yours to use however you want.
- *Transparency*—If you're using AI in your work, be open about it. You don't have to bore your colleagues with the technical details, but a simple heads-up can go a long way in building trust. Plus, it's a chance to show off your tech-savvy side and your commitment to innovation.

These suggestions will guide you in using AI effectively and responsibly, helping you make the most of this technology in your professional life. AI is an incredibly useful tool, but it's not a magic wand. It's up to you to use it responsibly and in a way that aligns with your values.

## 17.5 Putting it all together

Congratulations on making it to the end of this book! By now, you should have a solid foundation for using AI to grow your IT career. We've covered everything from leading AI projects at work to finding new opportunities, and we've seen firsthand how these tools can transform your professional growth.

Here's what we've found matters most when working with AI:

- Look for real problems you can solve. AI works best when it addresses actual business needs.
- Keep learning as AI evolves—what worked yesterday might be outdated tomorrow.
- Share what you learn with your team. We've found that teaching others helps everyone grow.
- Show your work through presentations and writing; make sure people know what you've achieved.
- Use AI responsibly. Just because you can do something doesn't mean you should.

AI in IT keeps changing fast. As you put these ideas to work, stay curious about new developments and keep adapting your skills. Knowing how to work effectively with AI will set you apart in your career.

## 17.6 Prompts used in this chapter

- I've attached some riffing about how I got AI tools started at work. Can you help organize this into sections like lessons learned, etc?
- The wrap-up is bland but has good info. How can I make it more engaging AND better relate to what we actually covered?
- Is the format of having AI give feedback after each answer effective?
- I need to convert the Adopting AI Success study into the format of the other case study. Please rewrite it with the proper formatting.
- Manning does not use Title Case, please find all instances in chapter17.adoc and change it to sentence case

## Summary

- AI tools make IT career growth easier by helping professionals take on new challenges and build skills.
- Getting companies to adopt AI means showing them what it can do by solving real problems and proving the business value of automation.
- Modern AI turns complex projects into clear presentations that leadership can understand.
- AI saves time with learning and certifications by pointing out which skills matter most and offering focused paths to stay current.
- Ethics matter when using AI for career growth. Staying authentic, respecting others' work, and being open about AI use are important.

# *appendix A*
# *Local AI models:*
# *An accessible alternative*

Local AI models offer more control over your data, enhanced privacy, and a greater ability to customize AI tools for your projects. Unlike cloud-based models, which focus on ease of use and scalability, local models can be tailored to unique workflows and run without an internet connection—ideal for industries handling confidential data, like healthcare, finance, and government. By keeping data processing local, these models make it easier to comply with strict data protection regulations and meet industry-specific legal requirements.

Running local AI models does have its challenges, particularly in terms of hardware constraints. Whereas cloud models offload computational burdens to remote servers, local models need dedicated equipment to train and run efficiently. Small language models (SLMs) are a practical solution here. They're designed to operate on limited hardware, allowing organizations to deploy AI locally without needing high-end infrastructure. In this appendix, we'll guide you step by step through what it takes to implement local models, showing you that it's more straightforward than you may think.

## A.1 Getting your hardware ready

If you've considered running a state-of-the-art AI model locally, you might have wondered what kind of hardware you'd need. For models like GPT-4 and Meta's Llama, the requirements are substantial. ChatGPT itself has estimated that running GPT-4 would require hardware costing upward of $300,000—something out of reach for most individuals and many organizations.

Not every model is like GPT-4, however. Meta's Llama, for example, with 703 billion parameters, can be run locally but comes with its own high hardware demands.

Let's break down the components you need to run these models. But first, we'll clarify two key terms—*fine-tuning* and *inference*—because these concepts will determine the kind of hardware you need:

- *Fine-tuning*—Taking a pretrained model and training it further on a specific dataset (like making a model that follows your company's best practices and style when coding PowerShell, instead of general PowerShell practices and style). It's how you adapt a general model for your particular domain. Fine-tuning needs a lot of computational resources: high-core CPUs, significant RAM, and plenty of storage.
- *Inference*—Using a pretrained model to generate outputs, such as answering questions or creating images from prompts. Inference generally has lower requirements, but you still need a capable GPU and adequate cooling.

Table A.1 provides a quick look at the hardware you'll need for each task.

Table A.1  Hardware requirements for running language models locally

| Component | Minimum requirements | Best for |
| --- | --- | --- |
| Processor (CPU) | 64-core AMD EPYC/Intel Xeon, 3.0 GHz | Fine-tuning |
| Graphics processing unit (GPU) | NVIDIA A100, 80 GB VRAM | Both inference and fine-tuning |
| Memory (RAM) | 512 GB DDR5 ECC RAM | Fine-tuning |
| Storage (NVMe SSD) | 8 TB SSD | Fine-tuning |
| Networking | 100 Gbps Ethernet | Distributed fine-tuning |
| Power supply | 2,000 W | Both inference and fine-tuning |
| Cooling | High-performance air cooling | Both inference and fine-tuning |
| Model parameters (example: Meta's Llama) | 703 billion parameters | Inference |

This setup is costly. Fortunately, much smaller models, like OpenAI's GPT-2 and Meta's Llama 3 (7B), can run on standard workstations, making local AI more accessible to small teams and individuals. The 7B stands for 7 billion parameters: the higher the parameter count, the more CPU and RAM you'll need to run the model.

For our personal use, we've had success running local models up to 32 billion parameters (32B) on a Mac Mini M4 Pro with 64 GB RAM. We don't consider an M4 Pro Mac Mini cheap, but it offers great bang for the buck, and it's within reach.

## A.2 *Tools for simplifying local AI setup*

Running AI models locally can feel daunting at first, but tools are available to simplify the process, particularly for developers. These tools provide a more user-friendly way

## A.2 Tools for simplifying local AI setup

to configure and run models, allowing you to focus more on experimentation and less on infrastructure.

### A.2.1 VS Code AI Toolkit

If you're a developer, you probably already use Visual Studio Code. Microsoft's AI Toolkit extension has made running models—whether locally or remotely—incredibly straightforward. In just a few clicks, you can set up a model like GPT-4, Mistral, or Llama directly in VS Code's familiar environment (see figure A.1).

Figure A.1 VS Code AI Toolkit interface, showing model deployment options

The AI Toolkit integrates seamlessly with model marketplaces like GitHub and Azure Model Catalog. This integration allows you to log in and use remote models or download them for local use. It gives you complete control over deployment. The toolkit becomes part of your existing development workflow, with features like code generation and documentation creation available right in the IDE.

The toolkit also includes a Playground feature, shown in figure A.2, which lets you interact with models in real time, generating code or text as needed. It's perfect for experimenting without leaving your development environment.

**326**  APPENDIX A  *Local AI models: An accessible alternative*

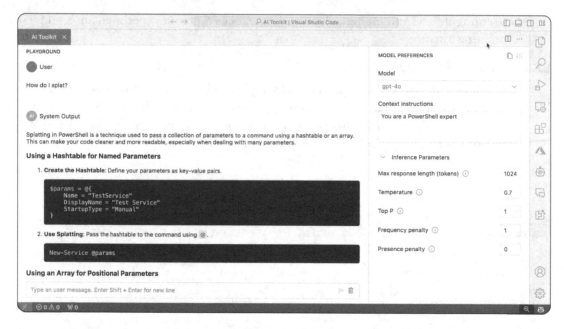

**Figure A.2** AI Toolkit Playground in action, showcasing the use of GPT-4o for code generation

What we appreciate about the AI Toolkit is that it allows us to figure out how models work, at least to some degree. We think it's interesting that the primary model file is a large binary file, as you can see in figure A.3.

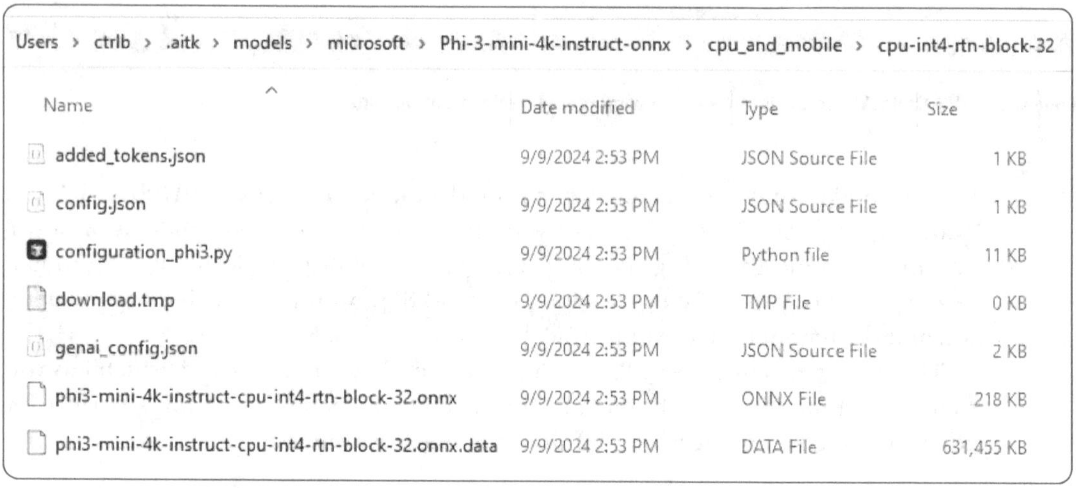

| Name | Date modified | Type | Size |
|---|---|---|---|
| added_tokens.json | 9/9/2024 2:53 PM | JSON Source File | 1 KB |
| config.json | 9/9/2024 2:53 PM | JSON Source File | 1 KB |
| configuration_phi3.py | 9/9/2024 2:53 PM | Python file | 11 KB |
| download.tmp | 9/9/2024 2:53 PM | TMP File | 0 KB |
| genai_config.json | 9/9/2024 2:53 PM | JSON Source File | 2 KB |
| phi3-mini-4k-instruct-cpu-int4-rtn-block-32.onnx | 9/9/2024 2:53 PM | ONNX File | 218 KB |
| phi3-mini-4k-instruct-cpu-int4-rtn-block-32.onnx.data | 9/9/2024 2:53 PM | DATA File | 631,455 KB |

Path: Users > ctrlb > .aitk > models > microsoft > Phi-3-mini-4k-instruct-onnx > cpu_and_mobile > cpu-int4-rtn-block-32

**Figure A.3** Files for a Phi3 local model

This binary file isn't something that can be easily examined or opened with standard text editors. Instead, it's packed with weights and parameters that the model relies on during inference or fine-tuning. These files can range from a few gigabytes to hundreds of gigabytes, depending on the model's complexity and size. Naturally, these binary files are unreadable by humans and require specialized tools or frameworks like PyTorch or TensorFlow to interact with.

The AI Toolkit makes handling these files much easier, simplifying the complexity of file management and deployment, which would otherwise be a highly technical process. Still, it's fascinating to know that behind all the smooth IDE integration, these powerful AI models are ultimately stored as binary data—essentially, containers for vast amounts of data and power.

### A.2.2 Setting up your own local AI chatbot in Visual Studio Code

Setting up your own chatbot may seem daunting, but with the AI Toolkit in Visual Studio Code, it's very manageable. Here's a step-by-step guide to get you up and running:

1 Install the AI Toolkit extension: Open Visual Studio Code, and go to Extensions (press Ctrl-Shift-X or Cmd-Shift-X). Search for "AI Toolkit," and click Install to add it to your environment.

2 After installing, you'll be prompted to log in to GitHub. This will allow you to use hosted models and repositories.

3 Open the AI Toolkit sidebar, and browse available models. Click Download for local use or Run Remotely to access cloud-hosted models.

4 Click Playground to start a chat session. Select the model you want, either local or remote.

5 Interact with your chatbot. Type messages or prompts, and the chatbot will respond in real time. Adjust your questions to refine the responses.

6 Customize settings (optional). Open the AI Toolkit settings to adjust parameters like response length, temperature, and frequency penalties. Experiment with these settings to find what works best for you.

7 Access the API (optional). After loading a model in the AI Toolkit Playground, you can interact with it programmatically using an API that follows OpenAI's conventions. Many AI platforms have adopted this standard, making it a common way to work with different models.

By following these steps, you can quickly set up a local chatbot in Visual Studio Code and start interacting with AI models in your workflow or better understand how local models work.

The following listing shows a simple PowerShell script that retrieves a list of available local models by sending a REST request to the AI Toolkit's API endpoint.

Listing A.1 Showing available local models

```
Invoke-RestMethod -Uri http://localhost:5272/openai/models
```

This script sends a GET request to the `/openai/models` endpoint, which returns a list of all available models, not just the loaded ones. It's a good way to check whether the API is accessible and models are available.

You can do more interesting things with the API, like sending messages to a loaded model and getting responses. The next listing shows an example.

**Listing A.2  Chatting using the currently loaded model**

```
$baseUrl = "http://localhost:5272"
$model = Invoke-RestMethod -Uri "$baseUrl/openai/loadedmodels"
$body = @{
  model = $model[0]
  messages = @(
    @{
      role = "user"
      content = "What is a PowerShell splat?"
    }
  )
} | ConvertTo-Json

$splat = @{
  Uri = "$baseUrl/v1/chat/completions"
  Method = "POST"
  Body = $body
  ContentType = "application/json"
}

(Invoke-RestMethod @splat).choices.message.content
```

Here's what the script does:

1. Gets the currently loaded model by sending a GET request to `/openai/loadedmodels`
2. Builds the request body with the model and user message
3. Sends a POST request to `/v1/chat/completions` with the request body to start the chat
4. Gets the model's response from the API's returned data and displays it

The script's performance depends on the hardware and model optimization. In our tests, a machine without a GPU took about 45 seconds, and an optimized MacBook Pro took about 31 seconds.

As you get comfortable with the OpenAI-formatted API and its structure, you can access many local models using different servers, such as those from jan.ai, LM Studio, and others. This flexibility lets you choose the best model and platform, whether it's for chatbots, automating tasks, or improving system operations. The consistent API conventions across models and platforms make it easier to switch between them as new options become available, so you can always find the right tool for the job.

### A.2.3 Ollama

Ollama is a powerful command-line tool that simplifies the management and deployment of local AI models. It allows you to effortlessly pull, run, and push models, similar to managing containers, as you can see in listing A.3. Mistral can be used for tasks like code completion, and DeepSeek Coder is ideal for chatbot interactions. Whether you are running locally or on a server, this flexibility lets you choose the best model to achieve your goals.

**Listing A.3  Downloading and running the Phi3 model**

```
Welcome to Ollama!

Run your first model:
ollama run llama3.1

> ollama run phi3
pulling manifest
pulling 633fc5be925f... 100%                                 2.2 GB
pulling fa8235e5b48f... 100%                                 1.1 KB
pulling 542b217f179c... 100%                                 148 B
pulling 8dde1baf1db0... 100%                                 78 B
pulling 23291dc44752... 100%                                 483 B
verifying sha256 digest
writing manifest
success
>>> Send a message (/? for help)
>>> What is a PowerShell splat?
```

If you're familiar with Docker, you'll find Ollama very intuitive to use—you can see the similar terminology and commands in the next listing. The tool's straightforward interface makes it easy to manage models, whether you're pulling them from a registry, running them locally, or pushing them back to the registry after modifications.

**Listing A.4  Using the `ollama` command**

```
Usage:
ollama [command] [flags]

Available Commands:
  serve     Start the Ollama server
  create    Create a model from a Modelfile
  show      Display information for a model
  run       Execute a model
  pull      Retrieve a model from the registry
```

```
push    Upload a model to the registry
list    List available models
cp      Copy a model
rm      Remove a model
help    Provide help for any command
```

Ollama and similar tools greatly simplify the process of integrating AI models into development workflows. They provide a straightforward way to access and manage models, making it easier to use AI in your projects.

For those who prefer a graphical user interface without the need for VS Code, jan.ai, local.ai, and LM Studio provide user-friendly interfaces. These GUI-based tools make it even easier to work with AI models, catering to a wider range of users and skill levels.

### A.2.4 Using structured outputs with local models

Like cloud services, local AI models support function calling and structured outputs to provide reliable data. Whereas function calls wait for external data or actions, structured outputs give you immediate formatted responses with no expectation of a return call. This makes structured outputs especially useful when you need to extract specific information or change data formats quickly.

SLMs are most effective when processing small, structured tasks instead of tackling complex problems. By specifying the exact output format you want, whether through function calling or structured outputs, you get consistent, usable data every time. The following listing is a simple example using Ollama to check whether two terms are related.

#### Listing A.5 Structured comparison request using Ollama API

```
# the two terms to compare
$msg = "Pacific Palisades, Los Angeles"

# Load the JSON schema from the file
$schema = Get-Content -Path similar.json -Raw | ConvertFrom-Json

# Construct the request payload
$payload = @{
    model    = "llama3.1"
    messages = @(
        @{
            role    = "user"
            content = $msg
        }
    )
    stream = $false
    format = $schema
} | ConvertTo-Json -Depth 3 -Compress

# Send the request to the Ollama API
$parms = @{
```

```
    Uri         = "http://localhost:11434/api/chat"
    Method      = "POST"
    Body        = $payload
}
$response = Invoke-RestMethod @parms

# Display the response
$response.message.content | ConvertFrom-Json
```

The schema defines exactly what format we want the AI to use when responding. This helps ensure that we get consistent, usable data that our applications can process reliably. In this case, we're asking the model to break down two topics, determine whether they're related, and explain its reasoning.

The structured output ensures that the model will always return these four specific pieces of information: the two keywords it identified, a Boolean indicating similarity, and an explanation. This approach eliminates the need to parse ambiguous free-form text, as the following listing shows.

Listing A.6 Structured JSON schema for comparison

```
{
    "type": "object",
    "title": "Comparison schema",
    "description": "Schema defining the structured comparison of two
    topics using the Ollama API.",
    "properties": {
        "keyword1": {
            "type": "string",
            "description": "First news topic you were provided to compare."
        },
        "keyword2": {
            "type": "string",
            "description": "Second news topic you were provided to compare."
        },
        "similar": {
            "type": "boolean",
            "description": "Indicates whether the two topics are similar."
        },
        "explanation": {
            "type": "string",
            "description": "Reasoning behind the similarity or
            dissimilarity of the two keywords."
        }
    },
    "required": [
        "keyword1",
        "keyword2",
        "similar",
        "explanation"
    ],
    "additionalProperties": false
}
```

#### ASKING TINY, SPECIFIC QUESTIONS

Breaking down larger problems into targeted questions yields better results with SLMs. For example, with file renaming, you can ask the model to suggest better names based on file metadata instead of writing complex rules.

For media files like movies or music, you might send these details:

- Original filename: Movie.2024.1080p.AMZN.WEB-DL.DDP5.1.H.264
- File type: video/mp4
- Creation date: 2024-02-09
- Size: 2.3GB

Using a simple schema, the model can return a clean name like *Movie (2024)* and suggest tags for your media library. This approach works well for organizing photos, music collections, or any files where naming matters.

The key is specificity. Instead of saying *organize my files*, you're asking *what should I name this specific file based on these details?* This focused approach usually works better than trying to handle everything at once.

#### WHY STRUCTURED OUTPUTS MATTER

Structured outputs are improving how we work with AI models. You get data in a predictable format that's ready to use in your applications, instead of having to parse free-form text. This is especially valuable for the following:

- Extracting data from documents
- Automating file organization
- Generating metadata
- Formatting API responses
- Populating databases

The main benefits are consistent responses, less post-processing work, and smooth integration with existing systems. IT professionals can now automate tasks that used to need manual review and formatting.

When running SLMs through tools like Ollama, structured outputs help connect AI capabilities with practical business tasks. They're particularly useful for processing large amounts of data or adding AI responses to automated workflows.

This feature becomes even more useful when combined with other IT tools. You could use structured outputs to automatically sort support tickets, organize documentation, or check configuration files.

## A.3 Popular local AI models

Choosing the right local AI model is important, as the model you select affects your application's performance, efficiency, and capabilities.

Factors to consider include model size, architecture, and pretraining data. Larger models like BLOOM and Llama handle complex tasks but need more computational resources. Unique architectures, such as Mistral AI's Sparse Mixture of Experts

(SMoE), offer efficiency for handling longer contexts. Table A.2 compares notable local AI models and their key features.

Table A.2  Popular local LLMs and chatbots

| Model | Description | Key features |
|---|---|---|
| Phi-3 | Microsoft's model for language processing and coding tasks | Handles up to 128,000 tokens; works well on GPUs, CPUs, and mobile devices |
| Llama 3 | Meta's open source model with 8B to 405B parameters | Great for translation, dialogue, and reasoning tasks. Available in various sizes. |
| Mixtral 8x7B | Mistral AI's model using a SMoE architecture | Efficiently processes contexts up to 32,000 tokens |
| BLOOM | Hugging Face's multilingual model with 176B parameters | Supports 46 languages; can run locally in smaller versions |
| Gemma | Google's lightweight models; 2B to 7B parameters | Comes in pretrained and instruction-tuned versions; optimized for mobile |
| OpenELM | Apple's on-device model focused on efficiency and privacy | Brings AI capabilities directly to Apple devices running iOS and macOS |

By aligning your project requirements with these models' features, you can select the best one to power your AI applications. Whether your focus is on performance, efficiency, multilingual support, or platform optimization, there's a local AI model that suits the task.

## A.4 Bringing it all together: Security and ethical considerations

When you run AI models locally, the responsibility for securing them falls entirely on your shoulders. This is both an opportunity and a challenge. You have full control over your data, but you also need to make sure it's well-protected and used ethically.

To help you navigate this, we've broken down the most important security and ethical considerations. Table A.3 covers both the technical aspects of keeping your data safe and the ethical guidelines you should follow to ensure fairness and transparency.

Table A.3  Security and ethical considerations for local AI models

| Aspect | Best practice | Why it matters |
|---|---|---|
| Access control | Use multifactor authentication (MFA) and role-based permissions. | Prevents unauthorized users from accessing sensitive data or models |
| Encryption | Encrypt data both in transit and at rest. | Protects data from being intercepted or exposed, especially during transfers |

**Table A.3  Security and ethical considerations for local AI models** *(continued)*

| Aspect | Best practice | Why it matters |
|---|---|---|
| Model isolation | Use containers or virtual machines to isolate models. | Minimizes the risk of one compromised model affecting others |
| Security audits | Schedule regular security audits and monitor logs. | Helps you catch potential vulnerabilities before they lead to breaches |
| Bias monitoring | Fine-tune models, and regularly evaluate outputs for fairness. | Reduces the risk of biased or unfair AI decisions |
| Transparency | Document AI decision-making processes, and be ready to explain them. | Builds trust with users and ensures accountability in AI-driven outcomes |
| Data minimization | Only collect and use the data that's strictly necessary. | Limits exposure to potential data breaches and helps maintain privacy |
| Legal compliance | Stay updated with regulations like GDPR, HIPAA, or other industry-specific laws. | Ensures that your AI usage complies with legal standards and protects users' rights |

By following these best practices, you can help protect your local AI models while ensuring that they're being used ethically. Security and ethics are two of the most important aspects of AI development. Keep in mind that SLMs won't match larger LLMs for complex tasks, but when you break problems into smaller, focused questions, they can be remarkably effective. With realistic expectations and proper implementation, local AI offers a valuable balance of capability and privacy.

# *appendix B*
# *OpenAI GPT Actions*

GPT Actions (previously ChatGPT plugins) let AI models work with external APIs to access real-world data and services. Although Actions can make AI applications more capable, they're currently limited to OpenAI's ecosystem, which is why this content is in this appendix instead of chapter 13.

Actions connect GPTs to outside systems through APIs. You can link GPTs to databases and other services using OpenAPI specifications that define how to access external resources.

In chapter 13, we cover function calling, which differs significantly from Actions. Function calling formats AI outputs so your code can process them easily. GPT Actions do something else entirely: they give AI direct access to external systems and data. You'll need OpenAPI specs for Actions, whereas function calling just needs structured output rules. Use Actions when you want AI to work with live data, and pick function calling when you need to process AI responses in your code.

Here's how GPT Actions work:

1. Set up an API.
2. Make a Custom GPT.
3. Include your OpenAPI spec with authentication.
4. Let users interact with the API using natural language.

Our tests showed that Actions work well for specific tasks, especially exploring APIs. We built an Action to examine the OpenAI API, which showed available models through simple questions instead of code. It works like an interactive guide that helps developers understand an API without reading documentation or writing test code.

Choose your GPT Actions projects carefully. When we created a documentation chatbot, we found that the AI often used its existing knowledge rather than checking the API for new information. Although GPT Actions need less setup than function calling, you get less control over the AI's behavior. The AI responds based on how it interprets the OpenAPI spec and API structure.

> **Microsoft Copilot Studio vs. GPT Actions**
>
> Although we're focusing on GPT Actions here, it's worth mentioning Microsoft's alternative: Copilot Studio. This tool lets organizations tailor AI capabilities within the Microsoft ecosystem, working smoothly with products like Microsoft 365 and Dynamics 365. You can create standalone AI assistants, enhance Microsoft 365 Copilot, and build AI agents for complex tasks.
>
> Unlike GPT Actions, which connect to external APIs, Copilot Studio helps create custom AI features right in the user interface. It's particularly useful for businesses already using Microsoft's tools, offering a more integrated approach to AI customization. GPT Actions work well with various APIs, but Copilot Studio is better for improving Microsoft-based systems.

GPT Actions have some key limits developers should know about. You can only use 30 operations per request, which means you'll need to choose carefully with bigger APIs. For example, OpenAI's API has more than 60 operations, so you can't include them all. (An operation is any single API endpoint or method, like `GET /models` or `POST /completions`.)

You may run into these common issues:

- *Speed*—Because GPT Actions need to call external APIs, responses can be slower.
- *API updates*—You'll need to keep your OpenAPI spec current if your API changes often.
- *Context issues*—The AI sometimes misses the bigger picture of how the API should work.
- *Hard-to-fix problems*—When something goes wrong between the AI and your API, finding the cause can be tricky.

Even with these constraints, Actions can be very useful if you choose the right APIs and design them well.

## B.1 A practical example: Using database monitoring APIs

Let's look at how GPT Actions work in practice by building an AI assistant for database monitoring. This setup lets users get real-time insights about their databases through natural conversations with the AI.

> **NOTE** Your database-monitoring API needs to be accessible from the internet for GPT Actions to work. For APIs in secure networks like Azure, you'll need the right network settings and access controls so the Actions can safely connect to your API.

## B.1  A practical example: Using database monitoring APIs

The first step is writing an OpenAPI spec for your monitoring API. This spec tells the AI about your API's endpoints, how to format requests and responses, and what authentication it needs. Figure B.1 shows adding an OpenAPI spec for a monitoring API.

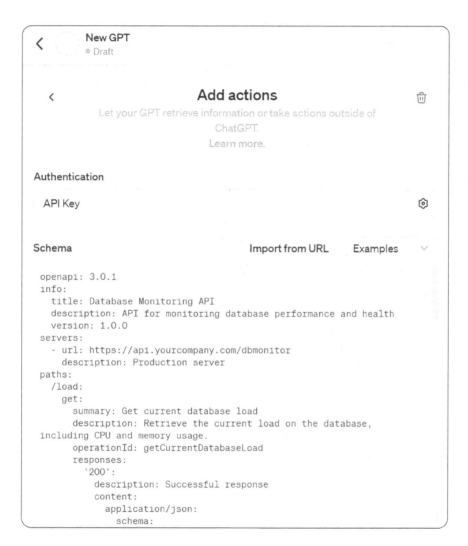

**Figure B.1  Adding a GPT Action**

The developer creates a custom GPT and adds the OpenAPI spec, which lets the AI work with the monitoring API. With this setup, users can ask simple questions like "What's our production database load?" and "Show me slow queries from the last hour." The AI then calls the API to get monitoring data and explains it in plain language.

These integrations are useful but need careful security planning. When you expose APIs to GPT Actions, you face risks similar to those when publishing any API. Be sure you have proper security measures like authentication and rate limits. For sensitive data, you may want to use an open source AI model inside your secure network instead.

## B.2 Real-world example: Using GPT Actions with the OpenAI API

We tested GPT Actions by connecting an Action to the OpenAI API. After adding OpenAI's API specification to a Custom GPT, we were able to ask questions about the API and get real information back. Here are some questions we tried:

- What models do I have access to?
- How do I create a completion using the Ada model?
- What are the parameters for the text-davinci-002 model?

The AI made API calls to get this information and explained it clearly. This showed how GPT Actions can help developers understand complex APIs through simple conversations—as long as the API spec is good and the project fits. But although GPT Actions are powerful, you need to think carefully about security when using them.

## B.3 Security considerations for GPT Actions

Using GPT Actions requires careful attention to security to protect your systems. Here are the important areas to watch:

- *Authentication*—Your API must require proper authentication, with these details in the OpenAPI spec. This stops unauthorized access and protects user data.
- *Rate limiting*—Set up rate limits to prevent API overload from too many requests, which is especially important with AI systems that can send many queries quickly.
- *Input validation*—Check and clean all user input before it reaches your API to block injection attacks and other security issues.
- *Secure communication*—Use HTTPS to encrypt data moving between the AI and your API, keeping sensitive information safe.
- *Data exposure*—Think carefully about what data you show to the AI. Sharing sensitive data or internal metrics with external services can lead to unauthorized access and breaches.

When working with GPT Actions, you'll need to consider all these security aspects to keep your systems safe. Sometimes it makes more sense to run an open source AI model in your secure network, particularly for sensitive data work. Another option is Azure OpenAI: it costs about the same as regular OpenAI but gives you better security controls and works well with other Azure tools. Just remember that running your own AI models requires substantially more resources than using OpenAI's API.

## B.4 Combining GPT Actions with function calling

GPT Actions and function calling work well together to create more capable applications. You can use Actions to fetch external API data and then process that data in your app using function calling.

A good example is a smart database monitoring assistant. Actions get your performance metrics from the monitoring API, and function calling turns that data into alerts, reports, or visual displays. This combination lets you build apps that handle data well and do more complex tasks.

Here are a few more ways to combine Actions and function calling:

- Use Actions to fetch real-time stock prices, and then use function calling to analyze the data and generate investment recommendations.
- Assist users in managing their schedules by using Actions to retrieve calendar events and function calling to automatically schedule meetings or appointments.
- Guide users through a travel planning process with Actions, and then use function calling to book flights or hotels based on their preferences.

By combining GPT Actions and function calling, you can create AI assistants that are not only smart and aware of context but also capable of executing tasks and delivering real results.

It's important to understand that Actions alone don't make an app AI-powered. Instead, they bring AI capabilities to your API, making it easy to explore with plain language. Actions work within the ChatGPT interface, so they don't directly integrate with your app's user interface. Rather, they enable AI interaction with your API through ChatGPT, which you can then use in your application development.

GPT Actions show a lot of promise for application development, even with their current limits. When used properly with well-built APIs, they can make AI applications more capable and useful.

# index

## Numerics

360-degree feedback, prompts  282–283

## A

access controls  248
advanced administration, analyzing memory configurations
   explaining method  191–192
   instructing method  192–194
advanced disaster recovery planning  173
agents, service desk  158–159
   agentic AI in enterprise CRM systems  158–159
   agentic AI offerings  158
AI (artificial intelligence)  3–20, 41–56
   applications powered by functions  240–244
   assuming understanding of  74
   auditing configuration files with  172–173
   best practices for AI-assisted development  212–219
   bots, bad  49–50
   building applications, validating SQL queries with examine_sql  244–247
   career advancement  320
   critical thinking and good judgement  140
   defining terms  42–44
      prompts  42
      statefulness  42–43
      tokens  44

   DevOps engineering
      breaking down instructions into focused passes  226
      choosing tools  222–223
      developing effective process  224–225
      implementation strategy  225
      lessons learned  227
      managing large files  226
      other uses for AI-assisted development  227–228
      results  226–227
   document handling
      document summarization  100–102
      ethics in  99–100
   free vs. premium accounts  50–55
   function calling  233–249
   future of communications  140–141
   generative AI  4–6
   in systems engineering  173–174
   instant messaging  126–131
   integrations and automation with  131–137
   management, performance reviews  279–287
   responsibly using at work  14–18
   service costs  13–14
   strengthening skill set  6–7
   text extraction from images  104–106
   tokens  45–49
AI use cases in upgrading tests
   breaking down instructions into focused passes  226
   choosing tools  222–223

341

AI use cases in upgrading tests *(continued)*
  developing effective process 224–225
  implementation strategy 225
  lessons learned 227
  managing large files 226
  results 226–227
Aider 222
Amazon Bedrock 267
Amazon Textract 108
analytics 5
anonymizing customer support logs 109
Anthropic Claude, paying for chatbot access 53–54
Anthropic Sonnet models 206
API updates 336
APIs (application programming interfaces), token limits and 48–49
Apple Intelligence Writing Tools 139–140
applications powered by AI (artificial intelligence) functions 240–244
assistant role 237–238
Assistants API 234
ATS (Applicant Tracking Systems) 316
auditing, configuration files with AI 172–173
automation
  automating tasks for efficiency and compliance 171–173
  integrations and automation with AI 131–137
Awesome Prompts Lab
  act as AI writing tutor 71
  Excel sheet 71
  interviewer for positions 70
  JavaScript console 71
  language teacher for ESL 70
  Linux terminal 70–71
AWS Certified Machine Learning - Specialty 311
Azure OpenAI Service 267

# B

basic prompting 83–84
benefits 275
best practices and common mistakes, pitfalls to avoid
  assuming AI understanding 74
  ignoring context 74–75
  misalignment 74
  over-specification or under-specification 73–74
best practices for AI-assisted development
  advanced techniques 217–219
    diff approaches 217–218
    library analysis 217
    troubleshooting AI loops 218–219
    whole-file approaches 217–218
  foundation principles 213–217
    comprehensive logging 213
    source control integration 216–217
    test-driven AI development 214–216
    working with AI effectively 213–214
bias and fairness 15–16
bots, bad 49–50
browser-based development 212

# C

career advancement 304–321
  ethical considerations and best practices 320
  external 314–319
  overview of 320
  training and certifications 310–314
change requests 161–162
Chat Completions API 234
chatbots 21–40
  text-to-image AI models 37–39
  token limits and 48
ChatGPT 8, 318
  ChatGPT Plus 267
ChatGPT Operator 158
ChatGPT's recommendation 256
CI/CD (continuous integration and continuous delivery) 225, 311
citing prompts 17–18
clarity 86
Claude, Anthropic 8
CLI (command-line interface) 188
CMEK (customer-managed encryption keys) 15
code assistants
  Aider 210
  Cline 205–207
  existing skills 202–203
  GitHub AI suite 203–205
  privacy and security 202
  summary comparison of 211–212
code documentation 181–183
  assumptions made 182

examples of usage  183
   expected output format  182
   purpose of query  182
coding assistants  222
coherence  43–44
command-line power users  212
communication pattern analysis  254
complex multifile changes  212
configuration files, auditing with AI  172–173
conflict analysis prompt  257
conflict resolution, workplace conflicts  254–262
   and crisis management  253–271
   SharePoint standoff  255–262
   strategies for effective conflict resolution  255
context
   injection  72
   issues  336
   retention  43–44
   ignoring  74–75
COOP (continuity of operations planning), generative AI's role in  266–271
   communication plans for crisis management  269–271
   crisis simulation  268–269
Copilot Workspace  204
creative images  9
crisis management  263–271
   role of leadership in crisis situations  264–266
critical thinking and good judgement  140
CRM (customer relationship management) systems, agentic AI in enterprise  158–159
CTE (common table expression)  180
currency conversion  247–248
Cursor AI  207–208
custom AI using APIs  108
custom GPTs  152–157, 276

# D

DALL-E  40
data security, with AI  15
database administration and development  175–197
   advanced administration  188–196
   code documentation  181–183
   heterogeneous database environments  183–186
   maintenance jobs  186–188
   query and object creation  176–179
   query optimization  179–181
database copilot  235–238
   assistant role  237–238
   system role  236–237
   user role  237
database monitoring APIs  336–338
dbatools  188–190
DDL (data description language)  177
DeepSeek v3  206
development tools  201–220
   best practices for AI-assisted development  212–219
   Cline  205–207
DevOps engineering  221–231
   AI use cases in  222–228
   GenAIOps lifecycle  228–230
diff approaches  217–218
directed output  93
disaster recovery, generative AI's role in  266–271
   communication plans for crisis management  269–271
   crisis simulation  268–269
DRP (disaster recovery plan)
   AI document handling  99–102
   document anonymization  109–110
   document classification and tagging  107–108
   document comparison  106–107
   format conversion  102–104
   language translation  111–112
   text extraction from images  104–106
DKIM (DomainKeys Identified Mail)  124
DMARC (Domain-based Message Authentication, Reporting and Conformance)  124
DMVs (SQL Server Dynamic Management Views)  176
document anonymization  109–110
document classification and tagging  107–108
document comparison  106–107
document handling, best practices for  98–99
   structuring and refining outputs  99
   text extraction methods  98–99
documentation, code  181–183
   assumptions made  182

documentation, code *(continued)*
    examples of usage  183
    expected output format  182
    purpose of query  182

**E**

emails
    enhancing management with AI  115–126
    improving writing while maintaining voice  137–140
enhanced network design  173
enterprise development  212
error handling  248
error logs  170–171
ESL (English as a Second Language)  70
ethical considerations, local AI models  333
examine_sql function  240, 243–247
    AI-powered SQL assistance in action  245–247
    defining what makes a query dangerous  245
    generating user-friendly responses  245
Excel sheet  71
explicit constraints  72

**F**

feedback, constructive  292–293
few-shot prompting  62–63
fine-tuning  324
firewalld  163
Fireworks.ai  206
forex_python library  247
format conversion  102–104
free accounts  50–55
    choosing  54
    learning and experimenting  55
    paying for chatbot access  51–54
freemium model  50
function calling  233–249
    building database copilot  235–238
    Chatting with OpenAI API  234
    combining with GPT Actions  339
    currency conversion  247–248
    implementing  238–240
    security considerations for  248–249

**G**

GDPR (General Data Protection Regulation)  15
Gemini Advanced  267
Gemini Imagen  40
GenAIOps lifecycle  228–230
generative AI  4–11
    image generation with AI models  9–11
    job security  5–6
    language model chatbots  8–9
    role in disaster recovery and COOP  266–271
GET /models operation  336
GET request  328
get_sql_query function  245
GitHub AI suite  203–205
Google Cloud Document AI  108
Google Gemini  9
    paying for chatbot access  52–53
Google Gemini Imagen  39
Google Professional Machine Learning Engineer Certification  311
Google Project IDX  209
Google Vertex  267
GPT Actions
    combining with function calling  339
    database monitoring APIs  336–338
    OpenAI API  338
    security considerations for  338
GPT-2  324
GPTs (generative pretrained transformers)  150
Grammarly  139

**H**

hard-to-fix problems  336
heterogeneous database environments  183–186
    staying up to date  183–184
    teaching an old DBA new tricks  184–186
hijacking  49
HIPAA (Health Insurance Portability and Accountability Act)  15

**I**

IAM (identity and access management)  15
IDE extensions  202
IIS (Internet Information Services)  172
image generation with AI models  9–11

inference  324
input validation  248
instant messaging, AI in  126–131
integrations and automation, with AI  131–137
interviews
    practice  319
    preparation  317
IPS (Intrusion Prevention System)  118–119
iptables  163
IT support, custom GPTs  152–157
IT support and service desk
    help desk therapy  146–149
    technical support  150–152
ITIL (Information Technology Infrastructure Library)  171

## J

JavaScript console  71
job search, AI-powered  314–315

## K

key principles in prompt construction
    clarity  67
    conciseness  67
    relevance  67–68
    specificity  68

## L

language model chatbots  7–9
language translation  111–112
leadership role of in crisis situations  264–266
libraries, analysis  217
Linux
    distributions  163–164
    terminal  70–71
Llama 3 (7B)  324
LLMOps (large language model operations)  228
LLMs (large language models)  7, 41, 111, 150
local AI models  323–332
    hardware requirements for  323–324
    popular  332–333
    security and ethical considerations  333
    tools for simplifying setup  325–332
logging  248
    comprehensive  213

## M

management  272–288
    career development and growth  276–278
    performance reviews  279–287
    policies and benefits  273–276
management interventions
    guidelines for  290–296
    interviewing candidates  300–301
    time management for hands-on technical managers  301–303
many-shot prompting  63–65
mechanics of
meeting transcription and recap with AI  126–131
memos  290–292
Meta Imagine  39–40
meta-prompts  75–77
Microsoft Azure AI Document Intelligence  108
Microsoft Certified, Azure AI Engineer Associate  311
Microsoft Copilot  9
    paying for chatbot access  53
Midjourney  38–40
misalignment  74
MLOps (machine learning operations)  228
multiserver administration  164–168

## O

objective performance reviews  5
OCR (optical character recognition) software  98
Ollama  329–330
one-on-one meetings  277–278
OpenAI  8, 43
OpenAI API  338
OpenAI ChatGPT, paying for chatbot access  51–52
OpenAI DALL-E  38
OpenAI GPT Actions  335–336
OpenAI's GPT models  108
output filtering  248
over-specification  73–74

## P

PCI-DSS (Payment Card Industry Data Security Standard)  172

PDF to Markdown conversion 103
performance reviews
   self-evaluations, deep analysis prompts
     281–282
   team goals 285–286
PIPs (performance improvement plans)
   293–296
plagiarism 16–17
policies 273–274
POST /completions operation 336
predictive system failure analysis 173
premium accounts 50–55
   choosing 54
   learning and experimenting 55
   paying for chatbot access 51–54
privacy-focused development 212
problem formulation 77–81, 93–96
   incorporating 79–80
professional email responses 5
projects 276
prompt chaining 72
prompt engineering 42, 57–81, 83–93
   advanced techniques 72–73
   Awesome Prompts Lab 69–71
   basic prompting 83–84, 86–87
   best practices and common
     mistakes 73–77
   examples of introductory prompts 68–69
   finalized output 90–93
   future of 65
   problem formulation 77–80, 93–96
   prompting strategies 58–65
     few-shot prompting 62–63
     many-shot prompting 63–65
     single-shot prompting 59–61
     zero-shot prompting 59
   recursive prompting 87–88
   template creation 88–90

## Q

query and object creation 176–179
query optimization 179–181

## R

R1 206
RAG architecture (retrieval-augmented
   generation) 150
ransomware attacks 264–266
rate limiting 248
ready-to-use AI services 108
recursive prompting 72, 87–88
relevance 86–87
renaming files 168–169
REPLACE function 192
resumes, optimizing 315–316
role-playing potential responses and likely
   scenarios 258–259
Roo Code 206
root cause analysis 5
RPO (Recovery Point Objective) 267
RTO (Recovery Time Objective) 267

## S

salary negotiation 317–318
Salesforce Agentforce 158
SCCM (System Center Configuration
   Manager) 160
scripting 5
security
   code assistants and 202
   for GPT Actions 338
   local AI models 333
self-evaluations 279–282
   deep analysis prompts 281–282
sentiment analysis 254
sentiment directives 72
service desk
   agents 158–159
   custom GPTs 152–157
SharePoint standoff 255–262
   AI's role in detecting and mediating IT
     conflicts 257–258
   proactive conflict-resolution agreement
     260–262
   role-playing potential responses and likely
     scenarios 258–259
single-shot prompting 59–61
skills matrices 276–277
SLES (SUSE Linux Enterprise Server) 163
SLMs (small language models) 323
SMART goals 283–284
SMEs (SharePoint subject matter experts)
   255–256
SMoE (Sparse Mixture of Experts) 333
SOC 2 (Service Organization Control 2) 15

sort command 168
source control integration 216–217
Spark 205
specificity 87
speed 336
SPF (Sender Policy Framework) 124
SQL (Structured Query Language), validating queries with examine_sql 244–247
   AI-powered SQL assistance in action 245–247
   defining what makes a query dangerous 245
   generating user-friendly responses 245
SQL Server Dynamic Management Views (DMVs) 176
statefulness 42–43
structured outputs 330–332
   asking specific questions 332
   importance of 332
summarization document 100–102
system role 236–237
systems administration
   AI in systems engineering 173–174
   analyzing error logs 170–171
   auditing configuration files with AI 172–173
   automating tasks for efficiency and compliance 171–173
   change requests 161–162
   Linux distributions 163–164
   multiserver administration 164–168
   renaming files 168–169

## T

task automation 222
team cohesion 296–300
   anonymous feedback 297–299
   team building 299–300
team goals 285–286
   defining 285–286
   organizing and tracking 286
Teams, workflows 131–137
technical images 10
technical support 150–152
   practicing for real-time scenarios 151–152
   setting up environment 150
   troubleshooting issues 150–151

template creation 88–90
terminals 202
test-driven development 214–216
text extraction methods 98–99
text-to-image AI models 37–39
   Google Gemini Imagen and Meta Imagine 39
   Midjourney 38–39
   OpenAI DALL-E 38
tiktoken 44
time management
   for hands-on technical managers 301–303
   prompts for 302
tokenizer 44
tokens 44–49
training and certifications 310–314
   acquiring new skills with AI assistance 310–312
   identifying and filling skill gaps with AI 312–313
   writing conference attendance proposals 313–314
troubleshooting AI loops 218–219

## U

under-specification 73–74
unreasonable requests 262
user role 237

## V

Visual Studio Code, setting up local AI chatbot in 327–328
voice, maintaining while improving writing 137–140
   Apple Intelligence Writing Tools 139–140
   Grammarly 139
VS Code AI Toolkit 325–327
VS Code forks 202

## W

warnings 290–292
web interfaces 202
webhooks 137
whole-file approaches 217–218
workplace AI, integrations and automation with 131–137

workplace conflicts  254–262
    SharePoint standoff  255–262
    strategies for effective conflict resolution  255
write-ups  290–292
writing
    AI  16–17
    improving while maintaining voice  137–140

## X

xp_cmdshell  195

## Z

Zendesk's AI  158
zero-shot prompting  59, 83